To L. C., my lifetime collaborator

A
Woman
Making
History

MARY RITTER BEARD

THROUGH HER LETTERS

Edited and with an introduction by

NANCY F. COTT

YALE UNIVERSITY PRESS   NEW HAVEN & LONDON

A

Woman

Making

History

Title page illustration: Undated portrait of Mary Ritter Beard, probably in her twenties.

Set in Sabon type by G & S Typesetters, Austin, Texas.
Printed in the United States of America.

The paper in this book meets the guidelines for permanence and durability of the Committee on Production Guidelines for Book Longevity of the Council on Library Resources.

10 9 8 7 6 5 4 3 2

All photographs courtesy of Detlev Vagts unless otherwise noted.

Library of Congress
Cataloging-in-Publication Data

Beard, Mary Ritter, 1876–1958.
   A woman making history : Mary Ritter Beard through her letters / edited and with an introduction by Nancy F. Cott.
      p.   cm.
   Includes bibliographical references and index.
   ISBN 0–300–04825–4 (cloth)
      0–300–05252–9 (pbk.)
   1. Beard, Mary Ritter, 1876–1958— Correspondence. 2. Feminists—United States—Correspondence. 3. Women historians—United States— Correspondence. I. Cott, Nancy F. II. Title.
HQ1413.B39A4   1991
305.42'092—dc20   90–12699
                                                    CIP

A catalogue record for this book is available from the British Library.

Contents

Preface

This book is an attempt to restore Mary Ritter Beard's place in history by bringing to light her private letters, against her own wishes. Historian that she was, leader of a plan to establish a World Center for Women's Archives, she nonetheless intended to leave practically no archives of her own. She used the epigram "No documents, no history"—did she want, then, no history of herself? According to her own report in the mid-1930s, she did not systematically save correspondence sent to her. If she kept copies of letters she wrote (and that is doubtful), she destroyed them toward the end of her life. She wished none of her letters ever to be published.[1]

The closest Mary Beard came to explaining why she wanted to keep her letters private was in justifying her refusal to publish letters of her husband's. Two years after Charles Beard's death, she wrote to historian Merle Curti: "Charles destroyed some letters, indeed all his letters, a short time before he died. I did the same with all but current correspondence in my files about the same time. He had only kept confidential letters and he felt obligated not to release them. I shared that feeling." She felt that correspondents who had received private letters from her or her husband should respect their wish for confidentiality. "If one cannot write freely to personal friends . . . without fear of confidences being betrayed in print . . . then liberty as friendship can be sadly lost." "It should be a precious liberty to bypass the press and public life by communing in personal letters on matters of the heart or mind."[2] Beard felt that she was acting in accord with her late husband's intentions in limiting revelations about his private opinions and her own. Before and after his death in 1948 Charles Beard suffered virulent attacks on his character and judgment, because he outspokenly criticized President Franklin Delano Roosevelt's conduct of foreign policy leading to World War II and failed to endorse the United States' entry into the war. At the time that Mary Beard made these decisions about their letters (in the late 1940s and early 1950s) she was undoubtedly feeling defensive, even embittered about the "vultures'" attack.

In her organizational and scholarly work, however, Beard was devoted to locating and preserving women's documents of all sorts in order to make possible the recording of women's history. Without that record, she fervently argued, contemporary women could not fully understand their social role. During the years that she led the World Center for Women's Archives project she displayed marvelous creative talents in excavating women's documents from basements and attics, creating historical documents through oral interviews, and identifying, cataloging, and maintaining known records of women's history. Many answers—none fully satisfying—might be given to explain why she exempted her own documents from that search. The failure of the World Center for Women's Archives (in 1940) defeated her largest hopes for women's knowledge of their own kind. By the late 1940s, the lack of recording of women's history appeared less grievous to her than women's refusal to pay attention to the historical information that lay before them. She felt protective of her private communion and collaboration with her husband, who had ended his life surrounded by hostile commentators. Both Beards had always shunned and disapproved of journalists' wishes to delve into the personalities rather than the ideas of intellectuals. Moreover, Mary Beard's version of women's history always focused on women's activities in the public realm, and it is likely that she wanted the record of her own life to do the same: her published writings would stand for her accomplishment.

Yet anyone who comes across Beard's letters in the manuscript collections of her correspondents cannot fail to be impressed that they convey the aims and variations of her political and intellectual convictions, perhaps even more lucidly than her published work does. My own interest was piqued when, in the course of other research, I began to discover her letters among the manuscripts of other women. By looking systematically in relevant collections, I was able to locate several hundred letters that she had written between the 1910s and the 1950s. The letters do not range evenly over these decades, however; only a handful date from the 1920s, and virtually all from the 1910s have to do with her work for woman suffrage. Although she wished to protect them from view, Beard's extant letters show little of a markedly private or intimate character. They are witty, sarcastic, frank in expression of criticism. The voice, however, is always that of the thinker and historian—the woman devoted to her intellectual work. One gleans only an occasional hint of her sensual or aesthetic pleasures or of her qualities as a leader, friend, wife, mother. Historian Alma Lutz, after interviewing Beard in her rented rooms in Washington, D.C., in 1939, recorded: "The apt. was light and pleasant, freshly painted but the furniture was shabby. . . . I felt that none of this mattered to her at all. . . . She was decidedly the pure historian."[3] A similar impression is gained from Beard's letters.

In this volume her literary heirs—her grandchildren, Arlene Beard and Detlev Vagts—have allowed me to go against the wish that Mary Beard expressed late in life to keep her letters private, in order to follow her larger and more lifelong convictions about the importance of documenting women's history. I believe that her letters provide the most complete and usefully detailed overview of her life's work. I have provided commentary in between to knit the letters together. My introductory essay, "Putting Women on the Record: Mary Ritter Beard's Accomplishment," is intended to complement rather than to preview or distill what follows. Dwelling mainly on Beard's published works, my essay does not explore all of the themes and issues raised in the letters, and it is especially brief on the development of the World Center for Women's Archives, which the letters themselves more thoroughly cover.

In selecting letters to publish, besides looking for inherent interest and readability I have tried to illustrate Beard's character, activities, and intellectual interests as completely as possible. I have not included letters of the late 1940s and 1950s in which she vented her spleen at her husband's critics (although she wrote many of these). In all but a few cases the letters published are whole, not excerpts. My occasional deletions of mundane or inexplicable details are indicated with three ellipsis dots. (When Mary Beard used ellipsis dots herself in letter writing, she made them more numerous, and those I have left as is.) My insertions of a word or two to identify someone named in the letters appear in square brackets, as do dates that I have supplied. I have silently corrected Beard's typographical errors. Her handwritten additions to a typewritten letter (most of which were to correct a misspelling or make a clarification) are not generally noted as such. The locations of the original letters are listed at the end of the book.

This project was made much easier and more enjoyable by Jane Kamensky's cheerful and utterly conscientious work in transcribing the letters, and by the excellent research assistance that she, Ruth Oldenziel, and Jacqueline Dirks supplied. I am indebted to all three. I also wish to thank Gerda Lerner for suggesting that I explore the Miriam Holden collection, Merle Curti for responding with interest to my queries, and Dorothy Porter for sharing her recollections with me. The enthusiasm of both Gerda Lerner and Ellen Dubois for the project has been very important to me. I am grateful to the American Council of Learned Societies and the A. Whitney Griswold Fund of Yale University for financial support for transcribing and annotating the letters and for the goodwill, skill, and cooperation of my friends at Yale University Press, especially Karen Gangel, Caroline Murphy, and Charles Grench.

I have relied heavily on the willingness of archivists and librarians at the libraries where Beard letters are held to send me photocopies, and I appreciate their help very much. For permission to publish the letters, I thank the libraries listed at the back of the book. Most of all, I wish to thank Arlene Beard and Detlev Vagts for their agreement to publish their grandmother's letters. To Professor Vagts, who has been extremely generous with his time and effort on behalf of the project and has given me full use of the letters and photographs in his possession, I am deeply indebted.

Putting Women on the Record

Mary Ritter Beard's Accomplishment

Mary Ritter Beard spent the better part of her life trying to prove the utility of history, especially by recovering women's past. She insisted that history was not whole without women's story. She persevered in seeing women both as cooperators with men and as makers, themselves, of *civilization* (a word she imbued with particular meaning). A woman intellectual of major stature and a unique historian on her own, she was also the lifelong companion and collaborator of Charles A. Beard, the most influential historian in the United States in the first half of the twentieth century. Never an academic, always an organizer through ideas, Mary Beard spoke to and wrote for the community at large. She deserves to be better known to history.

Certain themes remained remarkably consistent throughout her life work (she objected to the term *career* for herself).[1] Her approach to history and society was holistic or integrative. She refused, for example, to isolate the woman question from challenges facing society as a whole. She looked for the social principle and the process of social interaction as driving forces of culture and history. Her history writing began from the premise that "everything is related to everything else," that it was essential to see the "interplay of government, politics, economics, modes of living and working, schools of thought, religion, power, class, society and family, the arts and ambition, and the biological and cultural aspects of sex."[2]

Beside her holistic concentration on the social she had a lifelong passion to count women in. In her books, that showed as early as the high school text *American Citizenship* (1914), the first work of the Beards' coauthorship. In the preface, they objected that previous civics texts had been written "almost wholly from a masculine point of view." They called "less than half a book" any that neglected "the changed and special position of modern women." In her own first book, *Women's Work in Municipalities* (1915), Mary Beard embraced the subject of women "not in an incidental way." So did she in her subsequent works, *On Understanding Women* (1931) and *Woman as Force in History* (1946). In her words, the "whole social fabric" was not woven without women's strands. Responding to a friend's criticism of her "obsession with women," she defended herself: "The work I have done in studying women makes me aware of the large social corollaries as I should not otherwise be."[3]

Mary Beard rowed against the stream. Perhaps that has relegated her to the backwaters. She rowed against the stream of professionalization and specialization that engulfed her generation. More like a nineteenth-century than a twentieth-century historian, she was a moralist and didact who addressed the educated public. She earned no degrees beyond the bachelor's and accepted no honorary ones; she had no employment but as a writer and invited lecturer; she had no particular audience but those who would listen.[4] In a principled way, she was scornful of belonging to any academic "gild," as she called it. All these conditions had their advantages but also their disadvantages as far as the continuity of her reputation was concerned, especially because she was an innovator in both substance and style. Her published works were loose-jointed, oddly organized, her prose florid, her references sometimes obscure. Not willing to simplify the wholeness of her vision for the sake of lesser minds, she sometimes sacrificed her reader, who was her lifeline to influence.

She also rowed against the ideological stream, provoking and needling the organized feminists who would have formed her likeliest constituency. Passionately convinced that sexual equality was a deficient goal for women if it meant measuring up to a male norm, she doubted that the framework of equal rights was the most promising structure for women's advancement. In her pioneering efforts on behalf of women's history she came to believe that women's rights advocates since the nineteenth century had terribly misrepresented the past, by emphasizing women's domination by men. Nonetheless she insisted zealously that it was "important to keep the insurgent spirit alive" among women.[5] She spoke before many women's organizations, associations, and colleges and collaborated with those that shared her political and intellectual goals, but, after the suffrage movement, she joined none.

She pushed on optimistically, for most of her life, feeling in good company because she was in the same boat with her husband. Her teamwork with Charles Beard from 1900 to 1948 was a central feature in her life, their jointly written works a representation of it. After *American Citizenship,* they moved on to textbooks of U.S. history. In 1927 they published the acclaimed *The Rise of American Civilization*—which "did more than any other such book of the twentieth century to define American history for the reading public," in a later historian's accepted judgment. Its sequels followed: *America in Midpassage* (1939) and *The American Spirit* (1942). They summed up with *A Basic History of the*

United States (1944), an inexpensive mass market paperback, which sold more copies than any of their previous works.[6]

Like many the accomplished wife of a more famous man, Mary Beard achieved much greater public prominence as her husband's collaborator than she gained on her own as a suffragist, reformer, or author. Charles Beard established his presence as a major social critic and intellectual early in the twentieth century and sustained that reputation until World War II. "Not only as an historian but also as a political scientist and educator, Charles A. Beard was one of the most influential social thinkers in the United States from about 1912 to 1941," reads the assessment of him in the International Encyclopedia of the Social Sciences. His wife rode his coattails into the limelight—yet she remained on the periphery even when the limelight was brightest. During her husband's life, she received inadequate recognition for her contribution to their jointly written work.[7] (The entry in *Current Biography* of 1941 under both their names, for example, sketched his life only!) In the 1940s, when Charles Beard's foreign policy views diverged from the mainstream and he advocated American "continentalism" rather than international war, her former advantage became her burden. She felt that she shared the ignominy heaped upon her husband, because she shared his views. His fading glory entirely eclipsed her. After Charles' death in 1948, his evaluators read her out of the record, calling *The Rise of American Civilization,* for example, "his" masterpiece, "his" greatest work. The postwar generation of historians who kept Charles Beard's reputation alive by concentrated efforts to demolish his works paid no attention to his wife's contributions. The normative thinking of male historians of that generation appeared in Howard K. Beale's striking non sequitur on the Beards' coauthorship: "No one knows the nature of their collaboration. . . . Hence, I have always spoken of the joint works as Charles Beard's."[8]

Little is known about the method of their work together, about which both were always reticent. It was "too complicated," Mary Beard said late in her life, after her husband's death. Both shunned personal publicity (as distinct from publicity for their ideas and programs) and hated to satisfy voyeuristic journalists' desires for descriptions of their working relationship. In response to the inquiries of male historians, Beard was never forthcoming and usually slighted her own contribution. To Merle Curti she wrote self-deprecatingly in 1938, shortly before *America in Midpassage* appeared, "I try to help CAB escape the burden of carrying me for he is so much a personality alone. I would not allow my name to be placed on our co-authorship if I could prevent it because the major contribution is his." Although Charles Beard told Curti that the couple worked in "equal" partnership, Mary Beard wrote to him, "you don't *have* to include me. . . . It is commonly assumed that I injected women into the thought of history and just that. Let it all ride." On second thought she suggested—curiously—that Curti might treat her contribution to the *co*authored volumes by noting that she had published independently, and not only on the subject of women. Her actual pride and investment in the joint works surfaced more visibly in her sarcasm (conveyed only to another woman writer) about a reviewer's calling a work of the Beards "inferior to a work on American history by Morison and Commager, naturally, because in the Beard case only *one* scholar had worked on the book."[9]

No letters between the Beards are known to exist. They were rarely apart. Besides, late in life they both protected the confidentiality of their private letters by destroying as many as possible. Mary Beard's letters found in her correspondents' papers suggest, however, a thorough and mutually supportive partnership in writing, politics and life. In her first published essay, in 1900, she had envisioned, among other things, that twentieth-century women's engagement in work and politics would change marriage from "a one-sided arrangement, a boredom, a farce," into "a life-long comradeship with community of interest in humanity." In their own lives the Beards attempted to realize that transformation. After her husband's death, Mary Beard reflected on their working life together in a letter to her son, William: "*As for my being free now*, I have had as much freedom all along as I really cared for. . . . I loved sitting at home with my darling every night and being at his side all the days. . . . Outsiders and even you and Miriam [the Beards' daughter] because of your comparative youth could not fully comprehend our mutual happiness in working, jabbering, and getting such exercise as we took in our simple ways. THIS IS AN ABSOLUTE TRUTH."[10]

THE BEARDS' PARTNERSHIP

Both Mary and Charles Beard came from Republican Indiana backgrounds, although her youth was spent in urban Indianapolis, his closer to small-town and farm life. Their marriage in 1900, when she was twenty-four and he twenty-six, followed a college courtship at DePauw University. They then lived in England for two years. Charles Beard had begun studying at Oxford in 1898; there he was instrumental in the

y Ritter as valedictorian of her high school graduating class in Indianapolis,
ana.

Mary Ritter at DePauw University. (Photograph courtesy of DePauw University archives.)

founding of Ruskin Hall, a precocious "free university" offering evening and correspondence courses especially aimed at a working-class audience. The Beards lived first in Oxford and then in Manchester, where Charles directed an extension division of Ruskin Hall, while he was also pursuing research for an institutional history of the office of justice of the peace in England (which eventually became his doctoral thesis). There Mary Beard, reared in bourgeois comfort, was first exposed to the "ghastly deprivations" of working-class life in an industrial center, an experience that "deeply influenced" her "whole life after[ward]" and imbued her with her "first and immortal feeling for labor and its history," as she later described it. The analyses and approaches of English cooperative socialists made a great impact on both Beards during this sojourn. In Ox-

Mary Ritter (at far left) and her roommate, Mary Goodwin (at far right), in a group of DePauw students. (Photograph courtesy of DePauw University archives.)

ford Mary Beard also read *Women and Economics*, the persuasive indict-ment of Victorian gender roles published in 1898 by the American feminist Charlotte Perkins Gilman. She began to read history, and she be-gan to write, publishing her first essay in the journal of Ruskin Hall, *Young Oxford*. Moreover, in Manchester the Beards lived across the street from the fiery widow Emmeline Pankhurst and her three daughters. They became "devoted friends" of Mrs. Pankhurst, the genteel socialist and labor sympathizer, who was shortly to become world-renowned for her outrages against order on behalf of votes for women. "It was she who spurred me to work for woman suffrage," Beard recalled many decades later. The friendship powerfully directed the visitor from the U.S. to focus on problems of the female working class and on the vote as a form of remedy.[11]

The Ruskin Hall experience seems to have crystallized convictions that both Beards shared for the rest of their lives about the sterility of learning not aimed at progressive social application. "Mere learning in the form of collection of facts will never free the world," said Charles Beard in a

Charles Beard calling on Mary Ritter at DePauw. The bicycle in the foreground may have belonged to one of them; both were avid cyclists at college. (Photograph courtesy of DePauw University archives.)

speech there in 1900; and in her last major book, Mary Beard wrote, "The value of learning lies not in sheer erudition, if there at all." To both Beards, freeing the world was the priority. They continued to share an optimistic belief that the study and writing of history could *change* the path of history. Their most admired work, *The Rise of American Civilization,* opened with the claim, "The history of civilization, if intelligently conceived, may be an instrument of civilization." Their conviction about the dynamic relation between past and present was typical of rebellious scholars of the Progressive Era, and Mary Beard carried it through her life, in her work in women's history.

Returning to New York City in 1902, the Beards joined the "revolt against formalism" of their intellectual generation. They shared an ani-

Mary Ritter, DePauw graduate, in 1897. (Photograph courtesy of DePauw University archives.)

Mary Ritter Beard stands third from the right, next to her husband, in the center of this portrait of the Ritter family taken about 1906. The couple is flanked by Mary's brothers, sisters-in-law, and sister. Her parents, Eli and Narcissa Lockwood Ritter, are seated in the center. Miriam Beard sits on her grandmother's lap, beneath her mother, with cousins on both sides.

mus against historical fact finding for facts' sake, which made them ene-mies as well as friends in the School of Political Science at Columbia University, where they both enrolled—she remaining only briefly—and he subsequently found academic employment.[12] During the fifteen years following their return, Charles Beard taught history and political science at Columbia. He also produced an astounding flow of arresting prose, both journalistic commentary and controversial books in political science and history, the most shattering of which was *An Economic Interpretation of the Constitution of the United States* (1913). His fervent scholarship quickly made a name for him. There is no ready information about Mary Beard's public activities during the first decade of the century, while she was raising their daughter, Miriam, born in 1901, and their son, William, born in 1907. The couple seem always to have employed household help, but the children, understandably, occupied their mother's time more in this decade than later. "I know how you feel about the restrictions of young motherhood as well as any mere man can know," Charles Beard wrote sympathetically to a woman friend in 1917, "for Mrs. Beard had

Three generations photographed at the Beards' New Milford property, about 1909. Mary Ritter Beard stands at far left, her parents on either side. Charles Beard sits on the grass, with his mother, Mrs. Henry Beard, in back of him, an unnamed maid next to her. The wagon holds the Beard children, Miriam and William.

everything fall on her young shoulders simultaneously." He continued, "But in spite of all its limitations I find her believing that one must somehow work from the family out to public activity." This suggested a prejudice that they shared, which he made more prescriptive by adding, "It does seem that abnormality is more apt to exist without the great human experience of close association with child life, and some family responsibility." [13]

In the early 1910s, when Mary Beard emerged a visible suffragist, still she made periodic amends to co-workers for delay because she "had to make the boy some suits—no suffrage" or because she had to be in their New Milford country house "for the family's sake," or because she "couldn't leave the children" to whom she was "glued together for a fortnight while Charles and the nurse were both away." Before her second-born was three years old, Mary Beard became active in several women's voluntary organizations, including the Equality League for Self-Supporting Women (a suffrage group) and the New York Women's Trade Union League. In 1909 and 1910, she worked with the former to defeat an assemblyman hostile to woman suffrage and with the latter to support

Mary and Miriam Beard, probably 1905.

Mary, Charles and Miriam Beard, resting during a hike on the Palisades (New Jersey), probably 1906.

women garment-makers involved in massive strikes. For a short time in 1910–11 Beard served as editor of *The Woman Voter,* the newspaper of the New York state Woman Suffrage Party (led by Carrie Chapman Catt). She then focused her energies on the Wage-Earners' Suffrage League, an offshoot intended to organize working-class women. Her intense commitment to that cause, and her belief that class exploitation could be addressed by women's votes, undoubtedly had been shaped by her sojourn in England. After the disastrous Triangle Fire of 1911 incinerated nearly 150 trapped garment workers, Beard worked closely with the New York Women's Trade Union League, serving briefly as treasurer. She wrote to a close colleague, the working-class suffragist and unionist Leonora O'Reilly, "It has been my dream to develop working women to be a help in the awakening of their class." Her earnest and unconsciously condescending tone, if not her awareness of class, was characteristic of contemporary middle-class women facing their working-class "sisters." [14]

Beard broke completely with the Woman Suffrage Party in 1913, angered by Catt's failure to speak up for Emmeline Pankhurst, who was now roasted internationally for her destructive acts of civil disobedience. Beard's stomach for suffragist militance was tested by her joining the Congressional Union, a new national suffrage organization founded by Lucy Burns and Alice Paul in 1913. Paul and Burns, both of whom had served apprenticeships among the English militants, jolted the established state-by-state approach of the woman suffrage movement by working for a constitutional amendment through pressure on the "party in power" (the Democrats) at the national level. Beard was a prime mover in the new group. She worked with it through 1917, approving its political approach and flamboyant tactics, although never fully in sympathy with its leaders' single-issue approach. "I am so much more radical than either of the old political parties that, when I get off and think, I lose my whole absorption in the one fight for enfranchisement," she confessed to Alice Paul in mid-1916. Beard approved of the tactic of picketing in the nation's capital that the group, renamed the National Woman's Party, began early in 1917. She led a New York delegation to Washington, D.C., to protest the imprisonment of suffrage pickets early in November of that year. Later in the same month, however, for reasons not entirely clear, she resigned from the group's Advisory Council. [15]

Charles Beard not only marched in suffrage parades but also, at his wife's urging, committed himself to the unpopular position of the Congressional Union in the pages of the recently founded progressive political journal the *New Republic*. (Strenuous and noisy arguments preceded his conversion to "positive and valiant support" for woman suffrage, in the account Mary Beard gave her son many decades later. Childhood memories of his grandmother's management of a country estate made Charles Beard underestimate women's disadvantages and overestimate women's control of resources; he did not see their need for the ballot until his wife's constant disputation—carried on "impersonally," she assured their son—convinced him.) [16]

In the early 1910s both Beards tramped the sidewalks, climbed stairs, and rang doorbells for workers' causes and for local reform candidates. While Mary pushed for urban playgrounds, Charles labored intensively at the New York City Bureau of Municipal Research; he published a survey and comparison on *American City Government* in 1912, she a similarly structured overview of *Women's Work in Municipalities* in 1915. His scholarly work on constitutional history—most notably, his reinterpretation of the motives of the framers of the U.S. Constitution to highlight their economic interests—intersected with the aims of both of them to change constitutional provision and interpretations. Both saw scholarship in service of social change. The high school civics text that they wrote together in 1914 derived from both of their interests and was written at Mary Beard's instigation, in order "to bring women into the conception of citizenship," according to a much later account of hers. The book affirmatively intended to address not only boys but also girls—the majority of high school students, as the Beards knew. Assuming that women as mothers, workers, taxpayers, and citizens subject to the laws were deeply interested in government, the Beards urged, "Civics concerns the whole community, and women constitute half of that community." [17]

Both husband and wife sustained the alternative vision of education that had inspired them at Ruskin Hall. Both remained deeply skeptical that conventional establishments of higher learning furthered the goals of democratic progress and social enlightenment. In 1917 Charles Beard resigned from the faculty of Columbia University in a celebrated defense of academic freedom during wartime, and thereafter neither Beard relied on support from an established institution of higher education. Both fostered unconventional "counter"-institutions. Charles Beard was one of the founders of the New School for Social Research (from which he rather quickly departed, however), and in 1920–21 both were among the initiators of the Workers' Education Bureau of the United States, intended to promote educational efforts among trade unionists. Mary Beard's *A Short History of the American Labor Movement,* published in 1920, was a contribution to the "Workers' Bookshelf" series of the Bureau. [18]

Both of them continued to criticize the barrenness of academically generated scholarship and to express exasperation with deficiencies in the higher learning. As her interests in women's history deepened, Mary Beard excoriated educational institutions for their muteness on women's constructive presence in civilization. "What we now have is the instruction of young men and women in the history of men—of men's minds and manners," she pointed out in 1935; "in not one college of this country—man's woman's or co-educational—is there any comprehensive treatment of women's contributions to civilization and culture." In the 1930s and again in the 1950s she envisioned and tried to plan for a "real" woman's

college or research institute, one that would instruct women neither in
the home economics that she deplored as an academic course nor in the
"masculine" knowledge that she felt was the staple fare in American
higher education. As a result of her disaffection with conventional scholarship, she distanced herself not only from institutions but from the very
name of professional. An advertisement for her last major book announced, "Mary Ritter Beard belongs to no professional guild and permits no designation of herself other than that of student and writer." [19]

From 1921, when their coauthored textbook *A History of the United
States* was published, until the late 1940s, the two Beards were always
involved in writing works of U.S. history together, whatever else they were
doing. Their base of operations was their farmhouse in New Milford, Connecticut, which purposely lacked a telephone but boasted a library eventually stocked with seven thousand books. From it they began their travels
and dispatched their missives via the printed word; to it their presence
drew intellectuals, policy makers, international visitors, and would-be
students. The style of life that both maintained as scholars and publicists
had more in common with the gentlemen historians of the nineteenth
century than with contemporary professional specialists. They were both
intellectual loners of a peculiar sort, wanting to address and be heard by
the wide audience of the public, frequently collaborating with others on
an ad hoc basis, and yet avoiding constant collegial solidarity. [20]

In the decade following the spectacular success of *The Rise of American Civilization,* both of the Beards reached the height of their public influence. During the New Deal years the couple usually spent the winter
months in hotel rooms in Washington, D.C., doing research at the Library of Congress and involving themselves in politics. Charles Beard
more than once prepared and gave testimony before the House Naval Affairs Committee in the effort to keep U.S. foreign policy anchored on neutrality. In part because of her work to found a World Center for Women's
Archives, which she took up in 1935, Mary Beard was among the dozen
"leading feminists" of that year, in the wisdom of the *New York Sun.* She
was also the only intellectual among the dozen organizational leaders and
professionals named as possible female presidents of the United States
that year, in a widely publicized interview with the editor of the *Pictorial
Review.* At that point Charles Beard's economic interpretation of the U.S.
Constitution had become accepted dictum in college textbooks. In 1938,
a symposium among intellectuals by the *New Republic* on "Books that
Changed Our Minds" placed him second on the list, ahead of John

Dewey and Sigmund Freud in influence (although trailing Thorstein Veblen).[21]

In their sequels to *The Rise*, the Beards expressed both their aggregated interpretation of American history and their shared political views. The work of the two in the 1930s showed their preoccupation with defining a workable "collectivism" in answer to economic crisis. In *America in Midpassage*, which covered the 1920s and 1930s and was published in 1939—"a kind of memoir of the time from 2 old birds," as Charles Beard described it to a friend—they stressed the need for national management of economic and technological resources and enterprise; they equally emphasized the crucial importance of democratic methods and values, using terms such as *humanistic democracy* and *economic democracy*. Their criticism of the New Deal was that it did not go far enough in these directions. These were their joint positions, Mary Beard explicitly told friends.[22]

The two volumes of *America in Midpassage* also echoed with their insistence on avoiding munitions build-up and on neutrality as an alternative to international intervention. Shortly after the Versailles Peace Conference, Charles Beard already referred to the Great War as the "First World War." As a result of his negative judgments of the conduct and results of the war and his perception of a parallelism between Japanese and American imperial intentions, he quickly became an acute critic of American military adventurism in the Caribbean and of dollar diplomacy. He was also perturbed by the foreign policies of America's European allies, which he saw as undemocratic and imperialistic. Such international ventures would threaten constitutional government and liberties in the United States, he believed. His wife shared his insistence on maintaining American neutrality and concentrating on national development rather than international order. "Our minds and hearts are devoted to the enterprise of trying to persuade Americans to care about the making of a decent order in the USA where they have everything to work with," she wrote to a friend in reference to *America in Midpassage*.[23]

The Beards' teamwork formed in mutual respect, shared intellectual and political convictions, and mutual dependence. Charles Beard's increasing deafness made him rely on his wife's help on many occasions. With reference to his testimony before a congressional committee in 1935, for example, Mary explained, "I just have to stick pretty close to CAB and his enterprises because he is so helpless without me, being so deaf and generally so dependent on my cooperation. Even so, we generally have the same urges and points of view, if not in every instance." In their last decade together, she wrote unembarrassedly to a friend that she would go with her husband to Baltimore, where he was to teach a year at Johns Hopkins University, because "we are still in love." Her own political projects and writing always intersected with her teamwork with him. "What I print has to be rushed along to get anything of my very own out between orgies of co-authorship with CAB," she seemed to apologize to Luella Gettys, who was also the wife of a more-renowned scholar (V. O. Key). Yet she went on, "The orgies have a pleasure all their own and so do the separate thrusts at self-expression." The balance between the two satisfied her.[24]

Mary Ritter Beard preserved her independence as a writer and public figure by never signing herself "Mrs. Charles Beard," yet constant companionship with her celebrated and enormously productive husband must have affected her self-assessment. Her private letters reveal a lifelong ambivalence. On the one hand, she was intensely sure that her reading of history was accurate and all-important; on the other, she leapt to call herself "insane," "the worst person" possible to launch a project on women and history, "a low-brow."[25] She understood her mission with utmost seriousness and yet had a hard time taking herself seriously. Probably the immediate comparison of her husband's position and influence magnified in her the insecurities and difficulties that any woman intellectual of her generation faced. Charles Beard won institutional rewards and prestige that eluded her, including the presidencies of the American Political Science Association in 1926 and the American Historical Association in 1933. Having earned advanced degrees and taught at a major research university, he kept his eager academic audience, while his wife never gained one. She knew that she was his crucial collaborator, yet she must have sensed simultaneously that she was not viewed as his equal. This made her inordinately self-critical; she found it stressful to be seen as an authority. On an occasion when she was addressing a group in Cincinnati, the concentrated attention of the mayor and university president (both men) made her laugh—"I felt positively ridiculous with respect to my role as speaker but then I came to grips with myself in that role and finished out my speech," she wrote to a friend. Yet she bristled at criticism and suffered from unfair barbs. Her magnum opus, *Woman as Force in History* (1946), was initially greeted by a newspaper editorial in Charlotte, North Carolina (where the Beards were spending their winter), which said that she had "wasted [her] time working on such a book." "All I needed to do," Mary Beard grimly recounted to a friend, "if

I wished to know about the force of woman, was to ask my husband and he would tell me!" The effect on her of this "slap in the face" was "stunningly bad."[26]

In the late 1930s and the 1940s, Beard shared the views of America's place in world politics for which her husband came to be condemned. They were both vigorous anti-Fascists but also (in her words) "'hard-boiled' noninterventionists" regarding the European war. Her stance distinctly separated her from mainstream American women's groups, as she was well aware. "The name 'Beard' is anathema in many quarters, I assure you," she warned a friend in 1944, "whether Charles or Mary is prefixed to it." Her lament was fiercer a few years later, after Roosevelt's death and the publication of two books by her husband raking over the late president's foreign policy: "Charles Beard is now viewed as a combined buzzard and snake . . . and [as] a Brutus slaying a Caesar venerated by a world which understands him and abhors Brutus." Not long after that caustic observation, Charles Beard was dead. Mary Beard carried on for another decade, acting on her conviction that "work on my part is courage," to be pursued "for the mastery of grief and the enrichment of the invisible continuing companionship." She was sustained by her "glorious memories and work," she wrote to her son: "I am so thankful I trained myself to work, in this way."[27]

THE EVOLUTION OF MARY RITTER BEARD'S VIEWS OF WOMEN'S HISTORY

Mary Beard's first article, published in two parts in the journal of Ruskin Hall, began: "The volumes which record the history of the human race are filled with the deeds and the words of great men . . . [but] The Twentieth Century Woman . . . questions the completeness of the story." From this until her very last, she focused on history and its meaning for contemporary women. Spanning the century break, "The Twentieth-Century Woman Looking Around and Backward" appeared in December 1900, "The Nineteenth-Century Woman Looking Forward" in January 1901— the two titles and their order foreshadowing her later creative play with narrative linearity in history.

At this point, Beard's reading of women's past was vastly different from the analysis she would later develop. In "universal history" she saw women contributing nothing but children; marriage was akin to slavery, and women were men's beasts of burden or their valued property. She put women in contemporary society into three categories: the frivolous and idle rich, the trivially productive domestic bourgeoise, the disadvantaged working-class woman. Echoing the argument of Charlotte Perkins Gilman in *Women and Economics* (1898)—although she did not cite the work—Beard declared, "Woman has never been human. The desire to be feminine and to please men has made her a most unnatural, oversexed individual." Her hopes rested on distinguishing the future from the "dismal" past. Again following Gilman, she envisioned collective solutions, such as communal cooking and laundry, to end "household slavery." To make woman "a world-servant instead of a house-servant" she stressed the importance of education and direct involvement in the production and distribution of wealth outside the household. She appeared hopeful, because a "few bold spirits" were writing on "the woman question," and "woman is slowly becoming a factor to be reckoned with in politics, economics, and the solution of present-day problems." In these articles Mary Beard seemed discontent with her finding that "woman as a maker of civilisation" was "strangely absent from the pages of history," and only an occasional Joan of Arc or Elizabeth I supplied past models of heroism and idealism. That void in the written record provoked her: "'Has woman contributed nothing to the race-life, nothing to civilisation?'" her Twentieth Century Woman asked.[28]

During the next three decades, the question never left Mary Beard. While she bore and raised children, entered and departed from organized reform activities, began a life's work of historical authorship, and traveled to western and eastern Europe, China, and Japan, she pursued knowledge and developed her thinking to the point that she was able to answer it affirmatively in her book *On Understanding Women* (1931). The path that she took can barely be traced, by connecting one dot of information to another. Documentation of these decades of her life is sparse; what records there are concentrate on her suffrage work rather than on her intellectual development. By the time she wrote *Women's Work in Municipalities* (1915) she seemed convinced that, contrary to the habit of history books, women's contributions to civilization warranted notice. Addressing the annual convention of the National Municipal League on the subject of her book, she remarked that a visitor from Mars who read President Woodrow Wilson's five-volume history of the U.S. would hardly know that women had taken part in the nation from the landing of the Pilgrims to the present day. But "the knell of that sort of history had been rung," she reportedly said; "women were now studying history for themselves." Her own book began with a hint of apology turning quickly into assertion: "If this new evaluation of woman's work in civilization seems to err on the side of woman, we shall be satisfied if it helps to bring about a re-evaluation which shall include women not in an incidental way but as people of flesh and blood and brain—feeling, seeing, judging and directing, equally with men, all the great social forces which mold character and determine general comfort, well-being and happiness."[29]

Here were foreshadowed her later themes—most important, the vision of women as co-makers of civilization side by side with men and the implication that documenting their past shared leadership would help to cement it into contemporary reality. In articles published as early as 1912, Beard veered away from Gilman's analysis and insisted that women's home-based concerns were social (that is, involved in the common life), and political (that is, involved in the power relations and government responsibilities of the community). Perhaps her shift in emphasis was a consequence of her reform work. Like many suffragists, she emphasized that "the brute facts of life" for wives, mothers, and daughters in the working class (including poverty, industrial toil, contaminated milk for babies, tenement squalor, the dangers and temptations in urban entertainments) were "social facts—political facts if you please." In an essay criticizing the assumption that motherhood was an individual or moral task alone, she underlined that "everything that counts in the common life is political."[30]

Thus redefining women's involvements as political, Mary Beard set herself against—saw herself as advancing beyond—the past and contemporary generation of women activists who considered their warrant simply a moral one. In her affiliation with the Congressional Union, she understood its prideful embrace of a political approach not merely in the narrow sense that they were intervening in electoral politics (although they were decidedly doing that, to the horror of the longer-established leaders of the National American Woman Suffrage Association). She saw the Congressional Union's choice as a more meaningful assertion of women's right and need to take up civic responsibility. She emphasized to Alice Paul at one point of conflict with the other suffragists, "As our older women still think of responsibility as a moral thing rather than a political, it seems that we shall have to diagram the thing for them." Her husband echoed her sentiment on that issue.[31]

Aside from her depreciation of the moral and embrace of the political, Mary Beard's views of women as citizens mirrored those of most other suffragists, who saw the involvement of women in politics as contingent upon modern conditions. Their estimates of women's current citizenship did not erase the Gilman-like conviction that women had been a dependent sex in the long past. Neither had Beard during the years 1912 to 1915 yet formed a view of women's roles in long history. But as a booster of women's constructive social activities she was angered by the scarce esteem they received. Her developing belief in women as partners and equals with men in the common life of civilization contested with her awareness that men scorned or diminished women's efforts. The disparity between what she saw as the reality and what was acknowledged in men's eyes rankled her. More emphatically than at any other period of her life, she alluded to differentiation between the sexes in terms of separation, hierarchy, and injustice. In an unpublished essay, for example, she compared the overwhelming public welcome given to Hungarian revolutionist Louis Kossuth in the United States in 1851 with the hostility shown the English militant suffragist Emmeline Pankhurst in 1913. Both rebels, she pointed out, had come across the Atlantic waving the banner of political liberty—Kossuth to be lionized, Pankhurst to be denied admittance by the U.S. government until masses of suffragists demanded her entry. "Can it be, merely, that this is a man's world still and that the deeds women do are not of public worth?" Beard asked rhetorically, her own implied answer clear. As in days of old, she concluded, "Men still count most"; "what is feminine is hysterical, frenzied, or just idiotic—in a man's world."[32]

Beard's involvement in the suffrage cause compounds the difficulty of tracing the evolution of her views, for her rhetorical claims in suffrage propaganda may have been keyed to her audience's expectations, opportunistic rather than deeply felt. In an essay intended to arouse working-class men's sympathies for the ballot for women, for example, she focused on women of their class and claimed that without the vote, "they have no power to help themselves." She gave a different emphasis to an article two years later, one that drew on her research for *Women's Work in Municipalities* and was published in the *Annals of the American Academy of Political and Social Science,* destined for an audience of intellectuals and reformers. There she argued strongly for recognition of "the legislative influence of unenfranchised women," exercised through their lobbying, their organizational platforms, moral sanctions, and indirect "wire-pulling," as well as through their joint efforts with men in voluntary associations. Because she concluded that these activities marked "a long journey from woman's old spheres, the three K's," she presumably had not discarded the assumption that women had emerged to the political scene only recently. But she made the argument for women's influence thoroughgoing. "In the progress of modern social legislation of all kinds—the extension of educational functions, pure food laws, mothers' pensions, development of recreational facilities, labor laws, particularly for women and children, and measures directed against prostitution—not a single important statute has been enacted without the active support of women," she declared. She was speaking mainly about middle-class activists; she conceded that "women's weight has been almost negligible in many instances" with respect to "serious labor legislation affecting large employing interests." The difference between her earlier and later statement on unenfranchised women's influence may not reflect a change in emphasis over time but her perception that working-class women had less political clout than middle-class women and needed the vote more.[33]

If Mary Beard in the 1910s had not yet set herself the task of correcting the history books, she had seen the neglect of women in history as a major problem and had called history to her aid. Frequently drawing on her own and her husband's knowledge in American constitutional and political history in the suffrage cause, she argued analogies between the nineteenth-century attainment of white manhood suffrage in the United States and twentieth-century methods of woman suffragists; she went back to Jefferson and Madison to point out to Democratic congressmen that suffrage ought to be regarded as a federal question; she drew her suffragist colleagues' attention to the U.S. Supreme Court decision in *Minor v. Happersett* (1875). Just after the nation became a belligerent in the Great War she set before the Senate Committee on Woman Suffrage the history of American women's "vital services" and "equal and active participation" in the Revolutionary War, the War of 1812, and the Civil War as justification for giving women the ballot.[34] That leaning in the direction she would subsequently go did not continue into her next book, *A Short History of the American Labor Movement* (1920), which took a conventionally male-centered approach and treated women in trade unions very briefly.

Soon after, however, Beard's outlook on the long past showed that she had redrawn her portrait of 1900 in which women were either idle, engaged in trivial domestic pursuits, or purely exploited. When, in 1921, the suffrage goal attained, she wrote to her former suffragist associate Elsie Hill, she seemed convinced that women had typically attained more equality in access to work than feminists had been accustomed to admit, and she was, furthermore, newly critical of equality as a goal for women. During a trip to postwar Britain, France, and Italy, Beard had found that "there is so much industrial equality that women sweep the streets and till

The Beard family, met upon arrival at Yokohama, Japan, in 1923 by the son and son-in-law of the city's mayor. Miriam Beard stands at left, William Beard above his parents.

the land while men drink in the cafes." Her experience made her feel "how bourgeois our whole suffrage and equal opportunity movement is." She wrote to Hill: "Women have been having that equality in the fields of Europe since the days of the Roman Empire, for example. Of course real equality would have transferred the whip to her hands and let her hitch her husband and an ass together to the plow instead of having the sexes reversed; but is that the final answer?" Beard's European observations precipitated her new conviction that women had been occupied in "the world's work" all along, although there was nothing glamorous about it. Here she denied Charlotte Perkins Gilman's main accusation, that women had been excluded from meaningful and productive work in the world— work like men's. Beard also denied Gilman's assumption that what men had was worth women's striving for. She added by hand to her typed letter, as though she could not resist the impulse, "Half the goals they [men] set are ridiculous and [women's] pure imitation is both infantile and unin-

The Beard family seated for dinner in Japan (1923), with their host and hostess. Miriam and William are at the right.

telligent. A! Ha!" At the same time that she arrived at the opinion that women had shared "equality in the fields" of toil with men, she discarded equality with men as an adequate goal for women. Her revulsion from war and her bitter observation that women "rushed to recruit" reinforced the latter point.[35]

In her developing view, equality was not an adequate goal for women because the world at risk needed women to offer something different and better, more socially constructive, than war-making men had typically provided. A English-language newspaper report of a speech she made late in 1922 in Tokyo (where Charles Beard had been called to consult on municipal problems) put a unique spotlight on her thinking. If the report can be trusted, that speech marked the first time that Beard cited women's part in founding and sustaining civilization for the purpose of urging contemporary women to take leadership in social responsibility. "Time to Boast a Bit, Women Told," summarized the headline. Reiterating her earlier objection that history books had been partial—satisfying only men's vanity—Beard argued that such an account of the past was not only wrong but also "depressing for women to believe." Here, for the first time, she began to rewrite the long past. Women probably created settled agriculture, with the innovation of storing seed, she claimed; in archives and libraries lay materials that would show the vital part womankind had played in constructing and sustaining societies. Aware of herself as an American in a foreign land, she urged women of the world to join hands and make known their part in building civilization. She closed with a vague but telling admonition that women's newly gained tools of higher education, economic independence, equality before the law, and suffrage would mean nothing unless utilized socially, for the benefit of the whole community.[36]

Beard's Tokyo speech must have reflected her reading of anthropological works on women's contributions to the development of civilized society. The likely suspects were the books highlighted by the Beards in *The American Spirit* (1942), their intellectual history of the idea of civilization in the United States: Lewis Henry Morgan's *Ancient Society,* Lester Ward's *The Psychic Factors in Civilization,* Otis T. Mason's *Woman's Share in Primitive Culture,* and Anna Garlin Spencer's *Woman's Share in Social Culture.* All of these works revealed a primitive matriarchal social organization preceding the patriarchy of biblical times. Mason's, especially, reversed the theory that human society arose from paternal considerations and claimed that the kindly arts of civilization—agriculture, cooking, weaving, pottery, child nurture—sprang from women's work. All of these books except Spencer's were late Victorian productions, published before Mary Beard graduated from college. They could have been part of her intellectual repertoire long before 1922—but were they? The Beards wrote retrospectively in *The American Spirit* that works such as Ward's (1893) and Mason's (1894) had "brought more illumination and force" to woman's rights advocates at the time:

> Hitherto the sources upon which leaders in that movement had relied for information respecting the role of women in history had been largely limited to works on political, military, legal and ecclesiastic history written mainly by men for their own purposes. . . . Now anthropology penetrated the far past, ages beyond the oldest written myths and stories on which historians of politics, wars, laws and theologies had depended . . . . By its very scope it took into account all the arts and institutions for the maintenance and care of life. . . . And in its wide searchings anthropology found women at the very center of civilization in origin and development—as creators and preservers of the arts and of that perennial moral strength of civilization.[37]

This intellectual history sounded suspiciously like Mary Beard's own. True, late-Victorian anthropological theories of ancient matriarchy heartened some leaders in the woman movement (as the women's movement of that day was called). Elizabeth Cady Stanton, for example, cited the existence of a primitive matriarchate when she criticized the Bible in the 1890s, and Charlotte Perkins Gilman was inspired by the work of Lester Ward.[38] Most male scholars writing on the theme of matriarchy meant to document the superior virtues of the succeeding patriarchy, however. Their findings offered at best ambiguous encouragement for all but the most willful and purposive readers—such as Mary Beard.

The account in *American Spirit,* written decades later, does not clarify whether Beard read Mason's or Spencer's works when they were published, or not until shortly before 1922. It seems likely that she would have read *Woman's Share in Social Culture* upon its publication in 1913, since Spencer was part of the woman movement herself, one generation older than Beard. Spencer was a minister, writer, lecturer, and reformer active in child welfare efforts, a lifelong suffragist and leader in the National American Woman Suffrage Association. *Woman's Share in Social Culture* showed (even in the similar-sounding title) that Spencer was familiar with O. T. Mason's work; like Mason, she gave women the priority in initiating family organization and settled agricultural production. Much of her book, however, focused on family and social issues in the contemporary world, where she assumed that women's unique caregiving role might give rise to liberating ethical insights. Either Spencer's or Mason's book would have provided the framework that Beard needed to support her Tokyo talk, the title of which was, revealingly, "Women's Share in Civilization." Only Spencer supplied a link between the primitive past and the modern world, in an essay on the state that suggested a relative loss for women when men achieved the democratic "rights of man." Spencer argued that as the modern state broadened its social responsibilities beyond narrowly political to "ministrant" functions, it included "woman's sphere" of social services, thus making necessary the enfranchisement of women as members of the body politic.[39] Perhaps Beard read Spencer's book in 1913 or 1914—it would have supported her approach in her own book, *Women's Work in Municipalities*—and then, during the war years or after, sought more historical-anthropological confirmation of primitive women's importance in works such as Mason's and Morgan's.

Aside from traveling in the "old world" in the early 1920s, Beard was necessarily delving into its history, because she assisted with Charles Beard's textbook on European history (written with William Bagley), *Our Old World Background* (1922).[40] Her objections to male-centered histories of civilization also were gathering force. H. G. Wells' two-volume *Outline of History* of 1920 aroused her particular animus. In her Tokyo talk she accused Wells of partiality and vanity in treating only men in history. She continued to take him to task in the 1930s, criticizing his failure to discuss ancient female leaders and his use of the generic Man so as to imply that males launched civilization, when, in her view, anthropologists were "almost unanimous" that females had.[41] Although Beard had incorporated the relevance of women's invention of civilization into her thinking by the early 1920s, she did not speak of women's "force" coursing freely through history. In Tokyo, she described primitive women's skills as leading to their undoing: she reasoned that men, seeing value in women's arts and industry, used physical and mental power to dominate women and transform them into a species of property.

Such a bifurcated outlook was more or less her position when she and her husband began planning *The Rise of American Civilization,* in November 1923, as they traveled home from a second trip to Japan, viewing their own country anew as a result of journeying to the Far East.[42] Charles Beard characterized *The Rise* to its publisher for advance publicity in 1927: "Our book is essentially an organic book, not a collection of friable molecules. It is an attempt to get at the inner motive forces, acting continuously in time, that have driven the American people forward through three hundred years, displaying their unresting energies in the conquest of a continent and on the battle fields of two hemispheres. It is an effort to disclose the contacts of unity between economic, political, and cultural life." Here Mary Beard's integrative vision of history began to show itself. From the first reviewers' responses to *The Rise,* Charles Beard insisted that the work was truly joint, and that if personal mention were necessary in advertising, that feature would be the one to "play up." Indeed, he directed Macmillan Publishers to avoid quoting reviewers' extracts that singled him out as the author, because these were "not true to fact or just to my co-worker." "In reality the scope of the book outside of the politics is due to Mrs. Beard's interest and her labors," Charles Beard wrote. "The grand plan I should not have thought of or attempted to execute alone."[43]

A few times in her correspondence with women friends Mary Beard took credit for thus "widening the frames" of historical scrutiny in the joint work. To an old friend who praised *The Rise* she wrote, "Reviewers often imply that the whole product is C.A.'s in spite of the fact that he had never written on cultural themes before and so I appreciate your willingness to count me in, in view of the way I drudged on the work for three years and especially since the cultural side was my hunch—not just women." Decades later she confirmed that in their "cooperative enterprise" she had always insisted that "history is in fact the *whole* story of humankind including religion, literature, philosophy, and biology and everything else. . . . I have in my collaboration with CAB, from its beginning, widened politics, war and law and political economy to cover more aspects of human development. CAB has accepted my wide interest and done everything he could to work with me as I have done everything I could to work with him." [44]

Mary Beard likely supplied not simply the cultural side but the civilization concept itself, now deeply rooted in her thinking. Her husband's *Contemporary American History,* published in 1914, anticipated some of the interpretive themes and judgments of *The Rise* (for instance, on the significance of the Reconstruction period) but did not enunciate the concept of civilization. She, on the other hand, had long been sounding the theme that "woman as maker of civilization" was absent from written history. In line with her approach, the preface to *The Rise* alluded to women's agency in civilization, commenting sardonically that "there would be little more than caves and barracks or bare monastic walls in the wide world" without the very efforts condemned by "strong men" for "effeminacy." More specifically, *The Rise* proposed that twentieth-century women occupied a "strategic position in the unfolding of modern civilization," because their "power as the buyers of goods" put them in special "relation to the psychological centrum, the market, around which modern industry revolves." [45]

The preface to *The Rise* stated Mary Beard's now settled assumption that women were "involved in the whole process of human evolution from top to bottom, in war and in peace, as bearers of the heritage and workers in the arts and sciences." On women's participation in the European migration and establishment of a colonial economy the Beards were emphatic. "Absolutely imperative to the successful development of European civilization in America was the participation of women in every sphere of life and labor," they began, and after stressing the skills and strengths of seventeenth-century women in farming, handicrafts, and merchandising, concluded, "No doubt the migration of families was determined by domestic council, for the most part, and after the momentous step was taken, the women assumed their share of the hardships and their full burden of responsibilities." [46]

If the colonial era presented in *The Rise* thus accorded with Mary Beard's later readings of women's history, the treatments of eighteenth- and nineteenth-century women's work, politics, and education did not. Although the book cited statistics on women's proportion in the labor force at various points, its only discussion of women in developing indus- try took the point of view of the male labor movement, assuming that women, as also immigrants and blacks, were difficult to organize. Mary Beard had not yet entirely given up a mainstream feminist reading of gen- der hierarchy and sex discrimination. Remarking on the gathering force of the movement for woman suffrage, *The Rise* took the conventional view that "politics was a man's world." It asserted that "traditional discrimi- nations" closed girls out of schools beyond a very basic level, that men had an "age-old grip on higher learning" and that women school found- ers such as Emma Willard and Mary Lyon had to battle against the cus- tom of women's ignorance. It accepted the adage that war was "almost exclusively a man's business" until the late eighteenth century when the democratization of conscription meant that women as well as men were involved in national battles. It presented women's club activities and phil- anthropic ventures during the Gilded Age as evidence that "the gravity of women's interests steadily moved from the center of the family outward"; clubwomen discussed "questions long reserved for the masculine mind." In sum, by 1900, *The Rise* concluded, "American women had broken down the walls of the traditional sphere."

Credible as all of these interpretations were—and remain, for many readers—they are surprising only because in subsequent decades Mary Beard railed against them. She later refused to believe that politics and war had ever been "men's" domains, she insisted that women had found means of education equal to their brothers, she intentionally saw the home as central to rather than separate from the rest of public activities, and she never used the language or the concept of "spheres." While she and her husband made strides toward integrating women's vital presence into the history of American experience in *The Rise,* in other words, the narrative still half-clung to the framework of "woman as a subject sex" that Mary Beard later reprobated. As *The Rise* moved into the twentieth century and toward the present, the Beards emphasized the presence and power of women, especially their leverage as the nation's principal con- sumers, their share in producing goods and ideas, and their influence on public policy and political parties. "Having the means to buy and to com- mand, education to guide them, and freedom to superintend, women became powerful arbiters in all matters of taste, morals and thinking. In short, they called the tunes to which captains of industry, men of letters, educators, and artists now principally danced," the book summed up.[47]

Like the end of *The Rise,* Mary Beard's occasional writings in 1929 and 1930 took a very sanguine view of American women's attainments and prerogatives.[48] Possibly she saw the privileges of American women in a new light after direct observation of women in rural Japan and China during her travels of 1922–23. Although she left no such record, her husband later wrote that "after a trip to the Orient the Occidental is never the same" and that during their "first visit to Japan and China—both so different from the US and other Western countries—I became a changed person." Further eye-opening travels to Yugoslavia in 1927–28, where Mary Beard took special note of women eking out a living from the land, may have reinforced impressions gained in the Far East and influenced her to connect women's long past with their present through her own writing of history.[49] Many factors must have been involved in the shift in emphasis she undertook in her next book.

On Understanding Women, which was published in 1931, proclaimed Mary Beard's interest in women in *long* history. That interest diverged sharply from the coauthored work and from her husband's concern to encourage historians to write recent or contemporary history.[50] The book also clarified what was behind her insistence on the concept of civilization. Only that concept, in her view, made room for women in history. She argued that written history—"the chief source of knowledge about human affairs"—had been partial and fragmentary, "neglect[ing] one-half of the beings that have made up the human world." There was only one way to restore balance: "the narrative of history must be reopened, must be widened to take in the whole course of civilization as well as war, politics, gossip and economics."

> It is only by attempting to comprehend the wide course of civilization, therefore, that we can hope to understand women. In its evolution we see the interplay of government, politics, economics, modes of living and working, schools of thought, religion, power, class, society and family, the arts and ambition, and the biological and cultural aspects of sex. . . . Here are revealed the actions and reactions of social forces molding both the sexes.[51]

Such a concept of civilization justified placing women at the center with men, and thus was crucial to Mary Beard's inclusion of women in history. She developed that understanding long before the joint work, *The Ameri-*

can Spirit, explained both Beards' understanding of "civilization" not as
a neutral term or a synonym for culture but rather as an affirmative sign
for the purposeful movement from barbarism to humane living.[52]

Beard's venture into *On Understanding Women* may have been inspired by her reading of Robert Briffault's *The Mothers* as well as by her
travels outside the United States. The work of Briffault, a British maverick
anthropologist, published in the same year as *The Rise* (and by Macmillan, the Beards' publisher), confirmed Otis Mason's findings with
much greater sophistication of theory and method. More than once Beard
cited the significance of Briffault's three-volume work. In 1948, as Charles
Beard lay on his deathbed, she called it "her Bible." Not only Briffault's
words but also his references may have been highly instructive as she
wrote *On Understanding Women.* Of the more than two hundred works
she listed in her book's bibliography, she commented only on Briffault's,
"contains an extraordinary bibliography on the subject of women." A
few years later, when she composed a syllabus of readings and questions
for discussion called *A Changing Political Economy as it Affects Women,*
Beard remarked on Briffault's limitations. He was brilliant on the primitive era, she thought, but his accomplishments as a social historian were
less inspiring, because he believed that women's activities during centuries of recorded time were basically domestic.[53] That was where Beard
went beyond Briffault.

In *On Understanding Women,* Beard not only explicitly theorized her
historical approach but also built, on top of anthropological findings on
women's roles in *pre*history, an initial rewriting of women's roles in recorded history. Beginning with a review of the female-instigated origins of
settled society, her book amounted to a revisionist, woman-centered outline of European civilization, with some excursions to consider oriental,
Indian, Mesopotamian, and Egyptian examples too. It focused on the
high points of the standard history—the Greeks, the Romans, the feudal
and medieval periods, enlightened and imperial Europe. It found in each
setting female personalities and activities central to social and political
life and to the civilizing process. Beard eventually regretted the title she
had chosen, because it suggested a psychological approach. What she intended to show was that only history could lead to understanding. As she
later made explicit, she saw the problematic of feminist history that
stressed male domination to be, "how a creature who had been nothing
or nearly nothing in all history could suddenly, if ever, become something—something like a man, his equal"?[54] *On Understanding Women*

attacked the problem head-on, by subverting its major premise—that is, by denying that women had been nothing in history.

The book anticipated most of Beard's subsequent themes. First she pointed out many historians' partiality in neglecting women (as she would again, more caustically, in *Woman as Force in History*). Then she improved on their views, with her findings of women's appearance on all the stages on which men also paraded. More temperately than in her later work, she explained that women themselves had been partially responsible for the "one-sided view of their work in the world," because "unwittingly they have contributed to the tradition that history has been made by men alone":

> Women have been engaged in a continuous contest to defend their arts and crafts, to win the right to use their minds and to train them, to obtain openings for their talents and to earn a livelihood, to break through legal restraints on their unfolding powers. In their quest for rights they have naturally placed emphasis on their wrongs, rather than their achievements and possessions, and have retold history as a story of their long Martyrdom. . . . Feminists have been prone to prize and assume the traditions of those with whom they had waged such a long, and in places bitter conflict. In doing so, they have participated in a distortion of history and a disturbance of the balanced conceptual thought which gives harmony and power to life." [55]

This was the critique of feminist history that Beard would later accentuate, with less empathy. She did not yet heap particular blame on proponents of equal rights nor identify the theory of women's historic subjection to men as a great evil. *On Understanding Women* prefigured another core argument of *Woman as Force*, in its brief remark that a reliance on the jurist Blackstone's eighteenth-century *Commentaries* to explain women's legal status under the common law ignored the many "offsetting exceptions" in equity jurisdiction. Beard interpreted such reliance as a failing of "writers on historical jurisprudence" rather than (as she later would) a failing of equal-rights feminists. [56] Perhaps under the influence of Briffault, *On Understanding Women* laid more stress on women's differences from men, and especially on women's nurturant care-giving, than would Beard's subsequent works. The poetic cascades that opened the book—illustrating the "bewildering diversity" that the historian might hope to capture—were divided into two sections, one on the varieties of type in the "man's world" and one on the same in the "woman's world."

Mary Beard's later writings insisted that there was only one world in which both sexes acted; she used the term "man's world" only in sarcasm.

An ambiguity reigns through much of Beard's writing, oscillating between attributing special nurturant qualities to women, and assuming that woman manifested the full range of good and bad qualities also shown by men. *On Understanding Women* leaned in the first direction, her subsequent writings more toward the latter. The preface to Beard's next work of women's history, the anthology *America Through Women's Eyes* (1933), sounded with both voices. An innovative collection of excerpts from women's writings, the book followed a narrative of American history similar to that in *The Rise,* with a sharper edge of critique of bourgeois accumulation, befitting the era of the Great Depression. In Beard's preface, her doleful acknowledgement of women's instrumentality in the crumbling as well as in the construction of societies broke through her usual intent to place women "at the center of life—where operations are carried on efficiently for the care and protection of life"; she added "or where this fundamental cultural responsibility is discarded in the pursuit of self-interest." She tried to give the constructive side more weight, picking up paragraphs later with, "If there is in all history any primordial force, that force is woman—continuer, protector, preserver of life, instinctive, active, thoughtful, ever bringing thought back from sterile speculation to the center of life and work." Yet as if in counterpoint to *On Understanding Women, America Through Women's Eyes* was Beard's strongest statement of women's collaboration with men.

Beard intended the book to illustrate "the share of women in the development of American society—their activity, their thought about their labor, and their thought about the history they have helped to make or have observed in the making." Her headnotes to documents repeatedly stressed women's presence alongside men, in the Revolution, in peopling the wilderness, in social reform efforts, in the Civil War, in the era of robber-baron capitalism and imperialism. Typical statements were, "In this transformation of productive economy, women were actors"; "In all the activities of that conflict—economic, moral and intellectual—women participated on both sides"; "Having worked their way into every department of the political and social structure . . . women shared in the tempest of discussion." [57] In an important sense *America Through Women's Eyes* rewrote *The Rise,* for it avoided reference to male exclusionary practices in education, work, and politics. It also barely mentioned the women who rose to challenge such exclusions.

On the whole, this volume was as remarkable for its omissions as for its content. It virtually ignored the suffrage movement, including only one excerpt from a book by Carrie Chapman Catt and Nettie Shuler, which briefly summarized the campaign and its opponents and supporters among male politicians. The pioneers Elizabeth Cady Stanton and Susan B. Anthony were presented minimally, more as Civil War–era abolitionists and Union supporters than as complainants against male tyranny. Beard gave more space to Lucretia Mott than to Stanton or Anthony, highlighting, however, her social reform and antislavery rather than her women's rights views. Excerpts on women's emergence in the modern fields of law and medicine alluded to sex barriers there, but Beard titled this section "Breaking into Privilege" and, far from underlining male prerogative or female deprivation, observed that "inevitably, forceful and intelligent women demanded the full right to share in the golden profits of capitalism and attacked the legal and social restrictions that stood in their path." Beard's intent to document historical partnership rather than antagonism between the sexes was clear. Her approach was warranted by her developing interpretation of the nineteenth-century ferment over women's rights as a brief, almost anomalous phase in the longer history of women's agency, caused when "the domestic system of industry which revolved around the care of life—woman's prime concern—was demolished by the factory system." Beard reasoned that when the "sound" domestic and agricultural economy in which women "shared as workers, directors, and beneficiaries gave place to the feverish economy of capitalism," women "had to battle as individuals" and had "to think in terms of competition for place, income, and power."

Beard minimized the significance of women's rights advocacy as providing a framework for understanding women's history, but the premise of her book was that history looked different through women's eyes. Her headnotes occasionally suggested differences between women's perceptions and men's—for example, "Through the eyes of women journalists and diarists something besides elections, camp meetings and bar-room quarrels can be seen [in the West] by those who care to see." That theme was poorly developed in the documents, however, not only because Beard avoided revelations of gender conflict, but also and principally because she chose to focus on the public arenas of activity usually called men's, and found women speaking in ways parallel to men. For example, as she introduced antebellum Northern and Southern women's documents to show the development of two opposing cultures of "machine industry" and "plantation," Beard claimed, "Not a phase of the struggle . . . did they neglect and were all the speeches of Congressmen lost, the intellectual imagery of the verbal battle could be entirely recovered from the writings of women." Her intent to show parallelism and partnership between the sexes undercut her intent to distinguish women's ethical values and social contributions and thereby to revisualize history. The anthology amounted to what has recently been categorized by women's historians as "compensatory" or "contribution" history, which advances beyond a traditional narrative by including female subjects but places them within a conventionally male-defined framework of historical significance.[58]

The vagaries of the preface to *America Through Women's Eyes* (including a poorly developed proposition of the cyclical nature of the rise and decline of civilizations) reflected distinct shifts and complications in Beard's thinking about feminism and its relation to civilization, brought on largely by the depression. The economic crisis both vastly sharpened her critique of existing feminist ideology and raised her hope for a new kind of women's movement. Beard's own feminism had been forged in the early-twentieth-century civic, suffrage, and labor movements. She felt then that women would be much more effective in constructive reform work if they had the vote; the cause of justice for women alone did not ignite her unless it broadcast a social vision.[59] Beard's subsequent views were inevitably shaped by changing definitions and practices of feminism. Shortly after the Nineteenth Amendment was ratified, the National Woman's Party (NWP)—in which Beard had enlisted and worked for the vote—seized the name of feminism for its intent to "remove all remaining forms of women's subjection." Its program was a constitutional amendment assuring equality of rights regardless of sex. More than any other women's organization the NWP asserted that women as a group had to wage their own struggle for emancipation, although, paradoxically, their equal rights amendment proposed that the law treat women just like men.[60] Its leaders embraced a single-issue politics, which severed the party from the political left and from a multifaceted program of women's liberation. The NWP thus became in the 1920s quite different from what it had been in the 1910s, both its aims and its constituency narrowed.

In light of her holistic approach to gender questions and her postwar skepticism about equality as a goal for women, Beard did not support the equal rights amendment nor the National Woman's Party. (Many of the women in it remained her friends for decades, nonetheless.) Beard saw little meaningful difference between the position of the NWP and that of professional or business women who intended to strive for success on the basis of individual ambition and merit alone. In Beard's assessment, both outlooks amounted to advocacy of sexual equality with men in the context of laissez-faire individualism (something she reprobated before the crash of 1929). In brief remarks that she wrote for the journal of the National Federation of Business and Professional Women in mid-1929, for example, she reviewed feminist progress in terms of the commercial and professional gains that women had made, asking, "What is this equal opportunity in fact and in import? It is the mere chance to prove fitness and adaptability to a tooth-and-claw economic struggle reflecting the greed and destructive propensities of the traditional pacer. . . . If business and professional women had won their race in the days of rawest capitalism during the last quarter of the nineteenth century, would they have rested content and proud to be partners on a fifty-fifty basis in the practices and ethical justifications which marked the times?"[61]

Beard's evolving views rested on the premise that feminists had succeeded spectacularly in their immediate goals. Her rosy reading of American women's progress manifested a tendency recurrent thereafter in her historical writing, toward overly facile judgment that one woman's, or a few women's, attainment of a certain status or privilege signified that women in general had the same opportunity. In the late 1920s and early 1930s Beard seemed especially impressed with statistics citing women's control of economic resources. More than once she reiterated in print that women paid taxes on $3 billion of income and received 70 percent of the estates left by men and 64 percent of the estates left by women. The possibility that these facts represented only nominal economic control did not seem to have occurred to her. Beard asserted in 1930 that American women had gained a "genuine power of directorship"—a "status amounting almost to dictatorship in the nation's industrial and social order," she claimed by 1932. "In the old days," she wrote, "it was satisfying beyond present belief to prate of equality, for there was the wild freedom to philosophize about what women would contribute when they got the chance." Now, she believed, "the chance has come in large part." American women had raced through the doors of opportunity that feminists had flung open. They had attained "important political offices, novel business positions, unexampled wages and salaries, educational influence, laboratory advantages, scientific training, honorary degrees, prizes of many sorts, rare chances to explore the earth by land, sea or air, and international recognition." They had taken the "capitalist economy at face value—the face value assigned it by men," and had achieved, individualistically.[62]

Both Beards had long been critics of economic and philosophic individualism and of laissez-faire premises. The essence of the civilization concept, as adumbrated in *The Rise* and in all of Mary Beard's work, was communal or collective cooperation, as opposed to individualism. What was new in Mary Beard's work as the depression deepened was the plain identification of feminism with individualism. In *On Understanding Women* she saw feminism as a "sex antagonism" based on "legitimate grievances." It had seen "many honorable battles" but—being a phase "not fundamental" to civilization—it should pass, leaving open new possibilities for women to take part in social evolution. In *America Through Women's Eyes*, she pinpointed feminism as a reaction-formation phase occurring in the nineteenth century when men aggrandized political and economic control and women responded by mimicking the "rugged individualism" of the time.[63] Her assumption that equal-rights feminism was bred in laissez-faire individualism, and her objections to both, became major themes of hers during the economic crisis.

Beard's critique of feminist individualism was directed not only against laissez-faire but also against the sufficiency of the male model for female aspiration. The depression enormously enforced her view that equality— if it meant aping men's ways, as she felt it had—was a spurious and a world-threatening goal. "Equality with a spoliator of the nation's resources in commodities or life is a dead aim, whatever the exigencies may be of earning a livelihood; whatever the glories of a limelight fame," she wrote in 1930. "The opportunity to rise in professions, if they remain anti-social or plain stupid in their outlook, is of no importance from the standpoint of a progressive society or State. . . . Fixing the mind on man in a effort to pursue his course to the neglect of a consciousness of humanity in the large is a weakness—not a strength—in woman." Her most profound and seemingly most heartfelt commentary focused on women's adoption of men's view of knowledge and education. In contrast to her own efforts to change the male-centered reading of the history of civilization, she judged that women's presence in the academy, in general, had only meant more of the same. "That women frequently out-Herod Herod in academic sterility is an occasion for regret rather than exultation," was her withering assessment.[64] Worse, she thought, was that university-trained women absorbed and manifested typically male views of men's leadership and importance in human society and culture. Beard had looked skeptically on academic women before *On Understanding Women* was published, but the lack of enthusiasm for her book in women's colleges seemed to exacerbate her righteous indignation. More than once she recounted with rage and scorn the unsympathetic response of the women faculty at Vassar in 1931 when President Henry MacCracken invited her there to discuss the book. "The time has come to forget women," she remembered them saying. "We are human beings now." Beard retorted, "It is easy for you to forget women since you have nothing to forget, knowing none of woman's history." [65]

With the depression constricting university budgets and Ph.D.'s "actually selling ice-cream sodas at fountains," Beard pierced the veil of women's illusion, as she saw it, about university advantages. She seriously considered that women risked handicap rather than benefit from "university discipline," and not only for economic reasons. She perceived a danger that training mainly "by the male of the species in his own modes and manners . . . may unduly crush the initiative of the girl student and force her to believe that she must follow the masculine leadership or authority without deviation and at all costs." She went on: "There is considerable warrant for the thesis that university careers guided by men have deepened the intellectual cowardice of women instead of alleviating it. By accepting man's estimate of his own behavior, economic, political, industrial, and mental, at his own figures without considering the long and important drama of feminine behavior and feminine interests, women may lose ground both intellectually and economically." [66]

Not simply the matter of gender injustice in the universities but its social result concerned Beard. She had generally hoped and assumed that education and knowledge would equip women to exercise their particular genius at social construction and cohesion. Now, she realized, the result might be the opposite. Neither she nor her husband had ever seen the inculcation of knowledge in and of itself as a necessary good; both were constantly aware of the double edge of education. Back at Ruskin Hall, in a speech of 1900, Charles Beard had said, "Learning stands impeached in the court of history as the enemy of man as often as it stands glorified for its service to man." (He used as an example the teaching of antebellum Southern educators on the nature of blacks and slavery.) [67] In the 1930s, the rise of fascism in Italy and Germany piqued both Beards' sensitivities to the possibilities and consequences of mental indoctrination.

Mary Beard's constructive pessimism about women's indoctrination to men's views in the supposedly value-neutral universities and professions was virtually unique in the United States in this period. Critics of women's presence in the professions and the universities abounded, but they were critics who felt that women's place was behind men, at home. Beard was looking for women's leadership in social reconstruction, in values alternative to the ones that had brought economic crash and fascism. One other who sounded a similar alarm, warning that women who followed in the footsteps of educated men risked becoming like them, with all their destructive faults, was the British author Virginia Woolf. In *Three Guineas* (1938) Woolf brooded over questions similar to the ones that concerned Beard (although there is no evidence that either knew of the other's work). In an extended metaphor, Woolf imagined an imposing "procession of the sons of educated men," mounting to offices of power, and asked what it meant for the daughters to join them: "For we have to ask ourselves, here and now, do we wish to join that procession, or don't we? On what terms shall we join that procession? Above all, where is it leading us, the procession of educated men?"

Like Beard, Woolf looked to history to guide her, but she found little there to prevent an affirmative answer to her rhetorical question, "In another century or so if we practise the professions in the same way [as men], shall we not be just as possessive, just as jealous, just as pugnacious, just as positive as to the verdict of God, Nature, Law and Property as these gentlemen are now?" Woolf found a partial way out of this dilemma in the inspiration provided by biographies of distinguished women of the past, women who had made notable social contributions without having entered university discipline. These women, she wrote in a poignant combination of admiration and critique, had found their own teachers in "poverty, chastity, derision, and freedom from unreal loyalties." Only partially tongue in cheek, she recommended the same allegiances to modern professional women.[68]

Beard saw in history a much more continuous exertion of social leadership by women than Woolf did. By 1933 and 1934 Beard rejected and attacked outright the assumption that men had subjected women to their own will and domination in the long past. In her mind, certainly, the theory of subjection and the demand for equality were two sides of the same feminist coin. She did not attack the subjection theory directly until, at the turning point of the depression, the gleam on equality had thoroughly dulled for her. In speeches delivered in 1933 she referred to the notion of subjection as a "false theory which dominated the women of 1848"—her reference being to the "Declaration of Sentiments" composed that year, by Elizabeth Cady Stanton and others, denouncing male domination. In writings of 1934, Beard anticipated her main argument in *Woman as*

Force in History by pinning the prevalence of the subjection theory on credulous readers of Blackstone's commentaries on the common law. She attributed the "stranglehold on thought" achieved by that view to the writings of two nineteenth-century men, both advocates of greater liberty and equality for women: the German socialist August Bebel and the English liberal John Stuart Mill. Mill's book of 1869, *The Subjection of Woman*, indeed a bible to many feminists and a revelation to many liberals, gave the "dogma" its common name, in her view.

Beard had no doubt that both the subjection theory and the goal of equality with men had had historic reasons for being—"at a time when household industry was giving way to a machine economy"—and historic usefulness. "The dogma," she wrote in 1934, "knit them into a remarkably close sisterhood, simplified agitation, provided the emotional force for continuing the struggle for privilege on new lines, and left no room for disruptive questioning."[69] As a mover for social change (and as a veteran of Alice Paul's suffrage organization), Beard appreciated the utility and significance of these items but felt more strongly that this thinking, which once seemed to open the road, now led down a blind alley. As a historian, she recognized that an ideology might be progressive at one time and regressive at another. Charles Beard said as much, in a contemporary critique of "the myth of rugged American individualism." The individualist creed, he argued—in parallel to his wife's judgment of equal-rights feminism—had been "the great dynamic which drove enterprise forward" in the days of pioneering industry. But it was now archaic and destructive, superseded by the need for collective rationalization and planning.[70]

By the mid-1930s, Mary Beard moved from questioning and criticizing women's adoption of men's ways to expressing a renewed (if subdued) optimism that the world economic and political crisis would shock feminists into a more "cosmic" awareness. All of her historical findings were aimed toward rousing her contemporaries to reenact anew what she believed to be their historically documented role of creative social leadership. On her dark days in the mid-1930s, no doubt feeling that her message was falling on deaf ears, she blamed women—agents of their own lives as she saw them—for failing to see and grasp their historic potential. Criticizing Harry Elmer Barnes' *History of Civilization* (1935) for neglecting women, for example, she wrote to a friend "But I think his fault is women's fault in knowing nothing of themselves." "More and more I blame on women themselves their own supineness and oblivion," she wrote to another close associate.[71] Her own a priori belief in women's creativity usually won out, however, and in her most optimistic vision, she imagined that "rugged feminism" (as she called it in obvious parallel to nineteenth-century "rugged individualism") would retreat, and a new feminism emerge. The new feminism would be "less imitative than the old, more constructive and less acquisitive (therefore destructive), indicative of feminine concern with political economy as a whole as the old feminism was not, and in its collectivist vision betraying its realistic roots." It was such a vision, integrating women's struggle for gender justice with the encompassing "demand for decency of life and labor all around and security if possible," that Beard sought to foster in a course of readings and questions she composed at the invitation of the American Association of University Women in 1934, published as *A Changing Political Economy As It Affects Women*.[72]

Few other feminists understood what she was trying to do. "Mary Beard is a friend of mine but she has such a strange point of view. When have women had the power she gives to them?" one National Woman's Party activist wrote to another. To her friends in that group, Beard's announcement of her "disillusion" with the theory of subjection and the goal of equality was truly baffling. They did not sympathize with her intensified critique of a single-issue approach to gender justice during the depression. Loyal equal-rights seeker Doris Stevens identified Beard's interests in social renovation and collectivism with communism, not feminism—despite Beard's protestations that she was not a Communist. Stevens insisted "that a feminist can and must do one thing at a time," while Beard believed "that we have to do everything at once." Beard's desire to develop women's consciousness, values and leadership as such did not fit with the program of the Communist Party in the United States. She insisted—here in tune with Doris Stevens—on "admitting oneself to be a woman and making that reality and influence count as such." She deplored the "folly of pretending to represent something as neutral, as a 'human being' neither man nor women," an approach typical of women in professional and political posts (liberal or Communist) during the 1930s. Beard's claim that women had long been partners with men in the public domain also set her at odds with the educational approach of the League of Women Voters, which emphasized—to her annoyance— gradual training rather than immediate action for female newcomers to the political process.[73] Her support for U.S. neutrality (especially toward the end of the 1930s) was more thoroughgoing than that of middle-of-the-road organized women who also did not embrace her opposition to free-trade internationalism. At the mid-decade peak of neutrality sentiment in the United States, however, she found political if not necessarily feminist allies in the National Council for Prevention of War and the Women's International League for Peace and Freedom.

In the most salient division among women activists of the 1920s and 1930s, over the equal rights amendment, Beard "held aloof from the factional strife," in her own words. She criticized her former colleagues remaining in the NWP, perhaps because she expected more of them. Although she easily conceded that a "woman's bill of rights," as she called the equal rights amendment, was "long overdue" and "should have run along with the rights of man in the eighteenth century," she believed that current advocates of equal rights ran the risk of "positively strengthening anachronistic competitive industrial processes; of supporting, if unintentionally, ruthless laissez faire; of forsaking humanism in the quest for feminism as the companion piece of manism." If the ERA were achieved, she contended, "it would be so inadequate today as a means to food, clothing and shelter for women at large that what they would still be enjoying would be equality in disaster rather than in realistic privilege."

Her reservations about the equal rights amendment were balanced by no fewer reservations about its opponents who stressed the need for sex-based legislation regulating wages and hours. These women, not so unlike Beard, considered the equal rights amendment a narrow-minded, nature-defying expectation of sameness between women and men. Their conception of women's difference from men echoed conventional views of women, centering on the home, however. They usually portrayed wage-earning women as vulnerable, passive, dependent victims of the man-made industrial system. Beard not only refused to see women as victims but, more positively, believed that constructive work in the world as well as in the home defined women's essence. The protectionists' determination to prevent exploitation of women workers appealed to Beard, but she found their approach inadequate to the task of social leadership that feminists should provide, especially during the depression. "The minimum wage implies *a* wage and leaves out of account the millions of unemployed," she objected; it represented "too complacent, too sentimental, an acceptance of capitalism" and was "too consistent with the economic rule of a plutocracy." The agenda of neither equal rightists nor protectionists, she thought, would really "make a dent" on the "antisocial American labor system."

"Sex protection . . . embodies the objectionable idea of dependence.

Equality leaves out of account the objectionable mores of 'free' men,"
Beard said concisely, expressing her lack of sympathy with both sides. In
her most stirring statement on the issue, in a letter of 1937, she charged
equal rights advocates and opponents both with "inadequacy against
women's and democracy's ruthless enemies—war, fascism, ignorance,
poverty, scarcity, unemployment, sadistic criminality, racial persecution,
man's lust for power and woman's miserable trailing in the shadow of his
frightful ways." Her agenda instead was "plenty-for-all, to be attained by
democratic co-operative planning on a broad scale, with state help where
needed." As that suggests, her own vision was only schematic. She spoke
of "community planning for the meeting of community needs," a "collectivist" approach "less solicitous of the interests of the few." She looked
for "decency of life and labor all round and security if possible to attain"
and gave this as high priority as equal opportunity for women. To advance her vision of security for all, she urged women to be "creative leaders in the vanguard," *more* than equal to men.[74]

The vision itself was one she entirely shared with her husband. As
collaborators whose views on both domestic and international politics
agreed, both Beards were moving in new intellectual directions during the
1930s. Dropping the hint in *America Through Women's Eyes* that the
Italian historian Benedetto Croce and other social theorists were encouraging her to see a revolution in thought and a more integrative understanding of human history on the horizon, Mary Beard confirmed that
she shared the intellectual background of her husband's celebrated presidential address to the American Historical Association (AHA) in 1933,
"Written History as an Act of Faith." Indeed, her own work in theorizing
and writing *On Understanding Women* may have contributed signifi-
cantly to her husband's interest in disputing the propositions that objective history could be known and that it was the professional historian's
task to capture it. Although Charles Beard's new accent has been seen by
some historians as an "intellectual conversion," a break from his former
reliance on economic determinism to an unprecedented historical relativism, a more persuasive case has been made for the essential continuity
and consistency of his purpose from the 1910s to the 1930s. As early as
the Ruskin Hall experience, the relation between the historian's found
facts and the usefulness or interpretation of those findings was an imma-
nent theme in his work. His address of 1933 assumed the impossibility of
conveying the past as it was in actuality and the inevitability that the historian would select events or facts (often on the basis of incomplete docu-

mentation) to make a purported whole picture. It was for these reasons that he called the writing of history an "act of faith," which relied on a subjective "conviction that something true can be known about the movement of history." [75]

Whether Mary Beard influenced her husband to address· directly the issue of subjectivity in history is an interesting if unanswerable question. Before "Written History as an Act of Faith"—also before Carl Becker's presidential address of 1931, "Everyman His Own Historian" offered its relativism to the AHA—Mary Beard had perceived and asserted, in *On Understanding Women,* that "everything seems to depend upon the historian—his locus in time and space, the mere detail of birth, affiliations of class, and the predilections of sheer uncritical emotions." There she reviewed how partisan, rather than disinterested, were historians from Herodotus, Tacitus and Polybius on through Gibbon, Ranke, and Treitschke. She pointed out the political leanings of each one. Similarly, Charles Beard would a few years later focus on the political interests of Ranke, in order to burst the illusion of the objective and neutral historian. He seemed to echo his wife in retorting to a critic, "Is it possible for men to divest themselves of all race, sex, class, political, social and regional predilections and tell the truth of history as it actually was?" He had also, however, presaged the specific themes of his 1933 speech earlier: in a 1926 address he noted that historians' selectivity with their facts always constituted interpretation and in a 1930 speech posited the existence of "history as actuality," something external to the historian, the recording of which was to be sought. [76]

In considering the historian's subjectivity, both Beards were apparently influenced by intellectual currents in science and historiography. Croce's *History, Its Theory and Practice* (1923) stood out for both. Mary Beard listed the book in the bibliography of *On Understanding Women* in 1931 and mentioned the author in *American Through Women's Eyes;* Charles Beard frequently quoted Croce in the 1930s, and as president of the American Historical Association invited him (unsuccessfully) to attend the group's annual convention. Croce's position that "all history is contemporary history"—that, in other words, written history was inevitably "contemporary thought about the past"—powerfully appealed to both Beards. His underlying supposition that "only an interest in the life of the present can move one to investigate the past" expressed both of their predispositions. Croce was a more thoroughgoing relativist than either Beard, however—doubting that there was a distinction between facts and ideas, and pursuing the conviction that facts exist only in the consciousness of the observer to the conclusion that individual consciousness was the only reality.[77]

For Mary Beard, finding the facts of women's history was a life work. Both Beards stopped short of Croce's total subjectivism or solipsism, by retaining a conviction of the *actuality* of history—what was out there in the past, separate from the observer, real though not perfectly known. The relativism that Charles Beard enunciated in the 1930s was not anti-scientific or antiempirical but in tune with contemporary science: he drew on the thinking of scientists and philosophers of science, such as Alfred North Whitehead and Arthur Eddington, who tried to project the meaning of the new science of relativity for humanistic inquiry. The two Beards together and separately employed both the concept of actuality and the term *frame of reference* during the 1930s to describe the history writing at which they aimed, adapting these from the words of contemporary scientists, philosophers, and social scientists about the sociological implications of discoveries in non-Euclidean geometry and non-Newtonian physics. Both pursued their historical work of the late 1930s and the 1940s believing in the objective existence of "history as actuality," the wholeness of which the historian tried to grasp. Mary Beard's premise that "everything is related to everything else" in the "wide course of civilization" was akin to Charles Beard's claim that history as actuality would unite "all that has been done, said, felt and thought by human beings on this planet since humanity began its long career."[78]

To Mary Beard, the concept of history as actuality was not merely an instrumental but a necessary abstraction, crucial to her task of recovering women's history. In her actuality, women played full part. As she asserted in *On Understanding Women,* if women "dropped out of the pen portraits" drawn by historians in the service of states, kings, priests, or noble classes, they nonetheless "remained in the actuality."[79] Her perception of the disparity between past actuality and the fragmentary and tendentious historical record motivated her work.

Beard saw in fuller portrayal of women's history the antidote to women's underestimation of their own efficacy and the corrective to career-minded women's blithe dismissal of the relevance of gender. In the crisis of the 1930s, she was looking for a common and empowering consciousness among women that was not a sense of subjection or victimization. She was hoping for a shared consciousness among women that led not toward individualism but toward a movement for distributive justice of the most inclusive sort.[80] A unique vehicle for this appeared when Hungarian-born feminist-pacifist Rosika Schwimmer came to Beard with the idea to create an archive in which the documents of women active in the suffrage and peace movements of the early twentieth century would be preserved. As Beard initially saw the plan it represented a "way to recapture the imaginative zest of women for public life." "To recapture that zest I believe that some dramatisation of the woman's culture is necessary, is imperative," she wrote to a possible supporter. "It is perilous for society if they retreat to private interests to the exclusion of interests in the common life represented by the State."[81]

The story of the World Center for Women's Archives from its origins in 1935 to its collapse in 1940 is well told in Beard's letters. From Schwimmer's initiative, Beard developed a much more wide-ranging (and for a while, it seemed, quite successful and well-publicized) project to collect and house documents of women of all sorts. It involved dozens of sponsors and donors and served as the matrix of later major collections, including the current Sophia Smith Collection at Smith College and the Schlesinger Library at Radcliffe College. Beard conceived of it not as an antiquarian or curatorial project but as a political venture, the basis for an educational revolution, and the site from which women's public protests and social leadership might emanate.

Beard chose as the motto of the World Center for Women's Archives a phrase attributed to the French historian Fustel de Coulanges, "No documents, no history." It suited her purposes; yet her husband in the 1930s cited the positivist de Coulanges as a foil, a shorthand reference to a vision of history uncongenial to his own. "Where the records pertaining to a small segment of history are known," Charles Beard conceded in his AHA address, "the historian may produce a fragment having an aspect of completeness, as, for example, some pieces by Fustel de Coulanges; but the completeness is one of documentation, not of history."[82] Did Mary Beard choose "No documents, no history" with sharp irony, knowing that interpretation, point of view, the historian's conviction, mattered at least as much as the documents? Or did she mean to imply that documentation of and by women had unique quality in a history usually seen through men's eyes? The latter seems more likely. To sustain her conception of actuality, documents were the only proof. Because it was impossible to observe the past as a chemist sees test tubes on a table, Charles Beard once wrote, "The historian must 'see' the actuality of history through the medium of documentation. That is his sole recourse." In Mary Beard's aim to widen the frames of history to see women as they were in past actuality, documents were her eyepiece; only on documents could a new vision rest. She wrote with feeling to Dorothy Porter, the librarian at Howard University whom she enlisted to collect black women's papers for the Women's Archives project, "Papers. Records. These we must have. Without documents; no history. Without history; no memory. Without memory; no greatness. Without greatness; no development among women." [83]

Having gained what seemed to be a height of promise in 1938, the World Center for Women's Archives traveled a rocky road of factional disputes and failing financial support over the next two years. This was during the same period that public sentiment in the United States gradually moved from neutrality toward increasing acceptance of the possibility of war against fascism in Europe. Mary Beard related the two. That is, she hoped to acquaint women better with their historic role of building civilization in order to anchor them as opposers of war. "If we are ever to keep women from ganging up with men for war, we've got to give 'em a substitute in idealism meaning something to them personally," she noted to a colleague. At this time she was as much involved with her husband in the—as it turned out—futile effort to prevent the United States from joining the European war as she was with the archives. But by the late 1930s her reason and observation had crushed whatever hopeful belief she had held (if any) that women could be expected to show a pacific bent. *America in Midpassage,* for example, rejected the generalization that women tended to oppose war more emphatically—or more "naturally"—than men. It noted that the "white glare" of history showed women "as warlords of the most intransigent type at points in historic time when they ruled States or sought to rule States." In a full paragraph it recited women's methods of goading and supporting men in battle during the Great War. Yet Mary Beard (presumably she) could not resist following that recital with the claim that "in the main, fighting was man's business in history and women had been primarily engaged in the arts of peace, the making of civil society." She aimed her archives efforts to shore up that latter tradition, in which she did believe despite examples to the contrary. Neither Mary nor Charles Beard thought it impossible that "the cult of the irrational, exalting man's fighting above humanity's peace" might spread in America as it had in Germany and Italy. Their horror of involvement in the European war was in part a horror of that happening, thereby transforming the American tradition of civilian over military supremacy in the state, and also overthrowing women's constructive tradition. [84]

The edifice of Mary Beard's hopes for the Women's Archives came crashing down around her in 1940, at the same time that American war sentiment came to seem inevitable and Charles Beard's vociferous opinions to the contrary made him a pariah in the very circles where he had been lionized. Officially, the closing of the archives was attributed to the diversion of women's interests and funds to the European theater. Although Beard considered the leadership's internal weaknesses and disputes to be controlling reasons also, she did connect the end of the center with the movement toward war in a profound sense. Both showed her failure to get women to heed her clarion.

By 1940 Mary Beard must have felt doubly, triply rejected. Women whom she had seemed able to marshall now betrayed their civilizing role to march to the war drummer; feminists seemed more concerned to insist that "there can be no true equality until a woman becomes a Major General or Field Marshal" than to oppose American involvement in the war. Her depression-era vision that women would awaken to "cosmic consciousness" was blotted out. Her plans for an institution to document women's lives were erased, half-realized; and her husband was increasingly excoriated in the press and in person for views that she wholly shared with him.[85] At the peak of their influence on public opinion a few years earlier, both Beards had been pushed to the margin by 1940. To add insult to injury, the publisher of *On Understanding Women,* having agreed to bring out a new edition, refused to publish the revised version that Mary Beard submitted under a new title, *Woman: Co-Maker of History.* She blamed the rejection on the publisher's unwillingness to accept a new preface in which she dismissed fond beliefs of women's innocence of war-making and criticized Carrie Chapman Catt for naive denials of women's complicity in war.[86]

The writing of *The American Spirit,* the Beards' next volume and the only one thought by some critics to be more the wife's than the husband's work, must have been a supreme act of will, defying pessimism and defeatism as the United States entered the war. The book set out to trace American uses of the concept of civilization and, more than that, to show that the United States was uniquely situated to advance the concept. It was more purely intellectual history than its predecessors in their American civilization series, consisting of quotation and examination of one writer and thinker after another. Taking a cue from Henry Adams' admonition that one needs a polestar for guidance, the book re-viewed the American experience so that civilization, rather than individualism, became its driving concept. The idea of civilization was, as the Beards wrote it, a social principle, antithetical to individualism.

The American Spirit can be seen as an attempt to wrestle with the contradictions aroused in Mary Beard's mind by the entry to war. She had developed and clung to the conviction that civilization—the move toward individual and social perfection—did inhere in history and that women were central to its making. The descent to war, even more directly than the depression and the rise of European fascism preceding it, battered her theoretical balance. How could she hold to her conviction during World War II? Not only did civilization seem at risk, but women's instrumentality in bringing it to the brink seemed obvious to her. Time and again she pointed to the women leaders and disciples of Nazism, for example, as well as to the way that Nazism crushed the very aspirations that women in the United States cherished. The resolution in *The American Spirit* was that it was "sufficient for inspiration and guidance in conquering the forces of disorder and opposition and bringing the real closer to the ideal" if "ideals and illustrations of the true, the good, the beautiful, the social, the useful had existed in human experience from the beginning of recorded time."

The volume provided such illustrations—among them, the efforts of participants in the nineteenth-century woman movement. The book especially highlighted the ideas of Lucretia Mott and Elizabeth Cady Stanton, arguing that they both worked for civilization not as narrow-minded feminists but in a multifaceted way—"taking the full range of social issues into the scope of their thought and argument." In a treatment curiously at odds with most of Mary Beard's earlier and later pronouncements about the women of 1848, *The American Spirit* judged that "rights always remained, for the philosophers of the woman movement, only one interest among many—fundamental, it is true, but never all-inclusive respecting the purpose of the movement." Beard had already shown her admiration for Mott's social contributions in *America Through Women's Eyes*. *America in Midpassage* also made Stanton important among the "host of men and women" in the mid-nineteenth century who "undertook to make America conscious of human values, alive to the dangers of a purely acquisitive economy, and willing to carry out programs of reform." Had Beard extended that appreciative analysis, her later work in women's history would have looked very different.[87]

The Beards plucked the idea of civilization out of the burning, avoiding pure idealization or pure determinism, by contending that "the progressive realization of reason and good is *in* history, though not the sum of history." They thus achieved a dialectical view, emphasizing the human "struggle against the forces of barbarism and pessimism wrestling for the possession of the human spirit" while admitting that the latter—barbarism and pessimism—were also human features. They did not purport to offer an explanation of the universe or the "whole truth of history" (which Charles Beard, especially, had acknowledged was impossible) but "a construct, or view of life, summational and relative." And they offered it intentionally to combat pessimism, in the moderated conviction that humans inhabited "a partially open and dynamic world in which creative intelligence can and does work." Averring that "individual and collective efforts . . . can make the good, the true, and the beautiful prevail more widely, advancing civilization," they closed the book with a supremely ironic twist. War was the one invariable in human history, itself proving—since it depended upon some degree of civilization—that "the future of civilization in the United States has at least this much assurance." [88]

Thus, by effort of will (and absorption in research and writing), Mary Beard propped up her belief in the advance of civilization and women's role in it during the early years of the war. Her next project showed the bloom still coloring the rose of her creativity. Invited to submit revisions for the *Encyclopaedia Britannica* with respect to its treatment of women, she seized the chance. Selectively lashing male predecessors, she criticized the *Britannica*'s entry on the "American Frontier" for its ignorance of women's civilizing roles and of "mutual aid in community life, the cooperative enterprises which elevated the individualistic will to social prowess." She called the treatment "extremely narrow and bigoted" for following Frederick Jackson Turner too closely: "The tight little, provincial little, masculine thesis of F. J. Turner has had a death-like grip on the historical guild and has induced . . . historical writing by laymen . . . which has made [the frontier] barbarous—and made it men without women." With insight and constructive genius, she suggested several dozen new entries on topics including air-conditioning, bathing, bread making, women's colleges, cooking, domestic relations courts, etiquette, goddesses, Hull House, hunger, laundrying, matriarchy, militarism, non-resistance, patriarchy, priestesses, revolution, social implements (as a counterpoint to weapons), women, and war. [89] Her commentaries and revisions were probably much too radical for the *Britannica* to swallow. After she had done her work and enlisted more female talent to provide biographical sketches of notable women, the editor's interest fizzled.

By early 1944, after the Beards had completed their last (and best-selling) collaborative work, *A Basic History of the United States*, Mary was involved in a new writing project of her own. She finished the manuscript of *Woman as Force in History* in June 1945, although it was not published until the following spring. It went beyond *On Understanding Women*, not only criticizing male historians' neglect and showing women's public presence and participation throughout history but also making direct assault on the "dogma" of woman's subjection to man and on the corresponding feminist goal of equality with men. More decisively than ever before Beard indicted nineteenth-century advocates of women's rights and their successors for adopting the "subjection theory." She traced their mistake to the influence of Blackstone, in whose commentaries on the common law the legal position of the married woman was presented as wholly dependent on (absorbed into) that of her husband. Beard devoted much of her book to arguing the didacticism and partiality of Blackstone's view, because it neglected the equity courts. Under equity jurisdiction, Beard argued, women gained more leverage for their own interests than under the common law and did not suffer the "disabilities" that nineteenth-century women's rights' advocates stressed. Beard's reasoning about equity repeated the same flaw that her essays since the late 1920s had shown, for she assumed from the evidence of a handful of women using equity that their escape from the iron hand of the common law was typical or available to women in general. She was proud of her findings about equity, which were significant and thought-provoking if not conclusive.[90]

If women had always exerted force, what accounted for the widespread perception of female inferiority and male privilege? *Woman as Force* implicitly addressed this objection and answered that the feminist version of history was a prime cause. By adopting a Blackstonian view of their own "nothingness," Beard contended, women had taken a disastrously wrongheaded approach to their own rights and their own history; women themselves (as well as male historians) had hidden the truth of women's force. She thus resolved the contradiction between women's accomplishments in actuality and their apparent suppression by blaming women themselves, as if they had the power to have created an alternative outcome. Beard's woman-blaming was in accord with with her insistence on woman's force; it preserved her frame of reference whole. She roundly criticized male recorders *of* history but gave no room to men's resentment or subordination of women *in* history.

It is hard to measure the influence of her partnership with her husband on her mature view, in which she blamed women as much and perhaps more than men for past mistakes; but such an influence must have been exerted. The Beards' collaborative relationship may have provided the unconscious model and conscious corroboration for her thinking about women and men in long history. Her assumption that women's historic role of care-giving was consistent with their shaping of history in its largest aspects paralleled her own combination of family and public role. Her stress on partnership between men and women as the norm, sex antagonism as its distortion, paralleled her own harmonious relationship. The lack of acknowledgement she received for their joint work kept her from being complacent. She was constantly goaded into awareness that women's values and accomplishments remained underappreciated—but her own accomplishments, in her view, were undervalued by women as much as by men, and more gallingly so.

By the time Beard wrote *Woman as Force* she had a lifetime of collaboration with her husband and a dozen or so years of disappointments with women behind her. In comparison to her earlier work, in which she acknowledged the "legitimate grievances" and "honourable battles" of feminism, here she reduced the scope of women's historic demands to a partial and mistaken monotone on subjection. She construed the meaning of feminism narrowly, equating it with sex antagonism, atomistic individualism, and a misreading of history. Beard was very hard on men in the book, too. She used corrosive sarcasm against historians, social scientists, and men of letters for their misuse of the generic *man* and for their omissions and distortions of the record of women. But she blamed women as keenly for accepting the limited sense of themselves that men purveyed and for refusing to learn otherwise.

Beard knew the book would be controversial. She presented it polemically, announcing that "the dogma of women's complete historic subjection to man must be rated as one of the most fantastic myths ever created by the human mind." Reviewers picked up wildly divergent messages from her presentation. One male reviewer read her argument as vindicating men's behavior toward women, on the whole. He suggested that Beard's method could be used "against any other lurid caricatures of history. Wage slavery never was so abysmal as it appears from the soap-box. Not all overseers were Simon Legrees." A female reviewer wondered, on the other hand, "Why is Mrs. Beard so angry? For very early in this book you raise your hands and cry 'O.K.' Men have treated women shabbily throughout history." [91]

Neither of these responses was the result Beard intended. She meant to correct counterproductive interpretations of the past, to inspire women to meet the challenge of their social responsibilities not by imitating men but by working in tandem with them. The tone of the book predominantly reflected her wartime frustration and bitterness, however. The accomplishments of women during World War II, paraded before her as she wrote the book, presented a real dilemma for her thinking. The accelerated entry of women into men's industrial occupations and the integration of women into the armed services and into government posts and professions all served as good examples of Beard's claim that women were at the center of the common life, "equally directing" social forces. But the evidence that women were joining with men in the military machine, following men's model rather than providing a social leadership particularly their own, wreaked havoc on her faith that women's civilizing presence was worth affirming. Women's visibility in publicly supporting during the war threatened Beard's dearest convictions at the same time that it confirmed her basic thesis. Believing that women had chosen during the war to follow men's models and values, she thereafter felt freer than ever before to emphasize that women *had* freedom of choice and that the notion of women's subjection to men was "fantastic," a fiction. In letters of 1947 and 1948 Beard blamed sex inequities on individual women's indolence, childishness, lazy-mindedness, weakness, or elevation of men's knowledge above their own "by choice."[92]

In response to a male friend's praise of *Woman as Force*, accompanied by his assertion that he had always been a feminist, but not in the "opprobrious" sense she employed, Mary Beard wrote, "Whether I am a feminist or not depends of course on a definition and I am not bothering about this at all."[93] It is certainly possible, and in a narrow sense accurate, to call her culminating book antifeminist. In view of her life's aims that would be a great mistake—and yet the historical context of the book makes its antifeminism more important to notice. In a sense, *Woman as Force* was more in tune with its times than any other of her works, for a rash of antifeminist pronouncements during the war and postwar years sought to pin social malaise on women's betrayal of their familiar domestic roles. The brief against equal-rights feminism in *Woman as Force* anticipated the parallel critique in the most popular of the postwar diatribes, *Modern Woman: The Lost Sex*, by Ferdinand Lundberg and Marynia Farnham. Beard's book shared with Lundberg and Farnham's the glib description of feminism as a sex antagonism that complained of subjection and proposed only equal rights and women's imitation of men. Both books pronounced that the feminist tradition ever since the eighteenth century had grossly misled women by inducing them to follow men's model instead of their own destinies.

Where the two books differed—crucially—was on the question of des-

Undated portrait of Mary Ritter Beard, probably in her fifties.

tinies. Beard found women's historic mission in world-building, and Lundberg and Farnham found it in mothering. The audience and attention gained by *Modern Woman: The Lost Sex* infuriated Beard; she raged against its pseudopsychiatric analysis of the world and women's needs and saw the book as an overt antagonist in her battle to influence minds. "Naturally I am drawn into the contest for the capture of youthful thinking," she wrote to the president of Radcliffe College. "BUT I HAVE LITTLE DOUBT THAT THE PSYCHIATRISTS AND SEXOLOGISTS WILL BE THE VICTORS." To a friend she named Lundberg and Farnham's work the "nastiest book of this year (1947)." She was no friendlier to other postwar commentators who advocated refocusing women's sights on the domestic hearth.[94] Seeing only the conflict between her own and Lundberg and Farnham's aims, she probably did not recognize and certainly did not admit that their caricature of equal-rights feminism mirrored hers.

More than one commentator has noticed a tension in *Woman as Force in History* between Beard's emphasis on women as civilization builders and her alternative theme that women have been both creative *and* destructive, as good and evil as the best and worst men.[95] That dynamic tension playing through Beard's work matched her doubled vision of her subject both as Woman—a singular abstraction—and as women, diverse individuals. Advancing beyond the typically monolithic interpretations of Woman offered by predecessors (and by contemporaries such as Lundberg and Farnham), her doubled outlook was accounted for in part by her historical location. Beard's intellectual activism overlapped two generations. The organized women of her youth, in the late nineteenth century, believed in the coherence, the nurturance, and the constructive character of the group called Woman. Further inspired by her readings in late-Victorian anthropology, which stressed women's contributions to primitive civilization, Beard had a longing to retain that view of woman's role. But she also fully participated, in the 1910s and 1920s, in the emergent, self-named feminist generation's desire to get rid of Woman with the capital W, to revolt against formalism and enable women to choose their own destinies, in all their variety. Beard had both a political and historical commitment to see women as variety rather than one.[96]

Beard's uniting vision of women's past can be seen as her attempt to reconcile these two competing—and in her mind, equally true—frameworks, the first presenting women as one group, and a constructive one; the other presenting woman as many, as diverse, and as risky a population as men. Perhaps her historical vision did as good a job of reconciliation as possible, by finding variety and individuality in women's past, consistent with the overriding theme of women's work for civilization. Beard's vision of women as force in civilization was a consciousness-raising conception, intended to enable women to see themselves as a heterogeneous yet coherent group. Toward the end of her life, in a letter to an old friend, she summed up her life's effort to restore women to history: "What I have been trying to do for years is to awaken women to the reality of their historic power . . . to incite women to realize who and what they have been, with a view to their realizing better who they are and what they are now doing."[97] More than liberal feminism steeped in individualism, her vision had potential appeal for women across ethnic lines because of its basis in women's communal strivings. Yet where Beard wanted to eliminate one myth—that of women's subjection—she substituted another. In *Woman as Force in History* that tendency was visibly exaggerated. Offering women the strength of a vital shared history at the center, she granted no legitimacy to women's collective sense of grievance at exclusion or relegation to the margins. In her effort to redirect attention to women in history, she minimized and distorted the historical tradition of feminist protest.

In a fitting summary to Beard's work, both the strengths and the weaknesses of *Woman as Force in History* stemmed largely from her concentration on women in the public realm. As her earliest article had predicted, she remained interested in woman as "world-servant" rather than "house-servant." Although she saw women's care-giving in the familial context as archetypical of their civilizing role, she never attempted to plumb the historical depths of women's roles in marriage, for instance, or child rearing. When, in her early reform days, Beard preferred to regard women as political rather than as moral beings, that was not simply her secular voice speaking (although she was entirely secular)—it was her conception of the political as participation of the public community. She put the political first and judged morality by its social or political results—its collective or communal results. Similarly, her attachment to the concept of civilization (and her insistence on including women in it) relied on its origin in the Latin *civis,* which signified to her "the life, rights, duties, and moderation of citizenship—a care for public affairs." The Beards discussed that etymological origin in *The American Spirit,* where they distinguished *civis* from *cultus,* the root of the word *culture,* and linked concerns of the home and care of children and other private matters to culture, not to the category of civilization.[98]

Exactly why Beard stuck to the public aspects of women's presence in history is difficult to say. Possibly the interests and life work of her husband greatly influenced her. He, her collaborator, kept his sights on politics, economics, and international affairs and the gravity of his force perhaps kept her more centered on questions of public rule (the law, the state) and political economy than she otherwise might have been. Her emphasis may also have had much to do with her substantial dependence on secondary sources for her investigation of women in long history. Except for her reading of nineteenth-century women's manuscripts in the Library of Congress and her reading of *published* primary sources, she relied on other scholars' works—and those works largely concentrated on public figures.[99] Whether it occurred by intent or in effect, Mary Beard's attention to women in the public arena may be criticized as a capitulation to traditional historical priorities. One might even charge that as a result she failed to heed her own adage. For in looking at women on men's ground—as the public or political realm was ideologically construed to be—was she not taking man as the measure, the very method she reprobated? Her anthology *America Through Women's Eyes* risked that reading, and certainly her accounts of women as rulers and warriors could be read as such.

Yet Beard also testily criticized the traditional limitations of history to kings, wars, nations, and states. She intended to widen that framework. Her focus on the public should more justly be seen as a utopian leap. By emphasizing that what women did was political and social, she intended to eliminate the equation between the male and the public, to reinvent a conception of the public as a communal arena in which women as well as men acted. Whether or not Beard herself would have conceded it, she shared that perspective with her forebears, the mid-nineteenth-century pioneers of women's rights who wished to assert themselves as public actors and individuals, neither dependent on or represented by men nor confined to private influence only. Most nineteenth-century women who sought greater equality with men in education and legal status and in the professions and occupations—knowing well that their private characterization as sexual beings, mothers, wives, and lovers cut short their opportunities—stressed the civic side of their characters just as Beard did in her history. Beard differed in claiming that communal responsibility belonged to women in long history; she refused to see women as prevented from such exercise until the rise of feminism. She differed from some, too, in denying that individuality in itself was a sufficient goal and in always advocating instead a social outcome for women's self-representation. None-

*Charles and Mary Beard in a snapshot taken at New Milford,
probably about 1940.*

theless, her emphasis on the public personae and public responsibilities of women in history followed the path laid out by nineteenth-century insurgents who burst the strictures of the so-called separate sphere.

Mary Beard went so far toward expanding the boundaries of the public as to shrink the importance of the private realm. Evidence for this comes up in unexpected places—for instance, in her adamant opposition to home economics in the collegiate curriculum. Beard consistently maintained that "at college women like men should start their thinking and training with the subject of political economy as applicable to each [sex] and both together." She considered "training for home-making" a form of vocational education that belonged to technical schools. In a letter of 1936, she expressed concern that "admitting the claims of home economics to place beside public work" manifested a dangerous, even "fascist" tendency "to revert from full opportunity for women in public life." Going beyond the view of some feminist-minded pioneers of higher education for women, who believed that collegiate experience should provide an education as good as—by which they meant the same as—that available to men, Beard simply dispensed with the question of domesticity's claims on college-educated women. She wrote brusquely to a close associate who felt differently, "I have told you face to face and by letter that I do not regard the study of women's state of mind respecting domesticity and a career or their problems of domesticity itself as a proper phase of collegiate education." Although many women intellectuals and professionals who were her contemporaries acknowledged that modern women faced conflicting demands if they wished to pursue "full opportunity in public life" while also being wives and mothers, Beard looked away from this problem; she emphasized instead "the total economy in which women like men must function—whether at home or outside." [100]

Beard's position can be seen as a radical one. To an extent she was challenging the nineteenth-century ideological division of life into public and private spheres; certainly she was challenging the assignment of women to the latter only. As her claim that "everything is related to everything else" suggested, she wanted to merge the private into the public as she wanted to merge women's history into men's. But she was more comfortable and persuasive asserting women's civilizing power—placing women at the center—in reference to societies in which notions of public and private were not elaborately developed. In describing ancient or simple societies, she could speak of women's nurturance or domestic arts and feel sure that those accomplishments were recognized as both distinctly women's and distinctly public or communal, for the common good. She

Mary Beard in her study in the early 1950s, in a snapshot taken by a Japanese visitor. (Photograph courtesy of DePauw University archives.)

suggested *Encyclopedia Britannica* entries on baking and laundering, for example, but never addressed modern women's involvement in these activities. Intending to correct the typical treatment of women as private subjects in recorded history, she emphasized the public world even at the expense of examining the significance, historicity, or gender dynamics of intimate interactions. She turned a blind eye to the private realm rather than undertaking a political analysis of its construction. She never alluded to the separation of public from private in complex, modern, industrial society, unless her writings of the 1930s on feminism as a phase of historical development can be understood as implicitly recognizing that ideological development. To have explored that separation would have clouded her vision of women as world builders.

If Beard resisted historical investigation into private life because it would risk defining women in history as principally engaged in that realm, she had more complicated motivations also. She wanted to mark out an enclave of personal life that would not be subject to history—certainly not in her own case. Perhaps the tremendous irony that the archive-minded Mary Ritter Beard did not preserve her own papers can be understood in this context. Refusing to permit Merle Curti to publish her husband's private letters, she assured him that "as far as lies in my power . . . I shall see that his life as a public person is depicted in documents"—but no more than his life as a public person.[101] Her protection of the letters, like the Beards' refusal to discuss their collaboration with historians or journalists, manifested her defense of an inner sanctum beyond the historian's privilege. If the inner sanctum was, by the same token, not "in the common life," not revelatory of history, then her challenge to the bifurcation between public and private was not heartfelt. But her refusal to place gender-restrictive labels on any realm was genuine.

Beard spent most of her life reclaiming women's history as a necessary underpinning of the self-knowledge that would enable women to seize social leadership. If her coauthorship with her husband merits more attention than it has been given, her creativity in women's history was yet more farseeing; it most distinguished her and also set her apart from her contemporaries. Her major concerns and accomplishments were ahead of their time. No audience was fully ready to hear her unique message that the frames of written history had to be widened to encompass women's past. She affirmed women's agency in creating their own history and created the experimental vision that history looks different through women's eyes. Her insistence that women have always been central to history-making helped bring to life our current understanding of gender as a category of historical analysis.[102] Her deep-dyed conviction that women need their history in order to change their future is a most appealing part of her legacy. Given the boost of a vibrant women's movement and the welcome of an expanded and diversified scene of higher education, women's history has developed in the past two decades into a significant field—but neither of these circumstances surrounded her ventures of the 1930s and 1940s. And if women's history at present is still the "other," not the mainstream history despite its vital supports and the tremendous energy of its practitioners, how much more risky at her time—though crucial to ours—must we acknowledge the efforts of Mary Ritter Beard to have been? The full realization of her best insights and the practice of social justice that she did not call feminism (but we might) still lies ahead of us.

1 The Suffrage Years

Though she may have been active even earlier, Mary Beard's involvement in municipal politics in New York City on behalf of labor reform and woman suffrage becomes traceable beginning about 1909. Beard's real love and aim in the suffrage movement at this time was to involve working-class and wage-earning women, and in this venture she helped to organize a section of the Woman Suffrage Party called the Wage-Earners Suffrage League, in which the fiery trade-unionist Leonora O'Reilly was a leader.[1] It is probably a constitution for that section that she mentions in the letter below. Beard eagerly sought O'Reilly's views on the meaning of the ballot to publish in *The Woman Voter* alongside those of Columbia professor Henry Rogers Seager (a prominent member of American Association for Labor Legislation)—a presentation of "the working girl and the professorial views together," illustrating her lifelong tendency to rate academic knowledge no higher than grassroots wisdom.[2]

The letter below shows Beard in the midst of suffrage organizing with O'Reilly, preparing, among other things, a benefit performance of a play to be put on by working women. She expended as much time, money, and effort as she could muster. "If the [working] girls would only begin to wake up, it would be worth my life," she wrote to O'Reilly.[3] Like O'Reilly, the women mentioned in the letter—garment worker Clara Lemlich (whose words are credited with precipitating the garment strikes of 1909 in New York City) and social investigator Helen Marot—were both major movers in the Women's Trade Union League, a group that brought sympathetic middle-class or wealthy "allies" together with wage-earning women to foster the latter's education and unionization.

1. TO LEONORA O'REILLY

> The Woman Voter
> Mrs. Mary R. Beard, Editor
> January 1st, 1912.

Dear sister L. O. R.,

The enclosed constitution is what I got out of our conference that day. In this shape you can improve it as you see fit ready for its submission.

Where shall we meet next Monday night? Perhaps we had better meet at our headquarters in the hope that certain girls may turn up who have had handbills.

I was so absolutely worn out for a week that I had to drop all the threads and with you ill too we have not got very far perhaps; but I have had a rest of two days (only had to make the boy some suits—no suffrage) and feel ready for a fray again. However I hated to ask people to go to the trouble of rehearsing for the play for the 13th when there was no time for us to work up a crowd. When we suggested that night we forgot that holidays would interfere with meetings and then I have not known whether we could get the League [building] for $5 or whether we must pay $10. One week later we could have a well-attended performance and the girls would be able to help it go which is our reason for existence, isn't it?

I sent Clara [Lemlich] to call upon our suffrage leaders in several distinctly labor regions to see what they had done toward getting hold of working women, whether they had any meeting room where we might hold a meeting and whether they could give us names of girls. That was all right was it not for the time you were laid up? The child was nearly frantic with desire to work which especially interests me for the reason that Helen Marot said she did not believe we could get her to work. She seems to me to be keen about it and does everything that is suggested and does it well, I think. Of course we don't want to spoil her. She can help so much now with the New Year.

I shall be in to see you on Friday and if in the meantime you want me for anything, drop me a card or telephone at 4887 Morningside or 5860 Gramercy.

Yours as ever, Mary Beard.

The Woman Suffrage Party was working at the state level, trying to get the New York legislature to put a referendum on the ballot to enfranchise women. In that effort, Mary Beard negotiated cooperation between the educated and prosperous women in the College Equal Suffrage League and the trade unionists in the Wage-Earners Suffrage League. This was made more feasible by the membership of both kinds of women (the former as allies, the latter as workers) in the Women's Trade Union League. All the women mentioned below—Marion Cothren, a 1900 Vassar graduate, lawyer, and reformer; shirtwaist-makers Clara Lemlich and Mollie Schepps; and hat-trimmer Melinda Scott—were activists in the

.N.Y. Women's Trade Union League. The Wage-Earners' Suffrage League did sponsor a mass meeting to respond to the legislators' antisuffrage remarks and published their speakers' addresses in a pamphlet, *Senators vs. Working Women* (1912).

2. TO LEONORA O'REILLY

> Woman Suffrage Party of the
> City of New York
> Friday—[April 1912]

Dear sister L. O'R.

The College League has taken Cooper Union for April 22 for working up the wage-earners' section in the parade. I suggested to them that they get working women to answer the Senators and assemblymen who made such terrible statements in the debates on suffrage. If the bill comes up again to-day there will be more to answer. They absolutely ignored the workers—saying they "must defer to the *ladies* until they were ready for it"; they wanted "to relieve women of all burdens and responsibilities"; "suffrage would destroy the incentive to motherhood", etc. etc. *Now* if at this coming meeting you could ask "What is the incentive to motherhood to-day among the working women?" and Melinda Scott and perhaps Mollie Schepps and Clara Lemlich and a laundry worker could all go after these men with "hob-nailed" boots, we might interest the girls and have a terribly lively meeting. I have been instructed by the College League to work with Mrs. Cothren in getting speakers and have therefore left a note for Melinda, who made a fine speech at the New Jersey hearing, asking her to speak.

We had to get busy and I went ahead not knowing you were back. Am so happy to learn you are "home." Will you speak and act as chairman—April 22d then? Whom else do you suggest? Can you persuade Mollie Schepps?

Do tell me you like this idea for I am thrilled by it. We want to get out our announcements just as early as possible. We thought it might be good to give out tickets for the meeting to the union girls and girls at the lunch and other clubs around town.

We wish your mother would speak. Wouldn't she?

Here are two tickets for you and for her if you care to use them. If you can't, please let me have them again. They were given to me for you.

Love and a heart full of hope.

Mary Beard.

◦←⊷

Mary Beard recalled for a friend who was pursuing the ballot for women in Japan after World War II the "devices for getting out the vote" that she and her suffrage colleagues had used decades before: "mass meetings with stirring speakers; use of the press daily with news of *events* devised for the sake of this attention-calling; street corner meetings as well as rallies in halls; booths on sidewalks, made attractive with posters and literature, where women invited passersby to hear how, where, and why to vote; parades—what parades—at night with lanterns and by day with banners—'an army with banners!' and the very fact that women would parade unashamed for the 'cause'—a way of proclaiming its urgency; bands for the parading to enliven interest and help the marchers to stay in line."

Besides writing and organizing and raising money, Beard herself canvased door to door, especially in tenement districts. She recalled:

I did a lot of this kind of canvasing for the enfranchisement of women and of course ran into every sort of attitude and reasons offered for them. When a woman replied to my appeal for help in this campaign that she would not give it because the Mother of God did not vote, then slammed her door against further annoyance, I was for a moment too paralyzed to ring more door bells. But our women who agreed to work this way also agreed to report to district headquarters at the end of every canvas and we all wanted to make the fullest reports we could, which meant speaking to as many housewives as we could.

In some cases this door to door canvasing may have been somewhat or really dangerous but I never knew of any injury to any woman's body. Perhaps the instructions which were given to the canvassers helped to make the business orderly; such as, refraining from quarreling, behaving with good manners, leaving literature and in such a way, if possible, that at least the paper would be accepted, and be careful to remain outside the door and talk there if the place seemed otherwise risky. The real danger to many of us was that our legs would give away with exhaustion from the countless flights of stairs we had to climb in the workers' quarters.[4]

During this period the Beards lived on the Upper West Side in New York City, because Charles Beard was employed as a professor at Columbia University. In 1909, however, they bought an old farmhouse in New Milford, Connecticut, where they soon began spending summers

with their two children. Mary Beard's life of reform then had a seasonal cycle, in which she spent summers "in the country . . . for the family's sake."

3. TO LEONORA O'REILLY

[May 1912]
New Milford, Conn.

Dear Leonora—

I am sorry to have had to leave the fight so early but I am not so essential to it as I was earlier. There ought to be enough people interested in the Wage-Earners side of it now to make it go. The fact that such an army of tenement mothers and working women marched with Mrs. Belmont ought to stir the sluggish to action.

Though I must be in the country now for the family's sake, I am getting busy on a campaign Hand Book full of facts to be ready by autumn. So few speakers have facts and illustrative material.

I wanted to tell you goodbye. If, at any time, I can help at this distance, call on me. I wish you and your mother could have come up for a rest. My love to the girls in the W[age] E[arners] S[uffrage] L[eague] and to *you*.

Mary Beard.

Through her work on the Woman Suffrage Party of New York Beard was nominally affiliated with the National American Woman Suffrage Association—since the state work was carried on under the aegis of the national organization—but she, like others in similar local groups, was not working directly for national enfranchisement of women. That changed when in 1912 or early 1913 she came to the attention of Alice Paul and Lucy Burns, two young women recently returned from participation in the militant suffrage movement in England. Paul and Burns had in mind to reinvigorate the campaign to gain the ballot for all American women at once by means of constitutional amendment, an approach that had been dormant since the 1880s. They managed to be appointed to, and to revive, the virtually defunct Congressional Committee of the National American Woman Suffrage Association, which was supposed to deal with the federal route to suffrage. One of the first women whom they sought to join them was Mary Beard. They must have valued her not only for her reputation for effective work and connections with the labor movement but also for her husband's name. (Charles Beard published *An Economic Interpretation of the Constitution of the United States* in 1913, bringing himself even more publicity than he already had as a popular professor, municipal expert, and author of widespread articles, reviews, books, and textbooks on American government and politics). The Congressional Committee immediately began working up a huge parade to take place in Washington, D.C., on March 3, 1913, to upstage Woodrow Wilson's inaugural. Paul and Burns intended to pressure the president and Congress to make a constitutional amendment for woman suffrage a reality. They did, shortly thereafter, take up Beard's suggestion (below) to publish a national paper. A weekly, it was called *The Suffragist,* and Beard was listed on the editorial board.

4. TO ALICE PAUL

New Milford, Conn.
Sunday [early 1913]

Dear Miss Paul,

I am rather overcome by your own and the National [American Woman Suffrage Assocation]'s appreciation of me although I am very happy to be a part of the Congressional Committee.

The only hesitation I feel about marching in so prominent a place is lest the Washington women who are coming for the parade and who really have worked far harder than I—many of them—may think I am in this thing for personal notoriety. It is very comical to me to picture myself in that light but I would not do anything in the world to hurt the feelings of a single Washington woman when they all have been so fine about the movement there.

I have accepted the National's election and I shall do everything I can to help you. If you are sure there is no tactical objection to my carrying the banner, I'll be with you.

Leonora O'Reilly has had another change of heart apparently for she is circularising the trade union girls very hard for the parade. I wrote her a very long and very earnest letter pointing out what seemed to me the blind folly of ignoring political action.

The main thing I believe I can do for you will be to help start the national paper. That seems to me an absolute essential. If you are in Washington long enough, try to see Elinor Byrns about it as she will be greatly interested I know and would help solicit funds. I shall try to see her also. I am going to draw up the best scheme I can devise for my idea of the funds and organisation and send it on to you soon.

It will be good to see you on Saturday.

Cordially, Mary Beard

Participants in the demonstration planned for inaugural day were self-sponsored, so to speak: women were organized in state and occupational delegations, which had to cover their own expenses. A divisive issue emerged when a group of black women from Howard University offered to march in the college delegation; in response, several white women (it is not clear who) threatened to withdraw. The racist atmosphere and practices of the nation's capital at this time invited a segregated march. Alice Paul initially favored that resolution, but black suffragists did not give up their dignity so easily. Fortunately several white suffragists, including Mary Beard and the New York delegation, were resolute about finding a way to have an integrated march. W. E. B. Du Bois, a leader in the National Association for the Advancement of Colored People (founded a few years earlier) and editor of its monthly organ *The Crisis,* reported what happened this way:

> The woman's suffrage party had a hard time settling the status of Negroes in the Washington parade. At first Negro callers were received coolly at headquarters. Then they were told to register, but found that the registry clerks were usually out. Finally an order went out to segregate them in the parade, but telegrams and protests poured in and eventually the colored women marched according to their State and occupation without let or hindrance.

His assessment must have been based on black women suffragists' reports of their interaction with Alice Paul and the other leaders in the Congressional Committee. Du Bois affirmed that "after the matter was settled the treatment of colored participants was exceptional."[5] There must also have been a section principally made up of black women, for Mary Beard recalled decades later to her son: "I was marshal for that event of a section of the parade in which Negro women marched. I had insisted that they be permitted to participate and, since I was one of the first women to support Alice Paul and Lucy Burns, . . . my insistence that Negro women join in the parade was effective. But the fear that the hordes of people from Maryland, etc., who would come to Washington to see the parade, would be so furious to see Negro women in it, that they would resort to violence was so strong that I said I would get some men to assist me in marshaling that section. . . . I headed that division dressed in a Green Cape and some sort of cap. The men took positions at the sides of the Negro marchers—tall, impressive fellows. AND THERE WAS NOT A SIGN OF TROUBLE ANYWHERE ALONG THE LINE."[6]

The undated letter below, which must have been written shortly before the march was to take place, shows Beard's intention to resolve the racial issue to the satisfaction of the black protesters. The whole Beard family marched in the parade—Charles in the men's section, the children on horse-drawn floats.[7]

5. TO ALICE PAUL

[late February 1913]

Dear Miss Paul,

Here is a faithful report of the colored meeting. It was a small meeting but an exciting one. Three factions were represented:

1. Those who hesitated to make any demands which would possibly hurt the cause of suffrage. This position was taken by Miss Atweed of Wellesley who however wants to march with the college section if she marches at all. She is inclined to think it wise not to march.

2. Those who accepted the invitation from New York which I tried to convey to them as cordially as it had been expressed to me by Mrs. [Harriet Burton] Laidlaw. Mrs. [Mary Church] Terrell who was deemed in the early days a great acquisition to the suffrage ranks settled her attitude on the colored question by deciding positively to march with New York.

3. Those who were determined to put up a fight by marching where they belonged, they said, and not just where some women were willing they should march. These persons were certain that a southern minority was terrorising the northern majority and they felt it to be their duty now to take a stand for their own people. They are very indignant over the situation. Mrs. [Ella Rush] Murray, whose husband is a prominent man some way at the Congressional Library while she is a college graduate, represents this faction.

After a very heated discussion, I proposed that each woman sign her name on a paper saying where she wanted to march and that a committee representing all three factions take this paper to you to-day. You may not approve my action but I do want, if possible, to prevent trouble on parade day. Faction no. 3 will take the story to the antis and give it to the press, they said out and out, if satisfaction is not obtained at once.

Personally I am sick too of southern hold-ups and I do not believe that the political situation requires it for I do believe that we shall lose more in the north than we shall be able to offset by southern complacence if we have a row on parade day.

In conclusion I just want to say that Miss Hunt has not been able to stir up the colored women, had she desired, for she has not been well for weeks. The situation is entirely due to colored opinion itself and neither Miss Hunt nor I who were both present at this colored meeting could have made these women all of one mind had we so desired. They could hardly wait until I had finished telling them of the plan to put them with New York, etc., to rise and object.

We ought to be intelligent enough to avoid a race war. That is a perfect nightmare to me.

Yours, Mary Beard.

By April 1913 the suffragists following Paul's and Burns's leadership had founded a suffrage group separate from the National American Woman Suffrage Association (NAWSA), which they called the Congressional Union for Woman Suffrage. At the end of that year, relations between leading women in this group and their former colleagues in NAWSA were decidedly acrimonious. Mary Beard, as the letter below suggests, believed or hoped that the two suffrage groups could work separately without conflict, but her optimism was not justified.

The Congressional Union (CU) declared its sole goal to be achieving the vote through constitutional amendment and immediately began lobbying congressmen and attempting to send deputations of women—working women, Democratic women, women from various states—to see President Wilson. Mary Beard worked energetically on these early schemes. The letter below refers to plans for a delegation of women wage earners to see the president. Beard's connections with the New York Women's Trade Union League equipped her to aid the effort. The delegation, four hundred strong, arrived at the White House on February 2, 1914, although only twenty-five of the working women were allowed in to see Wilson.[8]

The CU was unique in seeing suffrage as a "party measure"—that is, in laying the onus on the Democratic party, which was in control of the White House and Congress. As early as 1914, the CU decided to marshal the votes of women in the ten Western states where they were enfranchised to threaten the Democratic party at the polls if gains toward a constitutional amendment for woman suffrage were not made. Mary Beard was wholeheartedly in favor of this strategy. Her speech at the hearing referred to below—before the Committee on Rules of the U.S. House of Representatives, where both NAWSA and CU suffragists testified in December 1913 in an effort to have a Committee on Woman Suffrage established—included a sophisticated analysis of the Democratic party's national electoral strength in the South as compared to the West. Beard argued that the party could not retain its power in the next national election unless it endorsed woman suffrage and thus ensured Western women voters' support. Her speech was well received by other suffragists, although Hull House leader Jane Addams reportedly thought she "hit the Democrats a little too hard." The hearing did not accomplish its object, however, for the House did not establish a Committee on Woman Suffrage until September 24, 1917, after several more years of suffragists' efforts.[9]

The great bulk of suffragists stuck with their local organizations affiliated with the NAWSA and felt either puzzled by or hostile to the aggressive new tactics of the CU. Early on the CU attracted mainly radical women and feminists, like Crystal Eastman (a lawyer, social investigator, and thoroughgoing socialist activist) and, on the other hand, some imperious elite members of the social register. The most famous of the latter was twice-widowed Alva Belmont, who had inherited great wealth from railroad magnate Cornelius Vanderbilt and industrialist O. H. P. Belmont. Beard (who was almost ten years older than Alice Paul but more than twenty years younger than Belmont) probably felt more at home with the younger radical women, but as the letter below suggests, she welcomed the reputedly cantankerous Belmont into the CU. In another letter of January 1914 she wrote to Burns, "Mrs. Belmont is justified in not wanting to be considered merely a money bag; but she says she does not intend to interfere with you—only she wants to be asked for her opinion now and then just to be a human being."[10] Beard also retained a certain distance from Alice Paul, unlike many of the suffragists magnetized by her leadership; her letters reflect what seems to be more ease and intimacy with Lucy Burns than with Paul.

6. TO LUCY BURNS

400 West 118th. St., New York
January 18 [1914]

Dear Lucy Burns,

The deputation goes on apace. Mrs. Belmont is going to pay for five women and I have promises for five more with expectations of others.

I'll send you names and pictures and speakers by the last of this week. We are planning to escort them to the station for a press story and to show them how we feel. We'll try to take working women with us on this occasion to make it seem that it is a spontaneous uprising of the proletariat. Will you be able to get hospitality for these women? . . .

Mrs. Belmont is very anxious to see you or Alice Paul. She is really very keen about the [Congressional] Union and its political acumen. I had a long talk with her this afternoon and if we treat her as a being capable of thought she will be a valuable ally, without interfering unduly too.

As for your attitude about putting it up to the Democratic party as a party measure, I am entirely with you. The other position seems to me messy and un-political. If we can just go on refraining from talking about the National [American Woman Suffrage Association] and do our job, the country is ours in a little while.

I dare say Alice Paul does not need to be warned against betraying any feeling about the National but if she has had so much that she does, you might say that she will keep her position by entering into no personal controversy of any kind. Let them say what they please and let us work. Mrs. Belmont is appealed to for instance tremendously by that policy. She never replies to any criticisms about herself, I believe.

I have some good people working on the congressmen and hope for reports soon.

Tell me what you know about the report of our hearing. They say it was lost or stolen, do they now? Do you think my talk is worth printing as a campaign document in case the committee fails to make good to-morrow in reversing that decision against us?

Yours as ever, Mary Beard

Sending a deputation of working women to see the president meant raising the money to finance their transportation and accommodation during the trip; Mary Beard was intensely involved in the details of nickels,

dimes, and dollars required to accomplish this, taking responsibility for
thirty delegates from Connecticut and eight from New York. Raising
money through the Women's Trade Union League was less feasible than
ever before, because most of its wealthy allies in New York, being
NAWSA loyalists, did not wish to aid a CU venture. Beard was apologetic
that she could not give more because she was "just so horribly poor." [11]
Costly in time and effort, the delegation paid off handsomely, if not in
President Wilson's conversion, at least in attention and adherents for the
CU. At this point Harriot Stanton Blatch, daughter of Elizabeth Cady
Stanton and leader of an independent New York City suffrage organiza-
tion, the Women's Political Union, which had been concentrating on the
vote at the state level, became quite interested in the national effort of the
CU, especially with Mary Beard's coaxing. So did Emily Pierson, a leader
in the Connecticut suffrage movement, several of her closest colleagues,
and some possible new donors. Mary Beard continued to cultivate Mrs.
Belmont, who not only promised financial support but brought into the
CU's publicity limelight her daughter, Consuela Vanderbilt, who had
married the duke of Marlborough and become a duchess.

7. TO ALICE PAUL

400 West 118—New York.
Feb. 4 [1914]

Dear Miss Paul—

I hope you are not very "mad" at me for not coming when you telegraphed for I was nearly dead I was so tired. Let me know sometime why
you wanted me so much.

I have some good things to report:

1. Keen interest on all sides in the national situation. The working deputation thrilled every one. The press was splendid and is hungry for follow ups.

2. Persons coming over who were opposed or indifferent: (a) Mrs. Blatch
who asked me to-day to come on the W[omen's] P[olitical] U[nion] Board
and said the w.p.u. would try to push the parade for May 2d. Wouldn't
that "jar" you? (b) Miss Symons of The Tribune now a keen friend—
whole spirit changed.

Mrs. Blatch told me she would help in a campaign. She and Mrs. Belmont are working for the parade.

3. Money in sight. I went on a hunt for Mr. G. W. Perkins to-day but
learned he is close to the McCormicks in the Harvester Trust so will have

to count him out perhaps for a little while but Mrs. Belmont was out all afternoon seeing men to get money from them. One she is to ask for $5000; two others $1000 each.

4. Chances that we can profit by putting Mrs. Belmont on the committee at once. Miss Reilly [Belmont's secretary] is very level-headed and she tells me how to manage things. This is confidential, of course. Mrs. B— loves the lime light as her social training was all along the line of rivalry for leadership. As she is always a good press story up and down the land, we can view her as business men would say as "a risk worth taking." She can now come to Washington and hold a suffrage meeting at a Mrs. Townsend's (biggest house in Washington?) to which every swell in town will be pleased to come. Our committee can't reach that element as she can and we need its money and support. She can preside at that meeting and have what speakers she likes and if she takes a collection or gets money, she'll turn it in to us. Miss Reilly will go along to handle the press side tactfully and she has a keen knowledge of the psychology of it all as well as a deep admiration for the Union.

Again—the Duchess of Marlborough is coming to visit Mrs. Belmont in July at Newport and Mrs. Belmont will make this play into our coffers and press.

She will give largely if she comes on the [Executive] Committee.

She can get us fine press notices if we could have meetings in the South and West where she might be present. Boston made big money out of her visit there. The national work will give her wider outlet so she may not tire as soon as she does locally.

The above are assets. The liabilities are possible inconstancy, break-out in the press, or promise without fulfillment. If Miss Reilly stays by her side we are secure and she will for a time. If Miss Reilly leaves, and trouble occurs, would we really suffer?

It is a gamble but I am a sport and I vote "take it" and do it quickly. It means money and press notices and big meetings and interest. All we need is to understand the psychology of the lady, I *hope*.

5. Emily Pierson was completely won over to the [Congressional] Union's policy and her delegates went home wild with enthusiasm.

6. Expect to have a good story in the Herald tomorrow on our policy.

7. I hope to find a contribution this week to pay for the $85 you sent me [to cover the costs of the delegation]. It is really $95 because Mrs. Nathan's check came back too. I had to use it all because I had the Conn. women on my hands. Emily Pierson could only get car fare and they had no money themselves. It was so important to see that the expedition did

not do more harm than good. Women simply would not give them hospitality and I took them to so cheap a hotel that we had to take in the Ball too. The New York delegates are pretty spoiled—some of them—and they wouldn't have gone or would have been crosser than usual if they hadn't been given money for meals on train. I felt nothing must be allowed to spoil the deputation and I would have gone right on and spent my own money if some had not come from the Union. Please tell Miss [Doris] Stevens this so she won't think it a hold up or strike. I intend to get it out of some one now.

Emily Pierson spend loads of money herself and she is grand to have won over.

I believe Melinda Scott's stories of hardships of hospitality are temperamental. Maggie Hinchey seems to have been comfortable at the place of which Melinda complained.

I hope everything went off well from your standpoint. Things are clearing up even in New York for the May demonstration and meanwhile I'll finish my reports on congressmen and try for money. *Can you* send me lists of coming congressional elections next autumn?

Hope you are not entirely used up.

Yours, Mary Beard.

Along with fund-raising and organizing, Beard continued to write articles and to testify on behalf of the CU's position—although she did not travel to the Western states to campaign, as childless organizers for the CU did. The hearing that she discusses below was held before the Committee on the Judiciary of the U.S. House of Representatives early in March 1914 to consider the woman suffrage amendment proposed to the U.S. Constitution. This was shortly after the Democratic caucus of the House had voted overwhelmingly to accept an Alabama member's resolution that suffrage was a states' rights and not a federal issue. Beard's address was a reasoned and historical attack on the Democratic leadership's position that granting of suffrage was a matter for the states to decide. Her concluding point—in an address that reached back to the Constitutional Convention and the Louisiana Purchase—was to accuse the Democrats of hypocrisy for their stand that woman suffrage was a matter for state action, at the same time that they were proposing a national presidential primary law.[12] The letter's account of the rudeness of grande dame Elizabeth Glendower Evans—a patrician radical the age of Alva Belmont—may suggest, perhaps, an exaggerated sensitivity on Beard's part.

Following this hearing, at which both NAWSA and CU suffragists testified, not the House but the Senate voted on a federal woman suffrage amendment for the first time in twenty-seven years. A bare majority in favor of the measure was achieved, far short of the two-thirds vote necessary for passage.

Undoubtedly Charles Beard's hand helped to craft Mary Beard's argument. He fully supported the CU's political approach as against the nonpartisan approach of the NAWSA. Indeed, in February 1914 the two Beards devised the idea, which Mary Beard wrote to Alice Paul, to establish in states where women did not have the vote "a democratic women's suffrage organization which would establish headquarters and watch every congressional primary to defeat in the primary every democrat who did not give a written pledge to support suffrage." [13] The CU did not adopt the plan, however, being sufficiently swamped with the effort to campaign among women voters in the West.

8. TO ALICE PAUL

400 West 118th Street
March 5th [1914]

Dear Miss Paul,

It is wholly impossible for me to go west at this time. I should like to help in that way but I am not the only one who can do so. I hope Crystal [Eastman Benedict] will be able to go.

The Hearing on Tuesday was certainly a strange one and I was very much disgusted at first. After thinking it over however I believe that there stood out very clearly (1) the fact that the Congressional Union was determined and would leave no stone unturned to reduce the Democratic majority and (2) the fact that there were two distinct types of women working for suffrage. Even if it was evident that we did not all agree, the Judiciary committee saw that one set was politically-minded and politically determined. They tried to bring out the question of our membership then to get an idea of our size. Mrs. [Ruth Hanna] McCormick called to the Union to answer and I popped up and said that our paid membership was no indication whatever of our strength; that our power lay in the appeal we had to the women voters and the financial responses we were meeting. That seemed to convince them that we were not insignificant.

As for my speech which Charles and I had worked on for two days as a complete answer to states' rights, I had to fight to get ten minutes in which to give it. When I arrived, Mrs. [Elizabeth Glendower] Evans said

"You can't possibly have more than five minutes and you must cut it to three if possible. Mrs. [Crystal Eastman] Benedict has ten and our time is short." I appealed to the committee for five more and they gladly granted it but Mrs. Evans clearly did not want me to say a word and under such circumstances my apparent desire to speak and the kind of a [speech] I had prepared under such necessity of showing up states' rights as I had deemed imperative, put me in a most outrageous position. It was the worst experience I ever had. Mrs. Evans treated me dreadfully afterwards. When Mrs. [Jessie Hardy] Stubbs insisted on the speakers having their pictures taken afterwards, Mrs. Evans pushed me from her side whither I had most casually and innocently strayed and grabbed Mrs. Benedict. The whole trouble as I analyse it is that Mrs. Evans was furious with me for wanting to show up the Democrats. She was always cordial to the extreme last winter and spring. She knew Mrs. Benedict would talk generalities and not go into their record perhaps. You have doubtless been told of how Mrs. Evans expatiated on her democratic devotion and loyalty and admiration for the President. It was terrible.

If any speaker had answered the states' rights thing which is all Congressmen talk, practically, I should have been only too satisfied but there was no comprehension on the part of Mrs. Evans that such a slogan should be met. It is because she is first of all a Democrat.

Still the Committee saw that we did not back up Mrs. Evans and so her position was weakened. Everyone will think I was just mad to hear myself talk.

I would not write you thus frankly but I know [that] you are able to work some and you will be anxious to know what everybody thinks of the hearing. We shall indeed rejoice when you are better and we all pray that you may improve rapidly.

Cordially, Mary Beard.

Although Mary Beard was certain that suffragists ought to encourage Alva Belmont's support, she wanted to keep her own distance from all that Belmont stood for. As the two letters below reveal, Beard declined to attend a strategy meeting of the CU purposely held at Marble House, Belmont's mansion in the upper-crust resort of Newport, Rhode Island. Doris Stevens, mentioned below, was one of the small group of young women who were paid organizers for the CU; she soon joined the Executive Committee also.

9. TO ALICE PAUL

New Milford, Ct.
Aug. 15 [1914]

Dear Miss Paul—

I can't do the Newport stunt. I shall probably be the only one who, for labor attachments, feels that participation in the Newport plans is inadvisable. I do feel that way and that I would lose more than I would help by coming myself. But your arrangements there are most important and I · wish them every success.

If you are thoroughly disgusted and want some one in my place on the Board, act accordingly. I can't help seeing my problems in this way. Doris Stevens ought to be an official instead of me anyway.

I'll help in the autumn in other ways if possible at all for my loyalty to the Union is steadfast. Service for it is not as simple for me, unfortunately.

Best wishes for the Conference.

Yours, Mary Beard.

Alice Paul tried to coax Beard to change her mind, citing the willingness of capmaker Rose Schneiderman, a leader in the Women's Trade Union League, to be seen at Marble House—but to no avail. Beard's independence on this matter suggests, in addition to her commitment to "labor attachments," how far she staked out her own path, combining her several interests in social reform rather than following exactly where the CU led. (Child's Restaurant, which she mentions, was one of the first inexpensive "chain" eateries; there were several in New York City at this time.)

10. TO ALICE PAUL

New Milford, Conn.
August 21 [1914]

Dear Miss Paul,

The Newport arrangements are far simpler than I had imagined but as a matter of fact Newport and money stand in the popular mind for one and the same thing and you might just as well play them up together in the press reports of the conference and get all the help possible from the combination. There is no advantage in having congressmen against whom we propose to wage war get an impression that we went into New-port and ate in Child's Restaurant and brought away no money. Let them think we invaded the seats of the mighty and brought away a war chest.

I just don't feel like making that play, invaluable to success and a speedy success as it is, especially since so many of you are brave enough to do it well alone. I think I am a pure coward in this.

Rose Schneiderman did go to Marble House but there is an inner his-tory in the labor movement among women here which I can't discuss on paper. I ought to be interested in suffrage first and labor second but I am frankly not. They are inseparable in my interest and I do not feel that on this occasion you have to have me while I do realise to the full that the Union doubtless does have to have Newport.

I hope you will understand and I wish you a victory there that will speed the fight splendidly this autumn.

Cordially, Mary Beard.

In the fall of 1914 Mary Beard was despondent about her lack of success in raising money for the CU's campaign among Western women voters to defeat Democrats running for seats in the U.S. Congress. She lamented her own inability to give, writing Alice Paul, "I haven't a cent myself this autumn but necessary car fare," and she seemed to feel inadequate to the tasks before her.[14] She was also furiously disappointed with the NAWSA suffragists, who, following the lead of Ruth Hanna McCormick, had in-troduced into Congress an alternative constitutional amendment on woman suffrage. This Shafroth-Palmer amendment stipulated that if eight percent of the voters in a state signed an initiative petition for a ref-erendum on woman suffrage, the state would be required to hold such a referendum.[15] The emphasis of this amendment on states' rights was di-rectly opposed to all the CU was attempting, and to all of Mary Beard's political convictions. "I'm so mad I can't think of anything else," she wrote to Alice Paul in reference to the NAWSA convention of November 1914. "Surely it is time for that group to get down and out of the way of suffrage. All of us become a laughing-stock through their action." At a slighter later date she was so enraged by the NAWSA suffragists' "re-pudiating us and blaming us," she wrote to CU organizer Doris Stevens, that "I felt like resigning from every association with womenkind I now have and forevermore—but," she continued, "I recovered and feel quite hopeful of the human race again tonight."[16]

Although Beard hoped that the CU and NAWSA leaderships could avoid confrontation, her emotions about the other suffragists remained volatile; indeed, so did her feelings about continuing with the CU. Her proposal to exit from the CU's inner circle in the following letter was not taken up immediately but she acted on it about six months later. The letter was written in the wake of the Congressional elections of 1914, during which the CU brought the federal approach to woman suffrage to national and congressional attention, although succeeding only partially in their electoral efforts. Only twenty-three of the forty-three Democrats against whom the CU campaigned were defeated, usually for reasons extraneous to the suffrage issue.

11. TO ALICE PAUL

400 W. 118. New York City
Nov. 7 [1914]

Dear Miss Paul,

I do not wonder at the exhaustion of the campaigners or at the exhaustion of the Washington workers. I seem to do nothing in comparison but almost no other worker has young children and no money like me. If I overwork, my children suffer and I can't go away because I have no competent person to take care of them. I probably can get some one for any big emergency but it is not a simple thing to do. I wish to God I could do more but I don't see how I can.

Do get some one in my place on the Executive Committee [of the Congressional Union] for it is useless to carry dead wood and this would be a good time to make this change. I shall continue to help whenever I can and in every way I can.

Faithfully yours, Mary Beard.

Fortunately Mary Beard could rely not only on moral support but also on material and intellectual aid from her husband in devising arguments and making contacts to further the movement begun by the CU. Charles Beard saw in the history of American political practice strong justification for the CU's attempt to make a minority group—that is, the voting women of the West—the "swing" voters who could decide the fate of a party and an election. His article in the new journal the *New Republic,* mentioned in the letter below, was the first of four he would publish there from 1914 to 1916 on the subject of suffrage strategy, all supporting CU policy rather than the state-by-state approach still taken by the NAWSA.[17]

12. TO ALICE PAUL

400 West 118th St., New York.
November 30 [1914]

Dear Alice Paul,

That ten dollars I promised eludes me all the time. If I can ever get hold
of it or keep hold of it long enough I shall surely help but I am always so
hard up.

I am trying to help however in some way. The New Republic has been
so hostile that Charles went down to see the editors whom we know
rather well and he explained and argued until they admitted that they had
been blind and foolish. Charles will have a reply in this next number.
Some member of the Union had a good letter in reply but it may be overlooked so far toward the end of the paper so that Charles will help too by
an article farther toward the front. I knew that one signed by him would
carry more weight than one by me as a member of the [Executive]
Committee.

I am serious about wanting to help financially but can't seem to make
good there.

Yours, Mary Beard

Late in 1914 the New York legislature approved a referendum on woman
suffrage to come before the state's voters in November 1915, and as a
consequence the friction between NAWSA suffragists and CU suffragists
in New York City mounted dramatically. The CU was considering opening a headquarters in New York City. NAWSA suffragists working on the
state campaign were sure that the CU's federal emphasis and attack on
Democrats would harm the local efforts. Many CU advocates, especially
New Yorkers like Mary Beard, saw tremendous advantage to their cause
in bringing a populous state such as New York, with all of its congressmen and electoral votes, into the "suffrage column." They thought it
appropriate to wait until after the November 1915 referendum to open
CU headquarters in New York City. As earlier, Mary Beard in the following letter suggests a path that will conciliate suffragists outside the CU.
On December 19, 1914, however, the majority of the CU's Executive
Committee voted to open headquarters in New York.[18] That decision set
Alice Paul on a permanent collision course with Carrie Chapman Catt,
who was leading the New York State suffrage effort and would be, a year
later, president of the NAWSA.

The first paragraph refers to the news that the Rules Committee of the U.S. House of Representatives would report favorably on the resolution for a woman suffrage amendment, which meant that the House would actually debate and vote on the issue.

13. TO ALICE PAUL

> 400 West 118th. St., New York.
> December 14 [1914]

Dear Miss Paul,

We are all delighted with the notice that the Rules Committee had to take even if it thinks it has played us a trick. I do not know of course what you hope to see done on December 23d. The House might vote to reject the motion of the Rules Committee and so let the Democratic Party slide from under all responsibility. I am terribly interested and anxious.

The sentiment of opposition to the opening of Congressional Union headquarters here [in N.Y.C.] grows among our friends. I have come to believe that it is a bad move for us to make right now for the reason that we could not open headquarters here without lambasting the democrats and we have far more to hope from them in this state next autumn than from the republicans, after all. Congress may adjourn about the time you would open here and it would not meet again until after our vote here next November. During that time while the campaign is on here you would be alienating, I fear, all the women and we should get no money, many more enemies, and be widely (instead of futilely as now) charged with having lost the state.

The day after election; that is, the first week in November however I am highly in favor of a move here if we get nowhere with the amendment this session.

I do not write this because I waver one iota from interest in the federal work or belief in your policy. I think we must work here among the women and on the congressmen but not through flaunting headquarters right now. Doris Stevens ought to come for a while and raise money quietly. She can do it I believe even better in that way and thus we shall keep the many friends we have and are steadily making.

I have come to believe too that it is a tactical blunder to open up with Mrs. Belmont. I can easily see that a refusal to do so will be difficult but on the ground that it is untimely to open any headquarters here that blunder can be avoided.

I can't very well write all I know and feel but I have been influenced by the great state of excitement over the situation that friends, and those valuable friends like Florence Kelley, seem to be in. She says she will resign at once if we take this step at this time though she is anxious to have us come a little later.

I think we shall be able to send a very splendid Democratic deputation on January 6th if the excuse for it then remains. Mrs. Robert Adamson is thinking of going (though you must not say so yet) and she is working it up among all the leading Democratic women. Mrs. Adamson and some of our common friends and people whom we are interested in making more intelligent about the Union want very much to see you and Lucy Burns and as many of the other members of the committee as possible while you are here. Can you stay over on Saturday night and spend that evening at Mrs. Adamson's for that purpose? Please let me know by special [delivery or] by telegram so we can ask people to come to meet you. I wish I could invite you here for the week-end but I haven't a single bed.

The Suffragist is a grand little paper. Here is my long delayed subscription. Am looking forward most eagerly to seeing you again and hearing everything.

Yours as ever, Mary Beard

•←

With the following letter, Mary Beard began her withdrawal from the CU's Executive Committee. She felt unable to give the group its due, but that feeling must have resulted from her own setting of priorities. Besides the demands of her family, during the time of her greatest involvement with the CU she was also busy with a writing project of her own. Her book *Women's Work in Municipalities,* which required a great deal of research into the activities of women's clubs and associations across the nation, was published in 1915. Although Beard does not mention it in the following letter, the suffrage campaign in New York, leading up to the referendum of 1915, was also commanding much of her attention.

14. TO ALICE PAUL

400 West 118th. St., New York
May 15 [1915]

Dear Miss Paul,

Crystal Eastman was to arrange with Mrs. Belmont for the conference on Monday if possible and I was to reserve any time and place up to Thursday, when I go to the country, that suited them. Crystal couldn't tell whether she would be able to get to Mrs. Belmont's for the meeting or whether we should all have to go down to her home but I have been waiting myself to hear definite plans before answering your letter. Crystal went to the country for a couple of days and has had to stay longer, it seems. She is not in a fit condition to do one thing and I don't see how she can assume responsibilities for some months to come.

As for me I must go to the country and I can't help one bit more or I shall break down too. I hate to have so little strength but there seems to be no choice between being a hermit and overdoing and I shall have to fluctuate between the two performances. I must consider my young children at times and they get no attention whatever during the winter.

You must find some one to take my place on the [executive] committee and others can do the work so much better than I because they have more time, leisure, money and wisdom. I shall be glad to meet the committee on Monday for I admire you and all in the same whole hearted way. It is only that I have reached the limit for the time being—for months—of assistance to you. I shall telegraph you to-night or to-morrow where we can all meet if I can get into touch with Crystal by that time.

Cordially, Mary Beard.

[P.S.] I read your letter again and I see the date of the conference is May 25. I *can't* come back for it but I think it a good thing for you to have it and I hope you will be able to decide on some excellent person for the New York work.

Mary Beard resigned from the cu Executive Committee in the last week of May 1915. The letter below suggests the mix of motives that led her to withdraw from the inner circle. Among these was her sense of inadequacy in fund-raising—an activity that she considered an obligation, even though it went against her "instinctive scruples." Notwithstanding her husband's support of her activities, she had little money to give. A few months earlier she had written to Doris Stevens that "my husband and I have a joint bank book and this winter I can't afford to get him in too deep."[19] Her unusual thought in this letter of getting a job shows how deeply she felt her lack of autonomy in spending.

At the time, Carrie Chapman Catt was accusing Alice Paul of having broken her promise not to open cu headquarters in New York; the accusation was specious, according to other cu members, for Paul had made no such promise. Beard believed Paul's account yet at the same time seemed relieved to be departing from the autocratically run cu

Executive Committee. Nor had her scorn for the tactics of the NAWSA in any way diminished. As in the letter below, through her whole life Beard frankly criticized—even despaired at—the choices and tactics of various groups of women, even while she cheered on women's achievements.

15. TO LUCY BURNS

New Milford, Conn.
June 8 [1915]

Dear Miss Burns,

I felt sure that Miss Paul had given no pledge to keep out of New York even before your letter came stating that she had not. I understand the whole spirit of your letter and share it. My resignation from the Executive Board was not due to condemnation of the C.U. but to the desire to enable a capable worker with more leisure to receive the recognition of committed membership and the stimulus that comes from such membership. It seemed the only fair thing to do. As for the Advisory Council, I'd rather not be on that now because it will only be a source of annoyance to me since I shall be called up constantly or visited by those who regard that body as advisory in character and want me to interfere with the acts of the [Executive] Committee. I leave you freer by staying off of it for outside I can abstain from interference and that is a comfort all round. Of course there will be no publicity on my action. I have tried to do the right thing and so quietly that only good will result.

I couldn't go to Hartford to-day but I sent my good husband and thereby endorse the C.U. very publicly and effectively. I think I shall get a remunerative job this winter and have some money at least to contribute to the Union. That will help more than anything and without such a job, I have no money to give as the children will both have to go to expensive schools this winter and part of our income has to be laid up for a rainy day.

I am sorry women of this country are giving such a lamentable demonstration of their political ignorance. Just as is the enfranchisement of our sex and necessary as it is, I find it very hard to be as absorbed in suffrage as I am in the labor struggles just because nearly all suffragists seem so hopeless. Our C.U. is at a critical stage of its existence perhaps but it has always been. Money is so essential that in declining to be the backbone of the support of the New York headquarters I felt it was better to make money-raising a real chore to be performed by one on the spot and more capable. I can do that but poorly when in town and not at all when out of town.

What a pity that all the National [American Woman Suffrage Association] suffragists can see is attacking other suffragists. They are in a mess about their old Shafroth amendment and I believe that is why they are so hot on our trail because they know they got in bad with that proposal everywhere. I was told that [Connecticut suffragist] Miss Ruutz-Rees said the other day she didn't care much for it now. They say through Connecticut that we declared war on the National with the leaflet "Which Amendment will You Support" and that war must be answered by war. Of course we did but they haven't sense enough to see that the c.u. has driven them into any sensible action they may now prove themselves capable of. Will it be sensible? I feel it can't be.

Yours as ever. Mary Beard

In spite of her resignation Mary Beard remained committed to the cu federal approach; at the same time she believed in the importance of working to gain suffrage in New York state. Her letter below to Carrie Chapman Catt, while personally deferential, forthrightly explains her political position and the sources of her frustration with NAWSA policies (and with certain NAWSA officials, such as Gertrude Foster Brown and Harriet Burton Laidlaw). It shows Beard's astuteness in recognizing the increased power of the executive branch in twentieth-century politics.

In 1915, state referenda on woman suffrage were pending not only in New York but also in Pennsylvania, New Jersey (the home state of President Woodrow Wilson), and Massachusetts. Throughout her letter to Catt, Beard implies the reasonableness and compatibility of working for suffrage at both the state level and the national level simultaneously. This would, in fact, be the policy the NAWSA adopted under Catt's leadership in 1916.

16. TO CARRIE CHAPMAN CATT

New Milford, Conn.
June 8th [1915]

Dear Mrs. Catt,

Some time ago I received your circular letter to the members of the Executive Committee of the Congressional Union. I have delayed replying because my personal deep admiration for you and my keen interest in the campaign you are leading so well made it hard for me to seem to have to answer except in hearty agreement with your point of view.

The more I think over the point at issue the more I deem it necessary however to explain my position in order that you may see how one whom you deem misguided does justify her position, in order that you may help to guide her out of her morass of political thinking if you deem her worth the trouble. I have always considered you so big because you have not considered those who differed with you as necessarily beneath contempt. Mrs. [Gertrude Foster] Brown has treated me that way. You, I know, will at least give me credit for honest intent if not for good sense.

Here are a few points then I wish to present.

First, granted that the [Congressional Union's] annoyance of the President seemed an importation of English militancy and a grievous mistake, what seemed an evil might possibly have been turned into great good by all of you who protested publicly if you had stated to the President that you regretted the incident *while* lamenting his stand on suffrage. That note was not sounded as far as I know.

Second, in your letter to the papers you stated your recognition of the fact that the federal amendment is solely in the hands of Congress and the state legislatures. Since we learned that technical fact as school girls however the power of the executive in state and federal government has so grown that it is the most striking thing in American political life to-day. One always has to take into consideration both the technical requirement and the facts of practical politics which are unwritten. President Wilson lashed Congress into every step it took and the chances are he will be still more a dominating figure in the year to come. At the hearing before Governor [Charles] Whitman [of New York] this past winter when we asked him to endorse suffrage in his message, I called his attention to the basis of our appeal to him in the increased power and influence of the executive. He listened very much interested to that point of view. We may not approve of usurpation by the executive but the fact remains.

Third, the President is interfering in state campaigns when he recognises with public effort the aliens who will vote against us in a state like Pennsylvania and when, in telling them everything else they need to know, he neglects to tell them to extend to American women in November the liberty that is freely and with glad ceremonies extended to them.

Fourth, his silence in his own state at the present is having a bad effect on his state. He should come out not against us but for us since he has stated that it is a matter to be decided by the voters of a state and in every issue in his own state before he has taken a hand by letter and by visit from the White House.

Fifth, the interests of the Congressional Union and of the state are compatible if followed along the lines which Marion May has probably presented to you. She and I have talked it over as individuals, not as members of any organisations especially, but as pure, politically sound, suffrage tactics. I believe that nothing would help New York like such leaflets and such type of work.

Sixth, while Senator [James] O'Gorman [of New York] took a stand against suffrage, his statement has been made in time for us to be able to make converts that count, by showing how a blind position like his will hurt his party incalculably and at once, owing to the close approach of the presidential convention and the keen interest that women voters are taking in the attitude of Eastern politicians toward the enfranchisement of their sisters. Not only can his statements be answered seriatim in speeches to the voters—who prefer to hear about politicians to hearing about the home and babies and justice unfortunately—but all politicians might pass the word down to the boys in time to help us if they felt we understood politics and proposed to use now what political power we do have.

I do not want to trespass upon your very busy life by writing at too great length but . . . I wish we might agree on the value of political work as well as educational work, on the power of the President, and on the advisability of always attacking the enemy rather than on laying defeat to women. When the Shafroth amendment, for example, came up in Congress, the Congressional Union in every public statement, I believe, and in every word to Congressmen and Senators refused to place the blame for the weakened hold the other amendment thereby had because of the machinations or blindness of suffragists but insisted that legislators must themselves be sincere in their desire to grant the essence of right and not the shadow.

I have long wanted to argue these matters with those of you whom I respect so much. I have never been able to achieve that victory of a calm argument of any kind with Mrs. [Harriet Burton] Laidlaw and Mrs. Brown has been inclined to insult me without a hearing of any kind. At least I know your spirit is bigger and if I seem hopeless in my attitude of mind I shall greatly appreciate your telling me so and why.

Sincerely, Mary Beard

P.S. I should be throwing my energies now into the state campaign if I could throw them anywhere outside the home. I can't afford to pay the right person to take care of my children in the country and they mustn't be in town this summer. I shall give with whole hearted devotion however the last two months to the state provided you all are not terrified at my cooperation. I shall not talk politics though then unless previous political plans have been made and you approve that.

⁕

The suffrage referenda in New York and the three other eastern industrial states were all defeated in November 1915. From outside the CU's inner circle, Mary Beard endorsed its aim to campaign against Democrats in 1916 and kept working for the Susan B. Anthony amendment (as the suffrage measure was now called). She also continued her focus on wage-earning women, suggesting, for instance, that the flamboyant suffrage musical, "Melinda and Her Sisters," written by Alva Belmont and Elsa Maxwell and put on at the Waldorf-Astoria on February 18, 1916, with a part-professional, part-debutante cast, be offered at "popular prices" as a benefit for the Women's Trade Union League. That suggestion was but one of her ideas to make the suffrage movement an inclusive and "real women's movement." Because Mrs. Belmont had earlier contributed to the relief of striking women garment workers, Beard imagined that she might favor the production. But it does not appear that Beard's suggestion was acted upon.

17. TO ALICE PAUL

400 West 118th. St/. New York
February 21 [1916]

Dear Miss Paul,

I have been thinking out some way to line up the organised labor movement behind the Susan B. [Anthony amendment] and there is a way I believe. The enclosed leaflet will show you a bit of the history of the relation of the A[merican] F[ederation] of L[abor] toward us. Having stood for the thing once, if feebly, perhaps we can make it stand for it again and strongly.

My idea is this. In the state campaign here the suffragists were always calling on the organised working women to help and playing up to the full every tiny bit of help. They did not reciprocate with any support of working women in their own efforts to organise and the union women have been talking it over since the defeat on November 2d. The Suffragists are trying to get them to agree to a long hard campaign. The labor men I hear are quietly working against the suffrage all the time. Now it would be wonderful as you know if the Women's Trade Union League here would send a public letter to all the organised groups of women in the suffrage states calling upon them to use their power and spare this league and others in eastern states from the necessity of the expensive and humiliating referendum again. The League is not at all keen about another referendum but as yet it is not with us keenly either. It is rather sick of mere suffrage talk and will slump in this work altogether possibly.

But—we could make it keen and get the letter to the west I believe if we could do something to indicate our support of a woman's movement that is big enough to include the efforts of women to organise in the industrial field. If we gave any open demonstration of this support too it would impress Mr. Gompers and the A.F. of L.

Mrs. Belmont is always ready to support labor organisation for women and so I have thought that if she would try to get those who gave "Melinda and Her Sisters" to give another performance at popular prices for the benefit of the organised working women united in the Women's Trade Union League here, that it would be one of the most wonderful things that could happen. Mr. Walsh and all good labor people would be proud of the Congressional Union for this stand and it couldn't hurt us any way. That is the advantage of the federal way of securing enfranchisement and the political way, that the labor sympathy is a real power. This would give organized labor faith in us and we would deserve the faith.

You may think me simple minded in this. If you don't, are you willing to put it up to Mrs. Belmont? If she would ask me to bring Melinda Scott to talk about it with her it could be put through beautifully. I would work on the ticket selling with might and main. The performers might take a fancy themselves to the idea of doing it for working women. It would not necessitate further work on the part of Mrs. Belmont and the players except for the settling of a date.

Let me know, will you, soon at any rate? This is the second big and glorious link in the Congressional Union's role of a real woman's movement if we can mold the link.

I shall write the Clayton Act article to-morrow.

Cordially, Mary Beard

◆◆-

During 1916, having withdrawn from the national leadership of the cu, Beard became more active in its New York State organization. New York suffragists decided to go for a second try at a state referendum, to be held in 1917. Meanwhile, to foster its work among women voters in the West, the CU there renamed itself the Woman's Party, with Nevada historian and suffragist Anne Martin as president. Against Woodrow Wilson's stand that woman suffrage was a matter for the states to decide, the Woman's Party sought a statement from likely Republican presidential candidate Charles Evans Hughes in favor of the federal route to woman suffrage. (Hughes did endorse a constitutional amendment, on August 1, 1916.)[20] The following letter from Beard to a colleague in the New York branch of the Woman's Party indicates some of the stresses of operating at the federal and state levels at the same time.

18. TO JANE NORMAN SMITH

New Milford, Conn.
June 23, 1916

Dear Mrs. Smith,

What fun to be going to Wyoming during the throes of the campaign! You will have much to tell us when you return and you must let us know it all.

I did not come down for the [Charles Evans] Hughes interview for I had a telegram from Miss Burns, in reply to mine, that Miss [Anne] Martin and Mrs. [Abby Scott] Baker could take care of it. I am waiting anxiously the result. Wilson seems yesterday again to have declared for the state method and so it looks like a campaign against his party positively.

. . . As for our [N.Y.] organisation and keeping open the rest of the summer, my feeling about it changed when I learned that Mrs. Belmont had pledged such a large sum for the Woman's Party. Her pledge frees our own money for local needs more and we therefore could keep open, I suppose, although I do not know how much there is in the treasury now. I think our chief value for the summer would be in answering inquiries and helping district chairmen to maintain interest in the federal way—the necessity of making the government recognise women. I really want to see the office kept open tremendously. . . .

I think there should be a meeting next week and that the point should be insisted upon of keeping open. If I was not in favor of it last week it was because I thought every cent would be needed for the West. It will look as if we had lost all hope if we close. Personally it does not seem to me that the Democrats are going to pass the amendment but that is no reason why we should not concentrate upon the federal amendment and try putting them out of office and giving another party a chance. I believe absolutely in the political way which is the only dignified way and in making the government enfranchise us. So if it takes us longer than we hoped, the state method takes an eternity and we have chosen the better way. We must maintain that point of view—those of us who have it strongly—and WE MUST KEEP OPEN to do it.

Do insist that the meeting be called and try to persuade the women that this course is best. The up-state chairmen as well as the local chairmen need to understand our point of view and if any one is discouraged like Mrs. Blauvelt, the office secretary should try to encourage her by telling her the whole situation and urge upon the chairman personal initiative. . . .

I wish I could be down more but the work I do in the winter is only possible because of my summer change. I have to catch up with the children and many other things which I wholly neglect when I am in town. I hope I shall hear that you have met and decided generously in the matter anyway.

Cordially, Mary Beard.

❦

The CU, or Woman's Party, gained more adherents in 1916, especially after defeats of major state referenda made more women see the virtue of a constitutional amendment. As in 1914, Mary Beard did not campaign in the West but provided articles and arguments—historical arguments—for the group.[21] For Beard as for radicals and socialists who supported the cause, it was difficult to swallow the fact that their anti-Democratic strategy benefitted the Republican presidential candidate Hughes, for he was more conservative than Wilson with respect to most domestic social policies. Yet Beard and others swallowed it, perhaps because they judged that Hughes had little chance of being elected, while their pressure was their only hope to make the Democratic party reassess its suffrage views. Beard had little appreciation for President Wilson. At the time of writing the letter below, she was angry because Wilson had made a special appearance to urge the Senate to act immediately and favorably on a child labor bill passed by the House; as a result, the Senate in caucus overcame Southern senators' resistance and announced that the bill would shortly pass. All the while, the president insisted to suffragists that he could not influence congressional committees and actions.[22] Happy with the result for child labor, Beard was nonetheless furious at Wilson's hypocrisy in dealing with suffragists.

19. TO ALICE PAUL

New Milford, Conn.
July 26, 1916

Dear Miss Paul,

Here's my hat off to you for your mastery of the situation when I was so annoyed at [Charles Evans] Hughes last Wednesday! You were true blue in pulling that kind of a statement out of the melee. I can do much better when I stay in the daily fight than when I get away for a time and look at things with a more distant perspective. I am so much more radical than either of the old political parties that, when I get off and think, I lose my whole absorption in the one fight for enfranchisement. I keep that absorption in town when I am at the office every day and have responsibilities that are heavy. The Socialists as individuals are usually pathetic and I remember that when I am working day and night for the CU because I am thinking solely of women but I can't keep away from wider surveys when I start to read and think along other lines in the summer too.

You see it is bad for me to come away. I have to though on account of the children. This summer it would be most impossible to keep them in town.

The kind of publicity that you are giving out about Hughes is perfect psychologically, I am sure. He told me he wanted what he said to come out as if it were perfectly natural. It will seem so when the way is paved as it is being paved by the activities of the women of the Hughes alliance and the confidence expressed by Miss Todd and others that he will speak up.

I have regained my balance since Wilson has behaved in such a hypocritical and insulting way about the child labor bill and the amendment. I do believe that instead of taking the Child Labor Bill as a sop, tremendously attractive as it is, women will be enraged by the President's insult to their intelligence. I believe his action will afford the very most powerful material for the campaign and that women will not yield the fight because he has put through the one thing and left undone the more fundamental thing. I could campaign with spirit now against him whereas I have had moments when I was very glad other women had to do the campaigning—moments when I have remembered [William Howard] Taft would go upon the Supreme Bench if Hughes wins, etc.

Mrs. Adamson has written you and me about letting Mr. Wilson off with endorsement of presidential suffrage. Of course I have told her that would never do in my opinion. It is her Democratic husband and own reactions getting in some work.

I have just sent an article to the Suffragist which will supply some more campaign material. It shows that Congress itself practically established manhood suffrage in the Mississippi region and the southwest and on to the Pacific. I hope to help in such ways as that.

Are you getting any more of that money from Mrs. Belmont? If you are not, I will send out a hundred letters to women I know who may be willing to give something more. If we can get our City Committee together by the first of August and reorganise we ought to be able to raise some more money very soon. Did you get the money from Mrs. Deane? I telegraphed and then wrote. I shall have to tell the women that the $500,000 is not coming in if I persuade them to contribute for they are very decided in their feelings about that. It ought not to be so, as all should play their part and the more money the better but they feel Mrs. Belmont has got so much credit for so little work in comparison with what they put in and get in return that they harbor the common standards of humans in this matter. It all seems pathetic and petty to me for I am always so glad when some other woman can be put into the headlines instead of myself as I hate so much to have to devote my life to this stupid fight which ought to have been settled years ago that I am terribly pleased we have the lady to use. She can say things I couldn't without losing all the radical friends I sympathise with and I grow more and more to thank heaven for her existence. But you see when Mrs. Deane admires Mr. Hughes so much and some other woman is keen about Mr. Wilson and they would one and all be very glad to be on the firing line of political committees or quoted as approving this and that, there are emotions which they have and we just have to understand their psychology and get what we can out of them.

I'll push the reorganisation so we can garner in all the women now who may have been impressed by recent events and achievements of the c.u.

Yours always, Mary Beard.

In spite of her recurrent doubts about the sufficiency and meaning of suffrage campaigning, Mary Beard worked hard to reorganize the New York branch of the cu.[23] By the end of 1916 her mood was one of frustration again, however, especially concerning fund-raising. She refers in the following letter to efforts to raise money to honor the memory of Inez Milholland, an eye-catching and news-making feminist and suffragist who died tragically in November 1916 during a speaking tour on the West Coast—not yet thirty, she was stricken by pernicious anemia. It is not clear to what, exactly, the opening line in the following letter refers, but it may be a temper tantrum of Beard's when asked to raise money.

20. TO ALICE PAUL

340 West 118th St., N.Y.
December 21, 1916

Dear Miss Paul,

I was a sickening disappointment to you last week, I know. I have been thinking much about it because temper—just plain temper—is a surprise to me and not a thing I shall let go any farther. I have been crushed to the earth and therefore physically tired by a conviction that the federal way even is interminable. You all feel the other way and I know the [New York State] referendum people have equal faith and so I allowed my zeal to slump. However I do want this question settled even as you do and I know it comes first in the revolutions I desire and the C.U. is wisest and most admirable, even if I do think it sometimes a bit confused in its statements.

I shall therefore atone for my temper by going to the Lewissohns and appealing with all by soul for a big gift. I am at this hour trying to make the appointment to see them and nothing shall prevent my making good on this. This was my first refusal to do any thing I really could do but the one thing I find harder than any thing else is to ask individually for money. I shall do it positively however and I have hopes that the Inez Memorial will catch their sense of beauty and idealism which they have in unusual degree.

While I have heaviest home responsibilities and must help swell rather than deplete the family income I shall rouse myself from lethargy and cynicism and plan to utilize every possible hour for C.U. work from now on.

Yours sincerely, Mary Beard

Early in 1917 the CU joined with its Western wing into the renamed National Woman's Party (NWP) and embarked on a new tactic of picketing the White House with signs and banners. "Mr. President, how long must women wait for liberty?" and similar slogans festooned the demonstrations. A few fragments of evidence indicate that Mary Beard approved of this new tactic, as she had approved of the group's earlier flamboyant actions. "You know I am never afraid of that kind of thing myself," she wrote to Alice Paul when she conveyed Florence Kelley's discomfort with the practice of heckling. Even after the United States entered the world war in April 1917 and the picketing was deplored by observers as traitorous to the nation and the war effort, Beard endorsed it. She wrote to Jane Norman Smith that in spite of virtual riots caused by the picketing, "it has done more than almost anything else could as matters stand at this moment."[24] By July and August the picketers were being arrested on charges of obstructing traffic. Refusing to pay fines, they were incarcerated; in jail, refusing to eat, they were force-fed. The ensuing publicity momentarily riveted national attention on the National Woman's Party.

In the first week of November 1917, the New York referendum to enfranchise women succeeded. Immediately Mary Beard and others organized a group called the Committee of One Thousand, made up mainly of working women, to protest the jailing of suffragists at the nation's capital and the conditions in the workhouse in which they were held. After a rally in New York, she and a few others carried a petition of the group of newly enfranchised citizens directly to Washington to President Wilson, asking him to endorse the federal suffrage amendment and to release the imprisoned pickets.[25]

Perhaps that trip to the national capital—perhaps a view of the actual picketing, which Beard had not witnessed before—led to the change of heart expressed in the letter below, written only five days later. Otherwise the cause for it remains mysterious. Beard despised the way that the NAWSA had jumped into war work in an effort to gain congressional approval of the vote for women; but she no longer approved of the National Woman's Party's tactics either.[26]

21. TO ELIZABETH ROGERS

430 West 116
November 17, 1917

Dear Mrs. Rogers—

I am slow to answer your letter as Chairman of the Advisory Council of the National Woman's Party. I am slow to answer because, while I have seen myself steadily pushed toward withdrawal from the Council, I have been so sorry to withdraw.

I can't fight the battle the picketting way even to win any more than I can use war work as a cudgel even to win. So please, let me depart quietly. Just omit my name in any publicity about the conference of advisors at Washington and omit it from the stationery hereafter.

I am willing to say no more and not even this much publicly for I have no desire to injure in any way.

We must each follow the light we have. In my case, it may be very dim. Best wishes to you!

Cordially, Mary Beard.

Apparently, Mary Beard took no part in activity on behalf of the National Woman's Party after November 1917. From the tone of the following letter, it seems plausible that she grew increasingly disaffected during the winter of 1918–19, because of the group's shock tactics, which included burning "watchfires" in front of the White House when Wilson went to Versailles, and setting his "fine words" on democracy aflame when these were announced from the peace conference.

22. TO ELIZABETH KALB, BUSINESS MANAGER OF THE SUFFRAGIST

336 West 95, New York City
April 9, 1919

My dear Miss Kalb,

Will you be good enough to tell me by what right my name appears as associate editor of the Suffragist?

I am well aware that the National Woman's Party calls one merely doctrinaire who cares about means to the end and that I am anathema because I do. I do object to this use of my name as if I sanctioned all the means used by the organization of which I am no longer even a member.

Sincerely, Mary Beard

2 The Activist Intellectual Emerges

During the suffrage years, Mary Beard had struggled to concentrate solely on the vote, preferring a more inclusive approach to reform. In ensuing years the National Woman's Party kept its single-issue focus, replacing the goal of a constitutional amendment for suffrage with the goal of a constitutional amendment for equal rights, while Beard's principles and inclinations led her elsewhere. A trip to postwar Europe in 1920–21 seems to have affected her greatly, leaving her more impressed than ever with the paltriness and futility of articulating a goal of sex equality apart from wider aims of social renovation. The trip fostered her anti-war feelings. If making women equal to men was not an appealing goal to her, that was in part because she saw the image of woman conscripted for war as the logical outcome—or epitome—of that goal.

In the following letter—one of a mere handful available from the 1920s—Beard gives her views of several NWP drafts of equal rights amendments intended to eliminate sex discrimination. Elsie Hill, a Vassar graduate of 1906 and daughter of a longtime congresssman from Connecticut, had been one of the earliest organizers hired by the CU and was named chairman of the National Woman's Party reconstituted in 1921; a venturesome sort, who ran (unsuccessfully) as a Farmer-Labor candidate for secretary of state in Connecticut in 1920, she was someone to whom Beard could write frankly and fully. Beard's principal objection in the letter is the same one raised by most women who initially opposed the ERA: the amendment's likely impact on the laws regulating women's hours, conditions of work, and wages for which trade-union women and others had fought for two decades. Beard is prescient in seeing deficiencies in the Wisconsin bill, which became the first state equal rights law in the nation. Unfortunately it is impossible to identify from the many early drafts of the ERA the language of the "third suggestion" to which Beard responds more positively, although it may have been one of the lengthier drafts in which areas of rights (such as jury service, child custody, citizenship) were specified.[1]

Beard's opening remark about "our" series foreshadows her major occupation during the 1920s: writing history books in tandem with Charles Beard. After her husband resigned from Columbia University in 1917, the Beards kept only a pied-à-terre in New York City and made New Milford, Connecticut, their year-round residence and the seat of their collaboration. Their *History of the United States,* a high school text, was published in 1921. Although she speaks of "our" series in the letter, her name was not attached to *Our Old World Background,* published in 1922 under the names of Charles Beard and William Bagley, who were also co-authors on two previously published elementary U.S. history texts.

23. TO ELSIE HILL

New Milford, Conn.
July 10, 1921

Dear Elsie,

I am surprising both you and myself by my instant reply to your letter. I can't possibly get down to Washington for I am working hard this summer again on the last book in our school series—the European Background of American History. But of course I am always ready to comment even at a distance on so lively a subject as your proposed new amendment, etc.

As for the federal amendment, it seems to me it would overthrow all protective industrial legislation for women and I can't see why it wouldn't also do things like conscript women for war. If "equal opportunists to the bitter end" want that result, the amendment seems to hit the mark. I am not one of that party especially since my return from this last trip abroad where there is so much industrial equality that women sweep the streets and till the land while men drink in the cafes. I believe that women will be conscripted for war in the future and the essence of democracy is that the whole nation fights as the king and barons and mercenaries once fought. Women have rushed to recruit in Silesia and there will be battalions of death outside Russia; but I am not interested one bit if that is all democracy has to offer. So much for the amendment as far as I am concerned.

As for the Wisconsin bill, it is so general in its scope that it seems to me it throws the whole matter of protective legislation into the courts, as well as all other special prohibitions because of the phrase "which they now enjoy for the general welfare". Any lawyer can argue and any judge can declare that all discriminatory legislation is for the general welfare. I don't see that the bill therefore gets anywhere in fact.

The third suggestion for a state bill I like better. It is specific, except for the final "Or in any other respect". It gets rid of the undisputed sex disabilities while leaving room for protective industrial legislation for those who believe in that. I am perfectly aware of the factions that rally around that policy. I am not an ultra feminist on that point because in my mind children do add a complexity to women that they cannot add to men and I see no way of removing it entirely for the best interests of both sexes as well as the children. {Then too women have little sense of humour about the actions and works of men. Half the goals they set are ridiculous and pure imitation is both infantile and unintelligent. A! Ha!}*

It is awfully good of you to keep me in touch with these doings and I would enjoy a talk about it all. Later perhaps we can have it for you can surely come here even if I can't come to you.

I saw Doris [Stevens] on the street in Florence one day. She looked so thin and white that she simply broke my heart. Do you still plan to go over this autumn? I want to talk with you about women in Europe as well as here—how they love war and mourning and sorrow and suffering; and how bourgeois our whole suffrage and equal opportunity movement is. Women have been having that equality in the fields of Europe since the days of the Roman Empire, for example. Of course real equality would have transferred the whip to her hands and let her hitch her husband and an ass together to the plow instead of having the sexes reversed; but is that the final answer?

You sound as if you were having big times in discussion with worth while folks. It will be nice to get their points of view through you. Best wishes to my erstwhile pals and please tell them that I am working as hard as they in the way that seems to open best for me.

Affectionately, Mary Beard

After travel to Japan in 1922 and 1923, the Beards occupied much of the mid-1920s with conceiving and writing the two volumes of *The Rise of American Civilization*, published in 1927, the most famous and admired of their joint works. Mary Beard fell so out of touch with Elsie Hill that in 1927, when Hill wrote to compliment her on *The Rise* (and to beg use of the Beards' town apartment), Beard received her note "like a voice from an unknown world" and admitted she had not for many years "seen so much as a mutual friend."[2] This suggests how far she had turned her back on her former associates, immersing herself in American history.

The following brief letter, apparently written just after *The Rise* was

* Lines within braces were added by hand to typed letter.

completed, gives on-the-spot evidence of Mary Beard's concern and perhaps responsibility for the cultural content of that work. Charles Beard carried on most of the general correspondence with Macmillan publishers, so it is notable that Mary Beard sent this query. Perhaps it also indicates the relative weight of work and holiday in the Beard household that the note was written on Christmas day! Which work by Canby—presumably Henry Seidel Canby—she is referring to remains a mystery, since he published no book in 1927.

24. TO CURTICE HITCHCOCK, THE MACMILLAN CO. (PUBLISHERS)

27 West 67, City
December 25, 1926

Dear Mr. Hitchcock:

Charles and I are decidedly shocked to read the enclosed sample of a forthcoming book by Canby for this bit so closely parallels our treatment of Irving that we are afraid Canby will steal our literary thunder. Have you any idea when his book is to appear and whether it is to do what we have also tried to do, namely relate the literature to the economics and politics? If Canby comes out first, he might think we had plagiarised and so it seems important for you to have our statement today that our work is alike on Irving at this moment and threatens to run along the same path for other writers if his book carries on as he seems to have begun.

We only hope we shall appear first and we stand ready to push as fast as we can on the proof when it arrives.

Cordially, Mary Beard

The following letter is the only contemporary evidence from Mary Beard's hand of the extent of her contribution to *The Rise of American Civilization*. Florence Cross Kitchelt, the friend to whose compliment Beard was responding, was a social worker, suffragist, and labor reformer in the 1910s and became a leader in the peace movement in Connecticut in the interwar period, while she continued to be involved in women's issues. It was probably because of Kitchelt's work for peace that Beard asked her opinion of the Kellogg-Briand pact, the treaty to renounce war that the U.S. Senate approved in 1928 after nationwide lobbying by women's groups and others.

The letter also reflects on the Beards' trip in 1927–28 to Yugoslavia, where Charles Beard was invited to consult on urban and governmental problems. During her months in the Balkans Mary Beard was very much impressed by the strength and vitality of peasant women living close to the land. Her interest in and acquaintance with peasants had been stimulated by the lengthy stay in Japan in 1922–23. Her research on American farm production during the writing of the *Rise* "especially excited" her, she later recounted.[3]

25. TO FLORENCE CROSS KITCHELT

New Milford, Conn.
May 18th [1928]

Dear Florence,

Can it be eighteen years since first we met! Like the ideal of good-will among men, our friendship thus deepens and intensifies with time. I am very proud of your contributions toward a richer social consciousness and you are certainly generous toward my feeble efforts to do a bit in that direction.

Another bond. We too have now sat on the Pynx (do you enjoy Gertrude Atherton's Immortal Marriage?) and we too have talked with M. Grouitch et al on the subject of minorities. Don't forget your promise to drop in on us here this summer—you and the good Richard—for a talk on our hill of the world and its affairs, including the ways of Macedonia, Bulgaria, and what-not. What a freak of Fate is the Bulgarian earthquake evoking friendliness in Jugoslavia and drawing the two peoples a little closer together. I was especially interested in the political game which France and England are still playing in the Balkans. Charles is preparing a book on Jugoslavia and one unique feature will be the comment by the young King on the Crown itself following the submission of the chapter on the Crown to the King for his criticism. But my good husband did not go on behest of the government as New Milfordites seem to think. He went for the American-Jugoslav Society to make a survey along the general line of his report on Tokyo.

We motored through Montenegro, among other adventures, and I am still dazed by the insight into the life of mountaineers which I got. Water gypsies had been my greatest previous surprise. And the sublimity of landscapes will be abiding joys!

Your excellent report on your activities in Connecticut I have filed away for use later in revision of books which demand being up-to-date. It is good to note the inroads you are making on the psychology of the children for that is the hope. How do you interpret the Kellogg peace move? Do you think it positively and indubitably a throw-out to the women voters this year? I met real Amazons this winter—women who had fought and truly found glory in war—but they were one of the minorities luckily.

The Rise of Am. Civ. is deficient all along the line, we know but it was the best we could do at that time. Now we think we could improve it one hundred per cent. Reviewers often imply that the whole product is C. A.'s in spite of the fact that he had never written on cultural themes before and so I appreciate your willingness to count me in, in view of the way I drudged on the work for three years and especially since cultural side was my hunch—not just women. We hope to improve it in a revision one of these days.

We shall hope to see you ere long. Better let us know in advance when you think you can come over so we shall surely be at home. May the common shelter for you two splendid people materialise yet and soon.

Affectionately, Mary Beard

No letters of any substance written by Mary Beard between 1928 and 1933 can be found. She wrote a few articles during this time, however, all in accord with the tone of her 1921 letter to Elsie Hill. She seemed impressed with what she called in a brief essay published in June 1929 the feminist progression, "the large measure of civil and political equality actually established after the long era in which it had been only a dream." But she seemed equally, or more, disturbed about the goal in view. "What is this equal opportunity in fact and in import?" she continued. "Is it the mere chance to prove fitness and adaptability to a tooth-and-claw economic struggle reflecting the greed and destructive propensities of the traditional pacer . . . or does it signify the power to lead as well as follow?" She was deeply concerned and dissatisfied with women settling for "sheer imitation" of men.

As the Great Depression broke, Beard was finishing her first major historical work, On Understanding Women (1931), attempting to show what women had done and been as women, not as imitators of men, throughout history. Her mood was very critical indeed; she blamed emulators of men for failing to foresee that by coveting equality rather than giving their attention to "the broad study of life," they would attain—in veiled reference to the economic depression—"equality in disaster."[4] Yet her outlook was less defeatist than hortatory; she chastised her contemporaries because she felt they were capable of better things, if they turned their minds from imitating men to conceiving original schemes for national economic and social recovery.

Although Beard was highly skeptical about the merits of clubwomen's activities in the 1920s and 1930s, she did appear to invest considerable hope in a grand international meeting of clubwomen in Chicago in 1933, convened to mark the fortieth anniversary of a similar congress held at the World's Columbian Exposition of 1893. The National Council of Women of the United States, an umbrella group in which a score of organizations representing at least five million women participated, hosted the meeting. Its president at the time was Lena Madesin Phillips. A consummate organization woman who became one of Mary Beard's closest allies and confidantes during the 1930s, Phillips was a Kentuckian who had learned law at the knee of her father (a judge), and then had come North during World War I as secretary of the national board of the Young Women's Christian Association (YWCA). She stayed to turn the YWCA Businesswomen's Council into the National Federation of Business and Professional Women (NFBPW), becoming its first executive secretary, then president, then lifelong honorary president. Devoted to women and to women's causes—she lived in intimate relationship with Marjorie Lacey Baker all her adult life—Phillips passed the New York Bar in 1924 and practiced law in New York City, meanwhile founding and leading the International Federation of Business and Professional Women's Clubs. During the late 1930s she was associate editor of the *Pictorial Review,* a popular magazine mainly directed toward women. During the same years she was instrumental in getting the NFBPW to endorse the ERA.

Just how much influence Mary Beard had in shaping the theme of the congress of 1933 is not clear, but its overall title, "Our Common Cause—Civilization," sounds suspiciously Beardian, and she gave one of the opening speeches, which she called "Struggling Towards Civilization." In a post-conference letter to Dorothy Detzer, the executive secretary of the Women's International League for Peace and Freedom, Beard took credit for putting the subject of munitions—a personal concern—on the agenda, thus giving speaking room to peace activists Detzer and Florence Brewer Boeckel, a former Woman's Party suffragist who at the time was educational director of the National Council for Prevention of War.[5] Beard also chaired the Manifesto Committee, which was supposed to produce a document expressing the spirit of the conference. From a sur-

viving letter written by Beard to Maud Wood Park, formerly Carrie
Chapman Catt's lieutenant in the NAWSA and the first president of the
League of Women Voters, it appears that Beard, Park, and Harriot Stanton Blatch were to compose the Manifesto Committee as of March 1933;
but when the congress took place, in July, of the three only Beard remained on the committee, and the document was written at the meeting
itself, as the letter below indicates.[6]

The manifesto, certainly by Beard's hand, displayed in brief her depression-era convictions that centralized national planning was essential to
recovery and that feminism had to be linked to broader social vision in
order to be credible and meaningful in the crisis. She meant the pronoun-
cement to succeed the Declaration of Sentiments written by Elizabeth
Cady Stanton in 1848. In it she proposed the start of a *new* women's
movement, dedicated not only to the winning of equal citizenship for
women but also to "the winning of security and opportunity for all humankind." It continued:

> We believe that every person, to whatever sex, race or nationality,
> or creed she or he may belong, is entitled to security of life, work,
> the reward of labor, health, and education; to protection against
> war and crime, and to opportunity for self-expression. Yet, even in
> parts of the world where feminism has made its largest gains, these
> fundamentals of security and the good life are sadly lacking. Hence
> it is against social systems, not men, that we launch our second
> woman movement. We enter now a social-planning era following
> the harsh experiment with *laissez faire* and national aggressions,
> with a World War, and its horrible aftermath in the economic col-
> lapse. All civilization is at stake and the condition of society cannot
> be ignored. . . .
>
> The care and protection of all life is peculiarly in woman's keeping
> and thus at one of the most tragic hours in the world's history, we
> pledge ourselves to assume this responsibility boldly and whole-
> heartedly.
>
> Where the feminist movement is fundamental in any country, we
> call upon the women of the world to give it their loyalty. Where the
> social planning movement is imperative, we call upon the women of
> the world to join us in carrying it forward.[7]

The manifesto was adopted unanimously, although not without be-
hind-the-scenes maneuvering, including overriding a version written by a

former president of the National Council of Women, Amy Wood. As the letter below indicates, Beard relied here, as she would later in the Women's Archives venture, on the support of Emily Newell Blair, a Democratic Party activist who was concerned with women's voice in electoral politics. Beard's relief at achieving assent from Florence Bayard Hilles, a longtime adherent to the National Woman's Party, is also interesting, because it indicates not only the party's reputation for noncooperation but also Beard's continuing notice of her old friends' politics. Beard left the congress buoyed up. Through the mid-1930s, she alternated between hope and despair about the likelihood of a new women's movement.

26. TO LENA MADESIN PHILLIPS, PRESIDENT OF NATIONAL COUNCIL OF WOMEN

New Milford, Connecticut
August 3, 1933

Dear Chief,

I am considerably perturbed in spite of your generous telegram over the possibility that I gummed your works, at the end. The Times report of Mrs. [Emily Newell] Blair's gallant fight for the scheme and the Manifesto cheered me immensely but of course I don't know the inner history of your contest with your Board [of the National Council of Women]. Clearly it thought the Manifesto weak. Maybe it was and is. Amy Wood preferred the one she had drafted late in the preceding afternoon but I think I did not prefer my later one just because it was mine. The whole thing was steam-rollered as I well know. But I couldn't see anything else to do in all the circumstances.

So by making the point of a planned society stand in juxtaposition or contradiction to the old individualist ideal, I hope to throw out a concept big enough to cover all the particular whereas-es which Mrs. Parsons or anybody else might have wanted to enumerate. And name it emphatically. For planning is the only means of subduing warfare and all else that we hate. The papers seemed to think that the Manifesto had punch if your Board didn't. But I try to look at the matter objectively, fully aware of my own mental anaemia. I pulled out at noon on Friday, as I did, because Mrs. Sternberger had greeted me in the lobby graciously and assured me that there would be no contest over the matter in the open. As I had been asked by you to meet the Board at the close of the morning session, I had

murmured to Mrs. Blair at the door of the assembly hall that my head
was probably coming off. She saw a dramatic and important opportunity
to save the day and apparently did her big bit handsomely. I am told she
has saved situations before!

But what is your status with the Board, if I may ask so personal a question? You are so far ahead of its members intellectually and spiritually
that I have relied on superior force to win. Am I right? You won't want to
put anything on paper but an "Oh yeah" would be enough for me.

The women can make the N[ational] Re[covery] A[dministration] work
as no one else can and apparently they have already set about to do so,
judging from the news about their pressure on chain stores in Washington, etc. But in the social planning they must also contribute creative
ideas and work with their social perspective in mind.

I was thrilled by Mrs. [Florence Bayard] Hilles' seconding of the motion to adopt the Manifesto, for that prevents Woman's Party opposition
and what is more—wins its recognition that social systems affect the
status of women and (as in the case of German fascism) may destroy
equality, once gained, by a single decree. I had talked with her at lunch
about this matter when she was inclined to condemn the whole Congress
for its "innocuous—ness". And she seemed impressed but I was amazed
when she accepted the Manifesto so publicly. I thought that a great gain.

I would ask you to come up here for a visit at once or soon to talk
everything over. But I can't do that right now. Yesterday there came a
message from Roosevelt "drafting" Charles into service without pay in
connection with the administration of the NRA. He is put on a board of
seven members to guard it for the New York, New Jersey and western
Connecticut district—the hardest in the country presumably. His instructions are to follow. Just what this may mean as to time and abode we do
not yet know. If he has to be in New York for continuous work we shall
take a little place there together and come "home" only for such free time
as he may have, if any. So I have to leave all invitations to that home
hanging. I should be able to see you in town at any rate. And maybe here.

You were a highly competent manager of the great show, dear Chief.
And I have thought of you admiringly for countless reasons. It seemed to
me too that the whole make-up of the Congress, with few exceptions, was
indicative of a revolution in women's minds. It was a mad-cap adventure
but under your chairmanship it did not work out meanly. On the contrary such publicity as I have chanced to see has reflected my own impression—that it marked a true advance for women.

You can be free to damn me up and down if you feel that I deserve it. I have no false confidence in my own powers. Your friend with her The-saurus may think so but I was fishing for ideas while she hunted for words. And there was the need of both. A day longer would have helped in the discovery of course—of ideas, if not words.

Au revoir, Chief, and

blessings on your head.

Mary R. Beard

Mary Beard's acquaintance with Harriot Stanton Blatch, who was twenty years her senior but had been her colleague during the suffrage years, seems to have been remade shortly before the congress of 1933. Per-haps Beard's anthology of documents published that year, *America Through Women's Eyes,* would have brought the two in touch anyway. Beard's attempt in the anthology to document major events in U.S. his-tory through women's words and experience was unprecedented (and would not be repeated until the flourishing of academic women's history in the 1970s). The book put women's accomplishments and partnership with men, not their disabilities, in the foreground. Its concentration on social, economic, and cultural history and its virtual neglect of the suf-frage campaign were remarkable. Neither Elizabeth Cady Stanton (Blatch's mother) nor suffrage was listed in the index, and Susan B. An-thony's words were recounted only in a Civil War–era speech against war and for emancipation. Stanton's voice appeared only to give a memorial for Lucretia Mott. Blatch herself was represented by an antiwar state-ment from her book *A Woman's Point of View: Some Roads to Peace* (Woman's Press, 1920), which she had written after a postwar trip to dev-astated Europe.

Blatch was infuriated by *America Through Women's Eyes.* Writing to the younger historian and feminist Alma Lutz, who was assisting her in composing her own memoirs, Blatch fumed, "Think of leaving out the whole of the story of the struggle—a unique and striking struggle of a disfranchised class forming one half the human race—for enfranchise-ment. If she had been taking as her title 'America From the Eyes of the Negro' would she have quoted Fred Douglas[s] only from memorial ad-dresses? completely ignored the abolition struggle, the passage of the XIII, XIV, XV amendments, etc[?] She apparently does not see the con-nection between political freedom & economic opportunity." In momen-

tary venom Blatch accused Beard of becoming "a leader among the ma-
nipulators" of history.[8] It is hard to imagine that Blatch would have
hidden her feelings from Beard, but since Beard did not save her letters no
evidence of Blatch's direct criticism survives. In any case, during the ensuing years a remarkable correspondence and apparent mutual respect developed between the two women. When Blatch's memoirs were published
in 1940 (the year of her death), the volume carried an introduction by
Mary Ritter Beard.[9]

In the following letter, Beard takes note of another critic of *America
Through Women's Eyes:* Beulah Amidon, a former Congressional Union
colleague, who reviewed the book in the *New Republic.* After a few
laudatory adjectives, Amidon called the work "inevitably disappointing,"
"broken and incomplete," because it "pulled [the contributions of
women] out of their relationship to the whole" and failed to "integrate
women into the total picture." Because Beard's aim was exactly to restore
women to the total picture, she was understandably deflated. Where
Blatch wished Beard had focused more on women's self-defined eman-
cipatory movement, Amidon disliked imposing a line "to mark off
woman's part from man's in what is an essentially human record."[10]
Beard satisfied neither. She always had to struggle to convey her view of
the past to her contemporaries just as she had to struggle for their understanding of her critique of equality. The letter also suggests that Beard
was constantly weighing her own views against those she associated with
the National Woman's Party. A controversial speech that she delivered at
the NWP biennial convention on November 4, 1933, brought their differences to the fore.

In 1933 the Beards' daughter, Miriam, who had married Alfred Vagts
in Germany in 1927, returned to the United States permanently—to New
Milford—with her husband and son, Detlev, born in 1929. Because of
the Vagts' connections, the Beards were very much involved (especially
financially) in aiding German exiles and refugees from fascism during the
1930s. Miriam Beard Vagts was one of the speakers who helped to pack
Madison Square Garden for a public rally denouncing Hitlerism, sponsored by the American Jewish Congress, in March 1934.[11]

Blatch too had her daughter near her: Nora Stanton Barney (only seven
years younger than Mary Beard), a suffragist like her mother and grandmother and one of the first women in America to be trained in and practice civil engineering. The *Women's Political World* mentioned at the letter's opening was a publication of Blatch's earlier suffrage group in New
York City, the Women's Political Union.

27. TO HARRIOT STANTON BLATCH

La Posada
Winslow, Arizona
[January 1934]

Dear Harriot,

Charles and I had to work at top pressure until the very end of the old year and in the process we could hardly go through our mail. So it was days before I so much as saw your postcard telling me that you and Nora had a copy of the Women's Political World which I might get. Just as I finished helping Charles get off his last contracted-for obligation and was ready for my mail, the time arrived for us to pack up and depart for the west—the man in the case to preside over the convention of the American Historical Association of which he was president in 1933 and I to do a little needed shopping and then join him en route to the desert where we are now socially lost for a whole month recuperating from a solid year's siege of terrible tasks.

We shall be here in this high mountain sunshine until the first of February when we go to Pasadena for a month. Then we shall return to New Milford by easy stages through the south and we both hope never to drudge away in such horribly confining stretches again.

We are trying to think in this solitude—in my case probably an utterly hopeless ambition. I am afraid you agree with Beulah Amidon if you happened to see her criticism of my anthology in a late issue of the New Republic as "wordy and dull." That is far from encouraging but it seems to me that she herself was not entitled to mistake the entire purpose of that volume. And that reminds me that I had a letter from a woman member of the Dairymen's Cooperative League hoping for an added extract in the event of a second edition which will give a new agricultural perspective by women and saying meanwhile that she has particularly enjoyed the quotation from Mrs. Blatch in the present edition. So you may feel complimented anyway.

In the spring Miriam and Alfred are going to build a house for themselves on one of our farms so that they may have a home which they can afford in the future when we are no more. That will help us all to stretch out a little more in the meantime and thereby have our friends in for the night with more comfort all round. They both brought so much stuff home from Europe and need so many rooms at present for carrying on their work, that we were simply unable to have guests after their arrival. We missed you particularly, for both you and Nora in your individual

ways furnish the finest kind of conversation and charm. There is little
enough of either in America still after a hundred years. I am especially
mindful of its lack after rereading Frances Trollope who, though British
to the Nth degree in her provincialism, nevertheless did make some exceedingly pertinent remarks on the USA. The Pioneer Press is going to
bring out a new edition of her Domestic Manners of the Americans
[1832] in a year or so with the original illustrations and I have been asked
to write an introduction. I may if I can forget Beulah Amidon long
enough.

You know that I am ever solicitous about your autobiography. If you
were not so interested in Charles' views of the world we should talk
about that more when we are together. However, I recognize as well as
you do the greater power of the man and must therefore bide my time to
read what I should enjoy discussing. What I count on from you is a more
trenchant comment on life than I was able to find for my anthology from
other contemporary sources. Except perhaps from Ellen Glasgow. I
thought that my quotation from her indicated a sharpness of mind and a
breadth of vision but scantily revealed in her fiction. Whatever I did not
accomplish by assembling the writings of American women about America, I find that the extracts have excited professors who are responsible
for the education of young men and women. It seems all new copy for
them. And that is something.

The National Woman's Party mistakes my point of view about equality
and I must do something to make that position clearer. I am not against
equality of course. I simply regard it as inadequate today. Men are so in-
competent and ridiculous when not base that I can't stomach the idea of
equality as the ultimate goal any longer. And in view of the fascist dicta-
tion to women which is setting in so strong a lot needs to be written still
on the subject of women in a twentieth-century setting. You and Nora
keep my faith alive in the vigor of women's minds and the reinterpretation of the old suffrage saw that "society can rise no higher than its
women" makes our sex's mentality frightfully important now. If we play
the game of the war band again there is no health in us.

I am so sorry, as is Charles, that Nora failed to be taken on for the
Tennessee Valley enterprise. If housing proceeds in New York under La
Guardia she may fare better. Tell her to use the letter Charles gave her in
that connection if she thinks it would help. Best wishes for your New
Year and Love to you three Stanton-Blatch representatives always,

Mary R. Beard

•←

Beard's hope for a follow-up to the congress of 1933 was not fulfilled, but its momentum kept her writing and thinking about how to join feminism with goals of social planning and perhaps prompted her enthusiasm for a World Center on Women's Archives, an idea born in 1935. Beard's connection with Lena Madesin Phillips, who frequently sent her speeches and writings to criticize, also kept her more in touch with the activities of organized women than she had been since the 1910s. As shown in her recollection below of Ruth Hanna McCormick (the NAWSA suffragist who pressed for the Shafroth-Palmer alternative to the federal woman suffrage amendment), Beard never recanted on her position of the early 1910s.

28. TO LENA MADESIN PHILLIPS

February 26th [1934]

Dear Lena,

That's writing! Go to it. I had a good laugh over the humor and a fine thrill at the ideas set forth. It is this ability to adapt which marks the sheep from the goats. And I use this figure more intelligently since seeing the two animals perform out in the desert. The sheep are so stupid that herders have to keep goats among them. They (the goats) are sensitive to danger and don't crowd together so closely as to smother themselves. I had no idea that being a goat was a compliment. It seems to be.

If you decide to go to Washington, I shall see you there before I reach New York as we are returning via the capital the last of March. Your decision will be of deep interest to me like everything you do and are.

As for Ruth Hanna McCormick Simms, I shall not be at Albuquerque again though I did come through there earlier. Years ago I saw her, during a mad trial of Alice Paul, Lucy Burns and myself conducted by the older suffrage group made up of Mrs. McCormick, Anna Howard Shaw and Jane Addams. We had just launched the Congressional Union and were trying to start the political tactic of having already enfranchised women demand the enfranchisement of the rest through their political power. It was dandy tactics and had great effect when we went ahead with it. But the older suffragists loathed us for breaking into their game. Dr. Shaw was insulting until Miss Addams had to protest. But I was impressed that day by the utter coldness of the lady McCormick. And by her lack of political astuteness in spite of her training under [her father] Mark [Hanna]. . . .

The chances of a follow-up conference do not seem encouraging as you reveal the Council's attitude. But I believe it ought to occur for many reasons: the wave of Fascist psychology with respect to women surging high in this country articulate in the magazines and educational reports, etc; the bewilderment of feminists about next steps; the need of definite nation[al] planning for a long period of time, our manifesto, women's sense of the humanistic proprieties which ought to be phases of the planning; the value of tying independent women of the country together in a movement in which they can express themselves freely and catch fire from fire. If nothing happens to make the outlook for such a meet brighter in the meantime, when I chat with you in March, let us canvas the field again then.

May the Fates be good to you—
Thine, Mary R. Beard

Perhaps Harriot Stanton Blatch read in the NWP weekly, *Equal Rights*, the report of Mary Beard's "Wilmington speech" at a NWP banquet of 1933. Beard had declared herself somewhat disillusioned with equality, especially in education, and positively opposed to equality in combativeness. She was quoted as asking how it was possible to have sex equality in property rights, "when about 2000 men at the most manipulate all our property rights?" She went on to ask, "Do we want to be preachers, bankers, Babbitts, merely for the sake of equality with men? Do we want to be labor racketeers?" In the following letter to Blatch she moderated her tone.

Beard continued to think that feminists, rather than training their eyes solely on sex discrimination, ought to think more inclusively. During the mid-1930s she was especially concerned about the munitions build-up in the United States and the effects of fascism in Europe. Beard supported antimilitarist organizations and efforts during the mid-1930s, the height of the domestic peace movement. She spoke at meetings on such topics as "Can We End War?" and tried to foster the publication of works about the waste, corruption, and danger in mounting arms production. Keeping the Beards up to date in a very immediate way, a stream of international visitors flowed through the New Milford household, swelled by the Beards' Japanese connections (from their trip in the early 1920s) and by Miriam and Alfred Vagts' German friends and interests. Mary Beard was also concerned about the rearguard attack on women's employment in the precarious American economy. Yet where feminists such as Lena Madesin Phillips in response emphasized women's right to work, Beard brought in other considerations, inclining "to the view that women may have to supplement this notion of their rights and that workers may have to supplement their notions of rights in the case of either sex by considerations of their value in a planned economy." [12]

29. TO HARRIOT STANTON BLATCH

New Milford
July sixteenth [1934]

Dear Harriot—

I can catch the full flavor of that sniggling about "even such an authority as Mary Beard." Of course it's ridiculous. But for that matter all authority is somewhat ridiculous. Things are true or they are not. That is all there is to authority in any case. And what any one else says about me is not my responsibility.

As for my feeling about that review by Beulah Amidon, I respect her so much that I was only sorry to have disappointed her. I was not hurt in the sense of being wounded because she did not like my performance. I can laugh at and criticise myself even better than any one can do either to me. That is gospel truth to which Charles himself will testify I feel sure.

You and I cannot actually be "poles apart", as you say—unless you have gone in 100% for laissez faire philosophy. I can't believe you have. I haven't the ghost of an idea how my Wilmington speech has been interpreted by the National Woman's Party. It was not written out and turned in by me. Hence comments must be second hand at best. What I was claiming is too bromidic for you and me alike to have to debate—simply that the women of '48 were keyed to the opening competitive regime which seemed to offer immortality at that time—when the free land appeared inexhaustible, etc., etc., etc. You know that story well enough to be able to "sing it to a harp", as we would say here. Then I expatiated on the well-known stuff about how driving for "sheer equality" in a competitive economy had its economic, ethical, and political limitations. I wound up with the thesis that the political economy in which feminism has to function is the prime consideration. For that is what determines in large measure its history. Are we poles apart?

Maybe we are. But we shall see. Don't jump to that conclusion before we chat some more.

The household will welcome you whenever you can come across its portal. Until Friday of this week we have guests, for instance Mr. Fukuoka of the Rengo Shimbun, a truly liberal editor of a great associated press in the Far East who has just come to this country and who needs to get a clear-cut idea of where the U.S. stands in its attitude toward Tokyo. Charles has to go to New York on Friday but will be back on Saturday. If you could come up on Sunday morning and stay overnight, that would be delightful for us. Or any time next week.

Miriam and Alfred have interesting views on Germany, some of which Miriam has been printing. Have you seen them—in Today, the Nation, the Sunday Times? Alfred is putting his opus on German-American Relations through the press. It is being published in England.

I want to hear about your book. Remember, if you will, that I am counting on you to provide the criticism of your times which so few women seem able to do. I had a long evening with Doris Stevens in Washington this spring. She insisted that a feminist can and must do one thing at a time. She maintained that I should work for Communism. "But I am not a communist," said I. I'll tell you how she impressed me for perhaps she has reported how I impressed her. I believe that we have to do everything at once. Of course we can't, if we accept the dominant philosophy.

Cordially always, Mary R. Beard.

Beard followed her first pathbreaking anthology with yet another, *Laughing Their Way*, a collection of women's humor—prose, poetry, and cartoons—jointly edited with Martha Bruere. If wags today still complain that feminists aren't funny, that was even more true in the 1930s, when highmindedness or glamour, never humour, exhausted the range of positive public images of women. In spite of Beard's and Bruere's creative searching, R. L. Duffus on the first page of the *New York Times Book Review* dismissively griped, "There is not much in this volume to shake a reader's (at least a male reader's) sides with laughter." The review as a whole was not unfavorable, but Beard was doubtless irritated too by Duffus' conclusion that "laughter for women is almost as modern an invention as equal suffrage"; that flew in the face of her convictions about women of the long past.[13] Criticism such as his she was able to deflect by sarcasm of her own, and besides, she was fired up with the idea for another book. The one that she would complete in the mid-1940s, however, differed from the plan outlined in the letter below.

30. TO HARRIOT STANTON BLATCH

New Milford
September seventh [1934]

Dear Harriot,

If you read Duffus on women's humor, you will remember that he talked about the undertow of feminine resentment at men. I thanked him for his review which interested me very much as a point of view and in his reply he enclosed the cartoon which I am sending on herewith to you as his notion of humor supreme—the "deep-bellied" kind which makes sides shake with laughter. So an uproariously funny article might be written on the ways in which different persons react to any given specimen called humorous. I am not witty enough to do the article but I am saving some reviews as the basis for it when some one else may try it. Edwin Seaver, for example, much prefers "ladies' laughter" of the Godey Book days to modern fun in the New Yorker, whereas Duffus can't abide the earlier form.

I am sending you a copy of LAUGHING THEIR WAY which will probably suggest to you countless omissions and improvements. I had not intended to do any of this book myself. I suggested it to Martha Bruere as a volume essential to my plan for a series on women and thought she was an excellent person to prepare it. But she got in a jam after she had collected a lot of the excerpts, we were under contract to turn in the manuscript, and I had to take over the job. My chief regret is, as I say on page 51, that the wit of your family and the feminists of your mother's time has not been caught and transmitted. I dare say a good deal of it could be assembled if one explored for it especially but I have another idea for the final volume on women in my scheme which *necessitates* the special study of the aforesaid women. This is to analyze the range and vigor of women thinkers and in this connection I am impressed by the early feminists' criticism of Church and State, among other things.

As I have visualized my series of books on women, this is it:

I *On Understanding Women*. Shows that women have always been at the center of thought and action throughout time.

II *America through Women's Eyes*. What they have written about the republican experiment in particular and how their own role appears in their pages.

III *Laughing their Way*. Women laugh as well as pray, etc.

IV Are Women Thinkers? I haven't the title yet for this and have done very little on it but I have in mind calling attention to such women as Rosa Luxembourg who could measure up to the best of philosophers even in abstruse logic.

My project as it works out is exceedingly sketchy but I hope it will be so suggestive that it may furnish a basis for "equal education" at last. For the present we have only education in men's history, men's ideas of their own thought and action, men's wit and humor, etc. If women turn in on themselves a little more, they may find out better what they really are. I don't know yet. The question of corollaries is a philosophic one. But if we are to *hold* any steps in equality, I have the hunch that we shall have to offer more to the community than straight "justice" and "right" since justice and right are never the basis of economic and political action. And in this connection I consider Fannina Halle's book on Women in Soviet Russia a grand thing. It shows that the spirit of the Slav woman from the age of the matriarchate to the age of Stalin has been so indomitable that the logic of contemporary equality in Russia is just the inexorable logic of her whole history. On the other hand Grace Hutchins' 1934 book on America called Women Who Work is such a ghastly picture of life and labor unrelieved by anything but a shriek for imitative communism that I wonder what is the logic of our own American life and labor really, in terms of woman's spirit in America. It would seem to me that the future of any society must bear an intimate relation to its past.

But while I work at these things I help to draw women into the common stream of American history as I did in the writing of The Rise of American Civilization and the various texts which Charles and I have circulating in the schools. The more I know about woman herself the better I can integrate her into the human story as a whole of course. And in every revision of a history text I am integrating her better I am sure. Just now CAB and I are having a try at a very thorough-going rewriting of a high school book and, as my opportunity is larger for including woman in the scene, at the same time I think I see her more clearly as germane to every step that America has taken. It will be so as we go from rugged individualism to ensuing necessities. (You know how Hitler has made German female maniacs serve himself?)

Forgive this long and rather detailed report of my half-baked efforts to think. I am not counting on a sheer epistolary discussion with you whom I hold in major regard as a thinker. Just a little later now I mean to have you for a sufficiently long visit for us to talk about this and all the other events and concepts which seem significant to you, to Charles, and to me.

In the meantime my best wishes for the rounding out of your memoir and for your good health—

Affectionately, Mary R. Beard

[P.S.] Charles is just finishing the proofs on the second and last volume in his study of National Interest—this one being called THE OPEN DOOR AT HOME. Next week we are both booked for a conference. On our return I hope to be able to invite you by giving you a choice of dates on which I may motor to Nyack for you.

Beard continued to encourage Harriot Stanton Blatch's history writing, which she saw as the complement to Blatch's historic actions. The following letter presages Beard's own intense commitment to the discovery and preservation of women's documents in the latter half of the 1930s.[14]

31. TO HARRIOT STANTON BLATCH

[New Milford, Conn.]
Sept. 22 [1934]

I wonder how you are getting on with your Memoirs. I trust you will let nothing interfere with their preparation and that, among the drawings you will make for it, you will give a rounded-out picture of the suffragists, showing their ideals and their courage, their fears and their weaknesses, the youth and old age inner contest (part and parcel of the strain and stress in India), the ordering and the obeying, and as far as possible the content of the propaganda. What did the women think they were doing in very fact? Wasn't your mother's group far more radical than the Shaw-Catt-Paul brigade? and didn't it have a much larger vision of the State?

Don't bother to answer these questions just to me. I simply present them as types of things I should love to see you cover.

Curiously and unjustly enough, unless you do set down your own relation to the public life of your time, dear Mrs. Blatch—for by that appellation your loyal army always talked of you—young men and women to come will have no way of understanding these times or your place in them. You were more of an orator than a scribe and so, while Mrs. Catt has manuscripts galore, taken to the naval conference at London as an exhibit, manuscripts which will pass into history possibly as the major record of the suffrage movement, your own glowing inspiration and wit and large-minded sweep of politics may not receive their due. You did not run to and fro across the continent, either, as I believe, and so nationally the one-night-standers or the national executives might have to crowd a tale the poorer for your exclusion. One who writes history has to have data he can put his hands on, you see.

So, you see again, I am tremendously keen on this point both for your sake and the country's. Your criticism would enrich the quality of American thinking and God knows it can bear the diet.

Yours ever, Mary Beard

During 1932 and 1933 Mary Beard made some of her most stirring and eloquent pronouncements about faults in women's higher education resulting from its imitation of men's. As a result of her address on "The College and Alumnae in Contemporary Life" given at the biennial convention of the American Association of University Women (AAUW) in 1933, she was asked by that organization to compose a syllabus on women—a set of questions and bibliography—for group study. The result was her fifty-seven page pamphlet, A Changing Political Economy as It Affects Women, published by the AAUW in 1934. This document— which she interestingly calls a "feminist" syllabus in the letter below— treated women's history in intimate connection with her concerns about aggressive nationalism and the relations between international trade, the search for markets, and war. (Her difficulty with contemporary syllabus of economist Dr. Harry Gideonse, "America in a World Economy," had less to do with his views of women than with his views of international trade relations. In the postwar years Gideonse became a major antagonist of Charles Beard.)

Beard's syllabus, divided into sections such as "the quest for sex equality" and "women and historic nationalism," full of encouragement to readers to uncover the women's history and activities in their local communities, was also notable for its acknowledgment of differences between women. She posed for discussion such questions as "Is race a factor in American sex discrimination?" and for close study "the inequalities which prevail as between women and women." Underlying the topics and questions in the syllabus was Beard's dialectical conviction that possibilities and prospects for women depended on the political economy in which they found themselves, while women's values and behaviors helped to create a given political economy.[15]

32. TO HARRIOT STANTON BLATCH

Carlton Hotel
Washington
Jan. 21st. 1935

Dear Harriot—

The judgment of my effort—as per the feminist syllabus—which you render sets me up indeed! But you would know better than any one what I was trying to do. I am not a little paralyzed by the fact that this thesis of mine is being distributed by the A.A.U.W. beside one by Dr. Harry Gideonse which is in complete conflict with everything for which I contend. Not only that, his syllabus is so messy in thought and logic that if he gets by, I should feel that mine must be in the same plight were it not for your commendation. I am flabby in spots no doubt and mine may not be a work of art but it is surely headed right, as you encourage me into continuing to believe. After a chat with President [William] Neilson [of Smith College] after breakfast a few days ago, I felt however like an infant crying in the night. There is just no glimmer of suspicion on the part of men or women apparently that women's education is not a perfect thing. If you missed the enclosed, you shouldn't. I'd like to have it back at your convenience.

Dr. Gideonse appears to be quite a favorite of the ladies. He is being advertised for the Cause and Cure of War program here this week, as quite a card.

January is waning and we shall be looking forward to seeing the Millers. And you.

And yours, Mary R. Beard

•←-

The Beards spent much of the winter of 1935 in Washington, D.C., conducting research and also working avidly for neutrality legislation. As the letters below suggest, they were welcomed among the influential members of the New Deal, while keeping a critical distance. The invitation from Secretary of Agriculture Henry Wallace likely had to do with Charles Beard's book *The Open Door at Home* (1934), which argued for limitation of American exports and international trade in favor of the development of American "continentalism" and concentration on a "standard of life budget" for all at home. This thesis took issue with Wallace's brief for trade expansion. Wallace, disputing Beard on this point, published an otherwise admiring review.[16]

33. TO HARRIOT STANTON BLATCH

> Carlton Hotel
> Washington, D.C.
> January 30, 1935

Dear Harriot,

Did your ears burn a few days ago about noon? They should have if there is anything in the proverb. Charles and I had just had the wonderful experience of talking for a few moments with Justice [Oliver Wendell] Holmes and we were full of ideas about his place in America and his generation. You are a kid in point of years by comparison but we joined you two in our thought and what we said should have made your ears burn—not with anger either. We wish we could have joined the celebrants on your 79th birthday. But we can't believe your story of being 79. I have hesitated to inquire your age but now that it comes out I thrill anew at the strength of body and of spirit that is Harriot Stanton Blatch!

I see that you are announced here for the Birth Control dinner. So I shall see you then.

Don't think I minimize the radical proposition put forth in my syllabus. I merely wonder how far it will carry, naturally. We had dinner last night with Secretary [Henry] Wallace and other guests in his home, including [Attorney-General Homer] Cummings. Oh, God, Harriot I wish you were President and Cabinet all in one.

> Love to you, Mary R. Beard

[P.S.] I have just been going over the education plans of the Fathers in the 18th Century. Nearly every one was impressed by the need of rallying to the young republic the support of women and was prepared to include them in the scheme of education. The west and the machine checked realization.

The letter below gives a more detailed description of the Beards' busy winter in Washington and their efforts to influence the shape of the New Deal and foreign policy. After *The Open Door at Home*, Charles Beard (with collaborator George H. E. Smith) also published *The Idea of Na-*

tional Interest: An Analytical Study of American Foreign Policy in 1934.
Mary Beard declined Dorothy Detzer's suggestion that she stand for election to the national board of the Women's International League for Peace
and Freedom; while deeply committed to work for peace and neutrality,
she was not an organization woman and obviously preferred to work in
tandem with her husband. She shared his acute critique of the American
attempt to create world order through international intervention.[17]

34. TO LENA MADESIN PHILLIPS

New Milford
April 28th [1935]

Dear Lena,

It is good to hear from you and we must have a chat together soon. I
must entice you here before long even if I have to devise a roulette wheel
to win you. That's a great tale connecting Charles and gambling—one
which he enjoyed with me to the full range of gaiety. He is pleased to have
you approve his treatise on national interest. The fight over his point of
view as there expounded has been a big one this winter in Washington
and goes on at the conferences where internationalists foregather from
time to time. Franklin D. [Roosevelt] read it from cover to cover and
marked passages galore. But he wrote on the fly leaf of his copy: "This is
a bad dish Beard gives us." We had lunch with H. G. Wells in Washington
who, without studying the thesis, was sure it was just chauvinism, until
we talked it over at length. Even then he thinks it "simpler" to establish
world order than to put a nation into shape. As soon as I can see a freer
calendar I shall ask you to come up and hear CAB "throw around some
of those choice occasional words" you seemed to read in his treatise. But
he has to go to Washington again and I have agreed to speak here, there,
everywhere in May. I wonder why!

This is neglecting to tell you that we left the capital the last day of
March. Thus I am denied the privilege of meeting Mrs. Wood. I should
gladly call upon her or ask her to lunch if I were still there. No doubt my
declaration in a winter letter to you that I am a "lone wolf" was intimi-
dating when you thought that I might do this or that in Washington. But
I must explain this better when I see you. It did not mean that I stood in
proud isolation way off on the periphery of events. It just happens that
I can do what I feel able to do in more curious ways than through
organisation work. The winter was dynamic with all the energy I could

muster but it flowed into a kind of underground enterprise such as private talks with government officers and congressmen by day and by night in small groups in our quarters or in theirs, with an occasional open speech and discussion at the Cosmos Club or somewhere. Without intending to, Charles and I in fact ran a perfect office at home—interviews piling on interviews, appointments made to speak at hearings on sedition bills and what-not, etc. without end. I never was busier in my crowded life. There were dashes to Atlantic City and elsewhere for meetings. There was movement in a definite direction. And maybe some results have come. Anyway we did our best to help the drive for civilian government as distinct from naval control, for a check on those who would clamp nasty sedition bills on the country, and for a rational attack on public misery and poverty. So forgive me if I missed chances to report on housing and other discussions and if I seemed indifferent to suggestions for work. I was not indifferent. I did in fact slip into the housing meeting but when I found that anything seemed able to go forward by its own momentum I was inclined to push something more anaemic provided it seemed to merit a thrust.

And what is more—I just have to stick pretty close to CAB and his enterprises because he is so helpless without me, being so deaf and generally so dependent on my cooperation. Even so, we generally have the same urges and points of view, if not in every instance.

I am keen to know about your winter of touring and talking across the continent. Why didn't you write me more about it? The *last week in May* perhaps you can come and tell me here. I shall hope to find that time clear for asking you.

Yours, Mary Beard

Through the mid-1930s Harriot Stanton Blatch's needling made Mary Beard formulate and reformulate, in a self-conscious fashion, her views of women and their history, as in the following letter. Indeed, in a contemporary letter to Doris Stevens, Beard wrote, "Harriot Stanton Blatch thinks me plain insane." Below, she makes the interesting mistake of attributing to Charlotte Perkins Gilman a comment made in fact by Freda Kirchwey, editor of the *Nation,* in a review of *On Understanding Women.*[18]

35. TO HARRIOT STANTON BLATCH

New Milford
[May 1935]

Dear Harriot,

Your letter arrived just as I was starting on a drive to Wells College and I am just home again. I never took so long a jaunt alone in the car but only good fortune attended me. It was a marvelous trip with the buds bursting all the way until one could imagine their making music doing it, after living in the Orient where poetry says they do. But the ghastly housing in the amazing landscape! It made me sick to the bone. Do these people on the land have to have task masters to make them repair rotting timbers and clean up their messes generally? I can't understand their sloth, for that it seems, when their houses lie far apart in fields so rich beside those which the Japanese or Montenegrins cultivate that they seem like paradise itself. They could at least have gardens but I saw only filth.

I am deeply interested in your criticism of my obsession with women. I have pondered on it myself right along—critically. But the work I have done in studying women makes me aware of the large social corollaries as I should not otherwise be. If supreme philosophy is the search for the primordial—and is it not?—that search is closely related to my quest. Charlotte Perkins Gilman said that I have "repopulated history" and if I have that was better than writing history "directly" along the line of men's partial offerings. As for the interpretation of history which is the larger idea, do you consider that it is an impersonal proceeding? Anyway, let us have a good talk about all this soon. It is a good theme. Would a trip to us early in June be too difficult for you? Where will you be then?

May is horribly crowded. I am going to Goucher College next week. Charles has had to go back to Washington. We seem to be running around to excess this month. But June will be a different story and the weather warmer, let us pray. It is frigid still up here.

Love as always, Mary R. Beard

Besides speaking and aiding her husband's testimony before Congress in 1935, Mary Beard had some other ideas for helping the peace cause, as in the letter below. She wrote in this vein—showing her awareness of the importance of popular culture—to leaders of several peace organizations and received encouraging replies about implementation. Beard was aware

of a large peace demonstration to be held in Geneva in 1935, in which her
old Congressional Union pal Mabel Vernon was a leader. She regretted
not giving more money to this cause, but she had given priority to "help
get some of the German men and women out of prison camps," according
to another contemporary letter.[19]

36. TO DOROTHY DETZER, EXECUTIVE SECRETARY OF
THE WOMEN'S INTERNATIONAL LEAGUE FOR PEACE
AND FREEDOM

New Milford, Connecticut
August 2, 1935

Dear Miss Detzer,

As you know of course the students of this country have recently
achieved some notable successes in causing the withdrawal from local
houses of films and news reels clearly militaristic in design. They resorted
to the boycott and used this agency of protest with considerable effect.
But the strain of abstention from movies is a hard one to demand of great
numbers of people, especially for any length of time. The war films will
keep coming back wherever vigilance relaxes. War films still reap immense profits from the movie audiences. Night after night they fan the
war spirit while lovers of peace seem helpless to meet this situation.

But is there not in fact a way for the protest to gain true strength? I
have learned that while the war films are financial triumphs generally, the
films with peace as their theme are financial disasters as a rule. I therefore
make the suggestion to you as to other anti-militarists who direct national organisations that a serious attempt be made to reverse this patronage. Abstention from attendance at the play could thus be relieved and
the pleasure of dramatic experience encouraged. Better peace films and
different news reels would surely result from the larger demand. There
are playwrights who are ready to risk their all on plunges into anti-war
films, But should they be ruined in the process? It seems to me that no
more effective work for peace could be done than to bring about the shift
of patronage from the one kind of picture to the other.

How can this be done? I have secured the promise of Miss Helen
Havener of the Motion Picture Producers & Distributors of America, Inc.
(28 West 44th Street, New York City) that she will provide any inquiring
officer or interested member of a civic organisation with the list of films
founded on the peace idea and keep that information up-to-date for

them. If this information could then be distributed among the membership of such societies with the advice that the members make it a practice to give their patronage to these plays, a still more notable success in driving out the war films might be achieved than can be achieved by the boycott alone.

You may be fully aware of all this and regard my letter to you as naive. But I am too convinced of the value of this procedure to hesitate to write you about it through the fear that some one may already be pushing it.

Sincerely, Mary R. Beard

3 The Women's Archives Begins

The following letter inaugurated a new era in Mary Beard's life, during which she devoted herself to the establishment of an institution that would preserve and maintain women's history through documents. The project began with a proposal by Rosika Schwimmer, a Hungarian-born feminist, pacifist, and radical reformer residing in the United States, who had been active in international woman suffrage and peace efforts since the beginning of the twentieth century. Schwimmer, one year younger than Beard, was personally acquainted with most of the leading lights of the prewar suffrage and peace movements in the United States—Carrie Chapman Catt, Jane Addams, Harriet Stanton Blatch, for instance—and she had discussed with several of them her idea to create an archive of documents reflecting those struggles. Both Harriot Stanton Blatch and Dorothy Dunbar Bromley, a columnist for the *New York World-Telegram*, suggested that Schwimmer should enlist Mary Beard's help.

In July 1935, when Schwimmer first wrote to Beard suggesting a meeting, she had in mind "an international feminist-pacifist archive," to collect and preserve documents and thus to keep alive the truths of women's international efforts and achievements for equal rights and world peace before and during the Great War. In Schwimmer's view, the postwar years had seen retrogression on both fronts, as women's rights had been compromised in many countries, the "militarization of women" was proceeding apace, and peace efforts by women were diminishing in influence. Her view of militarization in the United States was greatly affected by the refusal of her own application for American citizenship. She pursued citizenship through the 1920s all the way to the U.S. Supreme Court, which in May 1929 handed down a decision confirming her ineligibility on the grounds of her unwillingness to bear arms for her country.[1]

37. TO ROSIKA SCHWIMMER

New Milford, Connecticut
July 21, 1935

My revered Rosika Schwimmer,

Your name signed to a letter to me fills me with infinite delight. It leads me to venture to ask you whether you could come to see us in the country and talk over the archive of documents here. I rarely go to town in the summer but I shall do so if that is the only way or the best way to have the talk with you. Any time that you might set for a visit here before August first, when my house will be fuller for a week or so, would bring rejoicing to all the Beards.

As for your project it has my fullest sympathy. I think it imperative to put this material together. No doubt we have many of the same reasons for seeing it that way but it does me great good to learn that one so competent as you stands ready to assume the task. I shall be only too happy to tell you how I visualise the thing, parts of which I have longed to tackle myself but have not done and see no way to do myself. I look forward with the keenest enjoyment to meeting you—a privilege far too long denied me.

Cordially, Mary R. Beard

Beard visited the residence of the sisters Franciska and Rosika Schwimmer (leaving behind her handkerchief by accident). It was "a memorable day," Schwimmer wrote to Beard: "It was quite rejuvenating to meet again someone who possesses a fiery spirit and intellectual superiority,— something that has become so rare in the ranks of feminists." [2] As the letter suggests, Beard immediately set about collecting supporters for the project.

38. TO ROSIKA SCHWIMMER

New Milford, Connecticut

August 6, 1935

Dear Mme. Schwimmer,

Your generous words about my personality convince me that I caught fire in your presence. But who wouldn't? I am an intellectual babe who should stay in the woods but who is delighted beyond words when you help me pretend that I am growing up. It was wonderful to have the chance to commune with you and your sister! I hesitate to risk spoiling another by sending you a copy of one of my books but I hope that you will see in it the raw material of a great book when some one more gifted than I writes it on some such basis. I have asked my publisher to mail a copy to you.

Now that your plan has arrived for the Archive, I shall proceed at once to push for its execution. Your statement is so completely convincing that I must believe that the scheme will capture the imagination and appeal to the practical sense of American women in a position to carry it out. I shall make copies tomorrow and send them to such persons as Marguerite Wells of the League of Women Voters whom I know to be vitally peaceful in intention, Mrs. Geline MacDonald Bowman of the [National] Federation of Business and Professional Women, and Dr. [Kathryn] McHale of the [American Association of] University Women. It is possible however that there will be delay on account of vacations. I will let you know what response I get without delay. I am writing Mrs. [Eleanor] Roosevelt and Ellen Glasgow too. Each and everyone whom I suspect of being capable of intelligence I shall ask to consider this proposition for, conceivably, such a dramatisation of feminism and the woman's angle on life might even do something now to halt the backward movement which you so graphically picture.

The last of this month when some of my husband's engagements have been filled and I can be sure of his being at home, I shall try to lure you and your sister here by motor, sending my car for you.

Thank you so much for my five cent handkerchief so beautifully laundered that it looks expensive.

Cordially, Mary R. Beard

◆━

The women whom Beard initially contacted to support the archives project were of several sorts: old friends from suffragist days who had continued in anti-militarist efforts, obvious big names in women's organizations, potential sympathizers who had risen to importance in the New Deal, and women with money. Florence Brewer Boeckel had been a Woman's Party campaigner and editor of *The Suffragist;* after the Nineteenth Amendment was passed she became educational director of the National Council for Prevention of War, an anti-militarist organization of men and women.

Beard's fury at Harry Elmer Barnes' *History of Western Civilization* (New York, 1935) and Will Durant's *The Story of Civilization* (vol. 1, *Our Oriental Heritage* [New York, 1935]) was neither the first nor last of her trumpets against male historians of civilization for leaving out women's part.

39. TO FLORENCE BREWER BOECKEL

New Milford, Connecticut
August 10, 1935

Dear Mrs. Boeckel:

Here I am at it again! The enclosed [description of the Archives plan] is self-explanatory and I am behind it one hundred percent. I saw Mme. Schwimmer the other day in town and found her having to decide at last about her own archives. I hate as much as she does to see them boxed or burned.

Beside I am enraged by the new books on civilization—Will Durant's and H. E. Barnes'. They just know nothing whatever of the woman in any case. It is our fault I think. And in our fault all men and women are at fault.

I think that if we could dramatise the woman's culture as this Plan suggests, we might recapture the feminine imagination for a woman movement on a grander design, revive some of the old indomitable spirit which centered around the old Cause, and regain a united front directed toward peace and creative enterprise. It is worth trying, isn't it? Do you believe so? . . .

It is proposed (by me) to collect a group of women in New York soon after Labor Day to discuss the matter and get a sponsoring committee. Can you come?

Love and best wishes, Mary Beard

Another correspondent of Mary Beard's during the 1930s was a woman exactly her age who had been campaigning, ever since the design of Mt. Rushmore by sculptor Gutzum Borglum in the 1920s, to have Susan B. Anthony's head carved there along with the four presidents honored. Beard's letter to Powell brings out her particular interest in women's contribution to *public* life; it is also worth noting that she invents the phrase "woman's culture" to use in these recruitment letters.

40. TO ROSE ARNOLD POWELL

New Milford, Connecticut
August 10, 1935

Dear Mrs. Powell,

Your familiarity with Susan B. Anthony's passion for preserving her own and Mrs. Stanton's archives—meaning more than the personal interest of course—will make you receptive of course to this broad plan for a great international feminist archive which Rosika Schwimmer has drawn up. I don't know where you stand on the issue of war and peace but I entertain, as one of my feminist props, the belief that time and again in history women have had to take over men's bankrupt societies and that the Schwimmer-Addams' and other feminists' attempts to take charge of the western world in 1915 was a great outburst of the same sort of responsibility. All the correspondence and the interviewing connected with that drive for peace are in Mme. Schwimmer's keeping. But she is getting on in years and is by no means well. Nor can she afford to house this archive any longer. It is good feminist material and should not be lost by burning or by boxing for no one to read. In my opinion.

What is even more on my mind in championing the enclosed Plan is some way to recapture the imaginative zest of women for public life. It is perilous for society if they retreat to private interests to the exclusion of interests in the common life represented by the State. To recapture that zest I believe that some dramatisation of the woman's culture is necessary, is imperative. And this seems to me the way. Reverencing our pioneers is important. But work in our own time for our own time is equally vital, is it not?

Let me know your reaction to this Plan anyway?

Cordially, Mary R. Beard

Not surprisingly, Beard called upon Lena Madesin Phillips' support for the archives effort. As noted in the letter below, she initially imagined that a woman's college might be connected with the archives to offer an alternative education grounded in understanding of women's contributions to world history. Beard's critiques of existing structures of higher education in the early 1930s resulted not only in utopian visions but also in a tendency to blame women for not knowing, or for willfully ignoring, their own history.

41. TO LENA MADESIN PHILLIPS

New Milford
August 20th [1935]

Dear Chief,

I have not bothered you for ages, have I, with a fantastic scheme of my own? But you have been thrusting out in new lines while I have been incubating for new thrusts too. I long for a chat about yours and mine for maybe we have both got a new lease of life. If the meeting which the enclosed proposes comes off soon after Labor Day, I'll stay over in town for a chat and a bat if you are "agreeable." In the meantime I have got to bow down night and day to the revision of a High School book on American history with blood in my eye for more material on woman for one thing, but not everything.

I hope you will be enthusiastic about the enclosed Plan. You may or may not think highly of Rosika Schwimmer. That, I think, does not matter. Her suggestion is enormously important. I see in it, beside what is set forth by her, the nucleus of a true Woman's College. We could have seminars at the Archive Centers and talks by competent persons on the role of women in society. No writer or orator or "statesman" should be able after this gets going to publish a tome, deliver a speech, or plot a national program without an apprenticeship to this institution. I feel enraged for instance over the just published History of Western Civilization by Harry Elmer Barnes which takes no account really of women as involved in the story. It is overwhelmingly masculine and consequently unenlightened about how civilisations are made. But I think his fault is women's fault in knowing nothing of themselves.

Will you come to a meeting at Mme. Schwimmer's soon after Labor Day to consider the Plan and a sponsoring committee? Have you a choice of dates to propose?

Best wishes and love,
Mary R. Beard

❦

The first meeting on behalf of the archives project was set for Tuesday, September 10, 1935. It did not include Alice Paul, mentioned in the letter below, although she became a sponsor. The national chairman (so called) chosen a few months later was a National Woman's Party figure, Inez Haynes Irwin. A successful author of fiction and journalism, Irwin had narrated *The Story of the Woman's Party* (New York, 1921) and had also published, in conjunction with the international congress of women in 1933, a popular history of women, *Angels and Amazons* (Garden City, 1934). The organizational structure for the World Center for Women's Archives (WCWA), as the project was shortly to be called, with a national board and state branches, was similar to Alice Paul's structure for the National Woman's Party. But Beard constantly strove to make the member-

ship and leadership represent and appeal to a much wider range of
women.

42. TO ROSIKA SCHWIMMER

New Milford
September sixth [1935]

Dear Mme. Schwimmer,

. . . As for our joint Tuesday meeting, I . . . had urged Mrs. Blatch to
interest the National Woman's Party because I thought that she might
have more influence now with Alice Paul than I have. But on receiving
your letter I wrote directly to Alice Paul myself. I worked very closely
with her years ago. Indeed I was the first and for a long time the only
backer she had in New York. But we have not seen eye to eye on post-
suffrage programs. We have not disputed personally but I have seen nothing of hers for a long, long time and so I had turned to Mrs. Blatch for
pressure for the Archive. I asked Mrs. Blatch also to write to Mrs. Hecker
about the matter. I agree heartily with your appreciation of Mrs. Blatch's
place in the movement of thought. We are close friends. She has reached
an age which may make her a little forgetful and we may have to repeat
the details or the spirit of our enterprise but maybe not.

. . . Don't let us worry about personalities hampering our campaign.
The more diversity we have the better for the plan, it seems to me. And
beside it must thrive on moral force such as you symbolize or it will not
thrive at all. We'll work out all together some kind of sponsoring organization which will seem to our pooled intelligence the best way to proceed.

I sound ridiculously wise, don't I? No one was ever in fact more infantile of mind. But I have sense enough to know that I am comical. And I
have at the same time the keenest desire to do what I can to push this
thing along.

I am anxious that the Tuesday conference may move as swiftly as is
consistent with efficiency—for the sake of you and your sister. I have
some women in reserve on that account—women who are endless ver-
balists but who can be drawn in later to do the talking which will be necessary to achieve our goal. In the meantime my warmest regards to you
and "Franciska".

Mary R. Beard

Beard's reply to Rose Arnold Powell, who had written her usual plaint concerning Mt. Rushmore, gives the flavor of her hopes and excitement about the project just after the initial supporters' meeting.

43. TO ROSE ARNOLD POWELL

New Milford, Connecticut
September 14, 1935

Dear Mrs. Powell,

Deeply moved as I was by your letter I am slow in replying. And the reason for the delay is that I just returned from days in New York filled with effort to launch the Archive Center about which I wrote you recently. And your letter increases my zest for this Center.

We do seem so helpless in our individual protests against the determination seemingly displayed by men to maintain the credo of the man's world. But if we make group protests, the present group set-up is marked by such special interests that protests from women's organisations savor of special interests and are limited to that extent in their social effects. So the problem of next steps and longer strides is one which lies much on my mind as on yours.

I therefore see two things in one through this Archive project: the collection in one place of the data on women, including the rich personal material such as letters, diaries, memoranda; and the using of this material right at hand by people competent to use it, with the force of the Archive Center behind them. If, for instance, from such a place could go forth the demands and the protests, issued by a watching committee with its power increased by its wealth of data at its hand, then possibly the woman's culture could be integrated into the study of culture in the large and all our common intelligence enriched. Such is my dream anyway.

The Plan of the Archive Center will be framed in concise and clear form and presented on October 17th to a large but picked group of women in New York for approval and pressure. I am not sure just where the meeting will take place but I shall let you know when I know. Do attend it if you can.

That is a wonderful quotation from Montaigne which you give in your letter: "Men are nothing until they become excited." We'll be less as women as long as we are less excited. But with excitement must go fine reasoning and finer organisation than exists at present if we are to be more than the excitable something.

I do value your writing me freely for that helps my understanding and helps to keep me stirred.

Cordially, Mary R. Beard

A second, larger meeting for the archives was held in New York on October 17, 1935. There, Beard was able to confirm the sponsorship of such women as birth control reformer Margaret Sanger, well-known physician Dr. Florence Sabin, lawyer and pacifist Elinor Byrns, novelist Fannie Hurst, head of the American Association of University Women Kathryn McHale, as well as stalwarts Emily Newell Blair, Harriot Stanton Blatch and Lena Madesin Phillips.[3] The American Woman's Association (AWA), a New York-based club whose thousands of members included professionals and society women, loaned its Manhattan building for meetings. In view of Beard's intense commitment to this project, her remark in the letter below that she would soon "cease concentrating to such an extent on women" appears to be tongue-in-cheek.

The reference below to flying from New Milford to Blatch's home in Nyack, New York, is curious, because neither Mary nor Charles Beard thoroughly approved of the fact that their son, Bill (then twenty-eight), had trained as a pilot and flew a private airplane.[4]

44. TO HARRIOT STANTON BLATCH

New Milford
October 28 [1935]

Dear Harriot:

You are lenient—by letter at least—with my corrupt practice in asking for funds in such an irregular way. I had no right to do it. I did do it without right simply because I must get this project launched, if I am to share in it, immediately, as I am forced to be tied up for the winter months. It has such a momentum now that it will surely swing along at a good pace. Denied the privilege of citizenship, Rosika Schwimmer is kept from earning as she might otherwise do and out of the sum collected at the AWA, the amount she had spent in trying to work for the Archives Center can be returned and more left for the initial sponsoring.

I am unhappy because you had to go to bed after this last trip to New York. I would have asked Bill to fly me over to Nyack to tell you of this sorrow if he had been on the spot. I came home myself feeling and certainly looking bedraggled after my own two days in town. But even so, I betook myself to one of the dingiest spots known—the coal fields of Pennsylvania. The teachers of Scranton had asked me there and as I had never got off the train to mingle with a mining community, I was glad of this chance to do so. I came back sooty but I did get a feeling about life and labor in the coal field. I had lived over a volcano in Japan and caught something of the flavor of life thus lived, by the Japanese. It helped me to understand life over coal mines with the earth trembling and actually caving in on occasion. Somehow I had never realized that the carved out caverns were actually under peoples' houses; that miners who try to buy little cottages have awful damages to face from time to time; that the earth may open and swallow street car, truck, or detached humans when it feels so inclined. Yet the teachers chatted about backs or no backs in evening clothes to a degree which appalled in another form. I am back to fresh air trying to recover if not in bed.

. . . By December first I think that I am intending to follow your advice at the long last—to cease concentrating to such an extent on women. But the alternative is surely not to concentrate on man. What a mess he is! What a tragedy of life he makes for himself! Do you know the last lines of Shelley's Prometheus Unbound? About "Love from her awful throne of patient power." Love should come from woman for the healing of hate. But that takes me backward to my obsession I suppose. Anyway my true love—

I hope to enjoy the news that you are up again and refraining from town for a good while.

Mary Beard

The resumption of Beard's correspondence with Doris Stevens, a former Congressional Union colleague, must have been occasioned by Stevens' request to Beard to consider another former CU suffragist, Helena Hill Weed (Elsie Hill's sister), for a job. Stevens was active in the National Woman's Party in the 1920s and 1930s, leading its international efforts to attach equal rights for women diplomatic treaties. She supported the archives effort, as did many former and current NWP members, although she did not become very actively involved. The friendships forged during the suffrage struggle lasted a long time—and even for someone like Mary

Beard, who usually looked little to it, the network of acquaintance functioned for a lifetime.[5]

45. TO DORIS STEVENS

Hotel Syracuse
Syracuse, New York
November 14, 1935

Dear Doris—

Reading your vibrantly beautiful letter again today here amid our heavy-witted Club women whom for some unknown reason I had pledged myself to "address," I come again to your lines: "Often I realize how little what I do counts. Life should be lived magnificently." How my mind and my heart respond! That's why I brought your letter along—to keep me company. Instinctively I felt that I should need it.

Harriot Stanton Blatch thinks me plain insane to keep jabbering about women and this I don't understand in view of her intransigent feminism. But that probably proves that I am insane.

Let's have a two-some chat—you and I in Washington soon. I shall be there early in '36. And that's very soon.

You have married, dear Doris. I have thought of you a lot and hoped for your deep happiness—for your living magnificently. Your radiance and quick wit stirred my very soul when I got to Washington in 1915. I was clumsier than any donkey then, as I still am. You were all glow and charm. Keep all of it you can. Take time to live while you labor. One must not expect to see much of the result of the latter. But she must catch a good deal of the former to be rejuvenated for giving to the other. I can't bear to think of your strength fleeing. But I am growing very old. And these Club women age me a thousand years!!!

If we do get the money for the Archives Center I should recommend Helena Hill Weed with genuine enthusiasm for the work you suggest. We are making headway. The thing looks good. It cheers me to have your approval. But it takes time to materialize naturally. I am writing Mrs. Weed. I'll keep you in touch with "progress."

Much love—Mary R. Beard

❧

After the second meeting it became clear that administration of the plan for an archives center rested with Beard, who plunged into issues of organization, funding, location, and the like. She consulted frequently with Lena Madesin Phillips and also welcomed the help of Emma Hirth, a career official with the Young Women's Christian Association. Lura Beam, a researcher and writer on education and the arts who had written up studies for the National Committee on Maternal Health in the late 1920s and early 1930s, was also among the first directors. Another valuable ally was Mina Bruere, assistant secretary of the Central Hanover Bank and Trust Company in New York, one of the first women in the United States to make a successful career in finance, and president of the American Bank Women from 1928 to 1930. (Her brother Robert was married to Beard's coauthor Martha Bruere.) It is not clear exactly who Beard was referring to in her mention of the "wild women" in the letter below; she may have meant Florentine Sutro and friends. Sutro, aging widow of philanthropist Lionel Sutro, had a lifelong commitment to reform, had been president of the Manhattan division of the Women's International League for Peace and Freedom, and was close with Schwimmer, but her ideas about publicity for the archives project were not always palatable to Beard. The initial interest of the New York Public Library in collaborating with the project, mentioned in the following letter, seemed a boost in 1935, although the collaboration did not materialize. Perhaps fittingly, when the women's archives dissolved Rosika Schwimmer chose to deposit her papers there.

46. TO LENA MADESIN PHILLIPS

New Milford
Nov. 17, 1935

Dear Lena—

. . . I had been invited to tell the heads of the NY public library about this Archives project and that I did on Friday morning. The heads of all the branch libraries were present. It was a large gathering and it became an excited gathering. The head of the organisation made it very emphatic that the library would like to take the project under its wing—put a division of the library building apart to house the documents and take care of their preparation and use. So at least we should be able to perform a true service to women and men if we went no further than to get the stuff for the library. But I did not turn over the project of course. We couldn't have the school feature and I should not like to give up that unless we had to. Anyway Mr. Lydendecker said in open meeting that the library would receive our archives as we collected them and keep them for us until we get a separate building, if we approved that offer. And it offered more yet—this time at my suggestion. I asked whether the chief could use his staff to make a list of present library material and catalogue archives as separate from casual and usually fuzzy commentaries on the female sex; I was told that the library would be charmed to do so. There is a lot of valuable material already on its shelves of course but so jumbled as sense and nonsense that it badly needs this division. We must have a similar catalogue made up by the Congressional Library. It would be a distinguished achievement, if we found nothing more to record, to have carried the present libraries thus far in their appreciation of the woman's story. I am cheered immensely by this advance.

But, let us not give up the larger enterprise at this stage anyway. I'd prefer the library to a museum piece at the NY World's Fair but it does no harm to acquaint the city officials with their present neglect to draw any women into that Fair. . . .

There is more comfort: Mina Bruere is so enthusiastic that she is perfectly willing to be treasurer. Are you as gay over this as I am? The banking women have apparently been collecting their documents just as the medical women and others have been doing. They like the idea of a common center for many very clear reasons. So with Miss Bruere's practical financial experience and connections, it seems to me that one big problem is clarified enormously. But I'd like your opinion.

We must get back to our general assembly of sponsors with the plan of organisation, etc. at the earliest date. If we set the meeting for the first week in December—say December 3—could you and Miss Hirth and Miss Beam be ready to report? Miss Bruere might come into your committee meetings and bring some good suggestions? She is at the Hanover Trust as you no doubt know.

I have asked the AWA which offers us its gallery lounge free whether we could hold the big meeting there the evening of December 3d and if not what other nights that week we could have. Dr. Sabin and many others want to attend and can only do so at night. This date would clear us from the approaching Thanksgiving engagements and clean us up before Christmas. The question of incorporation will be one to face. No end of thanks for putting your shoulder to this wheel with me!

The matter of a budget is well-nigh insoluble now. We can go as strong as patrons will permit of course. The design of a building could take account of all sorts of things: separate rooms for the materials of separate organisations: alcoves for such individualistic documents as those of Rosika Schwimmer, etc. including a lecture hall and alcoves for student tables. The expenses of filing and cataloguing and serving could be ascertained on some ratio basis from Mr. Lydendecker of the Public Library and/or from the Special Libraries Association the woman head of which has written hoping to help us on our way. I shall look up her letter and send in her name. If Miss Bruere could get her banking group to work out a finance committee for us, what say you? . . .

IF we can—as we must—go back to the general assembly by early December with a plan of organisation, an improved prospectus, and a proposed governing board, with Miss Bruere authorised to form a finance committee perhaps, we should really be scrambling to our feet, should we not? All the sects of feminists, now including Doris Stevens, are ardent for this thing. Mrs. Catt gives her full support and cooperation. Publicity must be controlled from this day forward a good deal better. Wild women have broken in but the china shop is not wrecked, luckily. Don't breathe a word about their having been such, for they are supersensitive in that relation; they consider that they can make no mistake.

If you and Miss Hirth and Miss Beam and Miss Bruere could complete, say in a week, everything short of the governing body, notices could be sent out for the forthcoming general meeting quite some time in advance. And as for the governing body, the four of you and I might bring in our respective slates to a joint conference before the general meeting long enough in advance to be sure that the members of our agreed-upon group would consent to serve if approved. . . .

Love and best wishes   Mary Beard

⊶

By the end of 1935 administrative complications had thickened. While Mary Beard was seeking donors among the Carnegies and Rockefellers and collaboration with the Institute for Women's Professional Relations in New London, Connecticut (which focused on vocational issues), a divide among the founders was shaping up. From Beard's point of view, Rosika Schwimmer and her important supporter Florentine Sutro were more interested in publicity—including planning a site at the upcoming World's Fair to be held in Flushing, New York—than in the groundwork for the substantive collection. Beard respected and admired Schwimmer, and regarded Sutro favorably as an "activist par excellence." (As noted in the letter below, Sutro reflected on her life in an autobiography published in 1935, *My First Seventy Years* [New York, Roerick Museum Press, 1935]). But the pressure of the two for quick actions and immediate publicity made Beard uneasy.[6] Perhaps stress accounted for her unwonted and unwanted comment in the letter below about "the racial urge." This must have referred to the Jewish background that Schwimmer and Sutro had in common, although Schwimmer was the daughter of an agnostic and a freethinker, and Sutro's father was a founder of Ethical Culture.

In the nation's capital again in 1936 for midwinter, Beard was investigating the possibility of funding the archives project through the Works Progress Administration (WPA), the New Deal federal relief agency that created millions of jobs to combat unemployment. She approached Ellen Woodward, head of women's projects for the WPA, in league with Sutro and Lola Maverick Lloyd, a Chicago clubwoman who was an intimate friend and loyal supporter of Schwimmer.

47. TO LENA MADESIN PHILLIPS

The Mayflower
Jan. 23 [1936]

Dear Lena:

It was mighty good to see you and have a good chat together. The subjects under discussion will keep on brewing in my mind. And as you say to me: "We shall see what we shall see."

This particular follow-up is to state that it now seems that Mrs. Sutro will have to be put on the executive committee. She is here and she insists upon this. I suppose the racial urge is part of it. But she is also deeply interested in the Archives and has, it cannot be denied, thrown herself into its promotion with zest. She has some good points: great energy and will, time, money, wide social contacts. Her autobiography gives her more eclat. She will not be denied. If we attempt it, she will give us a black eye and we don't want that. She might very well be made responsible for some particular phase of the work. She has infinite persistence which is what promoters of a project need. If it is guided it may have infinite value.

We are making important progress here in connection with the WPA. In addition to what I put down on paper for you, it is possible that we may get a good sum of money. I may know tomorrow when I have an interview with the woman in charge of women's projects [Ellen Woodward]. I am to put up to her—encouraged by men in this division—the archives project. I was told that men and women on the inside have been as disgusted as critics on the outside over the fact that only cooking and sewing could be concocted as women's projects. So the ground seems prepared for our bold attack. I shall make it as valiantly as I can. Mrs. Lloyd and Mrs. Sutro will go with me to Mrs. Woodward. Indeed to Mrs. Lloyd and her daughter who is in the government work we owe the opportunity to come thus far and to go farther. I am jittery with excitement today.

Much love—Mary B.

•~

Mary Beard's group meeting with Ellen Woodward and with Luther Evans, director of the Historical Records Survey under the WPA, was exciting enough to generate the heady suggestion of a "woman's Smithsonian." This gave her hope of instigating a lively group of supporters in Washington, D.C., as well as in New York.

In opening the letter below, Beard reflects on a Liberty League dinner for two thousand at which Al Smith, the unsuccessful Democratic party candidate for president in 1928, ripped into the New Deal, declaring it an un-American communistic experiment, a travesty of the party platform of 1932. In the *Washington Post* the crowd was described as "brilliant-gowned, tailcoated" and "hilarious" at Smith's oratory.[7]

48. TO LENA MADESIN PHILLIPS

The Mayflower
January 26th [1936]

Dear Lena:

The day after the Al Smith circus, my dear, writing you my daily! The enclosed report you might miss and that would surely be a loss. My sister and her husband, vice president of the American Cynamid Company, were down among the cheering plut[ocrat]s helping to roar appreciation of the thrusts at taxation for the poor. I listened in upstairs after watching the drunks prepare for the dinner below. This morning when I went down for extra copies of the Post, it was still colorful to hear the pages shouting "Mr. Du Pont?" Well, here we are.

I see in the paper too that you are to be toastmistress Thursday night for the B[usiness] & P[rofessional] W[omen]. So thought I'd write you more about the WPA. You might like to share in dramatizing us wimmen.

After arranging with Dr. L. Evans to get in on his listing of documents, printed and unprinted, as I set down on paper for you—at his suggestion, Mrs. Lloyd, Mrs. Sutro, and I went post haste to call upon Mrs. Woodward, chief of the women's division of the WPA. The interview had been arranged by Dr. Evans himself who came to it himself bringing a fellow worker and the WPA publicity woman, Miss Carol (I believe that's her name.) The upshot was that everyone called for a Hall of Women's Records comparable in dignity and importance to the Smithsonian, if you please! We three New Yorkers found ourselves expanding until we were unrecognizable to ourselves.

The Woman's Smithsonian. Well, you see the WPA can't give funds to any private institution. I had asked for money. But if we called for the making of a public institution such as the Smithsonian, we might have a standing. We'd have to get Congress to authorize it. It might authorize the whole appropriation. We were told to get busy before it is too late.

One of the men at this interview has worked years at the Smithsonian. He is keen about this newest proposal, chimed in in its support, said the government would not interfere except to accept (maybe help name) directors. Miss Carol and the women were tense with excitement. Mrs. Woodward was called away but her secretary sat at attention. The gang is coming to see me at the hotel.

Are we ganging up on a Woman's Smithsonian or something like that? Quite a step ahead to discuss with the wimmen! Why not?

Mrs. Lloyd and Mrs. Sutro then plunged over to see Dr. Charl Williams [field secretary of the National Education Association] and burst in upon her with this idea. It was surely sudden. What could she say?

So there is more to the ball we started rolling than we had any idea of in the beginning. Somehow it appears to me that we should let all the women who have sent letters in appreciation of the idea of an archives center know what the idea has produced up to date. A circular letter might be mimeographed and widely distributed? If you wanted to bring any of this into your toasting, it should bring publicity!!

Oh my dear!—Mary

Eleanor Roosevelt's announced interest in the women's archives brought a great flurry of newspaper publicity and put Beard in the limelight. The project had received some publicity when launched, mainly in the *New York World-Telegram* for which supporter Dorothy Dunbar Bromley was a columnist, but in February and March 1936, when Bess Furman, who covered Eleanor Roosevelt for the Associated Press, got into the act, articles and editorials were carried in the *New York Times,* the *Chicago Tribune,* the *Boston Traveler,* the *Washington Herald,* and newspapers as far flung as Houston, Cleveland, and Providence. Schwimmer was content to have her own role little noted, because she was aware that her radical and controversial reputation might jeopardize the gaining of sponsors.[8] As the letter below makes clear, under Mary Beard's leadership the project had expanded far beyond the collection of papers of feminists and pacifists of the prewar era, to include a broad range of women in history. Beard hoped and imagined that because of the scope of the project, women of many different ideological orientations would be willing to cooperate in supporting it. Thus her hope at the end of the letter—where she mistakes the first name of Emma Guffey Miller, a leading Democrat—for women of differing political loyalties. Beard's glee at the apparent momentum of the project in Washington was tempered only by her awareness of factional strife among the New York women involved.

49. TO ROSIKA SCHWIMMER

> Hotel Mayflower
> Washington, D.C.
> February 14, 1936.

Dear Rosika Schwimmer:

I should have made this letter arrive as your Valentine conveying to you my congratulations on the IDEA! But the best I can do is to write it on this day and mail it on the 14th of February.

The truth is that my phone bell, my door bell, and my fan mail have been so compelling since I went to Mrs. Roosevelt's press conference last Monday morning that I have had no single half hour in which to report events to you. I did hurry over a kind of report to Miss Savord thinking that a necessary thing in case you were all meeting soon again—only to learn from you today that she is no longer secretary. Well! Well! But before I comment on the inner conflict which seems to be strong in New York, I shall tell you what I see as the important items in my Washington drive.

So I begin with Bess Furman's visit induced by your and my common invitation. We had a wonderful morning together. She sent out an advance story before the meeting on Monday night which you saw—as much as we printed—in the NY Herald-Tribune but which I have not seen because I have been too rushed to look at the papers, knowing they were carrying things. Mrs. Furman is carrying on—preparing more stories, one for Sunday the 23d for instance in which she hopes to tell about such crimes and misdemeanors as the prolonged burial of the

Aletta Jacobs library in the Creerar [Library] vaults. I hope I am still right about that. If you know anything to the contrary please wire [at] my expense. It was Bess Furman who got the invitation to the White House conference. She seems to think that I did not disgrace you all there.

Immediately after appearing there, woman after woman who had been at that conference telephoned in for a longer private talk about archives. I have already filled several of these appointments—as today with Mrs. Griffin whose husband owns or operates a string of New England papers such as the Waterbury Republican and the Hartford Times. She is deeply interested and is going to write as many stories as she can, one immediately for the organ of the women Democrats. Winifred Mallon, now president of the press women who meet at lunch once a week, took charge of all the publicity for this enterprise of mine—including the night meeting. She was generous of her time and very efficient in management. Some newspaper reports were taken out of the hands of women for some reason I can't quite understand and garbled as second-hand stuff was sure to be. Thus I was made to say that Cleopatra was a Phoenician and that the women of the south were *responsible* for "reconstruction" after the civil war. Neither thing did I say of course. No woman at the conference would have been so mistaken. I did not use the word "reconstruction" at all. I did use the word "rehabilitation" which has a different meaning in that connection to every American. But never mind. I put out my neck and got a few cracks naturally. On the whole a lot was done—to the good. Kathleen McLaughlin [who] is writing a column for next Sunday's Times, sent for more copy and I gave her what I thought she might want.

The NY World-Telegram telephoned via some man on the paper that it was proposing to run six articles on New York women who ought to appear [in] works on history but don't. He asked for the names of such neglected women. I had to work fast but this is what I gave him:

Margaret Hardenbroeck of Dutch New York, sometimes called the most enterprising person, male or female, in the colony—great landlord and business woman who probably ran the first packet line between America and Europe.

The De Lancey and Livingston and Schuyler women who waged a civil war within the nationalist war for independence. Mrs. John Jay the name for the patriot leadership.

Elizabeth Cady Stanton and Susan B. Anthony—widening democracy with criticism of Church and State as thinking of high order.

Eliza Lee Schuyler, granddaughter of Alexander Hamilton, for social work. Katharine Bement Davis and social hygiene by way of good measure.

Dr. Mary Putnam Jacobi—medicine and public health

Etc....for bigger measure.

So the young man said: "The boss has given me two weeks off in which to do this series and I regard it as the best assignment during my 13 years on the paper." So I gave him bibliography.

Publishers are writing from near and far for persons to write books.

Mrs. Roosevelt really gave us a big boost. I opened my talk at her press meeting by playing with the phrases "off the record" and "on the record." I said that she had made the former famous and would probably make the latter equally so. I tried to show the relation between being off the record by self-determination, voluntarily, and being off the record involuntarily, unjustly, to the detriment of social understanding. She agreed, asked questions, commented. During the hour we all spent together, one of the journalists asked whether you were on the central committee. I was wary but I tried to be honest. I replied that you were not a citizen and so were handicapped when it came to being a committee member but that you knew about the location of many important documents and about the women abroad and in the USA whose documents should be in such a center and THAT YOUR LACK OF CITIZENSHIP IS OUR LOSS. I did not say more, being wary, I did not know the woman who put the question, you see. I did state that your loss is our loss. I hope that may do some good.

Today Gladwys Jones, executive secretary of the National Deans of Women, asked for twenty or so copies of the press releases to take with her to St. Louis to the national convention of educators which opens the 24th. She got them and will distribute them among the deans. I gave her two concise points to emphasize in talking with teachers and deans.

a. To make equality function, the intellectual climate—public opinion—must be favorable. Archives pave the way. Using the story of the Weimar constitution as an ill.

b. It is not only woman's "progress" which we have in mind to demonstrate but the progress of civilization through women too.

She had come to our AAUW meeting and got excited and thought up this way to push the cause along.

I am looking around for some faculty person to do the same for teachers.

You inquire about the resolutions passed at the evening meeting. I sent in a list of women who signified their approval by signing cards. But there were some who incline to favor the placing of the archives as collected in the Congressional Library or other general institution. I claimed that that would again take women off the record and they were open-minded. A resolution I feared would crystallize such opposition and so it was agreed that every one would clarify her mind on the point—and all those women have minds—and that we would come together soon—perhaps in a great public meeting in the ballroom of the Mayflower. That is an ambitious plan. I shall have to find someone else to swing it if it is accomplished. But it should be accomplished and I think it can. Say in two or three weeks. By that time the N Y committee should be sufficiently organized for us to be able to solicit funds and members on a wholesale scale. I left the money-raising to that follow-up affair to which may be drawn the leisure class with exchequers. These women have only intelligence.

I deeply regret the appearance of factional strife in New York. I know that almost every member of the group is damned by other members, except that I have never heard Lena Phillips go after others as they go after her. I know that some have candidates for paid positions. I know that she thought Helen Havener right for publicity person. On Miss Havener I should agree. I have seen her operate for a number of years in every kind of situation. She has the selfless devotion of a saint born of intense enthusiasms. She will work till kingdom come in an emergency. She is experienced and knows the ropes. She is available. Some of the candidates I know less well and yet I know that there are and have been wheels within wheels which have led such candidates in some instances to be like enemies in the past. Even Mina Bruere is criticised by one of the women whom you would least suspect. So we have not and cannot escape factionalism it seems. I am sorry, very sorry. I hope it will wash out without delay. It is always present in the beginning of an enterprise, isn't it? I don't know. I should prefer to have pure idealists at the helm—idealists with wonderful competence. But hunting for them would consume years and possibly a life time. Meanwhile fascism might arrive.

I am glad anyway that you are to be near that gentle and loving Mrs. Lloyd in Chicago now. Do remember me to her. May the medicine of today do you worlds of good! I shall send you any news that comes my way by my own manufacture or by the work of others. I have been ghastly tired for a little while but I recuperate quickly and the breathing spell of a weekend will bring me back to the norm. I want to leave behind in Washington the strongest possible committee to work with the N Y committee.

May it be strong too. Mrs. Carol Guffey Miller has asked me to lunch with her on Monday. She is on the Democratic National Committee and thrilled by the archives project. I'll get a Republican too. Maybe ranking partisans with a lot of non-partisans can form a coalition in the archives' behalf. I'll see.

[M.R.B.]

Beard's response to personal publicity shows her evenhandedness with sarcasm—pointed toward herself as well as others.

50. TO LENA MADESIN PHILLIPS

> Hotel Mayflower
> Washington, D.C.
> March the first [1936]

Dear Lena:

Thanks for the clippings. They show how badly I have been thrown to the wolves or rather how I threw myself to the wolves by meeting the people of the press. I wonder where Lem Parton got the idea that I said women were increasingly important and men were beginning to feel abased. But where does anybody get anything? Just out of his own hot air. Anyway I helped to put the archives on the map if in the process I became a cartoon. My "generous mouth" to which Parton refers has certainly wagged an awful lot. And he can testify to you and the archives committee that I have wasted no time in beauty parlors. But oh gals, I wish I could! I do need a shampoo terribly. I thought Bromley did a very neat job on her column.

It was cheering to have a chance to talk with Emma Hirth again. We had Friday evening together and I expected to see her again but lost track of her hiding-place. She reported how competent, as usual, has been your handling of difficult situations. Thus we manage to keep on our way. As I told Miss Hirth, I am going to try to raise some money here at once for the Archives.

You've been running around. I hope it has been some fun amid the physical hardship. March is here. I'll be turning back north before long and seeing you again.

> Yours, Mary B.

By April of 1936 Rosika Schwimmer was very troubled by what she saw
as self-seeking on the part of some women involved in the archives; she
did not approve of the method used to elevate women to the national
board. Mary Beard reassured her of "the amazing devotion of the committee to the project—how night after night women, responsible by day
for huge tasks, tried to put weariness out of their minds and contribute
their highest intelligence to the formidable work connected with organis-
ing the Archives undertaking." She attempted to mollify her: "Dear
Mme. Schwimmer, you must know that we all hold you in high esteem.
My interest in you and my affection for you have never changed. I have
been so delighted that we could find women capable of carrying out the
grand idea which you formulated for an Archives Center. I could never
have helped you to get it into circulation by myself. If we had tried to
perfect an organisation alone, where should we ever have got? One has to
trust others if accomplishment is ever to come." In spite of these coax-
ings, Schwimmer formally withdrew from the project early in May, because she felt mistreated (even bullied) by some of the New York women
involved, including Lena Madesin Phillips. She was dissatisfied with the
publicity efforts and enraged by a contact made against her wishes with
Rosa Manus, an Amsterdam woman who had plans for a similar archive
in mind. In a confidential discussion among Beard, Schwimmer, and Inez
Irwin, Beard too threatened to resign, but Schwimmer insisted, "You cannot do it Mrs. Beard. Without you this idea will die." Schwimmer resigned and Beard stayed on in her post as chairman of archives. Years
later Beard wrote to a close friend that Schwimmer "was in many respects
a very great woman but she was terribly difficult and really so self-sure
that she wrecked some movements by her will to dominate." [9]

51. TO ROSIKA SCHWIMMER

New Milford, Connecticut
May 12, 1936

Dear Rosika Schwimmer:

I have thought of little else for days than our coming together over the
women's archives and the ups and downs of the succeeding relationship.
No doubt if mortal were more perfect, there would be no downs in mortal affairs. But such is not his or her construction. As for myself I am
deeply aware of my shortcomings.

Despite all the problems, the difficulties involved in winning under-standing and support for the project, and the temperamental errors which perhaps all the rest of us have made, we move forward, I believe, toward accomplishment. In going forward, perhaps we have not made ir-retrievable mistakes.

A strong executive board is now collected and as it takes upon its shoulders the heavy task of getting members and gifts, surely this is ad-vancing in the best way that those of us who tried to put our strength behind this thing would make it advance. I have been unwilling to lash and browbeat the other women into going faster than the speed they thought wise. I have often talked to you about American women versus Continental ways. Maybe this is American notwithstanding the usual idea that it is a brash people. Anyway we all feel better now about first getting incorporated and then asking for papers and funds. I shall do a lot through the summer here at my home in seeking members and money, though I cannot interview many people directly.

Most of the women will be away—several in Europe. But we shall have the plan of organization, the incorporation, and the names of a commit-tee to go out now in responsible ordering. In various ways work will go on through the intervening months until a strong drive opens up in the early autumn.

I believe you should be not-a-little content at the way I got behind your idea and then got other women behind it—women of the kind who would really push it along to realization. You and I could have spent the rest of our lives picking and choosing purely intellectual, spiritual, femi-nists and pacifists as the guarantee of THE IDEA in its perfection. But we should have no outcome, I fear, if we undertook that fine work of selec-tion by elimination. As it is, a widely representative group, several with national and international reputations, representing peace, feminism, la-bor, the three major religions, racial and civic work and the arts, has been brought together.

You will "give me a hand" on this, can you not?

As for your invaluable documents, have you ever placed a price on their head? We must get around to that matter now as soon as we can. I can't say what luck we shall have with moneyed benefactors but we shall search them out without more delay. Indeed that quest has begun. I full realise your sitation with respect to your papers and none of us has a de-sire to exploit you even if we could. We were not prepared to offer your friend any sum at this moment for her letter about which you wrote. I meant to inquire however about the nature of the letter but I got worried the other day and forgot.

> Believe me as ever your friend and
> admirer—Mary R. Beard

•←~

While focusing on the establishment of a World Center for Women's Archives Mary Beard was still committed to furthering the vision, which she shared with her husband during the 1930s, of an ordered and "collectivist" civilization. Her comments on an essay on taxes drafted by Lena Madesin Phillips show her continuing concern to establish for the nation priorities other than international and military power.

52. TO LENA MADESIN PHILLIPS

> New Milford
> June 3d—1936

Dear Lena:

I have now read TAXES—a most attractively written challenge to women to think upon the subject. You know how effectively you present even complicated matters, in my opinion. And isn't it stimulating to tackle the biggest things and try to devise the armature for a piece of sculpturing? We must chisel and mold and rub though we have only typewriters as tools—terribly clumsy instruments. I said in a Washington meeting recently that I feel like a plumber with a huge monkey wrench when I try to write instead of like a skilled craftsman. A plumber was in the audience!!!! I heard a murmur about plumbers being skilled workmen!!!!!! After the meeting (one of Mary Van Kleeck's Inter-Professional affairs) the plumber himself came up and what do you suppose he said: "My dear lady, let me propose your name for membership in the plumbers' union." I told him that I would practice harder with my tool to qualify.

I have two criticisms of Taxes—probably not important.

One of these is verbal:

Page 1. Paragraph 1. Statement of fact: "the mother . . . . was always willingly chained to a fixed spot." Nay, nay, Pauline. Not *always*. Not always *willingly*.

Paragraph 2. Last line. Change "really" to "not"???? She does hate to pay taxes, does she not?

Page 4. Would cut "a municipal airport". One of the scandalous wastes is an airport in every village idea, as I see waste. But every village wants one. And many get them—at terrific expense. You would watch the cost. I would eliminate most of them.

The other is philosophical if I may be bold enough to say so.

Your point of view seems to be that of the League of Women Voters too. I sat in on a state convention of theirs at Hartford two years ago when they were going to school for a week on taxation. Officials instructed them. Expert statisticians reported to them. They gave their own views of efficiency. But there they were in the heart of a munitions-making district, where profits had been rolling up, where the inhabitants were in need of every species of social service, *concentrating* on restraint in taxation and elimination of waste in management. Now I don't uphold extravagance and I condemn mismanagement. But I would bring into review as well the idea of community planning for the meeting of community needs—real needs for a civilisation—and on that build a wise taxation to cover the cost of civilisation. That is a collectivist, or socialist, outlook less solicitous of the interests of the few.

I'll see you on Friday and try to obey the rules at the Board meeting even if I have departed from the social code herewith.

You know me—Lena.

Affectionately, Mary R. Beard

The tone of the following letter to Rose Arnold Powell (who was concerned as usual with memorializing Susan B. Anthony) suggests Beard's frustration in her efforts to make a dent in public consciousness about women in the context of world economic depression. Her comments in 1936 ran the gamut from great hopefulness to despair. To Florence Brewer Boeckel at one point in the fall she wrote, "Women are challenged as never before to work together for ends larger than self. I like to use the phrase The New Feminism, in this connection." Yet just a few weeks earlier she had written to Harriot Stanton Blatch, about her efforts to find institutional support for the archives, "I get as sick at my stomach in presenting this case as I used to do when I asked a Southern Congressman to vote for our enfranchisement. One has to start with the ABCS in just the same way. Men are just as afraid of women's discovering themselves now as they were then." [10]

Beard's brother's impeachment and conviction also affected her reading of her own political efficacy. Halstead Ritter, a federal district court
judge in southern Florida, was impeached in the spring of 1936 on allega-
tions of misconduct and corruption in office and filing false tax returns.
Although the Senate acquitted him of the specific alleged statutory
crimes, he was convicted of "conduct unbecoming a judge." His case set a
precedent by broadening the definition of impeachable offenses in the federal judiciary. Mary Beard later said she saw the conviction as unjust, a
political ploy to unseat a Coolidge appointee in a Democratic era.[11]

53. TO ROSE ARNOLD POWELL

New Milford, Connecticut
June 14, 1936

Dear Mrs. Powell:

The items you send me about memorials to "our great" and Congressional and Executive action therewith are certainly revelations of the
ridiculous in economic politics to the Nth degree! It is such fantastic
operation. But it is the incredible which alone seems to happen. How can
I offset madness with reason? What you do expect of me!

Last week I was captioned in the press which reported my Commence-
ment speech at the New Jersey College for Women as "Denouncing" or
"Decrying" the "Dominance of Men." In fact I used no such language
but your clippings make me wish I had. There scarcely seems to be
enough intelligence loose to put in a thimble.

You have been notifying women's organizations of what is going on.
They could make a mass protest, if they would. All I can do, if anything,
is to try to work pretty much alone for a more distant future as I live far
away in the hills and am but an individual with a typewriter. I keep that
pounding nearly every waking moment and I shall keep on doing that at
any rate. I wish it might be heard in Washington. But you see they impeached my brother this last winter in the Senate and I shall be tarred
with that stick for a while. I should only hurt our Susan B. [Anthony] if I
tried to befriend her on the spot. Some one deemed holier than I—the
sister of the brother—will have more weight on Capitol Hill.

Cordially as ever, Mary R. Beard

Mary Beard remained closely in touch with peace and neutrality activists
in the mid–1930s. Here, differing respectfully from a longtime acquaint-

ance, the peace educator Florence Brewer Boeckel, she concurs in Charles Beard's published views on cultivating one's own national garden rather than imagining international order or looking to impose it on others. Her distaste for H. G. Wells' internationalist pronouncements was seconded by her scorn for his *Outline of History*. Simonds, mentioned below, was an expert on international war and peace who had made his name as a commentator on World War I. (He died early in 1936.) The Joad to whom Beard refers was likely the British philosopher Cyril E. M. Joad, who wrote a number of popular pacifist and agnostic works during the interwar period.

54. TO FLORENCE BREWER BOECKEL

New Milford, Connecticut
July 28, 1936

Dear Mrs. Boeckel:

We are both so happy to hear from you and we too wish that we could have a talk, ensemble, away from the madding crowd, with plenty of time to cover the ground which may only in fact seem to divide us. I feel very sure that our idealism is the same. It is the way to see more of it realised which is the point at issue. If we too were not running off for August, I should urge you to come to us for a day at least before you leave for England. Maybe you can come to us when you return. We are going to Antigonish in Nova Scotia to spend a little time in that cooperative community guided by St. Xavier College idealism. Father Coody has invited us and we both look forward to being inspired by the rare combination of dream and reality, made manifest by such intelligence as he possesses.

As for the grand world dream of [H. G.] Wells, I heard him talk about it two winters ago in Washington at Frank Simonds'. He then maintained that it would be easier to put the whole world in order than to put one's own "house", or nation. With respect to England, that is a natural view today as utopia. But what competence has England or the English displayed to warrant one's believing that that nation and its people have the wisdom for putting the world in order? They have a vast part of the world already under their control. As for tackling the grand job with our assistance, what have we to contribute? Have you seen the study of our Homestead land distribution recently reported in the July number of the American Historical Review? It seems that 3 1/2 per cent of the "people" actually got free farms under its provisions—for the reason that the government land grants to railway builders plus the speculative accumulation which had already gone on by 1862 left almost nothing for the people despite the legislation. The story of our American business men on this continent of virgin soil and free from clerical or feudal restraints is too appalling for aught but a burning sense of shame. We might start to clean up our own house and in that experience get some knowledge of how houses might be cleaned elsewhere. But until we have that inner knowledge and will to be clean, I just can't see what we can do ranging round the world with advice and good-will.

Of course if free trade seems the economic solution, then the solution is simple. But the history of the free trade idea and the condition in which it rose and flourished, then fell, must surely be taken into account when one accepts that simple solution. But here comes in our—my—mania—history. Wells, it is true, is supposed to have a flair for history. But special history must always be considered for there is every kind of the thing.

There could be no question between us as to life values vs. property values. I have no idea whether you suspect or detect a concern with the superior values in either or both Beards. It is there in both cases. That concern with life values is our supreme concern as yours. But basic human needs must be gratified somehow and that brings us down to the matter of economy whether we enjoy it or not. We can come up for air but if we live in the upper air all the time, are we not merely precious?

Personally I think that Joad has done some very silly writing and I have not an iota of confidence in Wells' common sense. I rejoice in their liberal outbursts for they set other people to feeling. But as leaders, I should regard them as hopelessly muddle-headed. I never in my whole life heard so much sheer drivel in one hour as Wells delivered at Frank Simonds winter before last. His imagination is majestic! His force lies wholly in that direction.

It would seem that a united front however is imperative among men and women who want to live the good life and see societies rest on that concept. Trying to create a decent society in the USA would be a rare laboratory experiment, would it not? You may believe, with Wells and many others, that we can't do anything here unless we try to do the world thing. But at least don't take it for granted that Charles and I, who believe we must try out our own competence here, are blind to world values of international association. Our view is not provincial. If we could believe that free trade is the right world economy for the good life for all, we would seem to you perhaps to raise no question of our provinciality. That is the crux of our difference in thought about the practice underlying life values I dare to believe. We are not anti-English or pro-American. Nor are we pro-English, for there is a danger that Americans will let the English do all their thinking for them continuously. Internationalism can so easily become just British reasoning. And it was that which helped to drive the Germans crazy and into the World War.

Do let us see you when you return from England.

With genuine admiration
for you two, Mary R. Beard

•←

During another midwinter season in Washington, Beard was greatly enjoying reading American women's documents in the Library of Congress while plugging away at the plans for the World Center for Women's Archives. She was especially impressed with the papers of Anna Dickinson, who in the 1850s and 1860s was a much-loved orator for the cause of antislavery and the Union. The following letter indicates that she also read Gilbert Barnes' and Dwight L. Dumond's edition of the *Letters of Theodore Dwight Weld, Angelina Grimké Weld, and Sarah Grimké* (New York, 1934). The prestige of her speaking engagements seems to have been on an upswing: she was preparing the opening for the final discussion of the AAUW's convention in Savannah, Georgia, in March, the keynote speech at the one hundredth anniversary of Mt. Holyoke College in Massachusetts in May, and a speech before the general session of the National Education Association in June in Detroit.[12]

To the additional notoriety brought by the WCWA she responded ambivalently. The *Washington Post* featured her picture in an account of the *New York Sun*'s annual list of outstanding women of 1936, where she appeared with thirteen other women of the world, the "outstanding feminists" of 1936. At the top of the list were Wallis Simpson, for whose love the King of England gave up the throne, and politician Ruth Bryan Owen, daughter of William Jennings Bryan. (The latter was appointed minister plenipotentiary to Denmark by Franklin Delano Roosevelt, but because of her marriage to an aristocratic Dane in 1936 her new Danish citizenship made her unable to continue in her diplomatic post.) Mrs. Florence Kahn, whom Beard also mentions, was a six-term member of the U.S. Congress.

55. TO HARRIOT STANTON BLATCH

Carroll Arms Hotel
First and C Streets, N.E.
Washington, D.C.
January 2d [1937]

Dear Harriot:

We were on the wing—actually went to Atlantic City for a break!—at the time when other people were at their desks mailing the seasons' greetings as of course we would be, erratically. None the less we remembered the few men and women closest to our hearts and among these few you were remembered. Now belatedly we send you our love and best wishes for others' sanity in 1937, taking it for granted that you and we have it already.

Don't attribute to me the insanity which in the press blackened me with two errors this last week: one, claiming that I was coupling the World Center for Women's Archives with a proposed Woman's Charter of Rights and also approving that Charter as printed; the other, with being a "leading lady" of 1936 in the company with stars such as Wally, that depressing Ruth Bryan Owen, old Tory Mrs. Kahn, and what-not. Charles tells me not to make a mountain out of a mole hill a propos the latter but I reply that the tragedy for me is the mole hill. Anyway, it is nicer to remember friends than the press.

I have sent in your suggestion for a competent Archives secretary-promoter and the Board will be grateful for the name. I am glad to know that Miss Claghorn is interested too. The "project" has reached the stage of a drawing of the desired building with floor plans, a budget, and consideration with a view to financing on the part of a woman's Foundation. We shall know our fate in this quarter this month. Mrs. Holden has even been looking up land for the building! There is fine determination about victory.

Charles and I have tucked into a little apartment here in a very quiet part of D.C. within easy walking strides of the Congressional Library where we hope to go on working day by day until April. I came across Anna Dickinson's papers yesterday—five trunks of which were rolled into the Library in 1933. There are interesting letters—from C. D. Warner, Wendell Phillips, and others which I quickly saw. But I have not gone through the five trunks for all the treasure. She kept calling cards, theater programs, everything it seems.

In going over the letters of the Grimkés and Theodore Weld, just published a year or so ago, I found what was to me a most amusing comment
on your mother to the effect that the devout Angelina or was it Sarah?—
thought that her free mind needed subduing. What a breath of fresh wind
she must have been in those pious circles. I have laughed and laughed
over Angelina's nun-like fear that she was sinning when she fell in love
with someone not Jesus Christ. I had no idea that any of our women carried that bride of Christ idea so far. I am improving my mind at least.
Justice Holmes told us he got tired of that idea at the age of ninety. So
may I.

Come on back during the winter and we'll have a long chat, being freer
than ever before for it.

Our love to you—Mary R. Beard

[P.S.] I am so hot over the military emphasis for the Inaugural. Have
protested. But protests roll in—to no effect. "F.D.[R.] wanted this,"
Grayson says.

Mary Beard had made a particular, and she thought successful, effort in
the World Center for Women's Archives to include advocates of the equal
rights amendment as well as their opponents in such organizations as
the League of Women Voters, who favored sex-based protective legislation for women. The alliance was never entirely stable, however, and
was rocked by a brief controversy over Beard's role in the "Women's
Charter." In 1936, international social welfare worker Mary Van Kleeck
and a small group of women thought the time was ripe to speak out
firmly for labor legislation for women while also affirming equal rights in
the face of fascist and liberal attacks on women's work outside the home.
They hoped to draft a Women's Charter of basic rights and to mobilize
behind it women in both the equal rights and protective labor legislation
camps. Mary Beard was invited to participate in the initial deliberations
on the document, and did so, but she withdrew before the document was
signed because of disagreement about the language to be used. (Subsequent disagreements among the group prevented the movement from ever
becoming a reality.) Publicity about plans for the charter mentioned
Mary Beard and the name of the World Center for Women's Archives in
connection with the venture, however, raising the hackles of National
Woman's Party advocates, who were not conciliated by or satisfied with
the language of the charter. Beard's letter below to the chairman of the

NWP National Council, an archives benefactor, attempts to exculpate
herself.

56. TO FLORENCE BAYARD HILLES

Carroll Arms Hotel
Washington, D.C.
January 5 [1937]

Dear Mrs. Hilles:

The moment I saw in the Times the story of the Women's Charter with
my name attached and the World Center for Women's Archives attached
to my name as if I were representing the Archives, I telegraphed indig-
nantly to Meg Irwin, the Chairman of the Archives Center, asking her to
get a denial out to the papers at once through the publicity chairman.
There was absolutely no warrant for such a use either of my name or of
the Archives. I had never signed that draft of the Women's Charter which
appeared in the press. Nor have I signed any other.

Last summer I was invited to a conference purely as an individual as I
supposed and insisted to consider a "Charter" combining the desires of
all leaders of women. I was interested in the idea—though obviously not
a leader of women myself. I attended that one conference. I did not like
the draft there presented and have been critical of every draft I have seen.
I understood, until the press story appeared, that the whole thing was to
be for a long time in the discussion stage.

It is not my fault that the World Center for Women's Archives was thus
thrown to the wolves. None could have been more shocked than I was
when I read the paper.

I have sent in my rectification with a statement of my own position to
Dorothy Bromley of the N.Y. World Telegram in reply to her comment on
me and the Charter.

I can only pray that the World Center for Women's Archives has not
received a deadly blow through the irresponsibility of some news-giver
unknown to me. I am trying to locate her myself.

Of the contradictory nature of the proposed Charter as printed I am
fully aware and I have pointed that out myself to its sponsors. Now I refuse to have anything to do with further correspondence on it.

What a strange thing to happen, to me and my sincere loyalty to World
Center for Women's Archives! I am afraid to poke my nose out of the
door again.

Cordially yours—Mary R. Beard

Historian Alma Lutz, who was assisting Harriot Stanton Blatch with her memoirs, was also a devoted member of the younger generation of the National Woman's Party who helped to keep the party journal, *Equal Rights,* alive. She asked Mary Beard to clarify her position respecting the Women's Charter. Beard's answer is a lucid and eloquent description of her own third path, resonant with her insistence on linking feminist with wider social views and her alarm about the threats to human values and women's status embodied in fascism abroad and the economic crisis at home. Grace Hutchins' *Women Who Work* (1934), mentioned by Beard, was an indictment of the system of women's double burden of home and work by a pacifist social worker of Beard's generation who joined the Communist party in 1927 and remained active in it for several decades.

57. TO ALMA LUTZ

> Carroll Arms Hotel
> First and C Streets. N.E.
> Washington, D.C.
> Jan. 29, 1937

Dear Miss Lutz:

I deeply appreciate your goodwill in inviting me to state my position with respect to the Women's Charter for the readers of Equal Rights and the members of the National Woman's Party. The National Woman's Party has offered me its floor on several important occasions to "speak my piece" and this is another evidence of its consent to hear, even though what it hears may be a variant on what it defends. In accepting another invitation, I am dividing my statement into three parts with a view to being both clear and emphatic.

1) As to the past. Up to this hour I have held aloof from the factional strife within the woman movement despite the continuous attempts that have been made to smoke me out of my "ivory tower." And I have held aloof for the reason that the two major factions—the two great parties I may say—have both seemed to me very inadequate as to program. Thus the equal rightists, I have thought, ran the risk of positively strengthening anachronistic competitive industrial processes; or supporting, if unintentionally, ruthless laissez faire; of forsaking humanism in the quest for feminism as the companion-piece of manism. The woman's bill of rights is, unhappily, long overdue. It should have run along with the rights of man in the eighteenth century. Its drag as to time of official proclamation

is a drag as to social vision. And even if equal rights were now written into the law of our land, it would be so inadequate today as a means to food, clothing and shelter for women at large that what they would still be enjoying would be equality in disaster rather than in realistic privilege. This I have said at National Woman's Party meetings and banquets, in a voice sometimes decidedly shaky because it was emotionally hard to appear to be unsympathetic with the fierce pressure for a woman's bill of rights and emotionally hard to appear critical of many women for whom I have both affection and high regard. However I could not throw my heart and energy into the mere struggle for equality on a basis of laissez faire in the twentieth century.

Nor could I throw my heart and energy into the mere struggle for a minimum wage, even for women. The protectionists satisfied me as little as the rightists, sorry as I was to be so fussy. The minimum wage implies *a* wage and leaves out of account the millions of unemployed to whom a wage at all is sheer utopia. It has seemed to me to represent too complacent, too sentimental, an acceptance of capitalism and to be too consistent with the economic rule of a plutocracy. Neither equal rights nor a minimum wage for women could make a dent on such an anti-social American labor system as that pictured, for instance, in Grace Hutchins' "Women Who Work."

In short, while I have always recognized the value and "justice" of the equal rights principle and lamented its historic lag, and while I have also recognized the value of restraining exploitation, since neither the one program nor the other struck at the issue of employment itself—that basis of all culture—I have lacked the zest for throwing myself into the fray of the factional dispute among women—until this hour.

2) As to the present. Now I am hurled into its center through no intention of my own. For that event Mary Van Kleeck gives the explanation in a letter to the New York Times. For the inaccurately bold publicity with respect to the Women's Charter, she offers the correct version. I desire therefore to call a halt, as far as I am concerned, on further ill-feeling engendered by that mistake—for the sake of the future.

3) As to the future. Being thrust into this fray and kept in this fray despite Miss Van Kleeck's publicity correction, from the necessity for revealing my attitude at last to both factions of women, I offer my challenge to both factions within the woman movement. For their common inadequacy against women's and democracy's ruthless enemies—war, fascism, ignorance, poverty, scarcity, unemployment, sadistic criminality, racial persecution, man's lust for power and woman's miserable trailing in the

shadow of his frightful ways—I offer the ideal of adequacy. No doubt we should have our woman's rights to equal opportunity but with them let us combine the demand for a decency of life and labor all round and security if possible to attain. Let us fight neither over the crumbs that fall from plutocratic tables nor over the right to be plutocrats dropping crumbs.

Let us demand, for example, a set-up in every industry which will carry with that industrial set-up a high minimum of labor reward without discrimination of sex, widening the laws which exist and creating the broad principle of the irreducible minimum from the start in the formulation of new national codes for industry now in process of revival and development. Let us go beyond equality in unemployed disaster and beyond equality in the exploitive privilege to equality in social leadership designed to win security for all. Let us even go beyond equality of leadership and be creative leaders in the vanguard, if men drag along steeped in their vested interests so heavily that they cannot see humanity for seeing money profits and dictatorial power.

If we will not so envisage our future, no Bill of Rights, man's or woman's, is worth the paper on which it is printed, for eventually, if not immediately, democracy will go down with plutocracy into militarism and the time will have passed when women can get together even to blow off steam about rights and protection—even about a Women's Charter. Men will win—the cruel types of men whom no woman should desire to equal.

Sincerely yours, Mary R. Beard

The leaven in Mary Beard's winter was her delight in reading American women's documents at the Library of Congress. "Oh the precious speeches and letters of women that nobody knows! I nearly go dotty over some of them up in the MSS division," she wrote to Madesin Phillips. "I am hunting for basic women thinkers in America and finding *some*. A lot of their stuff is not printed and has to be gone over in fading lines on yellowing paper. I had the pleasure of an admission to the five trunks of papers acquired by the Library just three years ago in which Anna Dickinson reveals herself. Who she was is shown in that 4 vol. History of Woman Suffrage which nobody knows either. She saved the Republican Party in 1872, for one thing." [13]

This reading undoubtedly confirmed and fueled her convictions about the importance of the World Center for Women's Archives. Yet, curiously and ironically, her concern did not extend to her own papers, either the ones she received or wrote. When a New Jersey supporter of the archives inquired whether Beard had any letters written by Alice Paul in her own possession, Beard promised to look but admitted, "I have never kept correspondence systematically—even important letters. It has not been concern for my own archives which has thrust me into the big archives business and in many ways this is too bad for I have had valuable letters through the years. I am a typical woman, I suppose, in my indifference in this matter as a phase of my long life." [14]

58. TO HARRIOT STANTON BLATCH

> Carroll Arms Hotel
> First and C Streets, N.E.
> Washington
> January 24 [1937]

Dear Harriot:

I have longed to rush in upon you with my excitement over your mother! And to talk more to you about the progress on your memoirs after discovering how beautifully you prepared her papers for the Congressional Library and for posterity. All your penned notations, all your ties, and folders touch me to the core. I should never have known how to prepare papers so well. You whose youth was spent among the entourage of your mother must have felt about all the records you thus handled even more sensitively than I feel, though I am honestly stirred to my deeps. Those wonderful letters from your father to your mother, even though he was "scared" to have his Liz face the hooligans at a meeting on the outbreak of civil war. Every item in those folders excites me. I have written you countless letters in my mind as I turned over the documents.

I have made a complete copy of your mother's speech on Labor which I should like to use if I can manage to get together a book on American women *thinkers*. I have assembled other types of American women for consideration, putting off to the last the more difficult task of finding thinkers if such there were. I consider your mother a basic thinker and it is genuine delight to get closer to her in the way you have made possible. I understand now how you feel about the Susan B. For Susan's birthday, I have agreed to write the script for a broadcast, spurred to do so by that indefatigable Ethel Adamson. But I am as adroitly as possible making the point clear. I shall send you the script, hoping for your partial approval at least.

Now this week I come on to your W[omen's] P[olitical] U[nion] scrap-books—looking primarily for traces of your speeches. Have you nothing in the way of record for your Socialist candidacy in N.Y? Nothing, I mean in the matter of speeches? It is very evident that you are a chip off the old block re social consciousness. That reiteration of ignorance and poverty by your mother moves me intensely. I was so ignorant that I feared I should not find the fundamental economic thought. Thank god, it is there!

My rushing in upon you is only postponed.

Affectionately, Mary R. Beard

It is likely that Doris Stevens wrote to Mary Beard about an upcoming protest at Mt. Holyoke College because its trustees had broken precedent and appointed a man—a Yale professor, Roswell Ham—to succeed long-time president Mary Woolley. Perhaps Stevens suggested that Beard refuse to give her slated address at the Mt. Holyoke centennial. (As it happened, the alumnae raised a storm of protest about the appointment, and the college trustees proceeded as they wished nonetheless.) Beard's response to Stevens articulates crisply her insight that human experience has a gendered character. Cornelia Pinchot, mentioned as differing on this matter, was married to Gifford Pinchot, governor of Pennsylvania, and was herself a Republican politician in the 1920s and 1930s.

59. TO DORIS STEVENS

New Milford
May Day [1937]

Dear Doris:

My May Day is rendered gay by the discovery that you and I see eye to eye on the acceptance of woman as woman. I am surprised to know this but my surprise of course shows how far apart we have lived and only that. I think you are dead right about the folly of pretending to represent something as neutral as a "human being" neither man nor woman. But I did not keep sufficiently close to you to remember that you could never be anything so strange. I am so happy to have caught up with you again for in my younger life it was your very radiance as a human being which made you so enchanting for me. Now your letter will help me to shoot my bolt at Holyoke with less fear of its futility.

I shall send you copies of my two speaking efforts as soon as I can get the copies made—the AAUW speech at Savannah and this next one at South Hadley. I don't know whether the AAUW Journal will have room for all my words. You can be as critical as you like when you read them.

The household found Senora de Tejeira a grand experience. How clear her eyes are and her head! She told us as much as she could in the hours she spent here about the life and no-labor of Panama. So her visit was all to our good. There was here the same day a Brunhilde from Vienna and the contrast of these two women was dramatic but Brunhilde simply adored the Panaman[ian] and the Panaman[ian], if not a little terrified by the exuberance of the Viennese (Frau Anna Askanasy), was none the less tremendously interested in her take of life over a volcano confronted with sadistic men in arms.

As for the protest eventuating in a demand for [Roswell] Ham to resign from the presidency of Mount Holyoke, that I think I must leave to alumnae who will make it I think. But I am entirely in sympathy with your call for resignations. What is more I am sure we should all get further with everything if there were more voluntary resignations on the part of persons who find themselves blocked by Tory opposition. As Charles told several Republicans in the last campaign, it is really not imperative that Landon should win: it is even better to be in the right than to be president.

On the point of admitting oneself to be a woman and making that reality and influence count as such, I have argued often with Cornelia Pinchot. She claims that whatever she has accomplished has been because she has not agitated as a woman. The point of view is often hard to break down. I have told her that everything she may have accomplished has been because she was a woman.

Mrs. Abby Rockefeller has declared herself ready to give us a thousand dollars to open an Archives Center office, provided we can get five more women to match her thousand. I think we can. Then we shall really be in the field for a building and for documents.

My love to you—Mary R. Beard

❦

The Beards returned to Washington in January 1938 as they had the several preceding years. The previous spring they had started work together on the successor volume to *The Rise of American Civilization*, eventually called *America in Midpassage*, published in 1939. Busy with this as well as with the WCWA Mary Beard also assisted her husband in his extensive testimony before the Committee on Naval Affairs of the U.S. House of Representatives. Charles Beard was opposing increases in naval appropriations and arguing against an American foreign policy that sought to insure *world* peace rather than simply national defense. The following two rare family letters, the first to their grandson, Detlev, and the next to their daughter and son-in-law, Miriam and Alfred Vagts, give a unique presentation of Mary Beard's view of this task.

60. TO DETLEV VAGTS

> The Mayflower
> Washington, D.C.
> January tenth [1938]

Our dear Detlev:

You are having a birthday and maybe ice cream! Remembering this great event your grandparents wanted to find some rare and beautiful or especially original object to send you as an honoring gift—for a young man who has made such good use of his eight years, I mean nine.

Three dollars can be rare and beautiful if not original. Maybe you can put them to some original use however as a birthday gift for a boy of nine. I might suggest, for instance, that you spend them to take your mother to a Saturday afternoon concert. But that is only "for instance." When we get the big navy bill outlawed, I shall look in the shops for the object, with my whole mind devoted to the quest.

You guessed that grandfather would have the taxpayers in mind in opposing the big navy bill. But I think he forgot taxpayers entirely in thinking about fine lads who should be allowed to live. We are arguing this matter with the biggest navy and army men in this country and many of them feel just as we do. Tomorrow General Rivers is to testify and it will interest you to know that he went [all] over Washington trying to buy as many globes as he could today to place before every member of the Committee, if possible, while he talks geography to them. He told me that they have used only maps (I didn't hear exactly what kind he said) (or did he say charts?). He is sure that they do not know what the seas and lands are like. He is a fine old soldier who wants to stop another *levée en masse*. I can speak French with you of course. I wish you were here and I could take you with me to listen to General Rivers.

Your school sounds most attractive. Your letters are positively attractive.

Have a happy birthday now and many many more !!!!!!!!!!!!!! without number.

Our love, The Washingtonians

61. TO MIRIAM AND ALFRED VAGTS

The Mayflower
Washington, D.C.
Thursday [early 1938]

Our beloveds:

It's like running a presidential campaign these days and nights in representing the opposition to the president on his foreign policy. Only—we are candidates for jail rather than the White House.

I shall write a longer letter just as soon as the H of R Committee on Naval Affairs thinks it had better let loose of CAB. We are working some 20 hours a day and have been for quite a while. But in these nice rooms where sun enters and the air is good we are both keeping well. I sit beside CAB as he confronts those roughnecks on that Com[mittee]—and see that he gets every question. My being there he remembers not to get too angry but to take plenty of time to feed out information. And the guys today actually cried for "Light". Can you believe it true?

It's not an easy life either of us or any of us lives. I long to hear every detail of yours naturally. But you generously reported essentials and you have done better than I.

In a day or two—more from us.

Always our love—Mother

4 The Women's Archives Continues

On December 15, 1937, the World Center for Women's Archives was officially launched at a gala dinner at the Biltmore Hotel in New York City, where the charts, maps, and letters of departed aviator Amelia Earhart were donated by her husband, George Putnam. In this new stage of progress, two women became especially important to Mary Beard. One was Marjorie White, a self-styled scholar with interests similar to Beard's, who sought employment at the center and volunteered her full loyalty to the project. The second was Miriam Holden, a philanthropic New York City liberal, member of the National Woman's Party, volunteer for the NAACP and birth control movements, and an intellectual and collector of books herself.[1] Holden had volunteered on the board of the project since its early days but became at this point Beard's mainstay in New York. Holden and Beard carried on a voluminous correspondence concerning the policies and problems—especially the money problems—of the WCWA. In the letter below, Beard mentions her plan to ask for funds from the wife of Eugene Meyer, who had made a fortune in investment banking and was the owner of the *Washington Post*. (It is not clear who Mrs. Bremer was, but perhaps Edith Terry Bremer, head of social services for immigrant women within the YWCA.) Beard's testy remarks about other women in political life—including grande dame Alice Longworth, the precious only daughter of Theodore Roosevelt, and clubwoman Daisy Harriman, who had been born into wealth—suggest how frustrating it was for her to get response from women (or men) with financial resources. At the same time, Beard was pressed by her writing and political efforts with her husband.

62. TO MIRIAM HOLDEN

> Mayflower Hotel
> Washington, D.C.
> March 12, 1938

Dear Miriam Holden:

Do by all means tell Mrs. Bremer to come to see me here. I agree that her interest harmonizes with the archives plan.

But I get no word which seems to indicate that we can do our thing. If it has to be built up any longer around me who started it, then it must mean defeat. I simply cannot at my age and with my burdens carry this one as my sole responsibility. If the Center does not grip other women as it grips me, then there is not enough belief to make it a reality. If the Board members won't even go to meetings to help make a quorum, we should at least try to get women who will do that and more. You have been splendid in every way and so this defeat, if it comes, will not have you to blame.

I am going tomorrow for the day to the Eugene Meyers camp across the Potomac. But I got the sickening feeling at their house on Thursday night where we were invited to help honor Thomas Mann that women will only play up men and not respond to appeals to explore their own social role as knowledge. They spin theories. They do not want to know. I say this because, as I watched Alice Roosevelt sweep into the room with the air of a grand duchess and look straight beyond me, though she knows me perfectly well and not long ago at Mrs. Borden Harriman's rushed up to me to ask to meet my husband (!), and move over to join Mrs. Gifford Pinchot and Mrs. Meyer, I felt my first genuine despair. "Princess Alice" has not even answered my letter asking her to let me see her a few moments. I know Cornelia Pinchot exceedingly well and she denies her interest in women and reveals the truth of that declaration constantly. I have Mrs. Meyer tomorrow but she may take the same stand as she seems to be of their breed. These three standing together and so gaily like close chums that they are represent about *eighty million dollars*, according to hearsay at least. The Spanish ambassador and Senora and I in our trio close by represent only the thought of human tragedy. In this assembly was Thomas Mann. What a strange thing life is and society!

If we do not get some money soon, we must fold up. I am sorry. There is nothing I can say to Mrs. Bremer, I fear.

My love to you, Mary R. Beard

[P.S.] Your inquiry about an exhibit at the World's Fair is one I can't answer in view of the state of our project. Who can assemble the stuff? I can't.

It is useless to talk about moving the Center to Washington. I can't swing that whole thing here either. I can get a DC group of women to work intelligently but they won't want to tackle the nation as we had proposed to do. The shift would simply mean that New Yorkers wanted to escape their responsibility. I refuse to consider it.

I HAVE AS ONE OF MY IMMEDIATE OBLIGATIONS the burden of working also for an effective opposition to imperialist adventures on the

high seas. Charles and I have done everything side by side as that is the
only way he could accomplish as much as he has. My heart is in that
cause of course but if we are ever to keep women from ganging up with
men for war, we've got to give 'em a substitute in idealism meaning something to them personally.

•←

The essays Mary Beard published during the 1930s lodged in small-
circulation feminist journals, such as the National Woman's Party's *Equal
Rights* or the Business and Professional Women's *Independent Woman;*
her occasional efforts to reach wider audiences through intellectual
magazines such as *Harper's* or mass women's magazines such as the
Ladies' Home Journal were not successful. Articles that were published
to these wider audiences frequently enraged her, as witness her comments
below on two articles in *Harper's,* Pearl Buck's "America's Medieval
Women" of 1938 and Genevieve Parkhurst's "Is Feminism Dead?" of
1935. Best-selling author and journalist Pearl Buck, recently returned
from years in China, had written a terse and casually polemical essay portraying relations between the sexes in America as utterly bowed under
tradition, which demanded that women be little more than pretty, accom-
modating creatures at home. Only half-satirically, Buck argued that
women would be more satisfied with their actual portion if they were not
educated as though they had open horizons before them. Presumably
Beard objected to Buck's assumption that in the past—in the tradition—
women acted only at home, providing services to men, and had no wider
public role. Since Beard herself frequently criticized both sexes in similarly harsh terms, it is less easy to guess her response to Buck's portrayal
of American men's childishness and their hypocritical tolerance and fear
of women, or to Buck's claims that American women accepted the
crumbs that men left in the job market and failed to support other
women's professional or artistic endeavors.[2]

This letter also reflects increasing difficulties among the New York
supporters of the archives. Because the group included both employed
women, who could not attend daytime meetings, and leisured women,
who were accustomed only to daytime meetings for their volunteer
work, even the seemingly simple matter of arranging meeting times was
laden with organizational implications.

63. TO MIRIAM HOLDEN

[New Milford]
July 29 [1938]

Dear Miriam:

I am writing you right off the bat though longing to talk directly with you about that awful article by Pearl Buck. It made me sick to my marrow as it evidently did you too. We just can't let such stupidity circulate forever and I feel like hugging you for your mutual consent to fight.

After receiving your letter I dug out the article which Harper's had rejected more than two years ago. I had tried to reply to an article Harper's had just published, called Is Feminism Dead—just as absurd a thing as Pearl Buck's. But the editors would have none of mine. Probably the thing is not attractively written. Buck employs all the cheap and nasty gossip which makes a sensation. I attempt a little history but history is emphatically tabu in all the magazines.

For instance the Ladies Home Journal is trying to recover its old circulation by claiming to have aroused American women to take an interest in public affairs. To this claim Dorothy Thompson and Dorothy Bromley seem to have given loud cheers. But when I was invited to fill out one of its questionnaires about my attitude toward birth control, divorce, etc., I popped back with a comment that "women had always been interested in public affairs" and I should like to do an article proving it. The reply to me was flatly that no history was wanted.

I was thinking that perhaps Catherine Mackenzie could get in a reply to Pearl Buck when your letter came. I was about to send her the thing I had had rejected. Now however I am sending it to you so that you can better discuss the Harper attitude with [its editor, Frederick Lewis] Allen. It is really outrageous for Harper's to give women these raw deals time and again. I have forgotten who wrote the thing on Feminism and in that case perhaps the editors thought they were giving women a new deal but its total ignorance of history made the deal rotten. Anyway, I shall adore hearing what Allen has to say. My feelings do not have to be spared because I am not a prig pleased with my own composition—merely a woman cultivating the memory of women. It is silly for men to think of men's role in the world alone and sillier for women to play their game exclusively.

As for our Archives Board, I am grateful to you for letting me see Miss Brezee's letter. The problem is a real enigma. I fully agree that leisure-class women are apt neither to know what is involved in attitudes toward women nor as accustomed to accomplish hard work as women professionally employed. It will be a miracle if we get any of them to push on this job. On the other hand five o'clock is a frightful hour for meetings and it has been a major reason, I think, for our inefficiencies. Everyone has been sitting on the edge of her chair ready for a dash out of the door. The salaried women come tired. Others, except you and me, don't come at all. Miss Lewisohn is increasingly faithful and I am so very glad for she has much to give, and by that I don't merely mean money.

If we don't put salaried women on the Board, we ought to have them working on committees or in an advisory capacity, don't you agree? As for our present boss, I wish I were sure myself.

I'm delighted that you enjoy Kate [Hurd-]Mead['s *A History of Women in Medicine*]. She has had a lot of good reviews and Governor [Wilbur] Cross let me do one for the Yale Review.

Affectionately—Mary R. Beard

In spite of Mary Beard's intent to make the World Center for Women's Archives a rallying point for women of all political factions, supporters of the equal rights amendment did play a major role in it. The choice of author "Meg" Irwin as chairman—even if she was mainly a figurehead, as appears to be the case—warned off women who held a brief against the National Woman's Party. Carrie Chapman Catt, for instance, supported the archives only nominally; she wrote to Alice Stone Blackwell in 1937, "I doubt if it will succeed. It has no place in which to house the archives and no money with which to maintain it."[3] In the following, Beard tries to conciliate the aging Blackwell, who was the daughter of nineteenth-century suffragist Lucy Stone and had lifelong ties to NAWSA, which made her suspicious of any organization with strong National Woman's Party representation in it.

64. TO ALICE STONE BLACKWELL

Mary R. Beard
New Milford, Conn.
July 29, 1938

My dear Miss Blackwell:

. . . I had read your biography of your mother with deepest interest and great enthusiasm both for author and subject. The copy you sent me

I shall keep in sight all the time now and give my other one to my daughter to remind the younger generation of things it must remember. . . .

You cannot know how often your name is on my lips as I inquire from friends who have the honor of knowing you how you are these days. It has grieved me very much that the proposed World Center for Women's Archives seemed spoiled for you by the personnel in part. But the attempt had been made to make the collection of materials widely representative and it seemed wise therefore to have all groups and interests among women identified with the leadership. The chairman had to be someone who would act in that capacity—for a time at least. Now however the Board is undergoing a drastic revision with a view to getting more efficient action. I shall write you about the outcome as soon as it is known. The next elections to the Board and for its officers must wait until the autumn meeting.

It would be a very specialized set of archives if only one or a few feminine attitudes toward life and labor were assembled, you will agree I am sure. But it is equally important to have some one head this movement in whose intellectual powers enough women—all women who have such powers themselves—believe. That is our enigma but one we must solve as soon as we can.

I think you will be interested to know that we have some ten state organizations and a branch in Washington, D.C., all really exploring the region for women's documents. The Newspaper Women of Ohio had already begun this research and are about ready to publish the history of women in Ohio. Gradually therefore the total ignorance of the rising generation about women who have risen before should be alleviated.

With my truest respects and
devotion to you, Mary R. Beard

As the two letters above suggest, the board of the archives in New York was undergoing reorganization in 1938. Mary Beard had precipitated some internal dissension by her favoritism toward Marjorie White. White was very good at archival research. It was she who discovered, for instance, that Carrie Chapman Catt's gift of the NAWSA papers to the New York Public Library lay crumbling and rotting in several drawers, uncatalogued and uncared for. She was not interested in fund-raising, however, to which several board members gave higher priority. Mary Beard hired Marjorie White as executive secretary to the organization in December 1937, even though Glenna Tinnin had already been appointed to such a position. The conflict between the two appointments was temporarily resolved by the board's decision on December 19, 1938, to employ both women part-time, White tending to archives and state branches, Tinnin devoting herself to fund-raising and office management.[4]

65. TO MARJORIE WHITE

[New Milford, Conn.]
November 28, 1938

Dear Marjorie:

Hsh but it's a fact that a crisis has come in the Archives movement. I hope it can be resolved rationally and in the interest of an intelligent victory. If so resolved it will take all the skill that I can command and all the understanding that the Board as a whole possesses.

I brought it on unwittingly when I asked the Board to engage you—especially as I did not at the same time insist that Mrs. Tinnin be taken on at full time. I am now told by Mrs. Tinnin that I have broken all good budgeting practice and disrupt the credit of our organization.

Moreover she can't stand the crowded office and is generally upset.

She regards the pressure for archives themselves as unimportant at this time. Her view of the Exhibit is theatrical and nothing else counts. She is pleased to have found for the Board new members to offset the "radicals" as she calls some of us. She has an idea which must be promoted through thick and thin. She considers herself as having been very shabbily treated. Maybe she has; certainly she has been devoted and some of her own money has gone into bills she did not know how to pay otherwise.

In the circumstances, to avoid a "scandal", I must ask you to operate as if you were my private secretary only. I hate to do this for your sake but it is the only way to keep from destroying all the gains uptodate. The situation cannot be definitely defined until the Board meeting on Dec. 19th. I shall send you my check for the December 1 to December 19 salary and I am writing Mrs. Tinnin to report that. There will be an interim of but two or three days between the writing of this instruction to you and your receipt and "eviction" from the office. Those days will be included in the Archives office check to you.

Please oh please cover up everything in dealing with Miss Evresoff. Plan to see her outside the office. Don't lose her fine volunteer aid. Make excuses.

Your idea of the Exhibit is mine. The other is balloon ascension. The thing will have to be threshed out on the 19th by the Board. The worst of the business now is that it has gone so far in enlisting the interest of Miss Branch and the Grand Central Galleries and others that to fight its direction via Mrs. Tinnin may break up the whole archives "cause" in a row. I think I should not do that.

I may have to pull out of the Board to save my own mental integrity. That I shall do if need be. Quietly.

Your report which arrived this morning delights me as usual.

There is the special matter of the letters to the European women both on Miss Phillips' list and on the Schwimmer list. Proceed to get the criticisms and approval of Miss Phillips and Mme. Schwimmer quietly but hold up the letter mimeographing and mailing until after the 19th. Say nothing on the matter to Mrs. Tinnin.

Just go ahead as you have been doing. The letter to Miss Quaid is sound. Send that. Keep track of your stamp expense. From today. I shall settle that with you from now on. I am returning the Quaid letter as you may not have a copy.

If I can get down before the 19th I shall. Next Monday—a week from today, I hope to. Then we shall meet in retreat and have a good long talk. Don't quit.

My love—Mary R. Beard

Whether in spite of or because of the resolution of December 19, 1938, there was a major walkout—or "voluntary purge"—shortly thereafter by New York board members, including the executive secretary whom Mary Beard did not favor. Beard thought this "housecleaning" might be favorable to the organization. At any rate, she was glad to be free of Tinnin, whose political views were too right-wing for her taste.

In the following letter, Beard subtly encourages Holden to appreciate the political benefits of Tinnin's departure. During an earlier stage of the board's organization, she had urged Holden, "You must keep on the spot to help back up the liberal labor side of the archives collection." The first line below refers to a protest Beard had received from Florentine Sutro, about being eased out of leadership; Beard implies that Tinnin, perhaps for political reasons, had conveniently forgotten Sutro.[5] Congressman Martin Dies, Democrat of Texas, mentioned at the close, chaired the new Committee on Un-American Activities in the U.S. House of Representatives and pioneered the techniques and slogans later made famous by Senator Joseph McCarthy, charging groups and individuals with being "soft on Communism."

Beard was nonetheless reaching across the political spectrum for women's papers. The Mrs. Pratt whom she encourages Holden to interview was likely Ruth Pratt, a conservative New York state legislator who had no allegiance to feminism whatsoever. Beard was also hopeful about the archives at this point because a vigorous group of women in Washington, D.C., seemed to have taken hold of the idea, making her less reliant on New York supporters.

66. TO MIRIAM HOLDEN

Hotel Henderson
Aiken, S. Carolina
February 6, 1939

Dear Miriam:

The enclosed letter from Mrs. Sutro has a good deal of justification despite the fact that she is too old to keep books now and despite her kind words about me. It is a shame that she is not on the list of sponsors. Mrs. T[innin] is alone responsible for that. You will see, won't you, that in the next printing, her name is there?

Have you heard that Washington, D.C. has waked up and is planning a big archives luncheon for February 25th? On that day the women in the government can attend and I have suggested that the women of the diplomatic corps be invited, with Doris Stevens' Latin-American friends. Every woman who attends is to be asked to bring an archive for presentation and that should bring national publicity of the right and vivid kind. I shall run up for this luncheon if the promoters insist although they can of course swing it perfectly well without me.

So we are not dead or dying. I think our purge may work to our genuine advantage, apologetic though I am if I committed any injury. . . . Surely we need a money-raiser who can answer people when they ask "What good does an archive do? And don't we know enough about women already?" The reply which Irene Wright, vice chairman of the Washington Branch makes is so direct and effective. When some of the women remarked that the documents which might be brought to the luncheon would not be important, Miss Wright replied that every one might be highly important even in its apparent littleness. And Miss Wright is so competent to say so; she was a professional archivist in Spain for the old government—having set herself up as of that profession and having got that big appointment. This was certainly a fine post. She now understands that we need to know more about Spanish women as about all the rest. Don't you want to tackle an interview with Mrs. Pratt? She might arrange for you to see her friends too???!!! Why let her drop? I should think you would be ideal for interesting her, provided you could soft-pedal on labor, etc. And you could.

I feel that in our new circumstances we can go straight ahead toward a comprehensive archive without Mrs. T[innin]'s hostility to everything liberal. She told others she was all for the Dies investigation and that was her basic inclination, as I got it.

Don't be afraid to upset my equilibrium by writing me if things look very bad. I don't believe they do.

My love—Mary R. Beard

Not a letter, the following unique manuscript was Mary Beard's response to the Camp Fire Girls' request for a relevant project to carry out. It illustrates especially well Beard's absorption of cultural anthropology and her innovative thinking about what would be called, in the 1960s, "history from the bottom up." Envisioning that some of the materials for the WCWA would be generated through oral interviews and through digging into local history, she here provided the Camp Fire Girls with guidance for producing such documentation. The organization took up the challenge, instigating an "Older Girls' Americana Project—on Women of Yesterday, Today and Tomorrow," in the spring of 1939 in Buffalo, New York; Reading, Pennsylvania; Sherman, Texas; Tulsa, Oklahoma; Des Moines, Iowa; and Columbus, Ohio. The results of the projects are unknown, however.[6]

67. PROGRAM FOR RESEARCH ACTIVITY PLANNED BY SPECIAL REQUEST OF CAMP FIRE GIRLS

Your work for soil, water, and forest conservation is something that you will want to carry on through all the years either directly or by giving support to the conservation movement.

But you will also want to work for human life. And to work well for human life, including your own lives, the lives of great women should be helpful, as examples of intelligence and heroism.

Why not begin to know your great grandmothers? That might be a delightful exploration and it could take this form:

a) What do you now know about your own grandmothers?

b) Where were they born?

c) Did they spend their whole lives in one place?

d) If they lived in more than one place, where did they go? And why?

e) How were they educated? Did they go to school? Did they learn to read and write at home?

f) Did they produce crops or other kinds of wealth, such as textile and canned goods and clothes and millinery?

g) Was life easy for them or hard, in your opinion? Why?

h) What difference do you find between your lives and theirs?

i) What do you think they might have done that they did not do?

j) What have they left behind to indicate their work, their tastes, their interests?

k) Was either of them a doctor on horseback on the frontier?

l) Are there in your family attic old letters or a diary or journal written by a grandmother? Or speeches she delivered but never printed? Or a novel she wrote but not for publication? Or poems? Or things she wrote down as just notes about life and what she saw and felt?

m) Were your grandmothers interested in community affairs? And in the larger affairs of the state and the nation?

Suggestion: If you discover interesting old papers of the kinds described, the World Center for Women's Archives (address Hotel Biltmore, New York City) would like to know about this very important discovery. It would appreciate your writing to it to make the report. Perhaps the papers thus discovered might be given to this Center so that they would become a part of a great collection of materials about women which it is trying to assemble for students and writers to read and use.

While you are becoming acquainted better with your own grandmothers, you might think about *the most interesting living women in your community*. And think about them in this way:

a) Who are the most interesting women in your opinion? Why?

b) Are they interesting to the community as well as to you? Why?

c) Have you talked with any of them? About what?

d) Could you get them to talk to your group about the work they are doing and the other things in which they are interested?

e) Could you write a sketch about any one of them, and say what they mean to you and your village or town? Try it.

f) If you do not know enough for a good sketch, perhaps the women you have in mind would let you interview them so that you could write them up. In this case, you could show them what you had written before you placed it in an album of such sketches prepared by the other girls too in your group. (Such an album would be welcome material for the World Center for Women's Archives.)

g) In your sketches, remember to put down these items:
Birthplace of the woman about whom you are writing.
If not born there, from where she came and why.
The character and size of her family, including her parents, brothers and sisters.
What she has done as work for herself and family.
What she has done for others.
What she has written or said or made as a work of art.
What kind of person you think she is.

To widen your discovery of human life, you might inquire whether there are any *legends* in your community about women who once lived there.

If there are such legends, try to write them down after getting all the information you can.

Are there memorials in your community to any women? If there are, find out the reasons.

To deepen your discovery of human life, ask yourselves whether you know about any women in *written history.*

If you do, make lists of them, for your group album with something clear written under the names about them.

If you do not know any women in written history, try to find out where you could get the "news" that women have been important persons in history.

Then to think about human life as girls, try to decide which woman or women in all this exploration you would like most to resemble.

◦←

Late in 1938, with trouble brewing in New York but hopes for a vital unit in Washington, D.C., Marjorie White attended the convention of the recently founded National Council of Negro Women (NCNW) to solicit that group's cooperation with the World Center for Women's Archives. Mary Beard had drawn up a race-inclusive collecting plan, beginning with the "aborigines"—Native Americans—and continuing to women of Spain and France who arrived on the North American continent before moving on to the English settlers in the Northeast; her interest in collecting documents of black women's history was also genuine. Mary McLeod Bethune, founder and leader of the National Council of Negro Women (and director of the division of Negro affairs within the National Youth Administration, a New Deal agency) pledged her support. Bethune named Juanita Mitchell, a young woman from St. Paul, Minnesota, who later became an important civil rights lawyer, to chair a committee on Negro women's archives to work with the WCWA.[7]

68. TO JUANITA JACKSON MITCHELL

> Hotel Henderson
> Aiken, S. Carolina
> March 1, 1939

My dear Mrs. Mitchell:

Word has come to me here where I am having a little rest that you have consented to serve as the chairman of the Negro women's archives for World Center for Women's Archives. Nothing could give me greater pleasure as general chairman of archives. And nothing will mean more to this Center than a fine record of this side of American life.

You have asked Miss White for some specific and concrete suggestions for your procedure and she modestly seeks my help in that connection. First then you yourself are on the right track in listing types of materials as essays, magazine articles, official documents, letters, and pictures. Your "etc." may properly go on to include letters, diaries, journals, even mere notes and the jottings down of memoranda, speeches, programs of organized action, unpublished manuscripts, books, honors and awards, and publicity (the latter will cover the attention paid to novelists, musicians and artists, actors, social workers and others).

Classifications may be made: i.e. women in education, in science, in businesses and professions, in the arts, in agriculture, in industry, in domestic service, etc.

Not only shall we want the documents revealing Negro women since the civil war but everything we can get pertaining to their lives and labor under slavery.

There are Negro women's national organizations whose records we should welcome. And each of these might make a list of its most distin-

guished personnel and ask for materials telling about them. From Dean
Slowe of Howard University, about a year and a half before her death, I
learned that the Negro College Clubs had a good collection of materials
which they would probably like to place in this Center; unhappily for us
all she died far too young and I miss more than I can tell you the opportunities to see Dean Slowe from time to time. Perhaps you can inquire
about this college material.

Now and then a Negro woman has written me about her work. In this
way I heard some time ago about a Miss Parkhurst (if I remember her
name rightly) who went from Hampton Institute, I think, to Chicago and
who was making her research an exploration of her race. If you know
about her and what she has found, that would be splendid material.
There are no doubt other women in the field of research who are building
up the record of Negro women.

Such activists in the South as Julia Harris of Athens, Georgia, belong in
the Center of course. What papers she may have I do not know but her
work has been extraordinary since she left Atlanta to work with and for
her own people. The Negro girls who have gone to Smith, Wellesley, and
other colleges may have kept diaries. I do hope so. Years ago when the
first great suffrage parade was held in Washington, I insisted until I got
the consent of the promoters to have the Negroes included in that parade.
Anything else would have been absurd. In that relation I met many fine
residents of Washington and if a chairman for the capital could be found
to work up materials there, that would be a definite service.

The Negro woman in the home as mother, wife, etc., is a story nobody
really knows and one which should be known if it can be explored on
paper. Her development of cookery, nursing, and all allied occupations is
important to the story.

I am so deeply interested in the task of discovering the history of our
Negro women that I am inclined to write you now to excess. Do feel free
to ask questions at any time. All this work is new for us all and we shall
have to feel our way as we go, with the road constantly widening.

Cordially yours, M.R.B.

Few moments early in 1939 were so full of triumph and promise for
Mary Beard as the luncheon on behalf of the WCWA held in Washington,
D.C., on March 4. The following letter, written from the Beards' Southern retreat, reflects that flush—although she was still aware that problems lurked in the wings.

69. TO MIRIAM HOLDEN

> Hotel Henderson
> Aiken [S.C.]
> March 9 [1939]

Dear Miriam:

I hoped to write you immediately about the Washington luncheon but I couldn't do it, largely for the reason that I had to follow up instantly several leads which came there and demanded quick recognition. I made a report to Miss White on several details which concerned her work especially and added some items for her to report when the Board meets on the 16th. I thought it would meet later and so I shall have to miss one more meeting but no more.

The Washington affair was a marvelous triumph I think everybody agrees. I must qualify with respect to my speech. Otherwise it was a grand victory. Nearly 500 women turned out and they were the master women, such as Mrs. Roosevelt, Miss [Frances] Perkins, Fola La Follette, Dorothy Detzer—all of whom spoke. The wives of several Supreme Court Justices were present and stayed to the very end—that is, from 1:15 to 4:15. Leading women officials came. The leading women in civic affairs were there and outstanding political women, such as Emma Guffey Miller. It was an entire afternoon party with only three or four women slipping out, and that on Saturday when week ends make their claims. Cards were passed up to me declaring pleasure at the "renaissance" of the movement, notably from Ellen Woodward and Izetta Jewell Miller. Crowds ganged up around the table at the conclusion of the meeting to talk about documents they have or want to get and to offer to work. A rich sceptic seems to be completely converted and talked later to Mrs. [Emily Newell] Blair about the money.

Mrs. Blair has written me for suggestions about further procedure and I sent Miss White a copy of the things I wrote in reply. I suggested, for one thing, that the D.C. keep the documents it collects between now and next October, safely deposited, for a grand Exhibit at the capital in the autumn which could be followed by one in New York using the same materials and things which we shall have. I hope you think that a good idea. It seems to me that it makes a clear objective for the drive from the Archives side and will produce the kind of Exhibit which you and I and all intelligent men and women can fully respect.

But I promised especially to report to you just how this luncheon was handled. Well, I couldn't get precise details and the main reply was: "It was so spontaneous we hardly know how it did happen to be such a success." The time of preparation was very short. There wasn't much advance publicity. There was no time to send tickets to individuals in advance and a tremendously long line had to wait to get in. But it did not seem angry. The idea itself may have taken fire from the President's Archive publicity and the logic of one for women.

I haven't learned about the publicity after the luncheon and can only hope that it went far and wide. Miss Beatty will be getting that information.

Mrs. Blair made a fine presiding chairman. She had a very hard task but carried it through extremely well, knowing when to stop the meeting and how to provide for various forms of interest-provoking. She omitted reading the numerous congratulatory messages and introducing all the officers to save time for the ceremony of presenting documents. This was not allowed to drag on but the documents which were presented indicated the power of the project. I was particularly touched by Frances Perkins' concluding remark to the effect that this Center with its factual information could be a place where citizen-women could justify their ways. Mrs. Roosevelt wrote out and signed that statement she made at the Youth meeting in New York as her gift and nothing could be better.

Now the Washington Unit (the name it likes) will reckon up the membership and assemble the ranks and forge ahead both for money and for papers. Oh it is so beautiful to sink roots this way!

I long to be home and near the Biltmore again. There can be no doubt that we did the right thing in checking that wild theatrical proposal and revising the management of WCWA. We were on the verge of ruining a glorious movement I firmly believe.

No one has done more or as much to save the day than/as YOU.

My love—Mary R. Beard

[P.S.] And four Negro women attended the luncheon without disrupting the affair. They came up to the table like others—enthusiastically and safely. I did wish you were there. Mrs. Jerome Frank is keen to work for Jewish records.

In the following two letters (as in others to Phillips), Beard offers her perspective on women in public life in the context of her contemporary concern with militarism, the rise of fascism in Europe, and the threat of international war. While in 1938 she was minding the vexing details of WCWA, she was also extending the wider reach to finish *America in Midpassage* with her husband. This sequel in their series on American civilization was contemporary social, political, and cultural history of the United States in the 1920s and 1930s.

70. TO LENA MADESIN PHILLIPS

> Hotel Henderson
> Aiken, S. Carolina
> March 9, 1939

Dear Lena:

I am returning the speech as you requested, following a deeply interested reading of course. I always want to keep in close touch with your thought and action and the part of your address on this occasion which appeared in the press made me want to know all the rest. But what I could not get precisely was the character of the inquest to which you addressed yourself. It comes through in part and seems to signify rather a customary academic subject for the discussion—leadership more or less in the abstract.

Your own former emphasis upon leadership as an expression of underlying popular urges and surges is, in my opinion, close to the grass roots of the business. And I can also see great value in the study of great leader-personalities set against their backgrounds. Max Lerner in the recent New Republic reviewing a set of new books on Lincoln asks very pertinent questions in this relation. I think you did well to try to shatter the concept of women's expecting something of leadership now as if leadership were a thing outside themselves. It is my contention that, if women knew their own history down through time, they would realize their own historic leadership as they do not know it today. I would play less modestly than you have done on that string, for I believe their leadership to have been exerted always in every aspect of life.

And in playing more stridently I would tell men more emphatically who and what they are as leaders, rather than presuming that they can answer any of the questions you ask, for I don't believe they can. I am so afraid that when they are not brutes seeking war, they are hopelessly childlike with respect to business and other civilian enterprises.

In the thing which I want to do in print I shall attempt an interpretation of the roles of men and women—brashly of course. As you say: "sometimes the more ignorant, the more ideas, and certainly the more feeling."

I am glad you are going to write more and on your own purposes.

The Washington luncheon appeared to be a vast success. The committee decided it was important to have Mrs. Irwin, not only because she is chairman of the Archives Board but also because she is a Republican and devoted to Hoover. There would have been an undue New Dealish or Democratic atmosphere otherwise. Fola La Follette held up the frontier-Progressivism and I the mugwumpery. But your speaking skill was missed. Nearly 500 of the outstanding women of the capital came to the lunch and stayed on lingeringly from 1 : 15 to nearly five. Mrs. Roosevelt of course gave distinction. She was flanked at the speakers' table by Mrs. Justice Stone and Black, Frances Perkins, Julia Peterkin, Ellen Woodward and women of that ilk. Dorothy Detzer made the final speech and it was tersely exquisite.

The ceremony of presenting documents went off effectively. It could have been carried on for a long time but variations were sustained to make the session interesting. Afterwards woman after woman came up to say that she had important papers, notably Mary Meeks Atkinson who told me she would give to the Center 1000 letters from farm women.

Maybe best of all was the conversion of a rich woman at the capital whose name I will give you when we meet next time. She told Mrs. Blair after the luncheon that she believed now in this project very strongly and thought women would offer the land (we think she may mean she will offer it) and others raise money for the building if it could rise at the capital. There is a growing interest in locating it there and perhaps none of us would object seriously if the capital could achieve land and building. But that is not a decision for this hour.

Mrs. Blair and her committee are to follow up the luncheon at once with a fine organization including a finance chairman. The thing is positively on its feet in Washington.

so you and Mrs. Holden and Bessie Beatty have not been toiling in vain in NYC. I tried to bolster up the movement to assure you on that point. Volunteers will materialize in NY this month, I have reason to believe—the reason being imparted to Marjorie White—volunteers who are college grads and capable.

On April 11th I am to speak at a banquet at Syracuse being arranged by the alumnae of that college. A huge throng of collegians is expected from Syracuse and other colleges. I am to stay over for a day or two and meet groups and out of this effort perhaps we can find a chairman for NY state; we need her very badly.

I must not scribble on and on for you have plenty of reading matter on your desk and your writing paper at your hand for your own expression. I shall see you the last of this month unless you are to be on the road. The moment you return in that case.

Affectionately as always—
Mary R. Beard

[P.S.] Our Beard-Beard volume is being held up for publication for a bit. When it appears you may or may not like our notion about the USA bending to labor leadership. There are imponderables, such as the refusal of the middle class to be crushed between the plutocrats and the workers according to the Marxian deterministic view of life and history, which we have taken into account.

71. TO LENA MADESIN PHILLIPS

[New Milford, Conn.]
May 11, 1939

Dear Lena:

I have been slow to express my true enthusiasm over your proposed major discussion at the coming International meet[ing] of the B[usiness] & P[rofessional] W[omen]. Owing to Archives demands. But I retain this great pleasure which came when I read your Bulletin proclaiming the intention to have the summer meeting go into the matter of Business itself. I regard that as leadership supreme.

You know, Chief, I begin to think that the idea of Equality has become a world fetich above the sacrilege of analysis. For women are and have been themselves responsible, if to an incalculable degree, in bringing on all the crises. European women were in business in the 14th century, we know from a published treatise, and French women have always been.

It is surely time for women to understand that they help to make the world and that the world is thus a two-sex affair. Granted all the "discriminations" such as the growing refusal of our states to let mothers be gainfully employed, still we must remember that such discriminations are in part a fight between two types of women—the women dependent on their husbands' jobs and who are actively interested in their getting jobs; and the women who earn their own incomes. That fight was a factor in producing Hitler who won feminine support by promising husbands and babies to women.

You have a magnificent task this summer at your meeting and you are assuming it magnificently.

Meanwhile this Archives thing is becoming tumultuously important. The radio clamors for stuff. The country is excited. College presidents galore are lining up with us. The gals are getting assignments to study women in history. Groups are forming here and there to back up the project.

Gilbert and Sullivan: "This measure all sublime, we shall achieve in time."

You work too hard and I grieve when I find you exhausted. I hope your rest, if you really had one, has done you vast good.

My love, Mary

When Mira Saunders, a Californian, wrote to her lamenting the lack of women faculty at Whittier College (a California institution founded by Quakers) and the reported preference of both male and female students for male faculty, Beard responded with a compressed statement of the educational views she broadcast in many of her talks and articles of the 1930s and 1940s. In conjunction with the WCWA, she was seeking cooperation from a number of colleges and universities, attempting to affect their curricula as well as the collecting policies of their libraries with her emphasis on women's history.

72. TO MIRA SAUNDERS

New Milford
Connecticut
May 16, 1939

Dear Mrs. Saunders:

Of all associated people in this country or in any other, the Friends should, presumably, be the most friendly about women. The situation at Whittier is especially surprising, therefore, on that score.

But it has even a wider and deeper significance in that the exclusion of women deprives the students of a genuine chance to learn about life in its fulness. That should be the aim of education. If students only concern themselves at college with their natural preferences and prejudices, they miss the educational experience of enlarging their minds and emotions.

This educational task is one which educators seem so ready to escape. The easiest way is to make the students as comfortable as possible. In this relation I have been horrified to discover that the president of a women's college—Bryn Mawr at that—accepts the women's point of view, as she has found it on her campus for some twenty years, to the effect that it is merely boring to study or think about women of the past. But her attitude reflects her own total lack of interest in history for, without knowing about the women of the past, one cannot know much, if any, history.

I consider the situation at Whittier, as you report it, a *plight*. And it is this general plight, which I attribute to the utter ignorance of history-in-the-large, that characterizes even many colleges that have women on their faculties, even colleges that have women as presidents. I have discussed this with the president of Reed College who is apparently truly concerned about the relations between young men and young women on his campus. In a symposium which was printed in the Journal of the American Association of University Women last year, participated in by President Neilson [of Smith College] and myself, I argued that women must know their own history as well as the history of men which is all they get at college, to be effective members of faculties. Men are such great propagandists with respect to the "man's world" that students' attitudes . . . represent the success of this propaganda above all else. It needs both analysis and the taking up of the cultural lag in this matter by the widening and deepening of history.

The Italians and Spaniards of the renaissance had a cultural attitude toward women which we should acquire by our revival of learning about them, for one thing. Latin Universities in Italy and Spain had women on their faculties and were exceedingly proud of them. Queen Isabella brought Italian women to Spain, put her Court to school to the men and women whom she imported and put women and men to teaching in the great Spanish University. To this day Latin Universities are open to women, I understand, and have in fact never been closed.

We are infinitely provincial as Americans in fancying that women had no education—top-notch at that—until they were admitted to Mary Lyon's little academy or Oberlin or to our later colleges. This provincialism marks our men and our women alike.

BUT more than provincialism is involved of course. We cannot know how our own society has been built up without knowing women's share in establishing free speech, free assembly, freedom of worship, all civil liberties, all humanism, all the branches of learning and everything else we value. We are both infinitely provincial and horribly ignorant about the fundamentals of thought and action, ideas and interests, wills and purposes. This ignorance colors everything that is felt and written in America today—in books, in magazines, in education, etc. I have just caught a ghastly Radio Program entitled "Women in the Making of America" to cover 13 talks—in time to save it from the banal chatter about this drama's being merely a movement from "slavery to actuality."

This program starts on the air this coming Friday, the 19th, at 2 p.m. over the NBC-Blue network. If you receive this word of it in time, you may be interested in noting that that note has been offset by something larger and more intelligent. To know women's history and acquire an interest in upholding it on campuses, some of us in New York have launched a World Center for Women's Archives. History demands records of course. I enclose a little literature on this subject. If you would like to join this movement, pray do so. It must bear fruit quickly. Indeed it is already doing so. Witness the aforesaid radio program for one thing. But whether we can finance an impressive Center remains the awful question.

. . . It may be true that college girls like men teachers for holding hands, figuratively or factually. But other likes should be developed if they are to receive any real education. Even Harvard was willing to study under Dr. Alice Hamilton.

This is something that must not be allowed to remain as "plight." I drew up a syllabus for the AAUW about three years ago with a view to starting women to work on their own history as a road to intelligence, influence, and dignity. What we think with is MEMORY. Men have so much memory of themselves but none of women. Women try to capture the memory of men and throw their own aside.

I shall write you again and hope to hear if anything develops at Whittier.

Cordially, Mary R. Beard

A second letter from Mira Saunders clarified her interest in women experts in international relations. Mary Beard's response shows how far she concurred with the views that were making her husband, who published them, increasingly unpopular in liberal circles.

73. TO MIRA SAUNDERS

[New Milford]
June 29, 1939

Dear Mrs. Saunders:

I am so glad to know precisely what you have in mind about women and Whittier. I failed to realize that it was the Institute of International Relations about which you were writing me exclusively.

Knowing this now I am impelled to say that it is probable that any recommendations which Dr. [Kathryn] McHale [of the AAUW] may make will be of women who belong to a different "school" of thought about international relations from mine. I am against American intervention in foreign quarrels on the order of our excursion into a world war again, at least. So are many, perhaps most, of the women who are associated with the AAUW, League of Women Voters, and the large affiliation which composes the Cause and Cure of War annual conferences. But in my opinion the attitude they take on foreign policy is just another war risk.

IF we could really produce a grand civilization in the USA where we have every facility at hand or could get what we need by quiet decent barter with other countries, exchanging directly what we have to excess for what we need and what they may have in that line to excess, in my opinion, and my husband's, we could do more for economic world rehabilitation and decent international relations than we can ever possibly do by thundering at dictators and trying to work with nations whose own record is so horrible too.

But the other point of view can be expressed by women galore from the AAUW and other groups. The most aggressive of them now is Dr. Esther Brunauer of the AAUW who has taken the leadership in lining up her association and others behind the foreign policy known as "collective security." There are speakers galore on that—Mary E. Woolley and countless heads of groups who have been studying international relations under the guidance of a group of men among whom Prof. Shotwell, Prof. Fenwick, and Prof. Gideonse have been mainstays.

On my side an excellent speaker should be Miss Edith Abbott of Chicago University. She protested in a letter to the Times recently against the way in which the AAUW and the League of Women Voters have been veered in the interventionist direction and privately she has carried on that protest. She is, you probably know, the sister of Grace Abbott with whom she lived until Grace's death a few days ago. Edith might like intensely to go to California next season and present her view of international relations. No one should be listened to with more genuine interest on account of her record in public life. Miss Abbott might have suggestions for other speakers if you would write to her. Her side (which is mine) should be represented. We are not evangelistic but deeply concerned about the kind of a society which is developing in the USA. We can defend it, we believe, without participation in another world war. Quakers as a rule want it so defended but some of them have been caught in the idea of policing the world, I find, or avoiding the need by challenging dictators with a counter axis, or bloc.

I have heard about Mrs. Macpherson's gift of books to Scripps but I wonder whether rumor is correct in reporting that the collection is largely made up of books on queens!?

The Radio Program about Women in the Making of America has revealed a depth of ignorance of the subject which should instigate some good hard work in this connection without delay. This program I have not managed in every respect by any means. I have merely kept it within certain bounds of accuracy and knowledge. I had especial difficulty with this week's on Freedom of Education for the women in charge had supposed that women were never educated until they began to go to such little academies as Mary Lyon's or to Oberlin. If the Women's Archive can go on the air on its own next winter, it should do a much better program. This one is a beginning, however, and with the tendency all over the country to shut married women out of posts where they can earn money it is important to keep the insurgent spirit alive even if it is somewhat brash in its statements.

Of course we Beards value the memory of you Saunders and of your work. It is a gracious fate which renews our acquaintance if only by post.

Do give my warm regards to Mrs. Campbell and the women I met there—all of whom I hold in affection.

                                        Cordially, Mary R. Beard

[P.S.] You wouldn't like to undertake together, would you, a Southern California promotion of the Archives? If you are interested in the idea, I shall tell you what the work would be and how to go at it.

❦

In the spring of 1939 Adolf Hitler's armies occupied Czechoslovakia and Mussolini's invaded Albania. Hitler and Stalin signed a German-Soviet nonaggression pact in August; by September 1 Hitler's armies were in Poland, and two days later Britain and France declared war on Germany. To permit Allied purchases of armaments in the United States, President Roosevelt called Congress into special session to ask for amendment of the Neutrality Act. The rally to which Detzer invited Mary Beard as speaker was focused on that issue. Unlike her husband, however, Mary Beard did not take her views on U.S. diplomacy to the public. Whether the reasons cited in the letter below or some other unstated reasons were the controlling ones can never be known. Public sentiment for neutrality was not strong enough, in any case, to prevent the Senate from repealing the arms embargo.

74. TO DOROTHY DETZER

[New Milford, Conn.]
September 26, 1939

Dear Dorothy Detzer:

I am pro-neutrality without reservation.

I want to speak my mind on Friday night.

But it would be a tactical mistake for me to speak on this occasion in Washington. I might be attacked by the opposition through the disgrace that came to my brother—his impeachment by Congress. The opposition could say that I belong to a family........

The opposition could also attack me as having a German name. My father's name was Ritter though my mother was a Howard—as English as that—joined to a Lockwood. My people on both sides were colonial Americans and I never knew a German in my youth. But I was stopped on the village green here a few days ago by two women who accused me of influencing Charles in his neutrality through being a German myself.

Well, I must give you no possible opening for a thrust against me as one of your speakers.

Sorry to the point of grief.

At the same time enormously honored by your invitation.

Yours as ever, Mary R. Beard

In the WCWA Beard aimed (unsuccessfully) to unite women, but she knew that on matters of international relations her own opinions aroused controversy and disagreement. This letter was written after the Soviet Union had invaded Finland but before Hitler's blitzkrieg in Europe, in the period called "the phony war" by American journalists. In the following months full-scale popular debate between noninterventionists and internationalists became acrimonious in the United States. Mary Beard's opinion remained with the former group.

75. TO DR. MINNIE L. MAFFETT, PRESIDENT OF THE NATIONAL FEDERATION OF BUSINESS AND PROFESSIONAL WOMEN

New Milford, Conn.
February 22, 1940

Dear Dr. Maffett:

I have your forceful appeal relative to "good Samaritans" and I cannot be insensitive to that ideal and practice of course. Human suffering grips the heart strings of every one who has a heart and a lot of warm blood passes through mine.

But there is an aspect of the International Federation which bothers me very much indeed. Two aspects in fact. And these I feel that I should lay before you in order that I may not seem merely indifferent if I do not continue to send in my checks.

First. If feminist philosophy calling for full equality of women with men, requires that, in the world crisis, the National Federation and its International ally must do much about, or even care much about, equal pay and equal work in the fighting forces, then my heart does turn cold and dry up. Granted that in many countries women must now actually fight, in my opinion the emphasis on rewards makes fighting too laudable an occupation and I am unable to think of it in terms of titles and pay.

I heard an American feminist declare recently that there can be no true equality until a woman becomes a Major General or Field Marshal. I replied that that was the oldest stuff in the human experience; that women were top war lords in many ancient societies; that Isabella of Spain and Jeanne D'arc of France led the troops as women on horseback. In short, lack of historical knowledge of women blows up absurd cliches of harmful social consequences, as I see them.

Second. The Good Samaritanship of the I[nternational] B[usiness] & P[rofessional] W[omen] might, conceivably, be a factor in getting the USA into the world war. Sympathy with Finland is a sympathy no one of us can resist, naturally. But I consider extremely dangerous to American democracy and culture the kind of proposals geared to that sympathy which women seem lightly to accept. And I believe, firmly, that the apparent determination of Americans to stick their fingers again into a European "peace" is another equally dangerous thrust in the dark, based solely on sentiment. We did Europe infinite harm, as well as ourselves, in my opinion, by our performances at Versailles and I believe we have no more sagacity now than we had in 1918, as far as sense about European peace is concerned.

So, dear Dr. Maffett, I feel that I cannot just run along with any organization which may be headed toward a program which I cannot endorse. Simple incidents can drive us mad, I fear. For instance if the old King of Sweden has to abdicate and Scandinavia which we all admire so much has to fight Russia, we could forget that America confronted a fairly similar world situation in the Napoleonic era when Napoleon put one of his marshals, Bernadotte, to rule over the combined Norway and Sweden and that this King is the heir of that earlier world war.

Staying out of the Napoleonic wars was our salvation. Going into the present war or trying to help Europe solve its own continuous messes will be to jeopardize our whole economy and civilization.

And yet all the leading national women's organizations have sanctioned points of view—defined for them by men whose loyalty to their European nativities or cultures is clear-cut, if the women would only realize it, or induced by allegiance to the Vatican—which are not, in my judgment, wholesome for our America.

Moreover, I am far from happy over the strength within the National Federation of Business and Professional Women of sympathy with the operations of the Dies committee. I do not like drifting with crowds when I fear their drifting.

Yet I hate to resign and resign from women's organizations. On the other hand, I cannot be satisfied with participation in groups which my membership helps to strengthen when I doubt the wisdom of their courses.

I have written you frankly. And at length. You believe in frankness and I admire you wholeheartedly for that essential quality of high leadership.

Most cordially, Mary R. Beard

In the latter part of 1939 the WCWA risked what Mary Beard called genuine crisis because of squabbles among the office staff and the national board in New York, and lack of money to rent sufficient space or to hire adequate personnel to keep its operations going. At the same time, it had reached a certain height of accomplishments: over sixty names of distinguished sponsors graced its stationery; thirty college presidents had loaned their names to the effort; branch groups functioned not only in the nation's capital but in Michigan, New Jersey, Connecticut, Indiana, and Pennsylvania; and an impressive collection of documents had been donated and more pledged. Mary Beard was working directly, as chairman of the committee on archives, with a specialist on Indian lore, with Mrs. Jerome Frank on the collection of Jewish women's records, and with several women designated by the National Council of Negro Women. Her propensity to want to work with researchers such as Marjorie White, to discover more information and more documents, was not fully shared by other members of the national board. White felt unappreciated and snubbed by board members. "Everyone top-hats her. No one has the faintest idea of how she has slaved and what she has accomplished," Beard lamented to Lena Madesin Phillips. Miriam Holden's own interest in printed books (rather than in manuscripts) was causing some friction between her and Beard.[8]

Furthermore, while Beard was actively recruiting African-American women's archives, it appeared early in 1940 that the Washington, D.C., unit, on which she had placed so many hopes, was going to be riven with discord over race. The group of women designated by the National Council of Negro Women was busy. When Juanita Mitchell withdrew because of her distant residence, Mary Bethune appointed a Washington-based committee chaired by the experienced supervisor of the Moorland Foundation collection at Howard University, librarian Dorothy Porter. Other members were Sue Bailey Thurman, the wife of Howard's dean, and two distinguished former presidents of the National Association of Colored Women, Mary Church Terrell and Elizabeth Carter Brooks. These women were probably not aware, as Mary Beard was, that WCWA regulations required members to join a local branch, nor that the white Washington unit would not admit them because of their race.[9]

Beard's way out of this dilemma was to ask the "Negro Women's Archives" group, in February 1940, to work directly with her committee on archives, bypassing the Washington unit. The Washington unit was in some disarray anyway, because its chair had resigned—whether because of the race issue or other reasons is not clear. From the black women's perspective, it appeared no anomaly to work directly with Mary Beard on archives, and Dorothy Porter readily agreed.[10] While hoping that the Negro Women's Archives group would funnel findings into the WCWA, Beard also encouraged them to seek an exhibit of black women's documents at an exposition being planned for Chicago by Congressman Arthur Mitchell, who (after leaving the Republican party in 1930) was the first black Democrat to sit in the U.S. House of Representatives.

76. TO SUE BAILEY THURMAN

New Milford, Connecticut
March 25, 1940

Dear Mrs. Thurman:

It was such a pleasure to be received in your home last Saturday and to see there the interesting evidences of your visits to India! Of course I read the "archive," which you gave me, with genuine interest and I think I can fully appreciate what you felt in India as its esthetic charms. I have been moved myself by similar charms in the Orient. The memory of sensitive ceremonies continuously enchants my thought and imagination with the idea that our lives in America might become more beautiful and beauty-loving. You and I have one bond in our affection for the Old East.

But we are both Americans and that is another bond. We talked together on Saturday about work here and now. I am sure we both want to instill into our work here and now as much of the delicacy and sweetness of ancient societies grown old in wisdom as we possibly can.

When I spoke of the old Spanish-Portuguese culture which some New York families have inherited, I did not mean of course that this culture is to be cherished by the heirs alone. What I hope I was saying is that the rest of us can know it better if its best features can be assembled as archives in our WCWA where students and writers can learn about it as few could learn about it if the learning required close personal association with the "old" families who cherish that culture.

I find it so true that the women of those families and the women of all other cultural groups can meet socially and yet know nothing in fact of another as far as innate tastes and aspiration are concerned, that the idea of a World Center for Women's Archives is for me the idea of realistic cultural exchanges made impossible by merely formal occasions.

This underlies too my enthusiasm for a possible great participation by Negro women in the grand Exposition which the Hon. Mr. Mitchell is proposing. Such participation would be the preliminary to a grand participation by Negro women in the World Center for Women's Archives. I am seeking every archive I can get from your beloved East too. The collection of documents which Negro women would assemble for the Exposition at Chicago would come straight to WCWA for its collection I like to assume.

And so I hope that you will call upon Mr. Mitchell immediately and let me know what he is doing about women's participation in his proposed Exposition. My mind fills to the very edges with dreams of a great demonstration by Negro women there. On my way home from Washington I could think of nothing else and I am sitting down to my typewriter soon after my arrival home to ask again what you think about this great objective and the possibility that your Committee will make it theirs. Mrs. Bethune will be enthusiastic, unless I am terribly mistaken. And those fine delegates whom I saw at the convention in New York of the National Council of Negro Women will also be enthusiastic no doubt.

I can't refrain from jotting down some ideas I have by way of sugges-

tions on a separate piece of paper. As I visualize Negro women's participation in that Exposition—or failing its financial support—in one of
their own, that feature might run as I have suggested. Surely nothing
would stimulate the best culture for the Negroes—*and therefore for us
all in the USA*—like a great appraisal made visible with respect to the
cultural strife of Negro women.

Do please let me hear what your committee says on this point and what
you learn from your call upon Mr. Mitchell.

There will be objections on the part of many Negro women—perhaps
few on the part of Negro men—to a separate Exposition, and/or to
women's separate exhibition in such an exposition. But this is precisely
the objection we meet with respect to our Women's Archive. Many
women and many men deny the validity of a separate archive for women.
I maintain however that only by dramatizing women can women be recognized as equally important with men. And I now maintain that only by
dramatizing the hopes and achievements of Negro women per se can they
be recognized as equally important with Negro men. And I also maintain
that the proposed Exposition, by dramatizing an important minority of
our population, may aid in awakening a stronger realization of its cultural values. For I take for granted that the Negro women who would
have the responsibility for their division would lift the cultural values
above the cheap and purely imitative strife for acquisition and enjoyment.
This is not to say that the efforts of Negroes to enjoy food, clothing, shelter and recreation are beyond the range of cultural values.

I have chattered to excess in this long letter to you.

But the chattering helps my heart.

Most cordially, [Mary R. Beard]

●←

In the following letter Beard tries to justify her position regarding the
Negro Women's Archives group to Miriam Holden, who had for years
been involved in the cause of racial justice through the NAACP and local
efforts in Harlem. The bylaws to which Beard refers required women
joining the WCWA to affiliate with a state or local branch. The letter
makes clear both the genuineness, and the limits, of Mary Beard's inclusion of black women. She ranks the importance of the majority—
whites—in the sustenance of the project higher than justice to a minority,
yet believes she has a solution that will attain both. The black women
with whom she was working accepted her goodwill enthusiastically and
invited her to speak at the occasion launching a new publication by the

National Council of Negro Women, to be called the *Africamerican Woman's Journal.*

77. TO MIRIAM HOLDEN

New Milford, Connecticut
March 25, 1940

Dear Mrs. Holden:

The teachers whom I "addressed" in Washington seemed truly stirred by WCWA and I think we can count on their working hard for the records of their profession. This crowd belongs to the Delta Kappa Gamma Society, made up entirely of women teachers who are recognized by their profession and by their communities as outstanding for their contributions to education. They were the most intelligent crowd as a whole to whom I think I have ever talked. Handsome women with noble brows. Intelligent and active as such types must be. I felt encouraged by their response of course but how to take advantage of it?

The woman who had expressed a strong desire to aid WCWA in money raising at the NY AAUW meeting was also present at this one and seemed equally alert. You have her name, I think, via the office as one who thought she might collect a thousand dollars or so. Was it Evans? She lives in Yonkers and must be an exceptional teacher or she would not have been admitted to this Society. If you have not yet written her, you might do so now to even more advantage.

I ran again into *the* Washington problem as of WCWA. We cannot get a strong activity there for funds until we can handle this problem by our Board. There is firmness like adamant on this point. Shall we then permit the wreckage of the movement at the D.C.? I attempted to prevent it in this way:

Having heard that the Negro Congressman from Chicago, Hon. Mr. Mitchell, is proposing a great Negro Exposition to be held in Chicago and is asking for Congressional aid, I called upon Mrs. Bailey [Thurman] whom you had met in our office and who is still the chairman of the Negro Committee selected by Mary Bethune. I was most graciously received at her home and we had a nice long talk. Her husband is Dean at Howard University and they are both prominent Negroes. Again I asked whether her committee would work with my Committee on Archives directly so that we could be sure what they would do and be sure of their archives.

On my way to Mrs. Bailey [Thurman]'s I thought of this way out of the dilemma—the dilemma of a minority's possible wrecking of a majority and for what end? The way out to be a concentrated effort by Negro women throughout the USA for a woman's exhibition in the aforesaid Exposition, following which all the materials collected for that exhibition would come to WCWA. Mrs. Bailey [Thurman] had not heard about Mr. Mitchell's plan. She didn't know whether women had been or would be invited to participate. I urged her to go to see the Congressman at once and find out. I urged her to call for such participation if the idea had not yet been advanced. And I urged her to discuss with her committee the suggestion of mine that they call upon the Negro women far and wide to put on a magnificent exhibition either as a feature of the aforesaid Exposition or separately if that fails to materialize.

I argued that a concentration on their own archives for such a goal would do two things: educate their own women as nothing else could; promote the archives for the Center definitely.

I pointed out an analogy with the plan for a WCWA itself—dramatizing their materials in the interests of their women's recognition more fully.

The appeal seemed to "take." Today I have written a letter to Mrs. Thurman containing a summary of our conversation and its suggestions for united action. I had to agree to make a trip to the D.C. again in April to speak at a meeting to celebrate the launching of a Negro women's magazine sponsored by the National Council of Negro Women. It will not be easy for me to make the trip but I shall do so in the hope that this will help to iron out the trouble and possible misunderstanding of my position. Mrs. Bethune will of course be present (she was not in Washington this last week).

It must not happen that you and Mrs. Grove get a wrong idea of me and/or Washington. It is all a question as to whether we should run the risk of an awful row over a minority which might ruin WCWA. The most delicate diplomacy seems to be required unless our Board can make a decision which will lift it out of a dispute. If our Board refuses to do more or anything other than affirm its present By Laws, every white woman will resign in the D.C. and in their resignations we shall be accused of—well you know.

. . . In view of everything I hope that the Board will meet informally— not for the record—at a simple cheap luncheon somewhere at 12:30 or earlier—before the next regular Board meeting and discuss our situation thoroughly—prior to the decisions in the afternoon for the record. With

Miss Shouse absent we could even go into office affairs as we cannot do when she is present.

Unless we can have this extra time for informal discussion prior to our last Board meeting for months, I fear we shall wind up in a complete mess.

If we could get a little room at the Town Hall or somewhere—each of us paying for her own food—and paying for the private room to boot— perhaps we could hold our Board meeting right there too and save the time of traveling to your sweet domicile and save your expense of serving food again. We have been greedy and not confessed it.

There is one thing more at the moment. As you may know, the National Federation of Women's Clubs is collecting archives for a big anniversary—the 50th—a year or so ahead. We must try to get the archives pledged to WCWA for delivery after that event. There is no other institution to which they could be assigned with such profit to the Clubs. But they need to be aware of this now.

I asked the Washington women to do what they could at the Club headquarters there. But we must work all over the lot to gain this pledge. I can make the plea effectively in California, I think, for the woman who is now state president there may accept the state presidency of WCWA when her term ends for the Clubs. Mrs. Marsh can help in N.J. CAN you consult your NY friend-president about getting this put before the National Federation? Mrs. Hansl has been talking it up with Club leaders whom she knows. We should put in our claim immediately.

After these preliminaries we can have an official request go from our Board of course.

I "leave off" writing to you at this point for your own peace and happiness.

Affectionately, Mary R. B.

Miriam Holden and Mary Beard did not see eye to eye on the "Washington problem." In Holden's view, Beard had erred by deciding on her own how to handle the question of participation without consulting the black women themselves. Holden urged that the national board in New York be augmented by the addition of a distinguished Negro woman, such as Mrs. James Weldon Johnson. She thought that Beard was letting the white women in Washington off the hook too easily for their racism. Beard believed that the black women were satisfied with her decision and better off without knowing directly the exclusion they faced in the Washington unit.

At this point, Holden was less than satisfied with Beard's leadership on a number of issues. She did not favor Marjorie White as Beard did and was skeptical about other allies Beard made in local historical societies. She was positively angry at another researcher whom Beard encouraged: Jan Gay, a Latin-American specialist who had interfered in a way Holden disapproved in a Harlem exhibit in which they both were involved. Holden recognized that WCWA was in financial crisis. Moreover, she wanted to shift the emphasis of the center toward books and found Beard utterly and autocratically unsympathetic on that point.

Part of what Beard is responding to in the letter below is Holden's statement, in a prior letter, "To me the way we handle it (the Negro matter) is just about as important as whether we continue to have an archive center or not." Beard did not share those priorities. She was first and foremost for the survival of the archives. She was sufficiently frustrated and despondent about the future, however, to write to Marjorie White, on March 25, 1940, suggesting that White take over her own job as chairman of archives. She imagined that White together with a paid fundraiser and a field worker would make an ideal team. At the same time she knew that the funds to employ such a team were not in the center's purse.[11]

78. TO MIRIAM HOLDEN

New Milford
April 2, 1940

Dear Miriam Holden:

Your letter just received I am trying to answer at once but with the very best mind which I can utilize. This is to say I am attempting to think quietly and rationally about every item in it.

It is easy to cheer at your securing facilities for our meeting together as a Board in a long enough session this month to find out where each and all of us stand on all the essentials. I did not care about the Town Hall Club. I merely suggested that, not knowing we could get by ourselves in privacy at the City Club. Now I do hope and pray that we shall have a good turn out, for it is now or never respecting fundamentals.

I have always found you inclined to be impersonal. So you will let me be frank on points where frankness seems a little risky as friendship. This is to say that I do find you somewhat variable in your judgments of what I do. I refer to the matter of the Negroes. You haven't forgotten surely that you warmly commended our interview's outcome with Mrs. [James Weldon] Johnson. Well, I have merely been going forward on the principle, which you enthusiastically sanctioned, by inviting the committee appointed by Mrs. Bethune to work directly with my Committee on Archives. Mrs. Thurman appears to prefer having Mrs. Dorothy Porter chairman of that committee but she is a member. Mrs. Porter will be the representative of that committee on my committee presumably but this will be verified. If Mrs. Bethune approves this plan, the finest Negro women in the USA should soon be working to assemble their best archives. If Congressman Mitchell gets the appropriation for aid for a Great Negro Exposition at Chicago, and if the Negro women win the right to participate with a splendid Exhibit there, surely this will all be to the good of everybody.

As you saw in the copy of Mrs. Porter's letter which I sent you, she and her committee will draft a plan for their procedure subject to Mrs. Bethune's endorsement. This I had asked of Mrs. Thurman when she came to the office in the autumn and so we are back to first principles. Their plan we can make suggestions about if we have any. At any rate those Negro leaders will feel as they should feel at home at the center of our Center.

You would be willing to break up the whole w c w a for something else or something got in some other way? Well that is frank, my dear. . . .

You wonder what my plan of organization is? I have no plan which I am "putting over." I asked for a reconsideration of our arrangement for the branches because they just aren't acting under it. Washington quit pretty stone dead. . . . Finding the branches in distress over the financial set-up and as for the D.C. over other matters, I thought perhaps we could have a more elastic financial policy and relieve other distress through work directed by my Committee on Archives where the Negro women would meet with other grand members of that committee, such as Dr. Lynch, from time to time, and push hard for special archives. But if the attitude to be taken is that I am doing something myself or doing something wrong, then let me know openly at the coming informal discussion at lunch prior to the formal Board meeting.

. . . There was a finance committee, it is true. It had nothing positive to report. There may be nothing more to report in April. You have confessed to me, dear friend, that you don't like to ask people for money. Who does? Who will? I have tried to get it from everyone I thought could give. And I hear that Margaret Cuthbert is rooting for some for us. Mrs. Moffett's scheme still looks promising. But I begin to get more worried every hour as I confront more closely the issue of my financial obligation to this movement.

A committee could no doubt frame a nicer letter as a money appeal. But what committee? And could it ever decide to whom to mail the thing?

We are a flop as a Board because we won't organize for burdens. I try to keep the wcwa alive and keep it from ruin.

But if you still feel that your accusation of a year or so ago is still sound—that I am a Margaret Sanger unable to work with anybody else—then tell me so again and I shall get out of the way with pleasure. I have thought of doing that many times but refrained because it seemed so unfair to leave this important movement for you and the rest of the Board to carry alone. I felt I should be conscienceless if I did that both for your sakes and for the sake of all the women and men whom I have got interested in wcwa through my direct efforts. . . .

Unless at our coming luncheon, each woman will assume some task and stick to it, we are sunk. Otherwise everyone will merely knock me down and kick me. . . . I shall stop speaking for this thing as soon as I get through the April-May 3d meetings to which I am pledged. What's the use going on? The thing can't do with me or without me unless it can do without me. And how I wish it could!

Miss Gay knows that there is no hope of a position for her unless she and I can raise some money by ourselves for her to go on with her Latin-American project. Miss White has magnificently substituted for me in keeping the science project and Mrs. Mezerik at work and interested. I have written tons of letters, brought in money and members and friends. I have made hard train trips and tired myself speaking.

Then on a Negro issue, which does not have to be made an issue but can be taken care of so well that the Negro women will be the great gainers, you would let all this die? How do you know that in doing that and feeling that way you are doing anything for the Negroes? What reason have you for believing that you are a better friend to them than I am? If Mrs. Johnson comes on the Board, we shall have to add that as an issue when we have far more than we can manage now.

> Oh God! Have mercy on my soul!
> Affectionately as ever—Mary

In the following letter Beard laid her resolution of the Washington problem before an active (white) member of the Washington unit, Grace

Cooper. It was Cooper who had managed to secure an office for the group in the annex of the Library of Congress, because her uncle, Congressman Kent Keller of Illinois, chaired the House committee on the Library. By this point the continuance and vigor of the unit was an open question; it was functioning under an acting chair, Irene Wright, who was an assistant secretary in the State Department charged with improving Latin-American cultural relations.

79. TO MRS. GRACE KELLER COOPER

New Milford   Connecticut
April 29, 1940

Dear Mrs. Cooper:

I had a very fine conference with the Negro women in Washington on the 22d. Before the dinner at Howard University at which the magazine, Africamerican, was launched—the organ of the National Council of Negro Women—Mrs. Dorothy Porter, Mrs. Sue Bailey Thurman, Mrs. Sinclair, and a woman from Boston whose name I cannot repeat confidently (I have forgotten this name), talked with me for a long time about the problem of association with WCWA.

These are wonderful women indeed. Mrs. Porter is top-notch as a librarian with full knowledge of books on and by the people of her race. AND she has been given the task of providing the entire book exhibit for the Negro Exposition. I learned more about that Exposition: the fact that $75,000 are already available; the plan of the Exposition; the possibility that a good section can be reserved for the Negro Women and their Archives; the opportunities which a Congressional appropriation would enlarge.

We went over some possible items for the women's exhibit if it is to be a feature. Mrs. Porter will have the matter decided at once.

We also discussed the matter of drawing Negro women into state branches and it seemed to be the positive opinion of theirs that their women would be better off by working with our Center in NYC directly for the quest for their archives. The next step then, I think, is to ask the Washington leaders to call together a conference of the women who joined the Unit—calling it quietly and without excitement—and put before them this new and better plan. They know how to argue for it. They will be convincing with respect to its advantages. They have a lot of work to do in connection with the Exposition. The decision, I believe, will be in favor of their independent organization. This is the most democratic procedure and if it is approved by the conference, white and colored skies will both be clearer. I shall keep you informed of developments.

Meanwhile I hope that the majority members of the Washington Unit will proceed to collect the archives along the lines suggested in the original plan for the D.C. It is a unique plan for the country, as a plan for the nation's capital. The Negro women couldn't do much about collecting those materials but they should be asked to get everything they can about their lives and labor in the capital. I will stress this point with them while you all go after the materials of the majority folk.

It would be generous if some of you would subscribe to the new magazine—Africamerican. Mrs. Bailey is editor.

[M.R.B.]

Hitler's blitzkrieg—invading and overrunning Denmark, Norway, Holland, Belgium, Luxembourg, and France—began to strike on April 10, 1940. Mary Beard's sense of being beleaguered in her progress with the archives must have been exacerbated by the steady move of American intellectual and liberal opinion away from neutrality and noninterventionist sentiments. Charles Beard's vociferous opinions came under increasing and direct attack. Although the following letter to historian Merle Curti reflects none of this explicitly, it has a distinctly touchy tone—not untypical of Mary Beard's belief in her husband's wisdom and complexity (which no one could portray quite to her satisfaction) but surprisingly hostile, given the nature of Curti's question. Over the next decade and a half Mary Beard wrote to Curti, as a trusted friend, torrents of sharp criticisms of other male historians.

80. TO MERLE CURTI

[New Milford, Conn.]
May 14, 1940

Dear Professor Curti:

I find all the writings about CAB, with which I am familiar, either inadequate or rather vile.

[Max] Lerner's calling him just a village atheist was really vile.

Hubert Herring's sketch in Harper's made him a jitterbug rather than the hard-working scholar he has been all his adult life. That was surely inadequate.

Irwin Edman's tribute in his Journey of a Philosopher had the competence of a thoughtful student long associated with his teacher, although the adjective for his voice (one Edman applied to nearly all the rest) seemed inexact.

Certainly Johnny Chamberlain got CAB all wrong in his Farewell to Reform for CAB was never pro-Teddy Roosevelt.

A man who wanted to write a Profile for the New Yorker became very vexed with me because I wouldn't cooperate, as if I could join in a cartoon-making! He flung himself out of the house saying he wouldn't write it at all then. Well who wants just to appear in print for the sake of being there?

Herring wanted me to indulge in the personal and I refused. So this reply is the best I can give you respecting things that have been tried and written, which I have liked. I am sorry.

We surely must have another visit together.

Cordially, Mary R. Beard

Beard was facing the evaporation of the New York board's confidence in her, for what they saw as ill-advised forays into research when funds for the archives center did not exist. (She herself contributed a total of about three thousand dollars to the effort and was trying unique means to gain money to keep going: she initiated an arrangement with *McCall's* magazine in which five to seven outstanding women writers would contribute articles to the magazine and *McCall's* would pay the WCWA three thousand dollars for each—with fifteen hundred dollars up front. But the plan never materialized.) The attitude of one New York board member, Carol Willis Moffett, writing to Miriam Holden, was harsh but perhaps typical: she "appreciate[d] the contribution Mrs. Beard can make" but felt the board "must be absolved from responsibility for her erratic behavior." Moffett believed that "the idea of the archives is important, but not so important that I will drop all my other interests indefinitely in order to nurse it along in the face of recurrent personality problems." Holden clearly shared some similar misgivings.[12]

Meanwhile, in May 1940, just before the fall of France to the Nazis, Charles Beard's *A Foreign Policy for America* was published, restating his views on continentalism and neutrality, as against the internationalist intellectuals. Critics now lambasted him for moral indifference to the depravities of the Nazis and the ruthlessness of Japan. "The Irresponsibles," by Archibald MacLeish (*The Nation*, 150 [May 19, 1940]), which Mary

Beard notes below, was not an attack on her husband or any other specific individual but a wholesale condemnation of American intellectuals
for failing to confront the Nazis' repudiation of the forms of civilization
and moral understanding that intellectuals themselves lived by. MacLeish
attributed this egregious collective failing to the replacement of the "man
of letters," who had assumed a public responsibility, by the specialized
scholar and the aesthete.

81. TO MIRIAM HOLDEN

New Milford
May 25, 1940

Dear Miriam Holden:

   That's a hard spanking you give me in your letter of the 22d. It comes
of course from your desire to keep me intelligent about the meaning of
WCWA and dignified in proposals for its advancement. Your spirit was
"well-intentioned" like that of the sensitive parent who flagellates a child
in its own interest. And though the average child does not take punish-
ment that way, I have had such disciplining that I do try my best to get the
other fellow's point of view.

   . . . There is the issue of financing any archives project. The Board, I
suppose, has the right to examine and question and refuse any action of
mine looking to such financing. If such examining and criticising and refusing is to match the position taken respecting our Branches now in existence which I have mainly built up, then I may be completely stymied in
my archives work. I hear that the decision about branches may be brought
up for review on the ground that it was illegally taken. In this case they
may be voted out. And the Board may also reject any means I see of paying for archives projects which cannot be executed without pay. There is
the matter of Jan Gay's highly successful work for Latin-American documents which she carried handsomely forward last week in Washington on
my o.k. and partial financial aid. No one else can do for us what she is
doing and other people accept her without our anxiety about her domestic situation. I don't know what that is and I don't care except as I pity
(and respect) a young woman who is trying to keep her extraordinary
head above the storm. I also have a chance to get a rare California
woman of old Spanish ancestry, associated as curator with the Southwest
Museum, to document for us the women of the Spanish settlements in
that state, dead and living. She is widely recognized as the best person,
man or woman, in the State, to do this work. And I think I could relieve

her of her task at the Museum for a while to pursue this research with California money, *for our Center*.

But can I do any of these things as Chairman of Archives? Or is every single woman I bring into the picture to be destroyed for some reason assigned by other members of the Board? Have I any autonomy? LET THE BOARD SAY IN JUNE ONCE AND FOR ALL because I am helpless to do another thing in the present state of confusion about my function in WCWA.

In re Washington and the Negro women. The trouble there can be removed at once by the full and free consent of the Negro women, unless our Board refuses to let it be taken care of that way. Mrs. Thurman whom you met at our office, editor of the Africamerican Women's Journal, and the other women with whom I talked frankly in the D.C. in April, stated their feeling that their women would be lost or injured if they made an attempt to force their way into the local white groups. They said that in most states, certainly in the southern states, they would probably not have the quality for success in that business. BESIDES they are now so enthusiastic about studying themselves and working with the archives project that they acquired what is to me the utter DIGNITY of going forward with the widening and deepening of their own understanding as Mrs. Booker T. Washington the Third advised them to do. Thus they will outgrow their inferiority complex and command a sincere respect which the battle over archives on the social basis would never permit. BUT our Board from its own sense of "values" may, reviewing the decision of May, be so interventionist as to knock both the whites and the negroes in the head as of the archives? If it does, no one will be sorrier than those grand Negro women of the D.C. They are growing up.

There was a time not so long ago when all feminists felt compelled to force their way into every man's club and smoking car. That was the childhood of the sex in my opinion.

I would be in favor of inviting Mrs. Weldon Johnson to membership on our Board where she would learn to understand the total archives movement and help us to safeguard its purposes. I am also strongly in favor of solving the Washington dilemma in the way I have outlined, seeing no inconsistency but true statesmanship in that proposal.

Yes I read Macleish's Irresponsibles and thought it a maze of contradictions and grossly unfair to the Responsibles who have written all these years: i.e. Sinclair Lewis, "It Can't Happen Here." For this outburst I consider Macleish really disqualified to be the head of the Lib[rary of Congress]. He reveals no awareness of the literature of protest during recent years. I hate to go back on him after adoring much that he has written himself. But I think this outburst rather disgraceful. No doubt it is patterned somewhat on Benda's "La Trahison des Clercs" but Benda wrote in the longer ago.

We're delighted that you like "A FOREIGN POLICY FOR AMERICA." How CAB does get flayed in the press and elsewhere however! I do try to refrain from writing you so much every time but there is always the need of infinite explanation of my mind and manners. I AM NOT JUST STUB-BORN and egoistic. If I am all wet however the Board can declare me so in June and then I shall have its full understanding of what I am.

Yours as always   Mary R. Beard

Astonishingly, Mary Beard resigned from the effort she had nurtured for five years. The failure of the board's confidence in her, as well as all the foregoing problems, was undoubtedly the real cause. The precipitant was Charles Beard's acceptance of a year-long teaching post at Johns Hopkins University, which meant that Mary Beard would be in Baltimore for the academic year. Beard had alerted Miriam Holden to her decision a few weeks before the date of the letter below. Holden was utterly taken aback. Peeved, unaware of Beard's agonizing over the project, she wrote to another board member, "How can anyone walk out on their own project so calmly and so freely I just can't imagine. Apparently no sense of responsibility to us or the people who have sent their precious archives." [13]

Though she was perhaps willfully deluding herself, Beard did not assume that the project would fold upon her withdrawal. She sustained hope that either the New York or Washington group would continue the work. It is puzzling, however, that in the letter below she seems willing to leave the Archives in the hands of board member Eva von Baur Hansl, whose career as an educator and vocational counselor Beard did not seem to respect very much.

82. TO MEMBERS OF THE BOARD OF THE WORLD CENTER FOR WOMEN'S ARCHIVES

New Milford   Connecticut
June 26, 1940

To my revered and beloved colleagues on the WCWA Board:

I abhor having to be away from Board meetings and having to give up my direction of archives-collecting from this time forward but I positively must. I am deeply appreciative of your insistence that I remain at my post, but an absentee from the meetings and from the office cannot be either a Board director or a director of archives-collecting with any competence. I have been at work on this Center for five hard working years. I know a few women who can carry on my part of the work, as chairman of archives, if they can now be assigned to that job. I know a few women who could push organization and publicity if they can be given the conditions for doing so.

Unless strong new blood can be transfused into our movement's management, neither my continued service nor any other service, old or new, will carry us further toward our goal.

Mrs. Hansl and Marjorie White would make a fine team directing interest in and winning success with documents.

Mrs. Hansl and Miss Elsie Yellis of Allentown, Pennsylvania (whose correspondence with me is in the files), would make a fine organization and publicity team, I think. Miss Yellis would have to have a good salary however, even as Mrs. Hansl would. Miss Yellis is not well known in New York but she has qualifications which might elegantly offset that handicap. Her heart is so completely dedicated to wcwa and her business experience has been so exceptional that this combination is an asset. She was a very popular and efficient president of the International Quota Clubs and interested that entire organization in wcwa.

The suggested new members for the Board whose names were read at our June meeting do not impress me at all as good material for hard work for wcwa. I am afraid they will merely use words as we have all been so accustomed to do. Their advice will be excellent no doubt. But that is surely not enough. I do not believe that women identified with other historical societies, for that is [what] ours [is] really, will be tremendously active in pushing ours. Mrs. [James Weldon] Johnson will no doubt help us to get archives but can she help us get financial support?

I am resigning, in part, because I will not go on soliciting archives when there is no real push for money. The members of the Board never have brought in financial plans until I found Mrs. Moffett and she did. I forged ahead trying to get papers and support until I almost dropped dead with labor.

In my opinion we have marked time for months unnecessarily—by supposing that we could make a movement out of bookkeeping alone. The leadership of Miss Judson diverted a live thing into a deadish thing in my opinion and the moment that happened Miss Judson resigned even from membership in the movement, to say nothing of membership on the Board. I was never consulted about this decision to make good books the sole expenditure of our funds. While I honestly want no particular respect for my notions of the proprieties, it is honestly futile for me to try to lift our Center with my effort and get it considerably boosted and then have no other lifting done. The thing gets too lop-sided that way.

Other members of the Board have worked hard too. I do not overlook this truth or deny it for an instant. But sometimes they have done things on the assumption that those things had never been done or thought of before and sometimes they have thus unwittingly caused a check on work going ahead. WE HAVE NOT BEEN A WORKING-TOGETHER BOARD when we have been active. The fault has not all been mine.

If obstruction in what I saw to do and tried to do was rightfully exercised at times, yet it must be admitted by us all that rarely, if ever, was an efficient substitute provided wherewith publicity and organization could move along. I had to make nearly all the publicity myself, which we got, and I cannot go on doing that. It would wreck our movement if I did, for in that case everyone would get sick of the sight of my face and of my chatter.

If I were a rich woman I could set up this Center in a rapid way, I firmly believe. But I am not a rich woman. And for it to count large in the thought of women it should be set up by multitudes of women of course. Unfortunately for my enthusiasms, I am old and very tired physically. What is more to the point: I must leave the New York scene and its environs.

I'd like to commune personally with you, Mrs. Irwin, you, Mrs. Holden, and you, Mrs. Grove, to whom I am sending this message. But we are far apart now physically and that seems impossible. So please take my word for the deed of traveling to see you. I am yours forever and a day.

> With love and respect—
> Mary R. Beard

Just after Mary Beard's decision to resign from the World Center for Women's Archives, Rosika Schwimmer wrote to let her know that she had made a tentative arrangement to place her own archives and library in the New York Public Library and wanted to alert the board of the WCWA before the final settlement. Her closing lines were, "I have buried many dreams in these last decades. The World Center for Women's Archives goes now with the lot." [14] Mary Beard was still, willfully, somewhat more hopeful.

83. TO ROSIKA SCHWIMMER

> World Center for Women's
> Archives, Inc.
> New York City
> July 10, 1940

Dear Mme. Schwimmer:

I understand fully your feeling that your dreams are lost. I don't like to raise the question respecting the inevitability of shocks to dreaming but, as I now try to analyze the slow progress toward a great Women's Archive, I come to the conclusion that dreams must be subjected to sharp realities for their realization if anything approaching their designs is attained.

I have tried for five years to *force* the Archive into existence, my faith matching your dream. Now I realize that more groundwork must be laid—the reality. But I am also convinced that your-my dream of a great Women's Archive is not lost. In truth there is an active nucleus of the present Board membership which is determined to carry the idea and build up a visible collection of important archives of women. Though I have had to resign from the Board because of utter weariness, I am confident that the work will go on and I believe that it will go on better than if I were to continue my forced feeding.

On my part I shall try to strengthen the foundation in thought about women. I am going to have a new edition of my book called "On Understanding Women" this autumn reentitled WOMAN: CO-MAKER OF HISTORY. I hope to widen and deepen curiosity respecting what women have wanted of life and have tried to procure. For competence in such a report, I of course need your own archives and I regret beyond my power to say to you that World Center for Women's Archives, the idea of which you originated, is not functioning yet with your documents available to me.

As for purchasing them now, that is impossible it seems. I have spoken to all the persons I know who should have wanted to buy them for WCWA. The Board will not be able to get them within your ten day limit. It knows that you have invaluable papers. It does not have access to funds at this time. I can only rejoice that you are able to place them in a "New York institution". You will let us know what institution as soon as you can, I feel sure.

If some one else had been your spokesman for your dream, it is possible and probable that it might have borne fruit by this time. Obviously I have not been the perfect spokesman, if any good at all. Knowing my inadequacies I have been instrumental in turning over the task to other members of the Board who will now undertake to accomplish more than I could attain.

I wanted to call upon you on Monday night of this week which I spent in town. But my long day had been spent in placing the most important archives the Center has acquired in preserving wrappers, as the final step in my fiduciary trust. And I was so exhausted by night-fall that I just couldn't get to you.

I hope that you will be charitable toward me and my failure to find the benefactor who would endow the Center with your materials.

As for a peaceful world order, that dream I am completely powerless to discuss.

My affection for you and your sister is still sincere. I have gained in countless ways by being privileged to visit with you now and then. I would have seen more of you if I could have managed to extend this privilege. May the world approach the dream of order and decency as members of the WCWA Board are approaching the dream of a Women's Archive though admittedly it is a lesser dream.

Cordially as ever, Mary R. Beard

Imagining that the WCWA would continue without her, Mary Beard retained her confidence in Marjorie White and moved on to revising and supplementing her 1931 book, *On Understanding Women*, for a new edition. She had always felt it was "choked with typographical errors on which a critic could dwell with damaging effect," and when the publisher, Longmans, Green and Co., offered to bring out a corrected second edition, she took the opportunity to write a new first chapter.[15]

84. TO MARJORIE WHITE

World Center for Women's
Archives, Inc.
New York City
July 11, 1940

Dear Marjorie White:

The need for a "survey" of WCWA uptodate, pursued within the immediate weeks for basic decisions in the early autumn pertaining to the right kind of office, etc., is one which I recognize as an imperative. In the circumstances Mrs. Hansl is to study our history and our files and make the appraisal with the advice and aid of the executive committee.

I am resigning from all official responsibility and my release includes my release as archives chairman. On this account I am informing all the projects chairmen that the projects are to take a vacation until further notice comes in re Board decisions.

You and I together—mostly you—have created a fine legacy, as we know. I have every reason to believe that the Board will gradually understand what we have done. I have told Mrs. Hansl that, if questions arise as she goes into the survey of our movement, you, who are near at hand and who know everything else as well as I do and the filing system even better, can be consulted more profitably than anyone else. I have told her very positively that I have always found you utterly devoted to the interests of WCWA and that I could have done nothing without you.

I am leaving the directorate to others entirely now because I am just too weary to carry the load which I assumed any longer. But the load will be carried better, I am convinced, without my burden-bearing. I am not a good Board member of anything. I do not have the experience and sagacity for such team work; it requires infinite patience and conference and I have time and strength for neither. Luckily new members will be taken into the Board and a loyal and enthusiastic executive committee of the present Board seems to be hard at work to keep our ship on an even keel.

As advocate on the shore, I shall be the best rooter I can for WCWA hereafter.

Your relations and mine have given me deep pleasure based on our mutual concept of a great Center and our mutual effort to make it a realised fact. I hope that in the reorganization, your talents and fidelity and enthusiasm will be recognized and utilized.

Let us see each other when we can and commune on the overarching universe as we envisage it in our respective ways.

For a few weeks I must concentrate on the new edition of my book, On Understanding Women, which I am to have issued this autumn. I have promised to turn in the copy by the last of August, around the 20th if possible, and to carry out that pledge I must work with might and main, eschewing all temptations to leave this job.

If I have the sense, this revision will widen and deepen a foundation for thinking about women and history and thus about the universe. It is a high ambition. I am a low-brow. But if I can add a few stones to the understructure and strengthen its base, even a little, I shall still be doing my bit for WCWA. Give me your blessing and pray for my insight and vigor.

When I have sent in my copy, then come to the country for a visit with me where we can talk in peace and try to reason further together.

With genuine affection,
Mary R. Beard

The following postmortem of the New York situation from Mary Beard's point of view shows both how petty and how deep the organizational problems ran. It tends to confirm the view that Beard was deeply hurt by the board's unwillingness to place confidence in Marjorie White as well as herself.

85. TO MIRIAM HOLDEN

[New Milford, Connecticut]
August 15 [1940]

Dear Miriam:

I really can't bear to have us misunderstand each other after years now of close association. If I can just clear up one point at issue by this one more letter to you, my heart will be considerably lighter. This is still that miserable matter of Marjorie White. But it involves so much of our trouble that I bring it back just this once more. Please try to look at that affair through my eyes and then tell me once more where I err:

WCWA was supposed to work for Women's Archives.

It was not designed to be a library except insofar as some one might prefer to think of it in that way as having letters, manuscripts and other *source* materials (not printed stuff) as some libraries have. If we got books, we were glad but books were to be supplementary to the source materials and not the prime business of WCWA. Our first literature defined our aims and later literature explained the kind of materials we were seeking.

I was chairman of archives—

Unable to handle the whole quest for documents by myself, I pleaded for assistance and asked for M. White as the available secretary for *my* work.

I knew what she was doing when she was helping me. When the Board had too little money she volunteered because she was deeply interested and believed that my plan of research for important documents was on the right basis.

I was given no other help of any kind.

I was never asked whether M. Shouse could be of value to me. She was put in to her post, first by Miss Beatty, and then by Miss Judson, you and Mrs. Grove, as I understand, to keep books and run such office business as it was supposed she could run

I had to do what I could about archives by writing my own letters, with such help as I could get with interviews, letters, etc. from M. White alone.

When I saw that several of the Board were disliking her, I felt that my word of her value ought to be regarded as my competence on this matter. I felt that I was the one to be criticised if criticism was made. I tried to tell the Board on two or three occasions what she was doing for me but when I mentioned in one such report that she had got Mary Dreier's pledge of papers for instance, Miss Beatty declared that she had seen Miss Dreier and that was that. No doubt she did. I had written her and we are old old good friends but it took an interview by M. White to get the definite pledge. This is but an illustration of the difficulty I had both as to my position and as to my competence in knowing what I was doing.

I felt that to ask the Board to hear her tell of her work, when I barely got to talk myself about Archives, was not the right procedure and that if she was to be on the defensive, I was on the defensive first.

The winter I was in the South, I paid for M. White to carry on for me. We conferred constantly by mail and she made great headway at the office with ARCHIVES—

It was natural for her to like working at this particular thing for we both felt we were accomplishing real work, amid many difficulties, including M. Shouse's dislike of having the interviews, etc. take place at the office. As far as possible this was avoided and taken care of elsewhere.

I did not give M. White the office key. She may have asked M. Shouse for it. If she did, when she did it was because she could only get letters written and take care of interviews late in the day or on Saturdays with such persons as Dr. Clara Lynch who was not free to consult her about cooperation for my work at any other time. When I could be in town and stay for the last train, I was also present at interviews at those times. Without a key, they couldn't have been possible even for me. Miss White, having one, was some times able to receive such persons if I myself was a bit late. In this way Professor Reimer conferred with us—the only hour she could come.

Whatever the limitations of manner this woman possesses, as long as she was getting results for me, as chairman of archives, it still seems to me that if I had any value as chairman of Archives, I was the one to be disowned or reproved instead of my assistant. Or given another one more agreeable to others

But Miss White was used by you and others for other purposes now and then, whether I was paying her salary or not. Thus she acquired an anomalous position—made necessary in part by the lack of a staff sufficient to do all the necessary work of sorts other than the archives business

NOW isn't this picture of the past a correct one? Or is there something fundamentally wrong with it?

The fact is, I gradually learned, that your devotion lay in books. I was glad that the Gallant Am. Women [radio] program gave play to that interest of yours. I hope it will continue. I share it of course myself as my approach to this whole WCWA enterprise grew out of the years I had been reading books. But all that we need to know about women is by no means in books. And it is my knowledge of that truth PLUS my concern with the preserving of contemporary documents for books yet to be written that makes me so keen about WCWA.

Practically nothing has been written for many years on Women in Science. That is why I plugged away at the materials for it. But Mrs. Hansl got the idea that I was just trying, with M. White's help, to do a Who's Who on scientific women. That is not true.

No I am terribly sad to have WCWA fail and to be out of a movement which is so dear to me. But you cannot deny that I got precious little backing. You did all you could, dear Miriam. I am appreciative to the deeps of my being for your friendship and for our association for the idea which we were trying to realize—for the dream we were attempting to make come true.

Perhaps I should have come to the luncheon at Mrs. Hansl's. I am so moved to learn that those of you who did expressed your own strong affection for our movement. Perhaps too sensitively I felt that I had become a bete noire.

The future? Mrs. Moffett took us up a blind alley. Unintentionally of course. So we are stranded financially.

But I am hoping that Washington will still want to have the Center itself. That would be a dignified solution, don't you agree? Its interest may have petered out but I am trying to discover whether it is possible to revive its proclaimed desire to establish a great Women's Archive there.

This is more than a project for librarians. We are not ready for an archivist yet. No Historical Society, in my opinion, is the right patron at all.

When the Board reassembles in October, I shall come to the meeting with or without a ray of hope from Washington. A decision about our future will of course have to be taken then. My resignation takes effect at the end of the present annual roll call. In view of our destitution there can hardly be another Annual Meeting and a new Board in New York at least. I must help like all the rest of us who have been loyal to clean up our debris.

Forgive me for writing you another such long letter. I have now said really all I can say about the past.

My love to you   Mary

[P.S.] I am sorry I can't take Charles to East Hampton this summer. He is too busy to go off anywhere

●≻─

In August and early September 1940 Beard tried desperately to see if the Washington unit would lead the World Center for Women's Archives, for the New York board wanted to dissolve the corporation. She stressed arguments that had been brought to her earlier, about the appropriateness of locating the center in the nation's capital. But by September 9 she had to admit that no rejuvenation in Washington was likely, for "a new leadership would have to be found to overcome the 'blight' which settled over our Branch there."

The letter sent out to members over Inez Irwin's signature on September 16, 1940, announcing the dissolution of the World Center for Women's Archives, Inc., cited the fund-raising difficulties occasioned by the threat of world war. Mary Beard could take comfort only in the fact that the African-American women whom she had encouraged *did* succeed on their own in mounting an exhibition on women's history at the Negro Exposition in Chicago in August 1940. Indeed, the group within the National Council of Negro Women that formed to cooperate with the WCWA effort became a permanent archives committee and continued to function for decades afterward.[16]

In the letter below Beard says she does not like using the notion that the WCWA failed as "a war casualty," yet she gave that reason to her old friend Florence Kitchelt, explaining, "WORLD ORDER or a World War seems to engage EVERYWOMAN's attention now."[17] No doubt she equally disliked dwelling on the mountain of petty squabbles that preceded the demise. Given Beard's commitment to preserving and enhancing women's memory of their own activities, the last line of this bitterly sarcastic letter is especially wrenching.

86. TO MIRIAM HOLDEN

[New Milford, Connecticut]
October 10, 1940

Dear Miriam:

Thanks for sending me the minutes and for your gracious-as-ever letter. Of course there will be, could be, no dissolution of our friendship.

I shall always have a guilty feeling about us all as a Board Unit. We had
no right to suppose that we could get anywhere the way we were going:
with no publicity, no finance chairman, no membership chairman, no
plans ahead. I don't like to hide behind the idea that we are a casualty of
war because I think we are hiding behind our own inefficiency but this is
the best we can do in the circumstances. Inez Irwin meant so well when
she wrote to everybody that my leadership had been followed. If I say that
this makes me ashamed or a scapegoat, I am told that I have an inferiority
complex.

But there is no good in reviewing this story. I have learned that my true
place is in the home!

I have only myself to blame for not saying a year or more ago that we
were making a failure of the whole thing by our ineptitude.

I have only goodwill for every one on the Board who, no more than I,
could do other than she did. You certainly were lavishly hospitable to us
all and I know that I was a source of worry to you many times and more.
We shall have to work through this experience emotionally and mentally
in our respective ways but I hope to forget as much of it as I can.

Affectionately as always
Mary R. Beard

5 Alternatives to the Archives

In Baltimore for the academic year 1940–41 with her husband—who was constantly under fire for his political views—Mary Beard carried on. She went about finding appropriate locations for the papers that had been donated to the World Center for Women's Archives. In October 1940 she gave the Littauer lectures at Hunter College in New York on the subject "Women in the Modern World," drawing an audience she estimated at two thousand. She and Marjorie White were also germinating a new plan for an encyclopedia on women, referred to in the letter below as the CYC. In the spring of 1941, upon the invitation of Walter Yust, the editor of the *Encyclopaedia Britannica*, this instead became a project to evaluate existing entries and to write new ones for that established institution. Beard led three researchers (including Marjorie White) and engaged other writers besides, on the venture, which produced a stunning critique of the male-centeredness of the *Britannica* and set forth vivid models for change. Yust's promises for transformation never came to fruition, however.[1]

The letter below also refers to an unprecedented event at the annual meeting of the American Historical Association (AHA) in 1940: the appearance of a full panel devoted to women's history. Under the chairmanship of Merle Curti, the program committee of the AHA set up several sessions around the theme of "the common man," including one on "The Negro in the History of the United States," chaired by W.E.B. Du Bois and one on "Class in American Labor History." As Beard notes, she was asked to chair the session called "Some Aspects of the History of Women" but declined. Instead, the dean of Vassar College, Mildred Thompson, a historian who had published works on Reconstruction, chaired the panel. Jeannette Nichols of Swarthmore College spoke on "The Nurture of Feminism in the United States," and Lillian Fisher of Oklahoma College for Women gave a paper called "The Influence of the Mexican Revolution on the Status of Women." Vera Brown Holmes of Smith College and Alma Lutz commented.[2] While Beard continued trying to influence the curricula of colleges and universities—even more avidly after the demise of the World Center for Women's Archives—she distanced herself from standard academic ladders and professional organizations. Or did they distance her? Her letter suggests that Curti's invitation, well meant as it was, did not to her mind sufficiently respect her own pride of place. She was, at the time of this letter, almost sixty-five years old.

87. TO MARJORIE WHITE

> The Wyman Park
> Baltimore, Md.
> January 18, 1941

Dear Marjorie:

So much I want to say to you. So little chance to say anything. I greatly appreciated your long critical letter and look forward to a long talk with you just a few weeks ahead.

Enclosed are some items for the CYC, taken, with the exception of the obituary of Dr. Kate [Hurd]-Mead, from a WCWA batch of papers which I brought down from Mrs. Hansl's office recently. The loss of Kate Mead is a deep sorrow to me. Her second volume of women's medical history will have to be brought out post mortem by some other woman doctor. I shall do all I can to see that this is accomplished. It was about ready for the press.

First I want to clear up for you the matter of women's appearance at that Am. Hist. Assn. Annual meeting. I had nothing whatever to do with the planning of the first session in the history of this Assn. for the discussion of women. I was invited to preside over this session after the speakers had been selected and their themes chosen. I refused to preside for I could have said so little as a chairman and would have seemed to be delighted with the set-up of this program. I couldn't knock it, for it was a gain—perhaps?—to have it at all. In fact I even covered up my refusal by saying simply that I could not be present as I would not be in New York at the time. Merle Curti was so eager to do something and meant to honor me. I wish I could have made a speech. I sent a lot of material to Jeanette Nichols for hers but I judge she used little, if any, of it, though she had asked me to help her, as she had never given any attention to the matter of women in history. DON'T REPEAT WHAT I AM TELLING YOU ABOUT THIS.

But it is bully that the Assn has appointed a committee of women and men to take up the slack from now on. I am writing Mrs. Nichols to learn about its set-up.

I am waiting with considerable excitement a meeting this next Monday—the monthly meeting of the presidents of Bryn Mawr and

Swarthmore. Felix Morley is to bring before it my suggestion as his own thoroughly approved one now that the growing three-college program be extended to include a communal Women's Library and Archive. If he gets it across, boys and girls alike, of those colleges, will be made aware of a long-neglected "field" of exploration. Let's hope for this triumph. I know Mr. Morley and he wants to be creatively efficient.

As usual you were generous about my paper composed for the Women's Congress. I felt that I should put the discussion of the new objectives up to those women and not define them myself, give them background for their discussion. But all I hear seems to indicate that it was a very sterile congress indeed. However, I do not feel exactly as you do about the labor-union, or all-labor movement, approach to or solution of the social problems. I put into the Labor Chapter of Charles' and my recent book, America in Midpassage, my ideas on that point. I have worked directly with unions in the labor movement. I know John Lewis and Philip Murray and other leaders of the CIO. In my opinion, the American middle class is stronger instead of weaker via capitalism, contrary to the Marxist theory of destiny. So our labor movement's future is involved in that fact. The issues are not so sharply defined as they were in Russia, for example.

Anyway, my attitude is not one of "pulling punches" but of a concept of the complications. Marxists tend to oversimplify, in my opinion, for the American scene.

I am keen to learn about that "episode at the Grolier Club" at which you only hint. I might be able to see you for a weeny time on Feb. 14 when I come to NYC to "address" the AAUW. I'll let you know.

The Blatch Memorial? I know nothing of any proposal to collect the tributes paid her, much less any proposal to publish them. And as for the reproduction of mine in a national magazine, I have no interest among editors; I mean they have no interest in me. I fear they have none in Harriot Stanton Blatch—the graver sin of course.

Hoping for a pow-wow on

Valentine's Day   Yours—Mary

[P.S.] I am not sure whether I told you that the National Council of Negro Women at its recent annual meeting in the Labor Bldg in Washington voted to establish a Mary Bethune Memorial in the form of a Negro Women's Archive! They are wise women. I have sent them some of the material WCWA had on Negro women, such as the copy of an article on old Mrs. Bowles of St. Louis.

I am holding materials given by Alice Lachmund which were not just right for the Carl Schurz Center to give to the Three College Women's Library in the event that it is voted.

◆◆~

The following letter addresses an aspiring woman intellectual who, like Mary Beard, was married to a scholar more famous and distinguished than she was: Luella Gettys was the wife of political scientist V. O. Key. As Beard here reveals, the sad fate of the World Center for Women's Archives was succeeded by another blow, the refusal of Longmans, Green and Co. to publish her revision of *On Understanding Women*. She wrote with spleen to a closer friend that "the publisher didn't like" the character of her new first chapter. "In 1940 the sacrosanct Carrie Chapman Catt was declaring at the World's Fair in New York that women hate war and love peace and they must stop war. I demonstrated that this is too sweeping a generalization and the editor didn't want the 'great leader' criticized, while she was alive at least. So there was never a new edition." [3]

The revised version is not to be found, unfortunately. It would be fascinating to see how Beard "ironed out all the signs of sex resentment" from the original. Her intent to do so indicates that she was leaving behind any stress on men's domination in her analysis of women in history. Her experiences and failures during the 1930s had left her at least as disappointed in women as supporters of the interests of their sex as she was skeptical of men's goodwill—and perhaps more so.

88. TO LUELLA GETTYS

New Milford—Connecticut
April 25, 1941

Dear Luella Gettys:
   You are a "prolific" writer and editor but that is not the whole story of your writing.
   Thanks without stint—and not as a "stint"—for sending me your opuses, many-paged, and in pamphlet form. Your subjects are important. You write with scholarly care. If I had read my Political Science Review in the library at the Hopkins, I would have been familiar with your Canadian Federalism article before I left Baltimore, but we had not had our magazines forwarded during the winter and only now have we begun to catch up with this Review. Anyway I like Reprints and am so glad to have yours.

Having worked to get the legislation which provides more security for American women married to foreigners, your study of the large question of Naturalization means much to me as the larger if inclusive question.

You have the training and mind of a scholar. I am a blunderbuss by comparison. But I am daring to send you a copy of one of my blunderings through the maze of history searching for Woman. I have to be honest and mark the errata before you read it. They show me up horribly as a too-ready-to-print gal. But what I print has to be rushed along to get anything of my very own out between orgies of co-authorship with CAB. The orgies have a pleasure all their own and so do the separate thrusts at self-expression, though in the individual case I am more embarrassed by the weaknesses of the outcome.

Longmans, Green promised me that I could have a new edition of the book I am sending you, to appear late in 1941. I prepared the revision and, with their consent, ironed out all the signs of sex resentment which appear in the copy you are getting. I had changed the title to indicate that I was trying to review history and the new edition was announced in mid-autumn of last year as Woman: Co-Maker of History. But I had opened with a current story of women's helping to make war—today and through the yesterdays. That is not a marketable proposition at this hour of history and the publishers did not like the new opening. So the revision is in cold storage, as I am sure I told you. My main regret is that it had corrected all the errors which appear, marked, in the copy I am sending you. Anyway I have the right to get another publisher and, with longer time for improvement, the better book will be on the market some day.

The physical distance between us now is longer but not the basis of mental communion. I cannot say that I have attained the scholarship which would eliminate the mental distance but I can say that I appreciate exceeding care, caution, and that kind of reportage.

I think CAB will look less like an "asphalt flower" next week when he lectures again at the Hopkins. It will be better for him when he no longer has to climb all those stairs to his office, for when one is nearing the seventies the heart usually resists that particular kind of strain. Yet perhaps the heart follows the leadership of the mind (pace Christian Scientists) and forgets to palpitate itself when the mind decides that what it is attempting is supremely worth while. Best wishes to you and "V.O." as I heard him called so much.

Most cordially yours,
Mary R. Beard

The following short note suggests both Mary Beard's voracious reading—for the recently founded *North Georgia Review* was hardly well
known—and her intensifying one-woman battle against what she saw as
the falsities of a feminist worldview that negated women's past strengths
and vital historical role. The article on which she comments below was
written by the editors of the journal, Southerners Lillian Smith (later the
famous author of *Strange Fruit* and *Killers of the Dream*) and her companion Paula Snelling. Written as the United States joined in the world
war, Smith and Snelling's essay focused on men's war-making propensities, claiming, in effect, that the repeated resort to mass violence was the
result of one male group's projection onto another of their common ha-
tred, fear, and jealousy of woman. The essay was heavily informed by
Freudian concepts and gender stereotypes and replete with assumptions
that Mary Beard questioned or repudiated—for instance, that women did
not bond in group loyalty as men did, that men had an affinity for death
not shared by women, that men had logic while women had babies. The
historical claims in the article, portraying women as only mothers, "aloof" from the making of civilization for ten thousand years while "the
group life of the race has been, directly, a creation of man," no doubt
infuriated Beard. Little in the essay could be called feminist besides the
authors' comment that "in extenuation of our sex's sins, we remember
that we are an oppressed group, that man put our mind in prison."

It is a mark of Beard's growing single-mindedness that she castigated
the authors for unadulterated feminism rather than for being hostage to
psychoanalysis (a bête noire of hers later in the 1940s). Smith and Snelling were interested or brave enough to print Beard's negative as well as
her positive comments in the next issue of the journal, along with praise
for "Man Born of Woman" from several readers.[4]

89. TO LILLIAN SMITH AND PAULA SNELLING

[New Milford, Conn.]
April 30, 1942

Dear Editors of the North Georgia Review:

Your magazine has some superb qualities informational, interpretative,
stylistic. I consider it of high importance in the journalistic "field." I shall
call it to the attention of others, insistently, in the hope of getting more
subscriptions for you.

BUT I regret your assumptions respecting women of which your MAN BORN OF WOMAN in your Winter number smells to high heaven. In my opinion, those assumptions are not warranted by the actual history of women and are narrowly restricted to the feminist psychosis of the 19th century in America. I myself held your point of view for many many years; but I widened and deepened my ideas of man born of woman and woman born of man after I had explored woman in the time-depth of long history down to the very origins of society. Now I regard *unadulterated* feminism as one of the shallowest ideologies ever formulated. Please note, however, that I underline an aspect of it. Your exposition in that Winter number of your journal I consider unadulterated.

You are frank and you will let me be too, I believe.

I am greatly indebted to Motier Harris Fisher for calling my attention to your generally exceptional Journal, however, and I shall welcome its issues as generally enlightened and enlightening.

Sincerely yours,   Mary R. Beard

•◦—

Beard got back in touch with Anne Martin to have her ghostwrite her own biography for the *Encyclopaedia Britannica*. As she wrote this letter—and for two years thereafter, as she set other women to do sketches—Beard believed that editor Yust of the *Britannica* was going to insert her additions and revisions piecemeal into the multivolume series.

The following letter is one of the few in which Beard mentions the world war at all; her extant correspondence for the war years is slight, and her views on the American intervention are not spelled out. To the extent that women reached new positions of power and prestige in the government and in men's occupations as a result of the war, one must assume that Beard was deeply ambivalent and perhaps utterly repelled. Below, she slights a *Yale Review* article by Ada L. Comstock, president of Radcliffe College from 1923 to 1943, which focused on examples of women's wartime participation similar or parallel to men's involvement. Perhaps Beard was especially put off by Comstock's observation that women "were more numerous and effective on the side of early and complete commitment to the cause of the Allies, thus disappointing the predictions of those opponents of women's suffrage who believed that a country in which women voted would follow a pacifist policy."[5]

90. TO ANNE MARTIN

[New Milford, Conn.]
June 21, 1942

Dear Anne Martin:

I wish I could look forward to going west to Carmel and to a good talk with you there. Alas for pleasure-planning in these horrible warring times! But it is an unexpected and true pleasure to have a letter from you and news of your continued affirmations in the press.

I have read every word of yours in the Pine Cone and the Cymbal which you sent to me, with intense interest. A great book awaits its author on the Hero which will take account, I think, both of conventional ideals of heroism and of women as hero in a more revolutionary sense. So is *everything* yet to be written. But it seems to me that our fellow-women all too lightly turn to activities at the very moments of crises when they should be participating in intellectual and moral idea-formulations. On this point I am particularly distressed by an article in the last Yale Review written by Ada Comstock—head of a woman's college at that!

Maybe she would also acclaim "Ann Sheridan's Tour of Army Camps"? The Carmel Cymbal delivered what I consider a fully-merited blast at that. The New Yorker also drove at the degradation of soldiers and women alike in the present policies which do not seem to me to be above the level of the prostitution on the edges of the camps one iota. And how few of our women really seem to care how women are pictured to fighting men or to other men in fact!

The Britannica will be hospitable to some recordings of women—for a time at least. Great publicity has been given to my attack on its masculinity in an article on the Britannica which the Readers Digest, The Saturday Review, and the Time Magazine have just carried. It has awakened a lot of interest in the opening of more space for women. But my fear is that the editorial staff will be satisfied too soon with what is offered for the volumes. However, I shall at least be able to shoot in a lot of sketches of women and I am asked to make a critique on the whole set of volumes indicating where weakness exists now respecting women even in general articles and in relation to wives of men whose sketches are there and what special articles should be written to present peculiar historic knowledge, etc. Any ideas you have or get later, on these matters, I shall welcome and include in my report late this year as coming from you.

Best wishes to you and my very
warm regards—Mary R. Beard

~

In 1942, the Beards published the capstone to their series on the history of American civilization, *The American Spirit: A Study of the Idea of Civilization in the United States*. This work of intellectual history—in great part a compendium of quotations of writers in and on the United States—was the least successful in sales and in reviews of all their jointly written books. Charles Beard's *The Republic: Conversations on Fundamentals*, published in 1943, was much better received—hailed as "inspiring" and "a godsend"—except for reviewers' quarrels with his chapters on foreign relations. At the time of the following letter to Curti, the Beards were probably engaged in writing *A Basic History of the United States*, which was published in a sixty-nine-cent edition in 1944 and outsold all of Charles Beard's and the couple's works, except for school texts. Curti published *The Growth of American Thought* in 1943.[6]

91. TO MERLE CURTI

[New Milford, Conn.]
October 18 [1943]

Dear Merle Curti, could any one fail to be depressed by a book he or she has published? Don't we always outgrow them the moment the last page has been written? What is the process of bookmaking but learning and growing? Any guy, male or female, who feels satisfied with a product of his mind, must surely suffer from arrested development.

If you get some rough treatment from reviewers, consider what the magazine Time calls CAB: "an old bald eagle," etc. And Louis Hacker again uses him in his review of The Republic, friendlier though he is to this volume, for his global dream.

And I? Well Lindsay Rogers in a charming review of The Republic in the Saturday Review closes with the remark that he understands I am writing a history of women, a subject about which he knows nothing, and hopes I will get a reviewer. Lindsay doesn't even suspect that I may have [already] attempted a book on that subject, that it did get immense reviews all over the USA. BUT, with reference to the aftermath of author depression, I know myself how deep it can go. For that book was dreadfully amateurish. I must of course try to handle the subject better in my tomorrow.

In brief, we who write are all in the same boat, if we are survivors of torpedoes, and we hope to reach the shores of thought with strength for more activity.

Forgive my pretension in feeling that I might be in the same boat with you and CAB.

Respectfully yours,
Mary R. Beard

•••—

The establishment of a Woman's Rights Collection at Radcliffe College, based around a donation of papers and books by alumna Maud Wood Park, leader of the NAWSA and League of Women Voters, was announced in 1943 at the same time that historian Wilbur K. Jordan was appointed president of the college. President Jordan envisioned the foundation of a broader women's archives, and Harvard historian Arthur Schlesinger suggested that he consult Mary Ritter Beard.[7] Beard appears overjoyed in the following letter (written from Tryon, North Carolina, where the Beards were spending the winter). Jordan revived the possibility that her dream might be realized, however belatedly, at Radcliffe. Her warning him against a collection based on the narrative of struggle for equal rights presages the theme of her next book, *Woman as Force in History*, on which she was possibly already at work. The collection built around Park's papers was a distinctive part, but not the whole of the Radcliffe Women's Archives when it opened to the public in 1949; thus Jordan moved some distance in the direction Beard advocated.

Beard related the anecdote about Chase Going Woodhouse, in the letter below, more than once. Woodhouse had founded the Institute for Women's Professional Relations in New London, Connecticut, and in the 1930s served as Secretary of State for Connecticut. In Beard's eyes, Woodhouse's definition of modern women's problem as the adjustment of home life to career was superficial, her advocacy of home economics training for women in college misplaced, and her failure to see that women had a distinct mission in public life infuriating. To a personal friend, Beard commented at about this same time that Woodhouse had "a limited if practical view of education, being wholly absorbed in the business and professional relations of women and men. She is not a reflective thinker. She is not concerned with the direction and upshot of careering. . . . I know Dr. Woodhouse and she has her place. But I regard it as a restricted and restricting place."[8]

The letter sums up what remained of Beard's accomplishments in the WCWA. It also shows her extensive knowledge of the location of women's documents at institutions around the United States. Practitioners in the field of women's history today owe her a tremendous debt for sponsoring interest in the preservation of women's documents. In 1945 Mary Beard gave to Radcliffe her own papers from the World Center for Women's Archives, the Leonora O'Reilly papers, the Inez Irwin papers, and other important collections over which she had control.

92. TO WILBUR K. JORDAN, PRESIDENT OF RADCLIFFE COLLEGE

Pine Crest Inn
Tryon, North Carolina
January 14, 1944

Dear President Jordan:

I am completely out of bounds with pleasure over your letter. A Radcliffe-Harvard combination is the ideal agency for exercising an enlightened leadership in the education of women and men with respect to men and women. Your "lively hope" matches my dream of such an enterprise. It would crown beginnings at Syracuse University, Scripps College, and Smith College with the halo of elder statesmanship. I shall be honored by the chance to participate in any way in the promotion of this vital educational movement at Cambridge.

Your conception of it, like mine, inheres of course in the definition of purpose. We are in complete agreement that it should be defined "quite broadly." And in the definition are enclosed your questions dealing with chronological limits or topical controls of the collection which you have under consideration.

If you should undertake to conform merely with feministic jingoism you could *restrict* your collection both chronologically and topically to what is called the equal rights credo. According to its proscriptions, women were a subject sex through all the ages until English and American rebels broke that "tyranny of men" and "emancipated women from slavery." In conformity with such a definition of men and women, with such an interpretation of history, a collection of materials on women could date only from 1848 when a conference at Seneca Falls launched a movement for full civil liberties—equal liberties—for women which had repercussions round the globe. In that case, the materials could be confined to documents about the rebels and their rebellion, to changes in statutory law, to the admission of women to institutional education, to their trend from domesticity to industry, capitalistic business and professional enterprise, and womanpower for war. The topical composition of collected documents could be quickly, easily, outlined. They could represent the most comprehensive archive of British-American feminism in the modern form to be found anywhere.

But in my opinion that would help to freeze like the icyness of a glacial age the interpretation of history as a history of masculine tyranny and feminine subjection until the first bright girls of the ages, conceived as English and American, "woke up" and made women who had been as nothing throughout history into something called a "human being." This feministic jingoism was compressed into six words by Dr. Chase Going Woodhouse in a recent speech delivered to a club of business and professional women, which I heard. She declared that she wanted engraved on her tombstone this dictum: "Born a woman; died a person!" I wanted to cry out: "Born a woman; died a stiff!"

The deep and deadening influence of the feministic interpretation of all history I have tried to oppose for many years, after discovering its character and observing its harmful effects on men and women alike. It has shaped the concept of equal education into the concept of equal education in the history of men only—a history embracing the development of all branches of learning, all the arts and sciences, all government and politics and war, all economy and culture, all important thinking and all philosophies. The effect has been to make woman a sex lost to history and to weaken a segment of society into infantile imitation, to the injury of all.

Believing that what we think about long history is the substance of what we think about current history in the making and our roles or functions in the process—in short our vision of the morrow—I regard the problem of educational leadership on the collegiate and university levels today, in respect of "equal education", as one of widening and deepening knowledge concerning the *force* of woman as well as the *force* of man in history. If you will look at my address at Mt. Holyoke, delivered at a luncheon (alumnae) in 1937 during the centennial celebration, you will see something [of] the large meaning which I put into this matter.

If defined "quite broadly," the research collection that you propose to build would, in my opinion, include materials running back to colonial times in America and further back in English history. I am discovering how right Elizabeth Decker (or is her name Dexter?) has been in her claim that our colonial women had and exercised all the liberties they wanted. Certainly her "Colonial Women of Affairs" is testimony to wide-ranging activities though far from an exhaustive story of them. Mrs. Lamb's two immense volumes on the "history of New York" from its

Dutch foundations indicate feminine liberties and prowess there. And as for women of all the frontiers, they were creative, productive, civilization-bearers, to a degree not even imagined by the Turner school of historians or by James Truslow Adams.

The identification of formal schooling with all education has done infinite harm to the mental feeling of, by, and for women. How could Abigail Adams write the letters she composed and Mercy Otis Warren write that extraordinarily penetrating "History of the American Revolution" if they had no education? How could the logical, eloquent, informed women of the ante-civil-war period write, speak, edit, and organize as they did if they had no education? One of my prime contentions is that formal institutional education has robbed women particularly of their consciousness of their previous intellectual power as learning and the ability to express themselves.

To comprehend the power of women of English stock in America, one must know about their ancestors of that stock. For light on American women as a whole, one must turn the lamp of learning on women of other stocks too.

Materials for keeping that lamp lighted must be found in published works as well as in unprinted materials. Hence it will be necessary to collect as fine a library of books revealing women in all history as may be possible.

But I must go on to your special inquiry relative to existing facilities and whether you would be duplicating them. I can assure you that there is not now available in any library a "wholly satisfactory collection" of materials dealing with the "historical status and cultural contributions of women in this country and England." Nor is there in any library even a wholly satisfactory collection of materials dealing with the equal rights movement alone. I make this statement out of knowledge gathered from an attempt to discover what institutions have materials on women and what they have. This attempt went far enough for that, as a project of a committee functioning under the Board of the World Center for Women's Archives now defunct as a war casualty. I was chairman of this committee. We were assembling a clearing house of information about materials in collections over the country with a view to enabling inquirers at our proposed great Archive to pursue their researches beyond its materials if need be.

I have in my files at home in New Milford, Connecticut, the results of that survey as far as it went. It discovered many collections of unprinted source materials in public libraries, in historical society libraries, in college libraries, in the D.A.R. and Colonial Dames headquarters, and in the Congressional Library. But the women's colleges which, in a few instances, have materials, have tended to collect only papers dealing with their own history and their own graduates, just as the women's patriotic societies have limited their collections to materials on the wars in our history. One of the richest collections of women's letters of the colonial age is at the Wm. Clements Library at Ann Arbor. Chapel Hill has recently gathered up a fine collection of Southern women's letters running back to colonial times and covering the war between the states. The Huntington Library has a miscellaneous lot of manuscripts, a list of which a friend of mine copied for me. Medical women have started an archive of their history at the University of Louisiana. Scripps College has been enlarging its book and manuscript facilities within the last four years. Syracuse University where a course on women in history is in its second year (in American history) has begun to assemble materials for students. Smith College is now reaching out for a broad collection and its promoters hope to launch instruction on women in history before long. At the University of Louisiana are rich materials, I am told, on women of the Mississippi Valley. There are some items on women of the old Spanish southwest in the Bancroft collection at Berkeley. The New York Public Library has important materials, in its great Theatre section, many manuscripts of assorted kinds, and it was given last year Rosika Schwimmer's magnificent immense volume of papers dealing with the feminist and peace movements in Europe in which she was so dynamic. After the nationwide agitation for a great Women's Archive got under way, the Congressional Library, directed by Mr. MacLeish, began to widen its collection of materials on women and it got some valuable documents, notably unworked letters of Susan B. Anthony and the unpublished papers of Mercy Otis Warren presented by her direct descendant, Charles Warren, whose wife recently gave a large fund to Harvard for the promotion of historical research.

The logic of that gift to Harvard, I wrote Mrs. Warren whom I had met in Washington, was the promotion of materials for the study of women in history. Her reply was: "Well you see, dear Mrs. Beard, I am not an intellectual." Fortunately you, dear President Jordan, are one.

You have near at hand the Galatea Collection in the Boston Public Library. I understand that it is exceedingly large and important. But unworked. You could refer researchers to that one and use it to avoid duplications. As for duplications further afield, you could strengthen your own collection by microfilming materials of basic importance from distant institutions.

In my opinion—one that led me to give nearly four years and several thousand dollars to try to establish a great central Archive—we need in this vast continent one place in which students, professors, writers, and serious researchers can concentrate their time and energy as well as save money from traveling costs. At this center with its clearing house of information, researchers could learn just where they must go to find materials not housed at the Center. The great and cheap modern process of microfilming can reduce even that amount of traveling.

On my return home the last of March, I can go through my files pertaining to the work for the central Archive, and turn over to you, if you would like to have them, documents which might be very helpful to your enterprise by saving you time at least. It will give me intense pleasure to come to Cambridge for a talk about the project early in April if that would seem worth your while, at least in prospect of advantage.

In the meantime if you will look into the books I have written on women (and ignore the dreadful typographical errors that mar my volume, On Understanding Women), you may be able to decide whether to invite me or to advise me to stay at home.

With every good wish for your progress as a creative intellectual and educator, I am

Sincerely yours,   Mary R. Beard

◦←

In this second letter to Jordan, Beard reviews her own recent educational efforts, especially on the *Encyclopaedia,* and lashes educators who had not caught her vision. The Vassar incident is one she never forgot; it seemed to epitomize, for her, the willful ignorance of so-called educated women in America.

93. TO WILBUR K. JORDAN, PRESIDENT OF
RADCLIFFE COLLEGE

Pine Crest Inn
Tryon, North Carolina
January 20, 1944

Dear President Jordan:

I am very glad indeed that you find my comment on your proposal worthy of your close attention. It is a privilege to discuss the proposal with the trustees and interested professors as well as with you through the medium of a letter. It may be too long for the best service. It would be wise, perhaps, in making copies for distribution to omit what I said about Mrs. Warren. I feel no animus against her of course and the story points the moral but her connection with Harvard might make it advisable to use the story, if at all, in verbal form to those who might be sure of my motive in telling it.

You are certainly right in proceeding "slowly and carefully". I shall be immensely pleased if you will come with Mrs. Hinckley to our home in New Milford for an examination of my files and for a larger talk about the project than correspondence permits. Any date that will be convenient for you both will be perfect for me—after April 5. Then, if you still feel, after discussing the matter with me in my home, that you want me to come to Cambridge before the project is formally presented I shall accept the invitation with full appreciation of the responsibility involved no less than the honor.

It will interest you, I think, to learn that very soon after the publication of my book, ON UNDERSTANDING WOMEN, President MacCracken invited me to Vassar to discuss its substance with the resident teachers. He had in mind the introduction of a course on the theme or some aspect. But to my amazement, among the great number of women teachers present, only one was not almost violently hostile. She was a Spanish woman teaching the Spanish language and literature. After listening to the discussion for a long time, she said: "I know what Mrs. Beard is talking about, as value." Her historic memory ran back to Isabella and she knew that both Spanish men and Spanish women have warm memories of more women of force in Spanish history. But the American women teachers cried as if with one voice: "The time has come to forget women! Now we are winning equality with men. We are becoming human beings." With no little heat I replied: "You can easily forget women. You know nothing to remember."

But President MacCracken suggested that they might at least have a course on the status of women. I said that that might only freeze the rigidity of mind that refused to take account of women in long history who were not bound by "status." Anyway the teachers did not want that course. Later President MacCracken, when he learned that the World Center for Women's Archives was not getting financial aid from any Foundation and little from other sources, came to our office in Radio City to ask whether Vassar might be the repository of the materials we had on hand. Our project, however, was far-reaching in scope and he did not have a fireproof place to take care of much material. He said it would take him ten years to get a building suitable for an important women's archive. I consider him highly intelligent respecting the need of widening women's and men's horizon for a vision of women. He is a great admirer of the Danish women who seem to him (a pre-war concept) so spirited and free.

It will also interest you to know that representatives of many university departments at Syracuse—men and women—have been cooperating to guide the experimental course there, in its second year, on women in American history. It is designed principally for the training of young women to be deans of women in colleges and the initiation in this matter was taken by Dean M. Eunice Hilton of Syracuse.

The Research feature of your proposal is essential to the utility of your collection of materials plan. I have read with care your Plan for its development. I have only praises for its excellence.

An illustration of the imperative nature of this feature is to be found in the thesis which Mary Benson wrote for her doctorate at Columbia University a few years ago. She called it "American Women of the Eighteenth Century", if I remember exactly. The Columbia Press printed it, I think [in 1935, as *Women in Eighteenth-Century America: A Study of Opinion and Social Usage*]. It depicted those women as seen through the eyes or wishful thinking of the colonial clergy, almost entirely. Their writings she explored at the Union Theological Seminary across the street. Who advised her? Evidently she lacked the knowledge of a single American woman of that century. Evidently her preceptors were in the same plight. As a kind of addenda, however, before her thesis was published, a little bibliography was inserted to indicate that others than theologs had written about those women. On the advice of whom was that addition made? After I had reviewed her book in Social Forces and pointed out its indirect exploration, Miss Benson wrote me of her regret and declared that she would try to make amends by studying directly the women of the antebellum period in the nineteenth century.

As for positions ahead accessible to women who may be trained at Radcliffe, let me say that there is immediately available one on the Encyclopaedia Britannica and no woman to fill it. This is the direction of a more enlightened treatment of women in the volumes. Something has been accomplished within the past two years under my direction in the way of biographies of women but I cannot carry on with this management owing to other work I feel I must now undertake. Ten years after my book On Understanding Women came out, some woman in Chicago called to the attention of the editor, Walter Yust, and his staff my "attack" in that book on the neglect of women in the Encyclopaedia. Immediately he asked me to discuss the matter with him in New York. Then he gave me three researchers whom I selected to assemble materials and write sketches. But these women could not write well in this especial field and I had to labor very hard to help them condense and yet give the utmost significance to each selected sketch. To carry on that work, trained writing as well as research is necessary.

I am not saying that I am trained. I am not. I am saying that women ought to be available for this important work on a great compendium so widely used. It was my firm conviction that the feminist dogma should not dominate the writing for this compendium. I tried to have the women of the sketches represent the force of women in as many centuries as possible and among as many peoples as possible in order that the narrowness of the mere "egalitarian" doctrine might be revealed. Mr. Yust is ready to go as far as competence in the research and writing go. While he admits frankly that he is not as interested as I am in pulling up the education respecting the role of women in history, he is hospitable to good work in that connection. I admit that my long history range of vision for the work on a compendium that embraces all times and places is overwhelming. But much can be done within its volumes *if* a woman with a long history consciousness, or even with a long view of American history, can be prepared to join Mr. Yust's staff of writers.

In the course of my labor with the Britannica, I made a report on the general articles in large number, with respect to their treatment of women, and suggested new articles that, in my opinion, should be written. I wish I could give you a copy of the report but Mr. Yust wishes to keep it confidential, naturally. He might be inclined, however, to give you a copy after you have won the support for your proposal. He is a very friendly person. He will be truly interested in your plan for research and literary training and publishing. Several women who go through your mill may find good writing opportunities under his aegis. In the great publicity recently given this Encyclopaedia, notably in The Saturday Review and the Christian Science Monitor, a prominent place was given to the fact that I had been taken on to overcome my indictment.

The World Book Encyclopedia also came into line with this trend toward a better understanding of women. I was invited a little over a year ago to rewrite an article on great American women composed by the League of Women Voters. Since "fools rush in where angels fear to tread," I did rewrite it and when I had sent in my own conception of such women, more space was assigned me to deal with more of them. Mr. J. Morris Jones had joined the staff of this educational project and he and I had worked together on a long radio series entitled "Gallant American Women" so that he knew my point of view.

Though I am writing far too long again to you, I think I can help to illuminate your educational task of leadership by reporting that this radio program, sponsored by the U.S. Bureau of Education and the National Broadcasting System, represented in the beginning, before I was invited to cooperate as a promoter of the Women's Archive, the purely shallow-depth feminist dogma to the effect that women had had no education in America until they were admitted to academies and colleges, had had no participation in the art of healing or anything else until the woman movement established the training that led to licenses, etc. I shook up that dogma as best I could in view of the speed of the programs and the dire ignorance that prevailed among the sponsors. When I get home I shall try to get for you copies of the whole series to indicate possibilities of research and writing and teaching for your graduates.

Here endeth this excessive epistle. I shall be waiting with intense pleasure for our conference in the early spring. Meanwhile I am deeply appreciative of your freedom of mind and power of spirit.

Sincerely,   Mary R. Beard

Catherine Drinker Bowen, successful writer of fiction and nonfiction, biographer of Tchaikovsky and of Oliver Wendell Holmes, apparently wrote to Mary Beard for ideas for a new biography on a woman. Bowen was a music lover like her sister-in-law Sophy Drinker, whom Beard also knew and had asked to sketch women musicians for the *Encyclopaedia*. Beard's marvelously frank assessments of individuals and books in the following is rather typical of her style in private letters at this stage of her life.

In spite of or perhaps because of Beard's recommendations, Bowen had second thoughts. She went on to write biographies of John Adams, Sir Edward Coke, Francis Bacon, and Benjamin Franklin. "A woman's biography—with about eight famous historical exceptions—so often turns out to be the story of a man and the woman who helped his career," she later explained her choice to an inquirer.[9]

94. TO CATHERINE DRINKER BOWEN

                                        Pine Crest Inn
                                        Tryon, N. Car.
                                        February 20, 1944

Dear Mrs. Bowen:

Your fascinating letter dated the fourteenth has been on my desk a whole week—unanswered. Though I have wanted to acknowledge before this day its illuminating story of Sophy Drinker and the exploration you have been making for a great woman theme for a new book of your own, I have wanted to give my most earnest thought to your inquiry about your project.

As I try to meet your question I am mindful of today's acclaim of your Holmes' volume. Congratulations, first of all, for making that grade! Oh I know Justice Frankfurter must be distressed. I have known him for some forty years and very well indeed! You disclaim the "scholarly" complex. I don't have to do that, when I remember an editorial not long ago in the Saturday Review written by De Voto which said, a propos a piece of co-authoring by Beard and Beard that it was inferior to a work on American history by Morison and Commager, naturally, because in the Beard case only *one* scholar had worked on the book. Yet I shall have to disclaim any scholarship myself, semi-publicly on Tuesday at a college near Spartan-burg since I am to be introduced to faculty and students as "a woman scholar." I am intending to remark that "distance lends enchantment" in respect of Mary Beard in all ways and that on my closer viewing undoubt-edly the effect will be that the observers will feel like the one who wrote the limerick on the purple cow: "I'd rather see than be one."

Sophy [Drinker] is in fact far more scholarly than I am!

But I have hunches which absorb me and I work along to express them and bolster them the best I can with some "data" at least. And I have tried to brighten them at times with the glamor of the journalese. So you and I apparently have a fellow-feeling of sorts.

I come to your inquiry about a great woman for a book—a woman nearer our own times than Mercy Warren and Eliza Lucas Pinckney. I have thought as hard as I could about this matter. I agree with your sage comments relative to Miss [M. Carey] Thomas' influence as a revoltee and she would be more real in your sculpturing than she will probably be in the hands of her official biographer. She should have your kind of reckoning.

Is there another woman educator as dramatic a figure by reason of her independence and discipleship? If so, I can't think of one. Lucy Salmon of Vassar was a real and vivid person, analytical, a somewhat original writer, free-spirited, and greatly admired by those students who liked those qualities. But I am afraid she could not be resurrected for a story of nation-wide interest. Miss [Marion] Park [President] of Bryn Mawr has seemed to me little more than a pussy cat owing, I think, to her total lack of a history-consciousness. She is so uninterested in the bold hussies who put over votes-for-women that she permitted the college girls to settle back in their distaste for that type of gal, without learning a thing about old Susan B., i.e., being beneficiaries and softer-minded concerning the voting privilege at least.

No other woman college president has made the rafters ring with the challenging affirmations of an M. Carey Thomas. Aurelia Reinhardt who has just retired from the presidency of Mills College in California had a precious sense of humor which all the rest seem totally to have lacked but, as far as I know, she upset no fixed ideas and was no pioneer in education. Ada Comstock of Radcliffe, Dean Virginia Gildersleeve of Barnard, Mildred McAfee of Wellesley, have been sheer puppets in my opinion. Constance Warren little more.

BUT if by education a woman-of-letters may be meant, I do believe that *Ellen Glasgow* has been and is to this day (with her last book) a genuine intellectual leader and a dramatic personality. She has seen two revolutions occur in her American society—the revolution in the South by a civil war and the revolution in the North by Global war via taxation, etc. Both the planting feudalism and the capitalistic economy have been upset in her time. And she has pondered on these events with a remarkably keen mind. Her novels, especially "Barren Ground", bespeak her penetration. Some of her articles do it too, especially one I quote in my book, America through Women's Eyes, that was entitled "What I Believe" and printed in the Nation. There are charming vignettes which could be used, such as her trying to live in a little New England cottage at Cornwall, Connecticut, among her literary friends, but finding that she couldn't do it, that she bumped her head on the tops of doorways, etc, though she is one of the tiniest women I know. Having seen her in her home at Richmond, her reaction to a little N.E. cottage amuses me to my marrow. I consider Ellen Glasgow one of the greatest American figures of our times.

For the age of "social meliorism", the age of Justice Holmes who was liberal about that outburst of improving energy, I think that the Chicago group of women with Jane Addams as their chief were the prime American educators—in humanitarianism. Ex-Senator Wollcott of Connecticut, himself a high-grade gentleman, wrote me that he deemed Miss Addams "the greatest moral force" of her generation. They had both been invited to address a meeting at Syracuse, if I am right as to place. When they arrived for that purpose, Jane was told that she was not to expound her pacifism. This was, if I remember what he told me as to time, at a moment when public morale was being directed to the first World war. She insisted that she would have to voice her true convictions or be silent. She was allowed to speak. And the Senator (U.S.) years later confessed that "she was right and I was wrong." His confession was made in a letter to me during the disillusionment after the war had ended.

That was a remarkable group of women who companioned Jane Addams at Hull House. It included Florence Kelley, Julia Lathrop who became the first head of the federal Children's Bureau you know, Mrs. Joseph Bowen who launched juvenile protection in Chicago, the Abbott sisters, Sophonisba Breckinridge, and Ellen Gates Starr who eventually entered a convent. Their story is immensely dramatic. It runs out as influence to the gubernatorial administration under Altgeld. It runs through the influence exerted at Hull House over innumerable men who spent some time there, such as Gerard Swope (who met the woman he married there).

Those women have never had a write-up the least enlightening in respect of their power and mentalities. A nephew of Jane Addams wrote her biography but it is a wooden Indian whom he discusses, not her dynamic creative force of character and purpose. Perhaps he was too near to her as a close relative to comprehend what she signified in American life and thought. Probably he just couldn't write either. Singly none has had a competent biography. Together they would make a glamorous tale of educational womanpower, full of "fight" on the home front.

It would of course be easier for you to write about a Philadelphian. There was Lucretia Mott whose materials you could get readily. I consider her a remarkable creature with a fascinating story of independence, pioneering, commingled Quaker quietism and forthright affirmation in her blended faith in Love as advocated by Christ (when most Protestants clung to old Jehovah) and her adherence to the way, or cult, of Reason. She read Tom Paine, Voltaire, etc. She upset fixed ideas in the U.S. and tackled them in England. She has been discussed in books but never as the dramatic figure whom I see in my mind's eye. She lived on a good while after the civil war which so tested her fidelity to her non-violent code of behavior. The *History of Woman Suffrage* (3 vols) gives important clues to her career.

Education does not all occur in colleges, as you surely realize. I am inclined to think that it doesn't occur there for women very much, if at all, because college training robs women of their own history and puts in its place only the history of men. This is why I want Sophy's book to come off the press and in fine form.

I should enjoy a long confab with you on women and *a* woman for your theme. In lieu of that enjoyment I can only scribble as I am doing on these sheets to you.

Most cordially yours,
Mary R. Beard

•←

Beard's old friend Florence Kitchelt, who had worked with the League of Women Voters in the 1920s, had long been opposed to the National Woman's Party's proposal of an equal rights amendment. By 1943 she had a change of heart. She recognized that much of the acrimony between the camps advocating and opposing the amendment was due to personality conflicts and to old wounds carried on from the suffrage campaign period. The passage of the Fair Labor Standards Act in 1938 and its confirmation by the U.S. Supreme Court in 1941 meant that protective labor legislation for men as well as women was valid. That removed a significant reason for objection to equal rights legislation. Kitchelt took the initiative of founding the Connecticut Committee for the Equal Rights Amendment, thinking that a new organization without the checkered reputation of the National Woman's Party would be more successful in mobilizing support for the amendment. She wrote to Mary Beard, as to many others, to argue anew for the measure. Beard's negative response—aside from her astute perception of the "rightish" trend of the National Woman's Party—is evasive. Elsewhere she explained her discomfort with the possibility of defining equality as the root of her opposition.[10]

95. TO FLORENCE KITCHELT

Pine Crest Inn
Tryon, N. Carolina
Feb. 22, 1944

Dear Florence:

Numerous of my friends in Connecticut and Washington and still further afield have longed to get both Beards behind the drive for the blanket amendment to establish equal rights. I shall probably lose every friend I have had because of my reluctance to do this. In this hesitation I am not swayed by Charles' concepts of the possible consequences of inserting this amendment in the Constitution. We have discussed it over and over and over. But those of you who are confident of its value and consequences will not accept, I am sure, the reasons for lack of comparable confidence, any more than you, dear Florence, could accept my and Charles' doubts about the great American international crusade.

I can't discuss the amendment matter on paper now. I am too bogged down with work—at last with more work on women. I think your weakest supporters for the amendment are such persons as M. Carey Thomas who knew no history apparently and Dr. Groves who assumes to know it but writes so absurdly about women in it. As for my feeling about the personnel of the National Woman's Party, I can report that a large part of it I associated myself with voluntarily and actively when it was called the Congressional Union. I backed up Alice Paul and Lucy Burns as their one firm original defender in New York, during a trial of the C.U. by the regular suffragists' council. I was wholly in favor of its plan for political action to expedite victory for the enfranchisement of women. I addressed Congressional committees—the Judiciary in the House and the Rules in the Senate—as a member of the C.U. But I am not as loyal an advocate of its present rightish wing. This fact, however, is not the basis of my reluctance to join the drive for the Equal Rights amendment.

I shall trust you to keep this reply to your letter of Feb. 16 confidential, knowing your true nobility of character. I have not answered or answered simply with "Sorry I can't" other appeals for participation. I believe that you and I have mutual respect for each other. I wish we could see eye to eye on every public issue, as we do see that way on problems of character.

My love as always—Mary R. Beard

While uncertain what the outcome for women's archives at Radcliffe would be, Mary Beard was also pushing in the same direction at Smith College. She had an ally, a friend, and avid correspondent in Margaret Grierson, the Smith College archivist. In 1941 President Herbert Davis of Smith, a scholar of English literature, had proposed to the college alumnae to build a rare book and manuscript collection on women writers. Adopted by the Friends of the Smith College Library the next year, the idea of the Sophia Smith Collection, as it was called, soon took a historical turn, perhaps because of the efforts of Grierson, who was also appointed executive secretary of the Friends. As some of the documents donated to the World Center for Women's Archives went to Radcliffe, so did some important collections go to the Sophia Smith Collection. Grierson welcomed not only Beard's suggestions about collecting but also her vision of courses or seminars to be attached to the archive. The historians on the Smith faculty were not receptive to the idea, however, as they had not been, according to Beard, when she had in 1937 encouraged the prior president of Smith, William Neilson, to interest them.[11]

Beard comments caustically, below, on Betty Gram-Swing, a former National Woman's Party suffragist and close friend of Doris Stevens who was experimenting with a women's history course at Syracuse, and on Alma Lutz. The few women who were really interested in women's history at this time—feminists concerned to preserve the memory of the struggle for rights—were committing a travesty of history, in Beard's view.

96. TO MARGARET GRIERSON

> Pine Crest Inn
> Tryon, N. Carolina
> March 6, 1944

Dear Mrs. Grierson:

I am glad that you are impatient for strong action. I share and appreciate its value—impatience. And yet I realize that a stable structure is taking form at Smith and that, in the long run [with] the combination of your tactful pushing and the firm consent of your colleagues to bring their weight to bear on the building, a power is developing within your institution which could not be matched by an independent job. Though you have been cautious about encouraging my hope, I have felt convinced that, provided you were not ill, genuine progress was being made. Your character clearly made the right impression on me. And of course in that impression was sensitivity to the force of your mind.

So I have ardent congratulations to send you for work superbly done! They include cheers for the preservation of the ideal from the invasion of superficial opportunists such as "Betty." I think I ought to warn you also against too much reliance on Alma Lutz who, though a colder personality, has precisely the same rigidity of mind. Her life of Elizabeth Cady Stanton was no more than an intellectual juvenile, as I told the publisher when he asked for my opinion, to his great disappointment. The book lacks any concern with Mrs. Stanton's mind—with her sharp analysis of Woman, Church, and State, for example, in their interrelationship. It was merely a story of physical activity for the most part. And I find Miss Lutz far from a thinker and laggard, I suppose, on account of her lack of knowledge or fear of woman in long history. She is a twin of Betty Gram-Swing as exemplar of what I mean by the sense of the hour only. But Miss Lutz can be immensely valuable as a contributor to the archives collection and everything she offers, such as the file of Equal Rights and its predecessor, will be all to the good. Understanding what she can do and what she should not do is the key to using her advantageously.

As for my name as a value, of course you are welcome to use it, though I doubt whether it has the pull which you think it has. The name "Beard" is anathema in many many quarters, I assure you, whether Charles or Mary is prefixed to it.

Maybe you have already sent the pamphlet and if so naturally it has gone to New Milford. In that case it will not be forwarded and I shall not get to see it before March 22 when we shall be at home again. We have been down here for the winter. We start toward home next Sunday, the 12th. We shall be at the Commodore Hotel in New York from the 13 to the 21st. If you want me to see the pamphlet before the 22 or 23d, you can mail one to me at the Commodore to be there on the 13th. I am sure that I *shall* like it.

I am not surprised that you have found the historians reluctant to fall into line. President Neilson found that also true when he tried to interest them in my idea of starting a course on women in history. But I took that as "a natural" since they have no knowledge for handling it and consequently assume that there is nothing in it. You'll be able to move them as Charles said his father moved balky mules—by building a fire under them.

You are so right that the faculty must cooperate by setting research projects for one thing. And it is fortunate that members are ready to do that. I am going to Syracuse on the 30th, anxious to see how cooperation of that kind has gone on there.

There is another sign of activity in another institution which seems spontaneous and if it has the vitality which it appears to have we shall have this year of 1944 a great educational enlightenment under way, fed by your illumination to a high degree. This will be a grand creative outburst among the terribly destructive forces of this time and in a generation it may produce a lot of American women, with student-women from other nations, who can do the basic thinking essential to a better way of life.

It is dangerous for you ever to write me because I pour out my words to you in a flood of joy over your initiative and competence. The "secret battle" wins in the end. I know so well its agonies meanwhile. . . .

If the dinner bell were not ringing, I would probably never close this letter. I do it with

> Sincerest admiration for you,
> Mary R. Beard

❦

Work on new biographical sketches for the *Britannica* was still proceeding in mid-1944, although Mary Beard's own contribution was supervisory only. Her letter to writer Elizabeth Schlesinger, wife of the Harvard historian who took unique interest in women's history during the interwar period, displays her shifting mood toward the pioneers of the women's rights struggle in the United States as she researched the study that would become *Woman as Force in History*.

97. TO ELIZABETH SCHLESINGER

> New Milford, Connecticut
> June 15, 1944

Dear Mrs. Schlesinger:

You must not be deprived of the vital association with your son during his furlough. Certainly not. His time at home will be all too short.

Your delay in hearing from Mr. Yust was due to his absence from his office for more than a fortnight and word of your consent to undertake the collecting of sketches had come to his office while he was away.

The 29th name for your list which I had sent you, Caroline A. Dall, seemed appropriate to me from my reading of her work and emphasis in the History of Woman Suffrage. It hardly seems to deserve a place in the Encyc. Brit., judging from the D[ictionary] of A[merican] B[iography]. But judging from the D.A.B. neither Mercy Warren nor Lydia Maria Child does either and so we must be on our guard against forming our opinions wholly on that D.A.B. When you get around to research on Mrs. Dall, you may form your own judgment respecting her calibre for a sketch in the Encyc. Brit. Mr. Yust accepts my judgment. He will take all sketches which I propose, provided of course they are convincing as to the quality of the women sketched and their social significance.

The sketches *are* to be sent directly to Mr. Yust. I would like to see them first but I cannot carry that load though I did for nearly two years read all the sketches written by three women who were working with me. They, however, were rather amateurish writers as you are not. They were superb researchers and that you are too. I am delighted that sketches now to be written at Cambridge and elsewhere will have authors who can both research and write. *Yes* I would like to have the list of contributors whom you will acquire.

It will interest you all to know that we are inviting such persons as Charles Warren to write up Mercy Warren, Sigrid Unset to handle several Scandinavian women, and other persons of similar competence to treat women within their domains of knowledge or of their accessible material.

The Britannica has been weighted so heavily on the side of European sketches that I am helping to establish a better balance. Mr. Yust fully agrees in this plan.

I am writing you this fully that you may know more about the place which you hold in this scheme of things. I have to confess that a new and intensive study of the speeches and resolutions of women in the History of Woman Suffrage, since I came home from Cambridge and following a close and hard study of the Common Law and Equity relative to women, almost ditched my belief that the highly articulate sisters were really great women. Their interpretations of long history were unquestionably crude. But they had a big job to do and their performance has positively changed the attitude of our nation toward women. So they definitely belong in the Encyc. Brit. As you work on their sketches, I suggest that you keep in mind, as a part of Mr. Yust's letter to you has emphasized I think, the significance of their determination to end the horrors of Canon Law respecting Woman and to cast off or socialize Common Law (as far as it remained in use) by bringing ethics and general welfare to bear on statutory law. Their commingling of legalities with the reforms of temperance and anti-slavery made them wade into some awful breakers— notably their abject identification of white women with Negro slaves. But their affirmations were no more extreme than the affirmations of the opposition. AND they were headed in the creative direction—from barbarism to civilization. Only Matilda Joslyn Gage seems to have known much about the history of women and she naturally saw it as a history of subjection to sadism via Canon Law in which she rather specialized.

I wish we could have a quiet long talk together. But that is not necessary as a prelude to your work for the Encyc. Brit. You have knowledge of all this background yourself. I am only reverting to it for your remembrance that sketches must be better than those in the D.A.B.

It is great good news that Professor Schlesinger was able to interest Mr. Scaife in the idea of a possible new edition of Mercy Warren's history of the American Revolution, with her proposals for its revision. If this edition is published its value would be enhanced by the addition of her Correspondence with John Adams over her portrait of him in this history. They were intimate friends of long standing, as you no doubt know. They differed over the objective of the Revolution. Their Correspondence is in the Cong. Lib. and it could be photostated there for Mr. Scaife's use.

You ask about Lucy Stone Blackwell or Alice Stone Blackwell for your list of names. Lucy has a sketch, if not a grand one, in the Brit[annica]. So I do mean Alice Stone Blackwell. Willkie has a long sketch! Alice S. B. has meant a lot more to the U.S.A. Aged women still alive are going in—to some extent.

Faithfully yours,   Mary R. Beard

Walter Yust had submitted for Mary Beard's comments a proposed article on "Woman" for the *Encyclopaedia Britannica*. Her response shows the flavor of her critical attitudes toward psychology, psychoanalysis, and sociology, as well as her commitment to long history as the main truthteller. Whether because of Beard's objections or for other reasons, no article by a "Dr. Beth" appeared in a subsequent edition of the *Britannica*.

98. TO WALTER YUST

New Milford, Connecticut
November 3, 1944

Dear Mr. Yust:

Dr. Beth's bibliography alone rules out this treatment of a theme as comprehensive as WOMAN. I find myself in purely emotional company there with my book in the list.

If Dr. Beth had not attempted to give any historical data and had used only types of biological and Freudian affirmations, her article would have had that range of vision and she might have summarized its findings with some consistency. Even so she would have been looking at WOMAN through the kind of mirror that I once saw in a child's doll house.

In fact Dr. Beth attempts to interpret all history and I consider her equally simple in this matter. For example she says (p. 4) "Greece shows." Well what was "Greece" in the historic time she covers? Greece was never a unified society in ancient times. You know this and I need not elaborate the point. At the bottom of the page she says "In Sparta" but in Sparta there were social upheavals and a history of changes which call for description and dating if any real statement about that community is to have the substance of reality.

Well this same criticism applies to every one of her historical assertions from her section on Rome, through the one on Christianity including her shallow discussion of chivalry, up to the present age. She takes the feminist dogmas at feminists' values without the knowledge which forces a larger point of view.

On page 11, near the bottom, she says: "Generally one may assume...... which preceded the subjection of women in Greek and Roman society"— the whole sentence and the assumption being utterly trite as naivete. Then she goes on "When comparing the modern situation with the mythological." Why compare the two? As for *Women at Work*, page 12, these items as far as they come uptodate, will be out of date by the time this article is printed.

With respect to what follows, *Differential Physiology* and *Differential Psychology*, all such contentions need subjecting to the history of women's thought and action. Whatever biologists and psychologists affirm about sex differences, it is a fact that women have asserted themselves in every kind of way. And not merely a few have ventured into lines of thought and action proscribed by biologists and psychologists. Women have often defied such proscriptions en masse.

NO, this treatment of WOMAN is rubbish, in my opinion.

I have talked with Dr. [Karen] Horney cited in the bibliography and read her publications. I consider her one of the most critical psychologists but even she needs to study the history of "cultures." I have said that to her.

Dr. Beth refers to [Johann-Jakob] Bachofen on her first page. But Bachofen was not writing about anything as governmental as a "matriarchy." He was describing Mutterrecht (mother law) and the two are not identical. Besides, the words "matriarchate" and "patriarchate" only came into currency in recent times and on this matter Maitland is most illuminating. The words are too strongly representative of governing systems for precision, in respect of sex relations. I need not go on with my criticisms but merely declare that Dr. Beth has taken in too much territory which she has not worked for exact knowledge. All these current sociological surveys are superficial in that they take no account of long history. They rest on observations at a particular moment in a particular situation and on chatter which lacks the intellectual depth of historical research.

If an article headed MAN were handled as this article on WOMAN is handled, what a howl would go up from men. But one could be written on MAN in this way and merely by taking from Dr. Beth's article those parts which deal with biology and psychology and the rhythm of dominance and subjection which she discusses relative to women. If this rhythm is true of woman, then while she is dominant, surely man is subject to her and he too is in the rhythm.

Dr. Beth is in my bailiwick—the history of women. But evidently she has not opened my book which she includes in her bibliography. And she cites no other work in history. I am in bad company there. Freud has done incalculable injury, I think. He has worked in the realm of pathology, not history. He was Oriental in his emotional life.

I regret of course to run counter to Dr. Beth. But she is out of her depth and women must not flounder with her in water over their heads.

Thanks for letting me see this article before you decided on using it. I hope you will return it to the author.

        & & & & &

I have wonderful material on the Pythagorean women and shall continue to hunt for some one to handle it for the Encyclopaedia. Prof. Hocking of Harvard certainly could *not* do it. Gertrude Atherton could, if she were not 87, as her study of Pericles and Aspasia indicates. But we must have a writer who is not a novelist and hence convincing in the realm of philosophy.

I shall report your approval of an article on Priestesses to Miss White and we shall let you know what we consider to be a reasonable length.

        Sincerely yours, [M.R.B.]

6 Toward *Woman as Force in History*

By the summer of 1944, Mary Beard was concentrating her energies on a new book. In mid-September the Macmillan Company, publisher of the *Rise of American Civilization* volumes, offered her a contract. Harold Latham, the editor in chief, had known the Beards since his college days when Charles was his teacher. The first idea for a title Mary Beard proposed to him, which she thought "exact," although perhaps "too ponderous," was "The Man-Woman Problematique"! By the date of the following letter she had given up that idea.

99. TO HAROLD LATHAM, THE MACMILLAN COMPANY

New Milford, Connecticut
September 29, 1944

Dear Mr. Latham:

I have been a bit slow about returning the Contract signed, owing to three days in town and the need of considering such contractual essentials as the number of words allowed me, on my return.

Now I have gone into all phases of the Contract. Except for the possibly too stern a restriction to 100,000 words, it is thoroughly satisfactory. I would like a leeway of 25,000 more words so that I can completely convince opponents of my thesis that the course of Equity has protected or newly established rights for women in every conceivable kind of case, submitted to Equity. This calls for many illustrations. But they should be fascinating reading, so curious are some of the problems presented to judges and the ways of adjusting them in judicial decisions. This won't be dull. It will be exciting, I think. I also need room for the final section on the great body of Literature dealing with women in history. This will overcome what I myself had assumed was a gross neglect of this subject. For example a great deal has been written about historic women warriors in books dealing with that specific theme. I shall also have to show that mediaeval law was not so hostile to women as the uninformed suppose. Agnes Repplier in "Pursuit of Laughter" found the woman shrew a common theme of miracle plays, etc. She assumed that this was queer in view of the law. She didn't know the law. Shakespeare tried to tame the shrew—a favorite villain.

I shall do my utmost to keep as close to 100,000 words as I can to give this book a permanent value. If I may interpret the "approximately 100,000 words" to mean, if necessary, as many as 25,000 more, then I can sign the Contract without further hesitation.

I note that no date is set for the delivery of the manuscript. Charles and I have discussed for several hours the problem of writing in a final form the stuff I have in the present form. We feel certain that at the very latest the copy can be turned over to you next June. That would mean an autumn publication as, we both thought—you and I,—the most desirable time. By getting that outside date I can cooperate with Charles in seeing that he has his easiest winter for 1944–45. That is, I can walk with him every day everyway, talk with him or listen like a good fellow, etc., have the leisure for really loving work on my book.

I'll send you a tentative title or two when I have one or two I like.

Sincerely, Mary R. Beard

Beard's work on *Woman as Force in History* during the final year of World War II coincided with the most virulent published attacks on her husband yet seen. Reviewers took the occasion of the publication of the Beards' *A Basic History of the United States* in August 1944 to excoriate Charles Beard's views on recent foreign policy, while praising the book as a whole. Reviewers assumed that the chapters that saw war against the Nazis as less than a necessity and criticized President Roosevelt for arrogating executive power as he led the nation into war were Charles' handiwork rather than a joint production. Nonetheless, Mary Beard was deeply wounded by the indictments, especially when they came from former friends such as Lewis Mumford, who wrote that Charles Beard, by advocating "national isolation," had "become a passive—no, active—abettor of tyranny, sadism, and human defilement." [1]

The following five notes to Macmillan editors show the author in the process of completing her magnum opus. Excepting her anthology *America Through Women's Eyes*, it was her first book of single authorship since 1931. Her husband assisted with details, the letters reveal.

100. TO JAMES PUTNAM, THE MACMILLAN COMPANY

New Milford
November 10, 1944

Dear Jim:

How does this title for my book impress you?

WOMAN AS FORCE AND AGENCY IN HISTORY

It is an exact statement of what I am dealing with. It sounds original enough to be attractive, it seems to me. And simple enough a verbalism to be caught by multitudes?

Don't rush an answer. It can wait until we meet again at the Commodore early next month. I shall want Mr. Latham's opinion too.

Yours truly, Mary R. Beard

[P.S.] I shall not expect to compete with [best-selling novel] Forever Amber, naturally.

101. TO JAMES PUTNAM, THE MACMILLAN COMPANY

New Milford, Connecticut
April 8, 1945

Dear Jim:

I was back on my heels and decidedly off my toes until your letter came on Saturday (yesterday) telling me that I am getting by the critics—Latham and Putnam. Now I shall get a good balance for my understanding and go to work with assurance that I shall not hurt your House.

You are very right about excess driving home of certain points, as I have done. I am well aware of that myself, in vital places. I shall prune, generalize, illustrate, and lick all that into better literary form.

In all there are to be twelve chapters. The last of this week I shall have carbon copies of all but the last one. These I shall send to you by the 16th. The final chapter will take about ten days more. This will bring me to April 23d.

Then I shall start afresh through the whole manuscript and have almost six weeks to refine it—by refining not meaning to put mere sugar into it of course; and to see that it is all proportioned well as to the fixed compass. A competent woman is working under my direction for what will be an excellent bibliography. That ought to be a book by itself but I am cutting it down and down to fit this opus.

Since you like the first chapters and will like them better when I have gone through them again and carved them more effectively, I feel sure you will like the following chapters which have already had that treatment. Thanks to you and Mr. Latham for your labors and sympathy.

Appreciatively yours,
Mary R. Beard

102. TO HAROLD LATHAM, THE MACMILLAN COMPANY

New Milford, Connecticut
April 18, 1945

Dear Mr. Latham:

Now that I have dug into the chapters of my book which I let you see, prematurely I find, I am humiliated over their shortcomings, as of the date when I gave them to you. The typist by omissions and for other less discernible reasons had obscured and distorted many pages. I had manhandled or womanhandled many others. If you thought that I had done "admirably", you will really like the final composition without the qualifications which must have been in your mind, even while you were commenting so favorably on the copy you had read.

I don't want to send you more copy that rough. Naturally I want you to know how I round out the legal story and where and how I go on from there. But I shall wait for a clean copy of the revisions of all the chapters up to the last one before I submit my manuscript to you again. This will be about the middle of May. Verifications made with the masterful help of CAB will then have been made and the rewriting will have taken account of any objections he may have expressed to the entire work or particular features. I shall work on the last chapter till the last day in the morn.

Of course I realize how crowded your very minutes are with pressures at home and in the office and with the exactions of your mind and interests. But I am spurred to do my utmost for a good and permanent book by the welcome which you have given it.

Most appreciatively yours,
Mary R. Beard

103. TO JAMES PUTNAM, THE MACMILLAN COMPANY

New Milford, Conn.
April 18, 1945

Dear Jim:

I have discovered with no little chagrin that you and Mr. Latham were both far too generous in your comments on the pages of my manuscript which you had read. I have been going over those pages and find a lot of them execrable. The typist that I employed at the Chrysler building is partly responsible but the major fault is mine beyond cavil. Anyway I have scoured and polished them much already and cast out stuff for the waste basket.

Instead of sending you and Mr. Latham more crude chapters I shall wait until about the middle of May to turn over better specimens of the material up to the last chapter. On that one I shall keep working to the very end of May.

Charles is taking up my polished sections, one by one, and giving me the benefit of his sound judgments with acute sight directed to accuracy of statements. He is really keen about the plan of the book and its contents. As you know, no one could be a better critic of all the legal story.

We have heard that the Saturday Review is to return to its attack on him, now that it has heard that Beard is up from his sick bed again. A prof we know asked to have this attack postponed that long at least. Venom of adjectives is not to reappear but a ganging up against CAB will be attempted this time, with the cooperation of professors if they accept the wide invitations which have been extended to them for aid and comfort. Cheers!

You and Mannie and Chris must come to us early in June at the latest. And be allowed to have real changes from town life while you are here.

Yours, Mary

104. TO HAROLD LATHAM, THE MACMILLAN COMPANY

[New Milford, Connecticut]
May 16, 1945

Dear Mr. Latham:

I had planned to have you receive today a carbon copy of the revised—much rewritten—chapters of my book which you had seen in their crude form and also all the following chapters except the last one.

But I need the carbon copy in fact for Charles to use in his hunt for possible errors in facts and for us both to keep reading for the rest of this month. It will probably make little or no difference to you whether you see the work now or the first of June. But you do need to know that I am keeping it all within the predetermined compass as to size; that the last chapter Charles thinks, as I do, is as original and significant in its way as the part that covers legal history.

I have had such complete quiet here for work all these weeks that I know I have a manuscript reflecting it. Never before have I been able to concentrate so completely on anything wholly my own.

Sincerely yours, Mary R. Beard

Beard delivered the manuscript of *Woman as Force in History* to Macmillan on June 8, 1945, and expected that it would be published by late November. In the fall she wrote to Margaret Grierson, "My book will be nobody's ideal. It may be wholly unnoticed or it may be attacked as jejune or traitorous to feminism. But there it will be as a demonstration of my understanding of the subject WOMAN—for better, for worse, or as nothing at all."[2] The following letter to Macmillan's marketing or publicity editor suggests more than predictable authorial anxiety and defensiveness: it appears that Beard had to justify her approach even after the book was accepted.

105. TO MR. CUNNINGHAM, THE MACMILLAN COMPANY

New Milford, Connecticut
July 3, 1945

Dear Mr. Cunningham:

In case the reader's comment on my book, to the effect that the average woman would not be attracted to my long section of legal history, troubles you, let me lay before you more items in its support as possible, even probable, appeal than I did yesterday. Knowing how harassed you must be with the burdens that had been placed upon you at this moment, I did not stay to talk longer about this phase of marketing.

I mentioned only a developing interest in my new approach to learning about women, among educators. But here are other centers of interest which I believe you will find impressive. They are known only to me and only to me because I have been speaking on many campuses in recent years and corresponding widely with women leaders in women's national organizations, etc. Hence I feel confident that such leaders will commend this book in their organizations' journals and help to promote it in influential ways of other sorts. For example:

The National Federation of Business and Professional Women through its Executive Secretary, Miss Louise Franklin Bache, and her executive associates. The address of this organization is 1819 Broadway, New York. I have lunched and talked with them and have worked with them for quite a long time, addressed meetings of their Board and members at annual conventions, etc. I have their friendship and confidence.

A national association of the highest-grade teachers—Delta Kappa Gamma—which made me an honorary member. The former President, Dr. Maycie Southall, who holds an important position at the Peabody Teachers College at Nashville, Tenn., is genuinely interested in my point of view. The woman who is to turn from her present position as president, to become Executive Secretary September 1, is on the faculty of the Wilson Teachers College at Washington, D.C. She is Dr. Margaret Stroh. On the invitations of these women I have addressed national and local meetings of this organization. I am invited to do this again at Denver in August. Though I cannot accept this invitation, I am in close touch with the leaders in this association who seem to value my study and writing and general point of view.

On tours through Alabama sponsored by the Assoc. of University Women and on a tour through Nebraska at the invitation of teachers prominent in the National Education Association I came into touch with men and women who manifested genuine interest in my conception of woman in history. I shall supply you with names of such persons who, I think, will want to have my book and *read* it. I addressed the N.E.A. at its annual meeting in Detroit in 1937 at its public meeting in the Masonic temple when about 10,000 teachers were present. And out of that affair came the invitation to speak at great teachers' rallies in Nebraska. I also was guest speaker at Scranton, Penna., not long ago, for a teachers banquet following which I was asked to return to give a course of twelve lectures. I could not do that but I have a nucleus of readers there.

I have literally been deluged with invitations to speak to branches of the Assoc. of University Women in such colleges as the University of Kentucky and in cities.

During a course of about eight years at such institutions as Syracuse University, Smith College, Connecticut College, and Radcliffe, (there on the invitation of President Jordan) I have both given my thesis of Woman as Force in History and left bodies of activists eager to promote what I call "A New Social Content for Education."

The Chancellor of Syracuse has not been convinced yet of my soundness but a course has been given there now for three years on Women in

American History and it has been growing in attendance and enthusiasm as the men and women behind it have themselves learned more substance for effective teaching. In my book which you have on hand I have given the data on women philosophers with considerable precision with a view to convincing the Chancellor at Syracuse that women have demonstrated force as philosophers. Philosophy is his specialty but he insisted at an evening meeting at Syracuse last autumn, after my exposition of my general thesis, that women had never done anything in his "field." For a similar reason, in other circles, I must be convincing about the history of law, by giving its precise details and at length—over a long period of time.

There are many Deans of Women in colleges, one at the Univ. of Wisconsin for instance, who hope to get courses established on women in history and I shall send you some names for promoting my book.

You will surely understand that I am not a publicity-hound in reporting all this intellectual awakening; that I am trying to acquaint you with a market that I believe exists for my book. I shall be attacked I know by the men and women who abhor having their simple and convenient-to-themselves dogma of woman's historic subjection to man questioned. I may have anything but a pleasant time over my counter-history. I honestly dislike personal publicity and that is a reason why I have done all I could to check it during my years of work with women and colleges. The ground, however, has been fairly well cultivated for the above-the-average man and woman to see the crop of knowledge about woman as force in history coming up now.

For your exceeding courtesy to me yesterday during one of your toughest days, I am deeply grateful.

Sincerely yours, Mary R. Beard

[P.S.] I'd better add that the young women of my collegiate sorority— the oldest one, Kappa Alpha Theta—are beginning to build up libraries in their sorority homes about which they are writing me—and, mirabile dictu, reading the unassigned books and discussing them out of class.

Moreover Dr. Mary L. Collins of Cincinnati, who, for more than twenty years, has inspired the graduate members of her sorority, Chi Omega, to keep up reading and learning, is a close friend of mine. At her invitation I addressed an annual assembly of these women at White Sulphur Springs not long ago. This sorority publishes an excellent journal.

•⊷

For publicity purposes, Macmillan composed a biographical sketch of Mary Beard, which appears after the next letter. Her letter responds to errors and problems in the sketch. Its prime mistake—mixing her up with another woman of the same name—shows how appallingly little these men had bothered to learn about her during more than two decades of publishing works written with her husband.

106. TO JAMES PUTNAM, THE MACMILLAN COMPANY

[1945]

So sorry to keep on being a fuzzbuzz, Jim. But it seems necessary further.

So you identify me with Mary Beard who organized nurses into a national body or helped to do that and then was a major leader in it? She is probably still on the staff of the Rockefeller Institute for Medical Research, though during this war she has headed up the Red Cross. There is no middle initial in her name. She is unmarried. She's a grand sort and I would be proud if we were one. We are frequently mistaken for each other, about the same age, and very congenial.

You have me "long active in the cause of women." But I don't like this statement here because this book is not designed to serve that "cause" whatever that cause is. It is, my dear, a book designed for the mutual enlightenment of men and women about each other as historic companions. Its cause is more *knowledge* on this subject, coupled with the conception of human force. I rather take the so-called woman's cause for a ride.

The Archive failed to materialize. I tried to found it with my associates on the Board but we couldn't finance it. So nothing should be said about that here. Anyway the reason for my activity in that connection is not exactly right as you state it. Any Archive or Bibliothek is promoted for the collection of materials on life in some or all forms and how the material is used is another matter.

If Miriam and Bill were tacked on to this piece, it could be assumed that the two books named are all they had produced. I'd like to have them advertised but to say enough means to say more about them to be fully effective and this doesn't seem to me to be the place for that. I'd be leaving our dear Alfred [Vagts] rather on the doorstep too, with his name only in parenthesis.

so, I've tried my mind and fingers at a revised edition of this page, asking your forgiveness.

[M.R.B.]

◄•►

Beard's objection to having her book identified with "the cause of women" is one of the most interesting features of her revision of the biographical sketch. So is her reluctance to have her children mentioned. Although she only refers to the partiality of this editorial information, one suspects that she felt that women authors ought to be no more identified with (or justified by) their human offspring than male authors.

Underlining in the prose below was inserted by Mary Beard; what she crossed out appears in square brackets; the words in parentheses, except for her undergraduate degree and her daughter's married name, are her own added comments.

107. PUBLICITY BIOGRAPHY PROFFERED BY THE MACMILLAN COMPANY

Mary Ritter Beard, [sociologist and historian,] was born in Indianapolis, Indiana, and received her education there and at DePauw University (Ph.B. 1897). Later she did graduate work at Columbia University.

Mrs. Beard has traveled widely in Europe and the Orient, and has long been active in the <u>cause</u> of women. Before the granting of the vote to women she was a leading suffragette. In 1937 she organized (no, just tried to in association with other women) the World Center for Women's Archives, <u>feeling that the</u> (not the sole reason) contributions of women had never received sufficient attention from historians of civilization. [She has also shown a particular interest in the improvement of nursing and the welfare of nurses.] (<u>No</u> this is the other Mary Beard—now of the Red Cross.) She is the author of "A Short History of the American Labor Movement" and "On Understanding Women," which has been described as "the most objective book ever written on the subject of women." She has collaborated with her husband, Dr. Charles A. Beard, in writing "The Rise of American Civilization," "A Basic History of the United States," and other books. She has also been editor or co-editor [of a number] of (two) volumes, including "America Through Women's Eyes" and "Laughing Their Way."

(Why this?) Dr. and Mrs. Beard are the parents of Miriam Beard (Mrs. Alfred Vagts), author of "A History of the American Business Man," (among other works) and of (Dr.) William Beard, author of "Government and Technology," (and other works.) The Beards live [in] (at) New Milford, Connecticut.

By mid-1945 Beard had no idea whether Walter Yust was ever going to publish the work she and others had written to change the *Encyclopaedia Britannica*.[3] Focusing more hope on Smith College because of her ally there, Margaret Grierson, she stressed that educational transformation might begin by means of an institute or series of seminars on women's history. Grierson had influence among Smith College alumnae because of her position as executive director of the Friends of the Smith College Library. "In my many dreams of ways and means for rooting the conception of woman as force in long history," Beard wrote to her, "one rather persistent dream has been that of a distinct organization, called 'College' if need be, and an alumna college at that to do the grounding in case no existing college would take the pains."[4] More immediately, Beard saw Grierson as someone who could build up a great collection of women's archives at the Sophia Smith Collection and perhaps organize information about women's archives across the nation. As the following letter shows, Beard had the idea—and had done some of the groundwork—for a comprehensive survey of women's collections. That was, of course, decades before Andrea Hinding and her associates at the University of Minnesota in the 1970s launched such a project, which resulted in the unique reference work, *Women's History Sources: A Guide to Archives and Manuscript Collections in the United States* (New York, Bowker, 1979).

In the following, Beard's memory of her role in making the suffrage movement political is sharp, except that she forgets that she spoke at three rather than two hearings before congressional committees. The speech she refers to below was presented to the U.S. House of Representatives Rules Committee in December 1913.

108. TO MARGARET GRIERSON

New Milford, Conn.
July 15, 1945

Dear Mrs. Grierson:

The movement for a better knowledge, hence understanding of women, is fortunate to have you as full-time promoter. Other persons are working at it but they have so many other tasks, even other library tasks, that they can only carry this movement forward in odd hours. Even if they could give their whole time to it, however, they might in no case have your conception of the task.

The enclosed list of institutions where materials are accumulating happens to be a list of places about which I know, as active spots, if in varying degrees of activity. Smith leads all the rest in fact, I believe, in respect of intelligent energy. But I have put the Detroit Library at the head of the enclosed list to indicate to you that it is getting important Michigan materials through the donations of Mrs. Hanavan who was the Michigan Chairman of the World Center for Women's Archives, and the intention of a fine group of Detroit women to make that a real center of archives now.

I appreciate your feeling of aloneness in trying to find out what is where. I have just suggested to Mrs. Hanavan that she procure a card catalogue of the fine collection of women's letters at the W. L. Clements Library at Ann Arbor to place in the Detroit Public Library for the use of students, writers, etc. And I have told her that she may be asked to send to you and others a report on present and future items deposited there. There are so many items in the Clements Lib. that Dr. Adams, its head, wrote me some time ago, via the librarian, that it would be impossible for the staff to undertake to list them for inquirers. But if you have an alumna in that region who could copy them, she would be welcome to do so. I understand that in that collection are letters of American women in great numbers running back to the 17th century.

I undertook to ask many college librarians some years ago to let me know what materials they have. But they also made excuses relative to sending me the items or frankly confessed that they had nothing or virtually nothing. On the Board of the defunct World Center for Women's Archives was Miss Mary Louise Alexander who, with Miss Ruth Savord (librarian now of the Council of Foreign Relations, N Y C) had set up a Special Library institution in N Y C. But Miss Alexander said it would be a herculean or impossible task to learn what libraries possess. Even so, I sent a lot of letters on my own initiative. And I learned that the *Huntington Library* in Pasadena, for example, has a lot of material. A friend of mine copied that list but I gave the copy to Dean Hilton of Syracuse before you began to operate at Smith, and just after the w c w a collapsed. If you have a fund at your disposal for making inquiries in all institutions, you could dispatch a form letter all round.

But a fine project for the Smith alumnae would be to explore college and great public libraries in their localities and make reports to you. This would be educational for them as enlightenment on collections or the lack of them.

About Hearings in the movement for woman suffrage. You will have to ask your alumnae for help there, I think, even in obtaining the highly important Hearings in both Houses of Congress. But I would concentrate perhaps first on the federal Hearings and be sure to get Hearings in which the old Congressional Union (later the National Woman's Party) participated, as well as Hearings which the NWP as such conducted. "Militancy", including Political Action which really brought Woodrow Wilson to the support of the Federal Amendment, can not be left neglected if the true and comprehensive story of the winning of the vote is to be on the record. I know the full force of the Political Action aspect of the campaign, which shortened the struggle, by direct participation in it. I spoke at two Hearings, once before the Judiciary Committee of the H. of R., and once before the Rules Committee of the Senate. If you should be able to get an extra copy of the Hearing before the Rules Committee at which I made my speech, I would be grateful for the gift of it to me. We got the amendment out of that committee as an outcome of that hearing as a result, I dare to believe, of my political "threat." Jane Addams was one of the spokeswomen but the Committee Chairman, from Georgia, lolled back in his chair and seemed to be going to sleep while she talked in her refined way. He sat up as if he had been stuck by a tack in his chair when I dared to attack the undue Southern representation in Congress and on this dominant Rules Committee, saying that the "West never does get justice" but in the West many women were voters and they would rectify this injustice in the coming election, etc. Anyway we got the amendment out of committee, with the aid of course of Miss Addams' personality and national position. I was speaking then for the Congressional Union; she for the regular suffragists who were making purely moral appeals.

Forgive me for seeming to inject myself into this matter. I do so to explain to you the need of getting *all* the federal Hearings. I have said this to Harvard-Radcliffe too.

Your idea of getting together a group to explore the present situation in colleges and universities in re materials on women, including books, is a fine idea—better than the alumnae idea solely, I believe. If a form letter of inquiry, i.e., were signed by such women as Mary Earhart of Northwestern, Dean Eunice M. Hilton of Syracuse, Chester McA[arthur] Destler of Connecticut College, it would get big results I should think. And all these persons would gladly sign I am sure. (If this idea were carried out, your alumnae might examine State & Local Hist. Soc. collections.)

I am glad you intend to visit Mrs. [Sophy] Drinker in her home. It is a great house and must be worth seeing itself. I have been urged to visit her myself, by her husband as well as by her, but as yet I have never got there. The Drinkers are top notchers in musical circles in Phila. I had lunch with

Mrs. Drinker in New York a few days ago and was delighted to hear that she wants to put her notes, etc., into A1 shape for you. She told me she had asked you for specifications in this connection. It is certainly best for you to go to see her stock. Take her as she is, of course, with all her ultra feminism. Her donation to Smith will be precious.

What you write me about Radcliffe and Harvard shocks me terribly. But do let me know what comes out of your talk at Cambridge when you have gone there.

About materials at Swarthmore. Fine stuff is there but I have heard that it has had no proper treatment for use or even for preservation. Ellen Starr Brinton came to see me once but maybe she has had no money at her disposal for ordering the materials properly. This is bad, bad.

I suggest your asking Pres. Felix Morley of Haverford what is in his library. Once I suggested to him, whom I have the pleasure of knowing and whom I admire, that the 3 colleges—Bryn Mawr, Haverford, and Swarthmore—who cooperate in many ways, build up a single fine library about women for their common use. Nothing came of it as far as I know.

That's grand about Mrs. [Elisabeth Anthony] Dexter's gift to Smith. The sources of her important book [*Colonial Women of Affairs* (Boston, 1926)] are imperative to know. I would appreciate your telling her (I am not lucky enough to know her or even to have her address) how much I value her one book and how I look forward to her No. 2. And it's wonderful too to get the records from Mrs. Hymer. If you have occasion to look at hers, after they arrive, and if you see the date of Mrs. Roosevelt's speech at the Cause and Cure of War when she began to turn to advocacy of a League to Enforce Peace, pray make a note of that date and pass it on to me. I tried to find it at the Yale Lib[rary] this spring in copies of the NY Times but failed in the time I was there.

HAVE YOU HEARD that among the candidates being proposed to succeed Pres. MacCracken [at Vassar College] is Eleanor Roosevelt?!

As for the records of Women Geographers I aspired to get them pledged to the World Center but got no pledge. I congratulate you on your victory. Also on enlivening Mrs. Morrow.

Here I sign off after signing on—to spare your eyes and moments.

With my devoirs to you

Mary R. Beard

[P.S.] But there's always a postscript. In this case about a larger book list. I am adding a very large bibliography, to my forthcoming book, of works depicting Woman as Force in History but omitting the grievances of women—leaving them to the specialists in that field. Meanwhile students

could be invited, to their profit, to read the Ancient and Mediaeval parts
of the Cambridge History.

◆━

There is no record of Mary Beard's reaction to the United States' atomic
attacks on Hiroshima and Nagasaki, or to the end of the war. Just weeks
afterward her mind was still on women's archives. Her inquiry to President Jordan below shows hope for a great collection at Radcliffe battling
with self-protective skepticism. Beard had for years been critical of the
Harvard ambiance and curriculum. Present at the celebration of the university's tricentennial in 1936, she was appalled at "the total lack of consciousness of woman." "The atmosphere of thought there has been as
masculine as any Mussolini or Hitler pageant," she wrote to Rosika
Schwimmer at the time. "Why do we make no impression whatever on
men?"[5] She was peeved that the gift to Harvard for a center in U.S. history in honor of Charles Warren—although made by the women of his
family—was made with no glance toward women's history. The Harvard
report of 1945, "General Education in a Free Society," did not encourage
her. President Jordan kept in touch with her off and on through the early
1950s, however, asking her recommendations about the Radcliffe
Women's Archives.

109. TO WILBUR K. JORDAN, PRESIDENT,
RADCLIFFE COLLEGE

New Milford, Connecticut
August 25, 1945

Dear President Jordan:

I shall be exceedingly grateful if you will give me direct information
about the amalgamation of Radcliffe and Harvard with reference to the
fortunes of the Woman's Archive and the building up of a library pertaining to women in long history.

At present I have nothing but rumor and I know full well how distorted
rumor can be. If a curt treatment of the project for enlightenment respecting half the human race has in fact been accorded this project, please tell
me this without feeling compelled to try easing my sorrow.

Rumor says that your plan for a proper Radcliffe building to house an
expanding library has been stymied. Having studied carefully the Report
of the Harvard Committee entitled GENERAL EDUCATION IN A FREE
SOCIETY and finding there only the conception of an education for the

male, naturally I am deeply troubled about the fate of what I have been hoping and expecting would be a new social content for education at Cambridge.

The section in this Report which deals with a call by Radcliffe alumnae and others for a course in "human relations" is anything but encouraging from my standpoint.

I do not wish to burden you, dear President Jordan, with the fear that I mean to reopen our heavy correspondence. I simply inquire whether the dream which I believe you shared with me has gone the way of many great dreams.

Sincerely yours, Mary R. Beard

Beard's disappointment in the delay of the scheduled publication of *Woman as Force* is palpable in the following letter. In fact the book did not come out until late in the spring of 1946.

110. TO JAMES PUTNAM, THE MACMILLAN COMPANY

New Milford, Connecticut
November 5, 1945

Dear Jim:

I never even dreamed that my book would not be published until spring. I did not know that this decision had been made. I did not know that you do not publish a new book in any December. I did dream that mine sold some at Christmas time. I am terribly disappointed although I know of course that I halted the date by my multitude of page corrections. I find it hard to bear your news but since I must do so, I shall the best I can.

In this situation, Mr. Gibson can have all the time he needs on the Index although it will help if he can let me see what he has done before I go away from home on November 20, two or three days before that so that I can make any revision I feel vital.

I shall have to send out a lot of postcards to persons who have expected with me that the book would be out this year. I shall do this at once. They have thought it would be useful very soon in their college and other jobs.

Well no further comment is necessary by any of us and I shall only add that I am glad you broke the news to me now, while I am still home and have access to addresses for these cards.

Our address will be Pine Crest Inn, Tryon, North Carolina where either of us can be reached directly after December first. Between November 20 and that time, letters will be forwarded from here. Our address in Washington we do not yet have positively.

I blame no one for the delay in publication. I should have written better for the copy I first sent in. I had to improve it almost at every pore. I should have only myself to blame, it seems. But if I had forseen this delay, I could have worked more at the MSS through the summer.

Yours as ever—Mary R. Beard

The following letter gives an unusually clear view of Mary Beard's continuing belief in women's nurturant function and her insistence on seeing that nurturance as part of public life. Often during the 1940s she seemed to take at face value popular claims that middle-class American women were leisured, even lazy, yet she retained confidence in the possibility that women could sustain a socially valuable and uplifting role differing from men's occupational emphasis. Despite her own sharp criticism of women's failures, she did not sympathize with male writers of the war era such as Philip Wylie, who, in *A Generation of Vipers* (1942) coined the term *Momism* and cast scattershot blame on women for all social discomforts and ills, from the high cost of living to juvenile delinquency.

III. TO FRIEDA MILLER, DIRECTOR OF THE
WOMEN'S BUREAU, U.S. DEPARTMENT OF LABOR

New Milford—Connecticut
May 6, 1946

Dear Miss Frieda:

Your article in yesterday's Times Magazine on Rosie the Riveter is both so packed with exact information and so thoughtful about facts that I am moved to write you of my esteem for this extraordinary presentation of the case of working women.

Sanity is terribly needed but an emotional attitude toward the subject is apt to dominate it. Secretary [of Labor] Schwellenbach's statement with which your discussion closes testifies, like your discussion, to the growing intelligence which should ease the long tension fostered by the dogma of woman's subjection to man throughout the ages and only beginning to be relieved by woman suffrage.

"Contributions to the world's upbuilding" have been made and with fundamental importance by women through the ages as I have indicated in part in my new book, Woman as Force in History. But some women, enormous numbers indeed, have had destructive urges. If our women can understand their powerful background as creative human beings in part and as destructive human beings to a high degree, we should be stronger characters in time. In current events, both types of women figure in every-day's news but American women—organized women who seek unity in slogans particularly—tend to lump all women into a single doctrine of sex. This I am struggling to make them realize. It is women themselves who put women over to men in so large a measure.

You are rendering a high service to both sexes by an article like this one in the Times.

There is one point which I would like for you to consider—the intellectual, moral, and social force which the "homemaker" could and should wield in the home. She is encouraged to excess to think of her role in the home as merely one of physical labor or baby-minding with its broader implications. But in long history the woman of the home was a force in lifting thought to new creative levels. In our society this woman continued to do that until recent years. Now she tends to get her release from housework and nursing children and guarding their health and behavior, as they grow in years, merely by playing bridge, running to the movies, taking guests to the theater or opera or night clubs, instead of reading and thinking about her historic function as an idea-maker. If intelligent discussion of life and its meaning, in the light of changing economy, politics, and knowledge, could be promoted in the home at the dinner table or during the evening, with the family and its guests, woman would again establish her historic leadership or cooperation in the "world's upbuilding." At present, and due I think, to the disgrace which was thrust into her mind by the exactions of the suffrage and other aspects of the feminist movement, such as the notion that the "woman of achievement" is only the woman who is physically active in business and professional affairs, the home-woman fails to cultivate her role as a builder of social philosophy.

If this woman does not regain her own sense of this kind of her inherited power, she will be the kind of material on which Hitler and other dictators of our age have preyed for their designs. The power of the Nazis grew from the uses made of just such housewives, for instance. And in our society we allow a man like Philip Wylie to make "Mom" just a "jerk." Here is a serious problem and one part and parcel of the problem of physical work for women, I firmly believe. The housewife must not be "out of the world" but *intelligently* within it. Otherwise her labor-saving gadgets will but stultify her brains.

With my tribute to you for your exceptionally fine handling of woman's labor in yesterday's write up in the Times, I am cordially yours,

Mary R. Beard

Woman as Force in History was published in March 1946. Mary Beard was almost seventy years old. Although reviews were mixed, there was much to please the author. Beard wrote to Jim Putnam at Macmillan on June 1, 1946:

> Reviews of mine continue to my surprised delight. They are of many kinds and several are really wonderfully understanding of my subject and my method of handling it as well as of inevitable attitudes toward it. For instance I get by the New Yorker remarkably well; the Toledo Blade gets my method perfectly and carried a long review commending the method, etc.; the St. Louis Globe-Democrat gets the meaning of force with a fine objective grasp; a Philadelphia paper . . . opens with the sentence that this book will not be liked by the "woman-hater or the professional Feminist" and this was sagacious in view of the damnation meted out to me by Independent Woman; and the Toronto Star has stirred interest in Canada.[6]

Her book was published amid a postwar cacophony of assessments of women's roles, flaws, and virtues. A redefinition of gender expectations and the sexual division of labor occurred in part as a backlash against women's public visibility as vital workers during the war. Beard's emphasis on women's historic strengths and capacities for good *and* evil combined with her critique of the defects of feminism into a unique approach. She writes here to a banker who was active in professional women's organizations.

112. TO DORCAS CAMPBELL

New Milford—Connecticut
August 4, 1946

Dear Miss Campbell:

It will give me genuinely great pleasure to autograph my book for you. I am deeply grateful for your interest in it in advance of your reading it and I hope your interest will be strengthened after you have read it.

. . . No doubt, thanks to your help in part, the first printing was sold out

within a month after its publication. Now no copies are available until a
new printing is made and when that will be finished I do not yet know.

We've got to make women historically sensitive to their true character
and force, unless we are to rest inert about the horribly loose talking and
writing they indulge in on the subject of women. I have had the satisfaction this past week of hearing that, at the Business and Professional gathering recently at Cleveland, only one woman, Congresswoman [Helen
Gahagan] Douglas, repeated all the cliches; that in conversations together, my book furnished fire, and it was widely agreed that women
must cease to chatter so foolishly about their kind. So I dare to hope that
a new era is dawning in which our kind will emerge from infantile innocence into the richness of adult intelligence. Your aid will be of immense
value.

The great popular women's magazines, Home Companion and Mc-
Call's, are dishing out the naive stuff in huge doses this summer via Philip
Wylie and Edward Bernays. It is women's fault that the masculine editors
get away with this business. For some of this writing, commitments had
been made before my book came out, it seems. But now I have received a
letter from a major editor who professes to have been "profoundly interested in it" and invites me to write an article on women's contribution to
civilization.

It is their [own] contribution to civilization, I find, that men themselves
long to have emphasized. They are inclined, however, to want only that
kind of article. They too lightly ignore woman's force for barbarism
though I have felt it vital to emphasize that too. We are not all of one type
and never have been; we have the inner-sex conflict no less than a conflict
between the sexes to consider if we mature mentally. But of all this we
may talk, may we not, together, after you have explored my book—perhaps in the early autumn? I could lunch with you some day if you would
like that?

> Most cordially yours,
> Mary R. Beard

The following letter is not the first nor would it be the last Mary Beard
wrote to her publisher about delay and inadequate publicity for *Woman
as Force*. (It is notable, too, that Macmillan editors addressed her, as if in
willful ignorance, as Mrs. C. A. Beard, rather than using the name she
preferred.) The initial publication of the book had been six months later

than she expected. The first run of 5,000 was sold out by late summer of 1946, but the second printing was not available until early December. During 1947 a third and fourth printing were made, bringing the total number of copies in print by December 1947 to 10,000. *The Rise of American Civilization*, in comparison, sold over 133,000 copies, and the Beards' best seller, *A Basic History of the United States*, over 600,000.[7]

113. TO JAMES PUTNAM, THE MACMILLAN COMPANY

New Milford—Connecticut
September 18, 1946

Dear James:

What is the meaning really of so long a holdup of a second printing of my book? You will remember, I hope, that when you and I had lunch with Mr. Latham about the matter of publication, I said that I was ready to sign a contract with another House that very afternoon unless I could be assured that Macmillan would truly get behind it. That assurance was given me and so, when I kept an appointment with a person who was waiting to know whether another publisher could have the book, I reported that I had placed it with your House and why—making our long association with Macmillan my reason. The other publisher seemed to want it badly and I now feel sure that he would have printed a larger first printing than your House did.

When I took the manuscript in for Mr. Latham to see in part, though in a very rough first draft, he said definitely that he was assigning the paper for it though I did not think to ask for how many copies. Later when Mr. Latham broke down and while you were away from the office, I took the finished MS to Mr. Cunningham and was greatly surprised when he remarked: "Now the problem is one of getting it published." Perhaps he did not know the history of Mr. Latham's confessed interest in promoting the book.

I have tried, in an effort to avoid overburdening you with a report to me on the status of a new printing, to get information about it from the publicity and sales departments. But of course the printing is not their responsibility and they have not given me the information though they have of course been friendly and hopeful I believe.

You must know that it may be very hard to revive the truly immense interest which this book met in the press of the whole nation, if the new printing is delayed longer. I fear it may be even too late now although several people have written me that they have had orders for it placed with Doubleday and other bookshops for two months or more. They seem anxious to get it but others who were stirred by the battle over it in the press may forget all about it as the flood of later offerings mounts, though it does not deal with my subject.

Word has come from Macmillan that a publisher in Switzerland asks for the right to bring out an edition there in French. But as far as I know a second printing with two corrections which I sent you long ago for it is not even in sight.

I cannot doubt that your personal goodwill to me is as strong as ever. I cannot doubt that you will drop me a line so that I may know what to expect and say to correspondents who put questions to me. Yesterday I had to give a Chinese delegate to UN the only copy I possessed when he visited us and expressed intense interest in my thesis, owing to his great learning about the women of his race as women of force. Property was passed down through them for a very long time, for instance. He is to send me important materials about Chinese women which are as yet no part of our knowledge.

This is a long epistle and I regret that I have it to write. But I am not just a huzzy—certainly not "The Glamorous Huzzy" as Hollywood represented Peggy Eaton to be, unjustly as to her.

I simply ask to be let into the know about more copies of my book.

Yours truly—Mary R. Beard

[P.S.] Be assured on your part that I deeply appreciated the fine publicity which emanated from your House when the book appeared. I get reviews still for the month of August. But the papers can hardly repeat them and that area of publicity is probably closed.

Although the *Encyclopaedia* project faded into oblivion, Mary Beard remained a fond friend of Marjorie White's. This nostalgic letter, more personal than almost all of Beard's correspondence, shows something of her emotional and aesthetic sides.[8]

114. TO MARJORIE WHITE

New Milford
Oct. 17 [1946]

Dear Marjorie:

How any one can kill a deer of either sex is more than my imagination can conceive—that is, how this can happen as a sport. I know your appreciation of that "jewel moment" when you exchanged greeting with the doe. We used to have them bound across our grounds here and pause close to our house now and then while we kept perfectly quiet for the exchange of sensitivities. And one morning when I had attempted to take a seven o'clock train to NYC but missed it, as I came back and walked up the hill from the street to my house, a doe with three adorable kiddies bounded across my path. Now once in a while we catch a glimpse of a deer in the woods behind our farm at South Kent in which hunters are not allowed to go. But the killing taste, once a necessity for survival and now a mere gloating over shooting skill for the most part, sickens me. Our grandson a few years ago at his home over the hills used to put food on his stone fence for the deer which he had seen close to the fence and once he caught it eating it. That esthetic experience he will never forget and it will help to keep him aware of the amenities of life, now in our age when amenities are more possible, as new conceptions of life.

While I have been brought up as a meat-eater, I am disgusted to the marrow of my bones by the pictures of the horrible slaughtering of cattle, hogs, and horses for human consumption. But I try to remember that manual laborers need their flesh and cultivate a restraint against preciosity. When I lived in England I knew some workingmen who would not touch meat and one carried his distaste for killing so far that he wouldn't even kill a fly. He was a Tolstoyan but I do not know that Tolstoy went that far. Oh I knew very well such magnificently idealistic laborers in England—locomotive engineers, miners (Keir Hardie for instance), weavers, etc.,—that association with them changed the whole course of my life.

They were nearly all cooperators in ideology and they mostly belonged to that wonderful cooperative movement in England. Charles lectured to large audiences throughout England composed of directors and members of that movement. It was all based on the idea of *civil*-ization and loyal to that great creative formula for living. Edward Carpenter wrote magnificent hymns for such a movement and their singing gave me intense joy. It was not violent in motivation—not martial music—not barbaric. It was a response to a high ideal of overcoming the tooth-and-claw struggle by respect for personal values. It was this type of labor movement which was adopted for Japan in the first decade of our century and I used to go to labor meetings there frequently and sing with the men and women there, see their sensitive labor plays, listen to their own composed music which was sung to their lovely biwa, thrill over what seemed to me to be a hope-

ful drive against exploitation and headed toward a *civil*-ization in that
land of esthetic tastes.

[M.R.B.]

The following continues Mary Beard's saga of understandable complaint
to her publisher about the treatment of her book. The second printing she
was seeking became available just as she wrote. Still, a year later, distressed that Macmillan had not advertised, she wrote, "I have felt justified in wondering whether Macmillan is really interested in my book."
Finally, the fourth printing was advertised in the *New York Times Book
Review* for February 1, 1948.[9]

115. TO HAROLD LATHAM, THE MACMILLAN COMPANY

Pine Crest Inn
Tryon, North Carolina
December 3, 1946

Dear Mr. Latham:

Since we last lunched together you have experienced deep sorrow and
great physical suffering. All your friends have longed to have you recover
your ground and I have numbered myself among them.

Now your letter with its invitation to lunch with you again seems to
indicate that you have regained vitality. I wish I could have a chance to
talk with you in that informal way and immediately, but Charles and I
have tucked into a cabin here for the winter and we shall probably stay
here this time until the first week in April.

Charles is writing you too, individually.

I am in the strangest possible position relative to my new book, dear
Mr. Latham. Nearly every day I get one or more letters from all parts of
the country and from teachers, club women who plan to discuss it in their
groups, and from women prominent in national organizations, among
others. Now and then a fine press comment still comes in, one from Can-
ada for instance about ten days ago. But no copies as far as I know are
available in book shops and I get no word whatsoever on this affair since I
was told months ago that the new printing was held up because of the
shortage of glue.

Since you do bring out new printings of other books, the one by Nor-
throp for example which was first published later than mine and which,

in my opinion, is commonplace in its conclusions though it gets a full page advertisement, I am really nonplussed by what I seem unable to believe is simply a matter of glue in the case of my book. Naturally I thought that it might have something of a sale at Christmas time in view of the swift sale of the first printing and such interest as was displayed by the Newsweek letter to clubs which in effect made my book a "must" for them. But it is not available as far as I know among Christmas books and for six months, as I understand it, it has been out of print.

Please tell me frankly what this means. If it means shortage of glue still, does that mean that my book is in the hands of some little shop, rather than a firstclass printing house? I am entitled, don't you agree, to know why I get this kind of deal, especially when I was promised that the House would get behind this book and truly promote it?

I have not bothered you personally about this matter during your long illness. I don't want to seem insensitive now by appealing directly to you when you may still have to eliminate all the labor you can. But after all it will be easier on you, I assume, to read these few lines from me than to hear me talk about the trouble I am having at a longish lunch time.

Meanwhile, as you may have heard, such interest in it exists in Switzerland that a publisher there asked your House for the privilege of bringing out an edition in French. The book has been written up in Germany and Japan—in Japan also discussed over the radio. And I had a letter recently from Brazil, where a librarian wrote me of her high regard for it and asked me to send her another copy if I could. I gave the last one even I had to Mr. Chiang of China who is prominent in the General Assembly of the UN and who spent some time with Charles and me at New Milford.

If for any reason my book has become objectionable to the House of Macmillan, let me know this so that I shall not be longer in the dark. I am refraining from suspicions of any kind and only seeking the truth about this curious situation.

Sincerely yours, Mary R. Beard

[P.S.] One of the most convincing letters I have had relative to the worth of my book is from a woman who said that from her personal experience she had believed that women were a subject sex but that she didn't want to judge all women and all men from her personal experience and that I had incited her to be broader-minded. She was grateful.

7 The Postwar Years

In the immediate postwar years Mary Beard spent many words publicly defending her thesis in *Woman as Force* and privately defending Charles Beard's character and reputation. She started a new writing project, which would eventually be published as *The Force of Women in Japanese History*. In her hopes to have *Woman as Force in History* supply an agenda for women in the present, Mary Beard saw as an immediate antagonist a contemporary book, the popular diatribe by Ferdinand Lundberg and Marynia Farnham, *Modern Woman: The Lost Sex*. Steeped in vulgarized Freudianism, the book argued that modern women—led astray by feminist preachers of equal rights from Mary Wollstonecraft onward—had, in aping men, lost touch with their real source of power, their sexual capacity to mother. Its litany of sorry results from women's wrong turn included all the evils of postwar society, from totalitarianism to modern nervousness. No doubt the eager reception of the book was due in part to its sharp articulation of the personal anxieties of the atomic age. That it located a convenient scapegoat for all problems—women—and moreover, a solution—women's acceptance of their sexuality and motherhood—made it all the more appealing.

Beard hated the book, for obvious reasons, and resented the much greater notice (and sales) it obtained than hers. While she was justifiably angered by Lundberg and Farnham's failure to learn from *Woman as Force* (which they cited), she did not acknowledge that her own truculence about the damage weaked by equal rights proponents to some degree mirrored theirs. The following letter is her reply to the editor-in-chief at Harper and Row after he had sent her an early copy of *Modern Woman*. Her remarks on its "extraordinary performance" are astute. The rage and despair this book caused her deepened her animus against Freud and psychoanalysis—although to call Lundberg and Farnham's work "Freudian" does a disservice to Freud. In a contemporary letter to President Jordan of Radcliffe, Beard wrote, "I dare to call psychiatry the new priestcraft and I consider it worse than the theological priestcraft in that the theological priestcraft offered some salvation from evil if only after death, thus providing some basis for thinking about the good. The new priestcraft offers nothing, I am convinced, but obsession with sex re-

lations and is making more neurotics every day every way instead of healing hurt minds and bodies." [1]

116. TO EDWARD ASWELL

Pine Crest Inn—Tryon, N. Carolina
January 15, 1947

Dear Mr. Aswell:

I hope that I have your name right and that you will believe me when I
say that the opinion I express here is given in a friendly spirit as a problem
in knowing and thinking, even if I seem to be speaking bluntly.

I appreciate your sending me a second copy of MODERN WOMAN:
THE LOST SEX and asking me again for my opinion of it. I read it immediately after it arrived as you will see from the dates of your second letter
and this reply.

To my great surprise and interest, the authors have obviously been impressed by my studies of women and have both made use of my studies
and commented on my comments.

In commenting on one of my comments, Appendix VI, page 421, they
say: "With Mrs. Beard's central thesis, stated in her preface (to Woman as
Force in History) that 'Women have done far more than exist and bear
and rear children' we would disagree. For no one of the many accomplishments of women she lists compares in historical importance with the
role of women as mothers."

In this instance of the Lundburg-Farnham collaboration I find superbly
illustrated their inability or refusal to let A equal A. My words "far
more" are a quantitative measurement and not a moral or other evalu-
ating judgment. But the authors give to these words their own moral, social, or historical judgment which makes A equal B.C.D.....Z. What I
demonstrated in my book was that whether women were mothers or not,
they did more things than mothering their offspring; that is, they carried
on many kinds of activities. I was simply stating a fact in the words taken
from my book, in proof that women were not confined by men to motherhood, as the dominant interpretation of woman in history avers.

But, for the moment, suppose women had been confined or had restricted their energies to mothering by their own volition, what kind of
human life would have characterized history? Would there have been
what is called "history" at all? That is a proper question a propos the
book which you submit for my judgment but I am not going into that here.

All in all, MODERN WOMAN: THE LOST SEX, seems to me to be an extraordinary performance in confusion and contradictions from beginning to end wherever the authors express themselves. Insofar as I can capture the substance of their volume, it appears to be a medley of talk about motherhood, one sex, pain over the industrial revolution, capitalism, the disillusionment with socialism as a social cure-all, and the cliches of contemporary psychiatry. Paternity escapes to excess, surely, from its co-responsibility for efficient child rearing.

Having apparently drawn to such an extent from my work, I am amused by the assertion on page 421 that I have "gathered together practically every example known to history of woman as achievers outside the sphere of nurture." The truth is that I have scarcely touched this business in the small compass of my books. I am doubly entertained by the accompanying statement that the authors have "inquired into scholarly studies dealing with antiquity as far back as Babylon." Their method of inquiry is peculiar, to say the least, in view of their declaration that I have cited "practically every prominent example."

But even if they had only looked at my examples, how could they have asked the questions they do ask on page 459? Or have asked them after examining the materials given in my Bibliography?

Moreover these authors need to go further back than Babylon with their research, as I did, to social origins as far as prehistoric materials open them, and so vitalize their thinking about woman by knowledge of what her creative intelligence accomplished at the dawn of human time.

There is no use for me to elaborate further my opinion of the book in question. In place of mine you have the opinion of Philip Wylie of course and, since he is now made omniscient by the house of Rinehart, evidently with your consent, I certainly do not belong in his class of verdict-givers.

Sincerely and cordially,
Mary R. Beard

●━━

This rare personal letter, written to their daughter and son-in-law from the Beards' midwinter retreat in North Carolina, renders Mary Beard's sardonic humor perhaps more authentically than any other single document. It also reveals an accidental meeting with Southerner James F. Byrnes, whom Franklin Roosevelt appointed to the U.S. Supreme Court in 1941 and then took from the court to head the Office of War Mobilization. Byrnes later served as Secretary of State under Truman from 1945 to 1947, playing an important role in atomic diplomacy.

117. TO MIRIAM BEARD VAGTS AND ALFRED VAGTS

The Inn [Tryon, N.C.]
on Feb 5 [1947]

Well well Hi, Beloveds, guess who came here to spend this week?

None other than Jimmy Byrnes—the Mrs. and his sister and a secretary (a woman). We were told he would be here and we said that if introductions seemed mandatory in the lounge to have us introduced as Jim Doakes and his wife. A few hours after their arrival as we were starting out of the compound for a walk, we met them coming in from their walk with a terrier on a leash. They did the first bowing; we bowed for bow, nobody spoke a name.

Today at noon the doors to the dining room were a bit slow in opening. We saw his Nibs coming through the front door into the lounge and we retreated to the far end. Dad was standing alone there. I picked up a New Yorker from the table. What did Jimmy do but go to CAB and say he was delighted to see him here? (this after his hostility to CAB's talk before the Senate For. Relations Com to the effect that Lend Lease was a war measure irrevocably). Uncle Charlie also expressed pleasure on this occasion (altho his sulpha treatment for pneumonia which he thought had destroyed his sense of smell had not deprived him of a sense of a whiskey breath). Most affable was the ex-Sec.; said he was enjoying the rest here from being eternally at the beck and call of some other person. So they chatted for a few minutes, partly about our change from Aiken to Tryon about which Jimmy inquired; he had been a judge there and married there rather above his class.

Meanwhile Mrs. Byrnes came to me and introduced herself very quietly and unpretentiously like a well-bred person. She also introduced Mr. Byrnes' sister and the secretary. Dad tells me that Jimmy's mother was a laundress (if I remember this precisely) and presumably his sister as well as his mother helped young Jimmy on his way up the scale in his youth. Well at least he seems kind to his sister who looks as if life had not been easy on her.

It seemed as if I ought to invite them all to our igloo but I refrained with an apology that we have no chairs which would be comfortable— the truth if I ever told it. But I pointed out the igloo and I think they will come on their own initiative. Our chairs are a severe sort, but o.k. for work and at other times we can soften 'em up with pillows. We have one of those sway-back wooden rocking chairs, i.e. which fits the architecture of the cabin but fits no human frame known to me today.

Perhaps everyone around this place is especially sociable today because last night was so bitterly cold—down to zero at our thermom[eter] just outside the door—that everyone had a funny tale to tell of how the night was passed. I myself, I said, slept in everything but a fur coat and this was a cue to those who had 'em to say they threw theirs over their beds. No fellow opened a window, it seems. I certainly did not and even dad broke his strict rule and kept his closed. But I had brought extra blankets and a steamer rug. With sweaters over pajamas—our cottage has cracks through which the wind blows—then blankets wrapped around us, then overcoats and for me the steamer rug—one thing CAB scorned anyway though I tried to insist on it for him—and my head wrapped in a woolen scarf and my feet buried in woolen sox, with swigs of brandy we slept a long night through. But in other tighter cottages women went from door to door, in some cases, to be sure their friends had enough wraps; they carried quilted dressing gowns, hot water bottles, etc. Some of them were colder than we were because they wouldn't use their mink coats or because the denizens of a cottage could not agree on where to put the thermostats before they were to bed. We two did agree in our cabin by CAB's taste and my steamer rug for extra cover.

We are as chipper today as can be. So is everyone who got colder. It is a warmer day but everyone is reckoning with another cold night. I see Jimmy out walking this minute in the sun which is very bright. We just came in—dad to write to Detlev and I to write you.

A man left early this a.m. by motor for his home in Oshkosh, Wis. His young son asked him to bring him a pair of skis. "But I am going south for a week's rest," the father replied. "No, you're not," said the kid. "I know you're going to *North* Carolina. You can't fool me."

Despite such flurries of cold weather here, I think today that this is the best place for us for the winters ahead and maybe for longer times—because here is one of the best dentists in the country as well as a very good hospital for an emergency. Yesterday the dentist performed a major operation by skilfully extracting the last tooth in the back of my upper jaw and doing it with all the care and interest of a great surgeon and artist. So many welltodo people are buying land and building here that he is thriving with his practice as a prime attraction for old folks.

A poor old Negro woman was burned out of house and home last week. All the Inns folk ran down the hill to try to save something. The house was big and old. Everything went but the old woman was saved. The cook at the Inn sent sheets for her bed at a relative's. I contributed a blanket from my store. Others donated some clothes. We got her fixed up for quite a while.

Meanwhile the last chapter of dad's second and last volume on foreign policy has not only gone to New Haven but been read and highly approved by Eugene Davidson of the Yale Press. So we have about decided to go from here to New Haven in the middle of March and have Paul drive there for us again at the end of March. That way dad can go over the copy and check nearly all of it so that the Ms can go into the works by early May.

Byrnes' "place in history," a la Beard? Never tell him shall we. He can read it if he wants to—then cry or fume. But he's a simple little fellow with the power to work great evil like all simple or all "sophisticated" folk.

Enough is sometimes too much. So I sign off here. Hoping though that you had a grand time with Detlev at home and that you are all as strong now as you are all brave, in your battles with the weather and with life; for your greatest good and happiness.

Mother

The following letter, to Beard's old friend Anne Martin, documents the curious evaporation of the *Encyclopaedia Britannica* revisions. Martin, trained as a historian, was also the first woman to run for the U.S. Senate—though unsuccessfully, in Nevada in 1918 and 1920. She consistently maintained that women had to gain political power through elected office to approach the reality of equal rights. Where Martin's daunting political experience made her criticize male politicians' exclusivity, Beard's inclination at this point was to look for women's participation in the problem. What might have been behind Beard's woman-blaming and seeming exoneration of men was her disappointment that women did not mobilize a united front. Her memories of the suffrage coalition ruled here. In another letter, she wrote to Martin, "As to those men of Nevada who don't want to open political careers to women, if women who are voters too won't work for women, the blame cannot be wholly placed on men. Can it? Remember how we won the federal amendment by getting enfranchised women to vote against masculine opposition? If a victory could be promoted in a national movement like that why can't it be used in a state for women candidates if good ones wish to hold offices?"[2]

In response to Martin's reading of *Woman as Force,* Beard launched into a vitriolic assessment of women's rights and wrongs. Beard had never imagined (as did some feminists) that women involuntarily internalized a sense of inferiority or helplessness because of the oppressive structure of gender hierarchy. In her view, the evidence that one woman had taken advantage of a given opportunity—such as the existence of equity courts—meant that all women could, if they tried. She cited more than once the limited divorce sued in chancery in 1945 by Doris Duke, heiress to the tobacco fortune, as modern proof of her case in *Woman as Force.*

118. TO ANNE MARTIN

Pine Crest Inn—Tryon, N. Carolina
February 27/ [19]47

Dear Anne:

You rightly ask again about your article written for the Encyclopaedia Britannica and I am so sorry that I can't tell you a thing about it yet. Mr. Yust has never kept me in touch with one of the numerous sketches or anything else which he authorized me to collect for this compendium. I have heard from a few women that they had received proofs of their short sketches of women but I think that Mrs. Henry Drinker of Philadelphia whose longish article on women in music was accepted has not yet had her proof. The system of revision, as I think I wrote you quite some time ago, permits only of insertions for new materials when a space is cleaned of material already filling it; or when pages are added and a whole volume thus renumbered. I was told by Mr. Yust that it was the plan to carry as many as 100 additional pages per volume when that amount were ready. It is possible that the taking over of the Encyclopaedia by the University of Chicago has affected the whole situation but Mr. Yust has left me completely in the dark for more than two years about events with which I was associated. I think the only thing to do is for you to write him again about your article. His behavior is incomprehensible to me as treatment of me. We never had anything resembling a quarrel. All that I ever said when he asked me how long the project of gathering materials on women would take was "as long as the Encyclopaedia enlarges." Whether that ended the matter for him, I do not know. It should not. But I am asking no more women to write for it, in the circumstances.

. . . Whether some one else is now editor, I don't even know. I think not, however, because Mrs. Drinker saw him not long ago when she passed through Chicago. Naturally she too longs to have her fine article in print. If Mr. Yust does not intend to print yours, he ought to tell you so and why. Once upon a time I asked him to let contributors know when, as, and if their work was not acceptable. The situation "puts me on the spot."

As for your comments on my book and its thesis, pray don't feel for a second that your unfavorable remarks are in the least "presumptuous." I do not demand praise though of course it is pleasurable when I get it. You do praise the book and me—me to excess. Your questions interest me and to them I reply the best I can, as follows:

1) "The very fact", you say, "that it was necessary for Equity to do so much," in my view, "seems to prove that women at one time at any rate were a legal and civil cipher under coverage and protected by the husband."

As to this opinion of yours, I can only reply that, if you can reread very calmly what I have written about the Common Law—about its origin and its relation to the feudal order which *bound both men and women* in servitude to the feudal State, perhaps you will "get me" better.

Deeply as I myself loved Mrs. Pankhurst and other great feminists who took Blackstone as authority, for rebellion against his conception of its perfection, I now understand, if with equally deep sorrow, their and my past limitations. In my book I have indicated that he did not know enough law when he either deliberately or negligently left Equity out of account.

2) But why Equity at all, you ask? Well, without it, how could law ever cover every affair in dispute between men and women? If you can examine again the problems brought before courts of equity, illustrations of which I give on pages 166–169, perhaps you will appreciate the impossibility of any written law's providing for such matters.

This difficulty is illustrated in the case of Doris Duke's contest with her husband recently over her property and divorce. Her husband, [James] Cromwell and his tough old mother tried to get some seven million dollars from Doris, she declared, and she went to equity about it—that is to the Court of Chancellery in New Jersey and won her case or cause of her rights as against their greed.

If the Federal Equal Rights Amendment were to become law, the issues of practice would become innumerable. The interpretations of Equality and no discriminations would have to be up for adjudication. Equity would have to be the resort. It would not guarantee judgments which in every case an extreme feminist might think the right ones or the wrong ones but it would have to be used.

Only where and when there is no litigation, is law a working fiat. Only where and when men and women are decent to one another is Equity not a value.

3) As to the rudeness of husbands, no law can end that now nor could it have ended it completely in the past. Law can't change all human nature. Women who simply cringe before nasty husbands are weak creatures by choice. Moreover women can be the detestable party, as you must know, and as they often have been and still are. Wives even beat up and even murder husbands, as husbands beat up and even murder wives. There is too much tendency among women, I believe, to think that indecent conduct all runs one way.

If men manage estates in which women have rights, that is or can be the women's reluctance or inability to manage them themselves. There was a case—there are more cases—in my village in Conn. where a widow got a huge estate by her husband's death; she had been his housekeeper and was too ignorant to know how to handle the estate; she called in a man to do it for her and he was so corrupt that he almost wrecked her. Countless women are either too indolent or put men's knowledge above their own by their own choice and so let men have the opportunity to control women's property and business. But the character of the law is not responsible. And in the instances which you encountered in England of men's running women's estates, the women didn't have to let this happen because of the nature of the law. They could have taken their trouble, if they were aware of trouble, to an equity court, if the man resisted, and got rid of his interference. Many women would rather endure men's egoism or rudeness than assume the obligations of thought and action themselves.

There was a horrible case in court which Mrs. Pankhurst knew about—which sent her to the revolt in feminism. The Judge himself was the father of the child which the mother wished to protect and he punished her. But you know that many women try to palm off on men babies which the men have not fathered.

In short, personal dispositions affect the relations of the sexes and law can not take account of all such vagaries without equity for their adjustments if men or women truly want adjustments. A lot of them seem to prefer to quarrel at home, resign themselves as far as they can to meannesses, to avoid a bad fuss, get lovers illegally, etc.

4) You refer to men's reluctance or refusal to share political offices with women. But what can the law do about this?

It might require that the presidency of the U.S. be rotated as between men and women. It might require that men and women be elected in equal numbers to both houses of Congress and to both houses of legislatures. It might demand that administrative offices be shared equally. But that would not necessarily work out beautifully in all respects.

The two major political parties have made equal representation a feature of their national conventions, etc.

But women themselves are generally so childish in their conceptions of politics and government that their leaders repeatedly affirm that women don't know enough yet to help run the govt and politics. Mrs. Roosevelt has declared that no woman knows enough to be president and Mrs. Tillett recently said that women must learn how to play "the man's game of politics." Women won't vote for women with much delight and women won't run for office to any extent. So many prefer to work with or behind men rather than to work at knowledge and carry the awful burdens of State that, in my opinion, it is very wrong to put all the blame upon men for so few women in public offices.

5) If I really "lean backward" in claiming that "inequalities" are fewer or smaller than they are, I tried to meet that objection by going after the credo that woman had been nothing in history, as a possible way to make such existing discriminations as *law* may cover by fiat seem *anachronisms*, which should be ended as such, instead of being viewed as long historic wrongs.

Anyway for your appreciation of any values discoverable in my book and for your sincere and firm friendship, I am

Ever yours—Mary Beard

Ever since her stay in Japan in 1922–23 Mary Beard had cherished a special interest in Japanese women. She particularly cultivated a friendship with Shidzue Kato (formerly Baroness Ishimoto), who was born into an elite samurai family just before the turn of the century but broke away to become a birth control reformer and campaigner for the civil rights of women. Mary Beard brought her to the United States for the international congress of women in Chicago in 1933, encouraged her to write her autobiography, and helped her get the autobiography published in the United States in 1935. Ostracized at home for the next decade, Shidzue Kato became an adviser to the U.S. occupation government after the war and was elected in 1946 to the Japanese legislature.[3] It was she who started Beard on a book on women in Japanese history, handing on to her a series of sketches of Japanese women in mythology and history, which had originally been written for the Japanese section of a women's world encyclopedia planned by a Viennese, Anna Askanasy. That plan collapsed when the Nazis invaded Vienna. In 1946 and 1947 Mary Beard was working with Dorothy Brush, a writer and birth control reformer active in the International Planned Parenthood Federation, to turn the Japanese sketches into a publishable book.

One of the women with whom Shidzue Kato worked in occupied Japan was Lt. Ethel Weed. A public relations professional before the war, Weed had joined the Women's Army Corps in 1941 and became one of a select number assigned by the U.S. occupation forces to strengthen the participation of Japanese women in postwar democratization of their nation. Probably on Shidzue Kato's recommendation, Weed contacted Mary Beard for advice about efforts to turn out Japanese women for the first postwar vote and to establish an agency like the U.S. Women's Bureau in Japan. Beard and Weed carried on a lively and friendly correspondence for years.

119. TO LT. ETHEL B. WEED

New Milford—Connecticut
March 30, 1947

Dear dear Lt. Weed:

There greets me as I come home today from North Carolina via New Haven your wonderful gift of the PUBLICATIONS ANALYSIS respecting the role of Japanese women in this crucial time.

I have read it, shall study it, share it on Tuesday with Dorothy Brush who is coming for the day to go into the book on women in Japanese history as a careful review of her work on it by this date, and make great use of it at an April conference to be held at Smith College on the higher education of our women.

This analysis comes at the perfect hour for me. I could have wished for nothing more clearcut as a discussion of social objectives, the relation of women to them, and the nature of the education which must be given to them (as well as to men, I amend) if the objectives are even approached. This will help me to make my participation in the conference at Smith very concrete, especially since it points the moral which I wish to draw sharply: that it is "natural" for women to help shape societies and their education must be in their long history to let what is natural take a new and better course.

If anything is printed or mimeographed as proceedings of that conference on April 18–20, I shall send it to you.

We are very backward in the U.S. as to enlightenment about the "nature" and history of women. Sexologists are helping to retard us. We have not done enough in our democracy in this matter to help the democratic way of life in other lands. But maybe we can effect this kind of a revolution in education soon now. There is a growing realization of its need but the opposition here, as in Japan and everywhere else, is strong and articulate. Yet it is surely a good sign that Smith College is summoning men and women to discuss the issue. One of the best women in higher education of women is the *new head* of Barnard College[, Millicent Carey McIntosh]. I wish she could have gone to Japan on that educational mission instead of Virginia Gildersleeve. The change in the directorate at Barnard is all to the good. *But you will of course not give publicity to this confidential appraisal of mine.*

I had an encouraging time last week at Hagerstown, Maryland, where I was guest of the Zonta Club (made up of women in high professional positions and women business executives, as you may or may not know) and delivered a "speech" after the dinner which was not only attended by men as well as women but paid for by their purchase of tickets for the occasion. There were prominent lawyers, doctors, professors, ministers, and other important men in the very large audience. Some people had driven from Annapolis and others from Baltimore. I condensed my book, "On Understanding Women," which in effect dealt with ways in which men and women are alike: in their conception of physical comfort as a basic need of the civilized way of life; in their idea of society as an idea of commingled human relations; in their love of power and pomp or in their desire to keep both within bounds; in their religious emotions whatever forms of faith and rituals they prefer; in their idea of science and the use of science in modern programs for social action; in their historic education and their sense of values inherent in education however they may differ in what should now be done as education; etc. I call this a "composite personality" of modern men and women and I traced, in this speech as I did in that book of mine, the origins of these common ideas and the course of their development in long history—as a development promoted by both sexes. My theme seemed to "take." I know it is sound historically.

If we can get that book on women in Japanese history into circulation, that will be an immense asset to this line of thinking. But publishing today in the USA is a terrible problem for publishers and authors of books which give basic information and so are not "best sellers." Publishers are really robots, bound to keep the presses running every minute of the days, and now they seem only able to put through the mill the non-fiction, non-sentimental, non-sexual informative manuscripts when a million-sales work lets up for a few hours. It is a hard situation for publishers of intelligence and for authors who truly have vital material to offer the public but the difficulties are not so depressive that nothing is being done to overcome them. When the Japanese story gets into good shape, I have confidence that it will find its place in the press. One reason for this assurance is the immense success of a novel on contemporary Japan just issued by Doubleday. (I find that I lent the review of this novel to Mrs. Brush but I'll tell her to send it to you.) It could feed the rolling press abundantly and got through on that account. But it should incite more interest in "our book," it seems to me. I consider it as a paver of the way to "ours."

Around the last of April Captain Mitchell and her husband will come to my home for lunch, according to our present arrangement. I look forward—and so does my husband—to a wonderful visit from them. They will be driving and so not too hurried, I hope, for a real talk about Japan.

My stack of mail, awaiting my return home, is high, wide, and sure to be in spots handsome. I snatched your communication from its volume as soon as I saw your distinctive envelope and I have been impelled to write you first of all this morning.

You will see, from what I have said here, I trust, that we women of East and West have many common phases of contemporary events to tackle—together.

> Always my real devotion to you.
> Mary R. Beard

[P.S.] Whisper or shout (if on the fly) my love to Shidzue.

◆────

As in the following letter to Frieda Miller, Beard was certainly correct in identifying Philip Wylie, Lundberg and Farnham, and Lynn White, Jr., as the vanguard of attack on women's self-esteem and social responsibility in the postwar years. White, president of Mills College, was a leader in the movement to attune women's college education to their futures as wives and mothers. In the speech to the American Association of University Women (AAUW) mentioned below, he fiercely criticized the male intellectual and vocational model used in educating women and argued—very differently from Mary Beard—that women's education ought to center around preparation for home and family. Beard's own approach never stressed sexual difference in this respect; she consistently opposed the idea that women's higher education ought to include domestic vocational training. But her skepticism about average American women in the postwar years fulfilling their historic potential for constructive contribution to public life sometimes took on, ironically, the flavor of postwar antifeminist strictures. Her view was often dominated by her frustration with the failure of women to catch her lesson, that knowing their own history would be collectively empowering. In her *Annals* essay mentioned below, part of a special issue on "Women's Opportunities and Responsibilities," she surveyed the extent to which women were acting in politics and public life in the modern world (for good and for evil), remodeling Japan, expanding Soviet power, advocating "peace by force" (her cynical reading of American women's contribution), embroiling Jewish-Arab tensions, taking leading positions on both sides in the communist-nationalist conflict in China. Some of her deepest feelings seemed to slip out in her comment that, compared to the past, the twentieth might "really be the most benighted century of human history."[4]

120. TO FRIEDA S. MILLER

[New Milford]
June 15, 1947

Dear Miss Miller:

Thanks for writing me and sending me the little pamphlet carrying information for which I had asked, and the copy of the Status Bill now before the two houses of Congress. I knew about this Bill in its preparation stage but I had not got its final form.

I advise you to do more than "skim" the work on MODERN WOMEN: THE LOST SEX and for the reason that its sales and influence on magazine writing about women, etc., are doing us no good but a lot of harm.

As for the president of Mills College, Lynn White Jr., I was appalled when I learned that he had been invited to address the AAUW at Dallas. I have a complete copy of his address in Boston last winter in the course of which he said: "most women feel insulted when one points to the undoubted historical fact that while there have been many talented women, there has never been a woman gifted with innovative genius." I have only the newspaper report to go by with respect to his talk at the AAUW convention but the report I saw in the Times (if that is where I read it) said that when Constance Warren asked him whether fathers were not involved as well as mothers in family responsibility he replied: "This is what the psychiatrists tell me." Evidently he was repeating in part or in toto his naive assumptions about women which colored his whole address at Boston.

"Never a woman gifted with innovative genius?" How did a distinctly human society ever get started? I keep asking this, if futilely. I use for my reply the weight of modern anthropological research which assigns to woman's original innovative genius the invention of all the prime industrial arts and offers strong grounds for the belief that she discovered agriculture. Prehistorical feminine innovations did not end woman's creative power. But if educated American women encourage male educators to eliminate all knowledge of women in long history and so to build up the idea of a man's world and masculine innovative genius only, then what modern American women get in consequence will surely be what they deserve.

My introductory article in The Annals which indicates the force of living women in tearing societies to shreds, for one thing—the Slavic and other Communists—seems to be just dead pan as feminists continue to pursue their line of talk, writing, and propaganda, reckoning naught of such contemporaries and of what could perhaps happen to undermine the "opportunities and responsibilities" which form the core of their ideologies.

A little brazen, am I? Yes definitely that.

> But cordially yours
> Mary R. Beard

Margaret Grierson became a major correspondent of Mary Beard's in the late 1940s and early 1950s—one to whom she confessed her hopes, fears, and often peremptory opinions freely and with whom she allowed herself more than typical self-promotion. The following letter suggests that Beard's searing awareness of women's disunity greatly influenced her discrediting of internationalism.

The Freedom Train, on which Beard comments acerbically, was a specially designed set of railroad cars—painted white with a gold American eagle in the center between blue and red stripes—which toured the nation displaying a hundred or more significant documents of U.S. history, including the Emancipation Proclamation. The sponsors of the privately financed venture promised that the train would not stop in segregated railroad stations. As Beard suggests, political groups took the occasion of the train's appearances to protest the as-yet-incomplete state of freedom in America.[5] Beard's reference to "Commies" reflects not only her own rejection of Stalinism but also her absorption, witting or unwitting, of contemporary political discourse. Her closing reference to the Almighty is so rare for the nonreligious Beard, however, that one suspects it is wholly tongue-in-cheek.

121. TO MARGARET GRIERSON

New Milford
Sept 18, 1947

Dear Margaret:

I've been waiting almost a month for a chance to think about my phrase "degrees of realistic intelligence" and whether I see with muddy eyes what I was doing when I put those words together. I am sorry they trouble you except as your trouble forces me to analyze them as carefully as I can.

I wish we could talk this thing over directly. Surely we can do that some time. . . . Last week I got another illustration of what I call "degrees of realistic intelligence". I had accepted an invitation to be guest speaker at the closing session of the national convention of women teachers belonging to the Delta Kappa Gamma Society. At their luncheon preceding this banquet, they had agreed upon a program for their united enterprise ahead. A very impassioned member had presented it and expounded it. It called for full-teacher effort in behalf of World Peace, World Democracy, and World Citizenship. When my turn came to speak I was in a hell-of-a-mess because I know as they apparently do not even suspect that women are embattled against women over the earth for and against these ideals which are certainly not realities today. I was unable to deliver a flaming message egging them on with their crusade while suppressing what I know to be terrific barriers in the way—and perhaps insurmountable.

I even confessed that I do not know what *world citizenship* means. *Citizen* hitherto has had a clear definition signifying a habitat, rights and immunities fixed by law. Intelligence respecting this fact, however, is of no moment to those women. They regard their mentality as a kind of super-intelligence transcending knowledge and customary realities associated with the word citizen. So, as I see them, they are good women living in a world of their dreams or rather of dreams fixed for them by men who assume to dictate dreams to women. These women are parrots, I think, taking this dream, with the crusade to realize it, just ready-made. And I? What am I? Maybe just an idiot.

According to MODERN WOMAN: THE LOST SEX that is what I am. The authors have some intelligence and some sense of permanent values. But there are realities which they overlook—fundamentally the one which offsets values in maternity by snatching babies from their cradles for the butchery of other babies.

Oh I don't know. It is silly for me to run along like this. Words are terrible-to-handle media of communication. Art and music are simpler.

But as long as people continue to write on such things as the philosophy of law, emancipation, freedom, history, political science, etc . . . ad infinitum as *specialties*, torn from the web of all life, there will have to be only partial intelligence if the word intelligence should be used at all, it seems to me. I fear it really has no meaning at all.

The Freedom Train? Some 50 women's organizations in Philadelphia the other day celebrated its dispatch with dancing, singing, and other exercises. But Langston Hughes in the New Republic of September 15 gave voice to Negro Blues over the nature of this Freedom Train exploit, while expressing his idea of FREEDOM. I prophesied a boomerang from Negro quarters and said that the Commies would swing one too. They have begun their swinging. Well there was a lot of *understanding* (that's the proper word, probably) on the part of the initiators of this Train project that Americans must love their exceptional heritage and defend it or lose this republic, but not enough understanding about ways and means of enlarging and defending this love, as events may prove, alas. When I first heard of this project, last winter, I thought that the sponsors might be induced to give recognition to women's contributions to our peculiar Heritage but I was mistaken—that bubble burst, before it flew at all. I thought I had a splendid secret soon to share with you and then for us to open up to others for cooperation.

. . . About the "progress" (let's hope it is competent) on the Japanese book, I can report that about half of it is ready for copy with carbons and that I have located a typist to do this work. I shall send a carbon to Japan for any necessary corrections and verifications, while I go on to the remaining chapters. I shall also send you a copy of this first part of the Ms for your frankest judgment. By the last of October, if all goes according to my plans and hope, I shall have the roundout of the business. Then, while in Japan the last part is being examined for accuracies and opinions of the treatment, I shall scout for a publisher. I think I can get a good one, provided my first chapter makes a hit as a Must for reading the rest. What a hussy I am! But you will be interested to hear that Lt. Ethel B. Weed insists I must not waver *because* my world vision of women is an imperative all along the line. She tells me of her contacts with British and other officers who, unlike our MacArthur, are perfectly contemptuous of women in public life and so she thinks that this book should help to shock them out of their complacency as well as bolster the democratic force of Japanese women.

PRAY FOR ME EVERY DAY EVERY WAY, even while you praise me unduly. That should make the ALMIGHTY certain that I am truly humble. I am indeed.

My great love to you   Mary

[P.S.] Don't let an answer take up any of your precious time. The only word I think I really understand is *civilization*.

In the immediate postwar period, a group of younger scholars who had learned from Charles Beard and were eager to honor him, in the midst of mounting rejection of his views, planned an anthology of essays on his work and influence.⁶ Mary Beard's response to Arthur Macmahon, who asked her about her contribution to Charles Beard's "shift" from political science to history, is typical of her self-effacement when asked such questions by male scholars. A professor of public administration at Columbia, Macmahon had been Charles Beard's student at Columbia University and also worked under his direction at the Bureau of Municipal Research during the 1910s. As president of the American Political Science Association in 1947, Macmahon asked Beard to speak before that group, in what turned out to be the last public address of his life.

122. TO ARTHUR W. MACMAHON

[New Milford]
September 21, 1947

Dear Arthur Macmahon:

If I seemed curt when you asked a question about Charles' apparent shift from concern with government and politics to history and my influence in this matter, it was because I want the book to be about him exclusively. I knew he would be back beside us in a second or two and I was anxious that he would hear nothing which might even hint at our private relation to things of the mind.

But this I can say to you on paper here. *First*, we have often said to each other—Charles and I—that it would be really impossible to isolate influence. We have lived so much at home together since his deafness intensified that it has been inevitable for us to talk almost everything over together as we did when the impulse to resign at Columbia surged up into speech. *Second*, each of us and then both together steadily realized that to work at history and know nothing of government and politics was to do no thinking about history. The opposite we know is equally true: to work at government and politics and leave their history background out of account is to miss their substance and play with shadows. The same is true if economy is forgotten, as well as education and the whole social "pattern."

So a shift to history is not actually a shift. Nor has CAB in fact ever completely shifted. What he has done has been to try to widen his knowledge and reflection to take in as much of the *whole* substance of thought and action as he could in his time and location. I have abetted and aided this broadening—but not merely on his account. I have labored to learn more and think better myself every day every way since I was a raw recruit among experts in learning.

You will, I am sure, adhere to my request that you say nothing about me in this study of CAB the Teacher.

It was a high and happy occasion—seeing you again.

Charles is strongly impelled to accept the invitation to the Pol. Sci. rally. I want him to do it of course if he feels like it. I think there will be mutual benefits if he can "speak his mind" again—in this year 1947 in this group.

Most sincerely yours,
Mary R. Beard

Merle Curti intended to write an essay on Charles Beard's influence on other historians and asked Mary Beard's suggestions. Her response contains probably her only existing catalogue of the distinguishing marks of her husband's scholarship. While her letter is friendly and typically self-deprecating, it carries a thread of critique: the neglect she chides Curti for in his intellectual history—that is, making Mercy Otis Warren "also there"—is the same way she suggests he may treat her.

123. TO MERLE CURTI

[Pine Crest Inn
Tryon, North Carolina]
December 2, 1947

Dear Professor Merle Curti:

I have pondered your letter but I am afraid that no very helpful suggestions come as a result.

We agree that a questionnaire would be "quite inappropriate."

Let's see whether we have other agreements. You say you will "of course have to include me" with respect to writings which we have both signed. I can ease you out of that difficulty by saying you don't *have* to include me. You might indicate merely that I was "also there"—in a respectable manner. But seriously—very seriously—this particular matter is impossible for any one but CAB and me to handle and neither of us nor both together would ever attempt to deal with it. It is too complicated for one thing and we prefer to have the writing stand on its own ground instead of that mysterious intimacy. It is commonly assumed that I injected women into the thought of history and just that. Let it all ride. Reporters have for years tried to get us to discuss how we have worked together but we have refused—partly to save time but more importantly to get on with work, and also to keep the personal out of the papers. Neither of us values personal publicity in the press features.

As for Beard's influence on others' writings, if you can get hold of a study of that made by a student a few years ago for his doctoral thesis, you could both save your time and get nuggets for your essay, I think. I forget his name and exact university but it was either Wisconsin or Ann Arbor I seem to remember. I am sorry I can't be sure. I shall try to get this information from Charles without arousing his concern with my reason for asking and do this today or tomorrow; then write you on this point.

I believe that it would be as unsatisfactory to you as to us to write a hundred letters to historians soliciting their confessions of Beard's influence on their writings or otherwise on their minds. Many, I suspect, would now be reluctant or unwilling to admit any influence. Others might wish flatly to deny it. The student to whom I have just referred went at the matter directly, by reading a great deal as you suggest you might do in a search for his influence. Yet to be absolutely sure that the writers had not come to their conclusions by their own mental labors would be impossible, it would seem to me, unless they acknowledged the Beard influence—by quotes, etc.

One rather original line you might take, it occurs to me, is to use denials of his influence, if you can find them. An outstanding one, of which I know well, is [Joseph] Dorfman of Columbia's treatise on Veblen. Oh yes there is [Harry] Gideonse's too who published a pamphlet of 50 or 60 pages on Beard's dense ignorance.

But you and professor [C.] Vann Woodward, who should be able to judge such judgers and who have studied history intensely, would provide the competence of critical scholarship if you just went at Beard's yourselves. I see no other way out of the dilemma than this kind of treatment:

a) Beard's writings on European as well as Am. Hist indicating his broad knowledge of that other world and a measurement as comparisons. That is the only way to measure, is it not—comparatively?

b) His text books for our schools in both aspects of history with emphasis on their critical and creative character—no other people going as far as he and a few others (succeeding text makers) in inviting Americans to look homeward, angels. In our mutual textbook writing, Charles and I got into the schools both recognition of labor and the labor movement and women as makers and sharers of Am. history, the seditious word "socialism", etc, in what is now the ancient of days.

c) His concern with the direction of events in the U.S. as more history in the making. His not being an antiquarian, a local colorist merely, nor a sheer academician unaware of economy and the general "culture patterns" developing in relation to economy and what may be called political "philosophy", or the "history of thought" (this without invading your specialty).

d) His attempts to integrate economy, economic theories, political theories and practices, war and the war spirit, in a "seamless web" of life, as history.

e) His being so much more than an "arm-chair" scribe, despite the amount of time he spends in chairs reading and writing. His burning desire to get at the "truths" of history, in their complicated interrelations.

You could never end your quest for a way to treat him as other historians may view him, I think. You know now the attitudes toward his writings by Nevins and other popular authors. Where you and CAB may part company a bit as writers is, I seem to detect, in your conception of European superiorities as cultural excellences. But I attribute this, in your history of thought, to your international socialistic philosophy. We shared that dream to a considerable extent at the beginning of this century during our sojourn in England when it was superbly insurgent. But I think you minimized such creative thinking as Mercy Otis Warren, for one, displayed in her history of the Am. Rev., etc. You merely put her in your book as "also there." I note that an effort is again being made to push international socialism but the absolutism of the simple Communist crowd will perhaps darken that dream quickly.

Forgive me for my brashness in assuming to be "in the know" at all. [Bernard] De Voto was wiser when he said in the Saturday Review a propos a volume signed Beard and Beard that, in this case, unlike a volume on history by Morison and Commager, only one scholar authored it.

I'll send you word the moment I can get the clue·to that student study of Beard's influence.

With the highest personal regard, the deepest sympathy with your problem in re Beard, and the warmest pleasure in your devotion to him with its repercussion in acceptance of me—

Affectionately—Mary R. Beard

[P.S.] We're here for the winter—working as ever where it is warm enough to keep well.

•←·–

Beard's next letter to Curti provides her longest say on her collaboration with her husband—but one that skirts the central question entirely. In passing she notes the infuriating *New York Times* review of *Woman as Force* by J. H. Hexter, which had undermined her argument by claiming that "through no conspiracy of historians" the colleges of cardinals, the courts, the parliaments, the great explorations that counted as history were "pretty much stag affairs." [7]

124. TO MERLE CURTI

Pine Crest Inn—Tryon, N. Car.
December 17, 1947

Dear Merle Curti:

I have at last learned that a student at Buffalo worked up the larger and more comprehensive of three studies on CAB's influence. Charles has just this day got off the last page proof of his second and final (he says) volume on American foreign policy and the conduct of foreign affairs. It has been a whale of a task to read this large volume of proof because it has called for infinite care with quotations and with things said about them for precision. I dropped into bed after the post office took custody of this proof. Charles has been sitting by the fire in our little log cabin, while I slept, longing for some way to reach the people with facts about the plight we are in which they might read and heed.

I hope you have seen Hanson Baldwin's article in the December Harper's: THE MILITARY MOVE IN. But the military moves in by the invitation and urging of civilians. This should not be overlooked. That not one professor at Columbia has protested against making the near-illiterate General Eisenhower head of Columbia eats me up too.

Books presumably have values. If there were none on history and the governments in history including our own, perhaps we should be a still less enlightened folk in this century. But certainly books are not enough. Pamphleteering is going on at a rapid rate in behalf of our obligation to the human universe—and with arms as well as goods—and pamphleteering in behalf of our republic is needed, I believe. I hope you won't write too feebly in relation to CAB's writing as his effort to get at the realities of our political and economic history. This new book will be off the Yale Press early in February. It may lead to a hanging. But you may be able to see it in time to take this latest history book into account as a mention of it.

Once more about ME. You are so beautifully generous to that Mary R. Beard. But nothing you could possibly say about my work on the B & B books could be more than indicative of your friendship for me. You couldn't really know about it. I have honestly no interest in any public attention to it. I am truly not a scholar. I have never wanted to sail under a false color in this respect. I am only an inquirer. The one published statement about me which I elicited by publishing my own book on "WOMAN AS FORCE IN HISTORY" and which makes me feel very good was that of Prof. Richard Leopold of Harvard in the American Year Book of 1946 when this book was offered to the public. Under General Works he said of mine: "A mature statement on a much-neglected subject."

I recognize that you have a problem of Charles' and my joint authorship in connection with certain books. But I suggest that you solve it this way:

1) Note that I have published independently.

2) Use that Leopold statement about my last book (as a contrast with the review of this book by Prof. Hexter of Queen's College prominently displayed in the Sunday Times Book section who said that my claim to the effect that women had helped to make all the culture patterns of history was not the truth; that in truth men had made them all).

3) Add merely that my interest has not been solely in women since that would be to cut out of history one sex—the female—and so err in thinking of its totality, as much as others err when they cut men out and ignore women.

A single sentence in this way could take care of the B & B problem. I would ask you not to touch it at all but if you refrained entirely, some one *might* criticize (some feeble-minded-sister perhaps) and Charles himself would be embarrassed.

But I want the volume to which you are contributing to be the full tribute to him, as it should be. I have always of course appreciated the affection for him on the part of students and teacher colleagues and other friends. By handling his wife simply and quietly in the manner I suggest, there need be no real diversion from the fulfillment of the task you and other friends and critics have undertaken with this book.

Pray be careful not to put your name on the outside of any letter you may want to write me further. Then Charles will not wonder why you are writing to me. Your letters will come straight to me.

> With affectionate loyalty
> grounded in true admiration
> Mary R. Beard

Owing in great part to Margaret Grierson's work and friendship, Beard thought by the spring of 1948 that the "growing and valuable collection of books and source materials on women" at Smith was "far ahead of Radcliffe."[8] In the letter below, Beard regales her confidante with a full discussion of what she is trying to accomplish in the book about Japanese women, although even her co-workers Dorothy Brush and Shidzue Kato would tell a different narrative.

125. TO MARGARET GRIERSON

> [New Milford, Conn.]
> March 26, 1948

Dear Margaret:

I'm really pleased as Punch over the privilege granted me of talking to the group at Smith about archives and their significance for understanding women. Whatever the size of the rally on May first I shall be happy over this chance to talk on the thing nearest to my mental heart (if I may thus combine thought and feeling) at a college which has come so far along the road to appreciation of Fustel de Coulanges' concise dictum: "No documents no history." If no history, what is woman but the prey of monomaniacs?

Having just read Emil Ludwig's "Doctor Freud," I fairly burn with renewed zeal for snatching man and woman from the clutches of the cult which is totally devoid of the values inherent in studying the facts of history as a lot more than sex.

But I'll try to appear sober if not too solemn when I arrive at Northampton on the first of May. May Day is not an occasion for ponderous solemnity and I shall indulge in some figurative May Pole dancing in celebration of the magnificent work you have accomplished at Smith.

Your invitation needs no other support. I shall be with you in time for lunch, letting you know later just when and how I shall arrive. I may have our man Friday drive me up. Anyway I'll be at your side when you tell me the hour for the lunch. If there is anything I might do after the p.m. meeting, I could stay on for that effort but you must be sure to spare yourself too much strain. Come Sunday you must stick long in your bed. I could get down to New Haven latish on Saturday and either stay there or be met by man Friday and hauled home.

Were it not for the fact that Charles will be bogged down until the first of June with the finishing of his revised college text, I would suggest to him that he come with me to Smith. But I know full well that he cannot do it in May. Our son who has been working for months in new research for this revision is coming the middle of April to go over the whole Ms with his father and both fellows will be in need of genuine rest after this hard and meticulous task has ended on the dateline of June one. I shall of course tell Charles that he is warmly invited. He thoroughly delights as I do that this college is in dead earnest and has demonstrated thus far its will to press exact knowledge of woman. I'll bring with me a statement from him to this effect which you may read to the audience in lieu of his direct presence. He has to go to New York sometime in May to accept personally the gold medal award by the Institute of Arts and Letters. More running away from his desk than that he really cannot do this spring.

I am impelled to speak out at Smith myself by a letter which I got yesterday from Shidzue Kato. In it she says that she has expected from me a "scholarly" work on Japanese women but that she is sorry that Dorothy Brush has not helped to make a "dramatic" story. She is not only loyal to Dorothy and to me. She expresses, if gently, the common preference for a fictionized writing of history. After all, this book in D's hands, would be of that character. Dorothy too was clearly bored by my historical approach to the job. But the moral as I see it is the fixed idea which Dorothy shares with Shidzue that woman was a subject sex in history, at least when the matriarchy dissolved in man rule (this is the formula you know); and with that firm attitude about history each would build the book on the drama of agelong servility suddenly exploding in emancipation from history. Most of the sketches which are the sources of the book groan with that dogma. But set in economic, social, and political history with war as common accompaniment they reveal women as actively helping to make all the "culture patterns" in Japanese history, as energetically supporting feudatories and the cult of clan loyalties, then actively waging the contest between Shogun and Emperor on both sides of that partisan struggle, eventually, long before their enfranchisement by MacArthur, breaking through all sorts of traditional feudal codes and breaking out into social civilian experiments whatever the difficulties of these acts. So there was in truth a dynamic preparation among women themselves for the enfranchisement which came to them in one bold act by the Commander out of the West. This is truly high drama—the drama of woman as force. But to make lesser drama of a feministic tragic kind would be a folly, I staunchly believe.

I shall send you in a day or two a copy of my reply to Shidzue Kato. I understand both her and Dorothy. Lt. Weed seems to understand what I mean by my approach to the book job. She is coming home from Japan by April 15 on a furlough of about 45 days, she writes me, and you and she must meet. She will come to my home. I hope you and Marine can be here then. What can be done about a book is this—but I'll put that into my reply to Shidzue which you can see as copy.

Now this is all. It requires no answer from you, my dear Margaret. I tell you this book story this moment to indicate to you the problem of convincing women that they have their own history and documented; that if they refuse to study it and grasp its meaning they can never be more than mental children. Our own women so far are so injured by their historical innocence that they seem to me to be less than mentally curious children—just parrots learning to speak what men teach them to say. I see that the AAUW is circulating the effusions of Pres. Lynn White, i.e., as if they were sound leadership of women.

Ah well a day. *All you need do* now is to tell me the hour for the lunch on May first and where I am to come at Northampton when I arrive there, God willing.

Devotedly yours—Mary Beard

Here again, in response to Rose Arnold Powell, is the harshly single-minded Beard of the postwar era, sure of her own answers, hostile to those women who do not see her light. Perhaps she was made especially testy by Powell's continued focus on Susan B. Anthony. And perhaps by the creeping knowledge that Charles Beard's weakness and illness, of which he had not been entirely free since he took sulfa for his pneumonia in 1945, now threatened his life.

Beard mentions below a *Life* magazine article that reported on a five-year project at the University of Chicago to take inventory of the great ideas of Western civilization. A huge research team emerged with the finding that Western civilization contained exactly 102 ideas (and their subsets). *Life* chose to print for its readers as samples the introduction to idea #51, "Man," and one of its subdivisions, "Men and Women: Their Equality or Inequality." The latter was rife with statements of the inferiority of women.[9]

126. TO ROSE ARNOLD POWELL

[New Milford]
July 3, 1948

Dear Mrs. Powell:

Your letter of June 23 was not one to answer as simply "more of the same thing," the kind of appeal and response which we have had as exchanges now and then through the years. For this reason I have had to wait this long to write you this time, until I could give this new letter of yours the attention which is your due.

There are new elements in this sex situation today—not least being that ganging-up by the University of Chicago crowd against women by means of those excerpts cut from the "world's great books" which deride women—the quotations used in Life magazine which I saw when that issue came out. Several women wrote me at once to urge me to write an "answer" to Life—a hot protest, they said. I replied that even a hot protest would do no good, even if Life printed it. This I firmly believe: that mere outcries are futile against that sort of thing.

Then what? Two things, I told those correspondents: (1) for women to boycott all magazines which treat women so abominably; (2) for women to reply, if at all, with exact knowledge of the distortions of great writings as mere cuttings from great men's small moments, the case in that article in Life. Every man quoted there, I either know or suspect, could be quoted as appreciative of woman. And to the list there could be added, in woman's favor, such great men as Seneca and Plutarch, i.e., Socrates, etc.

But women will neither use the boycott nor work at the stuff of learning to offset such abuses. The magazines are largely addressed to women, as you know. Women take them with avidity, perhaps fume in countless cases, but are helpless to meet men on men's terms in protests. In short, women are lazy-minded. I do not intend to spend my time on articles. They take a long time to write and they require a peculiar style which I do not care to learn.

Once I did write a letter to Life protesting against its tone of sex anarchy and its depiction of women as biology alone. But a woman on the staff answered (my letter was not printed)—I think I said it was not for publication—that the women did not feel as I did.

You know that I view women's innocence of their long history as a serious weakness which handicaps them in self-defense when that is their problem. But I doubt whether you take much, if any, stock in this view of mine. For example, in the letter to which I am trying to reply, you say: "I agree with you that women will split in many directions under masculine influence, seemingly satisfied with whatever minor sops are offered them—or none." Well I don't agree that "masculine influence" is the clue to all their splits. Women have influenced men to engage in all sorts of enterprises too—from exploitations of women and children to the crime of war.

The Seneca Falls women gave no indication of knowing a fact about women in history. Nor did dear Susan [B. Anthony] know much about it, it seems. Lydia Maria Child had written a remarkable volume on women in history. But the 48ers and Susan adhered to an absolutist dogma and in its propagandistic use for a long period they encouraged men to the conviction that women had been nothing in long history. So why shouldn't men feel "superior"? And why shouldn't young women begin to have an inferiority complex? To our day no students of either sex have any training in the conception and details of women and men making history, individually, or together.

That Britannica publishing project is ridiculous in its man-mindedness. But put up to women where women belong in its project as writers and themes, and what replies would you get? Women, I feel I have to keep on crying, have no language but cries.

I know very well Florence Hellman's bibliographical work on American women. But it is hard to use in the form in which it is presented and it is only American at that. The wealth of materials in the Cong[ressional] Lib[rary] on women in long long history is fabulously rich. But what women work it?

I don't even like the stamp issue honoring Stanton and Mott because it has Mrs. Catt in the center as the chief figure, owing to the pose, and she had nothing to do with Seneca Falls. Stanton and Mott should have been there without Mrs. Catt and have had better portraits and poses. I won't use this stamp at all. Among others, I protested against it, though not in time knowing too late about its design; but it is possible that Mrs. Catt, a stanch Democrat, was introduced by some political management. I don't claim this. I merely wonder how she got into *this* stamp.

A VITAL NEED IN EDUCATION IS TO ESTABLISH WOMEN IN HISTORY AS PARTICIPANTS IN THE MAKING OF ALL HISTORY AS THEY WERE IN REALITY. This is my firm belief; my "cause"; and I work at it all the time, in various ways.

This reality transcends the cult of feminism, of equality, of superiority and inferiority credos. Equality is not enough and while that is the cult ideal, in the dearth of historical knowledge it will be a mere sex war. Say I.

You are positive. So am I. If the "woman movement literally has been brought about in our own lifetime," that is not the biggest credit to our life time. I think it demonstrated its *inadequacy* in my books written since 1931 (my own books) and sharpened the demonstration in my last one: WOMAN AS FORCE IN HISTORY. NO? Then why not?

With sincere regards
Mary R. Beard

●←~

Charles Beard's allergy to sulfa, with which he had been dosed in 1945, led to aplastic anemia; by the summer of 1948—when he accepted the Gold Medal of the American Institute of Arts and Letters—he was mortally ill.

In the hospital, Mary Beard cites her faith in Robert Briffault's *The Mothers* (1927), a work she often relied on for her claims for women's role in founding civilization. Briffault, London-born son of a French diplomat and a Scottish woman, was exactly Mary Beard's age and died in 1948 of tuberculosis. He lived his last seventeen years in France, some of the war years in a Nazi prison for his left-wing views. Beard declared that Briffault should be "required reading for every Harvard and Radcliffe student," in a letter written a few years later to the director of Radcliffe Women's Archives. She claimed that colleges had "boycotted his anthropology and its showing of women's leadership in establishing social order and the arts of living." [10]

127. TO MARJORIE WHITE

Grace-New Haven
Community Hospital
August 18/ 1948

Dear Marjorie:

With your beautiful letter my hours are brightened. The deepest feelings cannot be expressed in words, as we both know. My beloved seems really much better today—at long last. I know how your husband and daughter must have felt when you were undergoing serious trouble at the hospital. I was anxious with them.

Keep the faith in that first creative woman, so that we may keep the faith in woman's greatest tradition—creativeness for life—creating society as civilization. Briffault is my Bible as far as he goes. One can hardly value his 3 volumes enough. The more one studies them, the greater they seem to be. Too bad life used him so harshly later. The greatest are the least appreciated, it seems. Too bad he had to care so much but he had hard living circumstances, one of the tragic Europeans.

You must not think that I deserved any part of CAB's Gold Medal Award. It was given for his total work—and justly. Don't carry sheer feminism too far.

A shrine to Ellen Glasgow—a very great person, in my opinion—is being made of her home in Richmond. More than that, a seminar in her own study is projected for the study of her work. Everything she wrote and everything written about her is being sought for her Archive—source materials for this seminar. We rejoice surely that the Archive idea lives. I have been asked to inscribe and autograph *Am. Through Women's Eyes* for her Archive. Reading over her statement in The Nation which I used in that book—"What I Believe"—I am more proud of her than ever.

I have been at the Hospital until midnight every night till this one. Now I'm tucking into bed—at ten—to catch up a bit on lost sleep. But I wanted to write this to you as a prelude to sleep. I like to believe that you and I have an independent line which we mark out for women and that more women will take to it with us and faster than we expected now.

Mary

Charles Beard died on September 1, 1948. Mary Beard was seventy-two years old. She was determined to keep on doing what she had been doing as an independent intellectual, as the following two letters show. Initially she intended to give up the New Milford house, which she refers to here as the Barnacle, because the couple who had long served the Beards in housekeeping and maintenance were also aging; but in fact she kept the house, and Paul and Selma stayed on faithfully, for seven or eight years more.

128. TO JAMES PUTNAM, THE MACMILLAN COMPANY

New Milford, Connecticut
October 9, 1948

Dear James Putnam:

I am an Executor of Charles Beard's estate, with William and Miriam as my colleagues. The three of us have no others as co-executors.

In connection with the request for a Polish translation of THE RISE, William and Miriam will have no problem. That can be my decision with their approval, since half the revenue would be mine. With respect to matters concerning THE ECONOMIC ORIGINS OF JEFFERSONIAN DEMOCRACY which you wish to straighten out, your questions had better come to me first; if they have to do with contractual relations or other items clearly involving the Estate they must also be submitted to Miriam and William, as executors of CAB's estate, as of prime business for them. Fully aware of the Beard will, I shall consult with them in that case, as sole beneficiaries if there is any *economic* benefit.

I have wanted to know the list of Macmillan books by each and both Beards which have had or are in process of translations. If you will ask Miss Hinrichs to send me the list, I shall be grateful to you for your part and for her in the satisfaction of this desire of mine.

About Mary R. Beard personally, your interest is buoying. "To carry on bravely" can mean much or little. I simply must do many things about which I have no choice, such as business details connected with the Estate, closing up my house for the winter (it is my own property and not a part of the Estate), helping Paul and Selma to change over at this long last to self-reliance except insofar as they have been remembered in Charles' will, and deciding where to go. In deciding where to go, living with either child's household is no factor. I do not believe that the parents should crowd in with their offspring and in-laws, however cordially they are welcomed, provided the elders can take care of themselves. I plan to spend the winter in Baltimore and if I can get my house closed the last of this month, I shall go straight there. I shall be within easy hail of the Cong. Lib. and friends in the D.C. when I feel the urge to go there. I shall have the advantage of Baltimore's good libraries, theater and concert if I am moved to attend performances, and many close friends who will respect my work—friends who will not pester me any more than I shall pester them and yet be companionable when we are in the mood to be so vis a vis. I am too old for New York or Washington as a resident. If I can get a small apartment at the Wyman Park in Baltimore where Charles and I spent a winter a few years ago, I shall be very contented. It is in the midst of adorable woods, not in the business district, and I may even take my car along for a drive when I feel like driving or get a driver when I feel like going some distance involving a sense of direction, which is not a strength of mine, or traffic.

That's a good plan, don't you think so?

Next autumn I plan to put the "Barnacle" on the market. None of us could afford to run it any more and none of us pines for the burden if we could afford to keep the menage going. Paul and Selma could never be matched and, without them, the place would be a White Elephant. Paul is near 60 and Selma begins to need an easier life though she is several years younger than Paul.

But Bill [Beard], according to our scheme for 1949, will bring his wife and children from California, when their school year closes in June, to spend a month with me in the home of their grandparents and get a feeling about the beauty of this part of the country. That too is as it should be.

So what is bravely carrying on? Work on my part is courage, and that I shall try to maintain. Not that I have any false notion of its value in other people's minds but it does have value in my mind as something transcending primitive wailing, dependence on dependence, and geared to things I firmly believe should be tackled—even by such as I.

Here's my story since my change of life on September 1, looking ahead till the beginning of winter in 1949. Charles can never be pitied however greatly he can and will be missed. I do not intend to pity myself for I do not regard myself as other than the most fortunate woman in the world in having had up into my seventies the life with Charles A. Beard.

Your interest buoys me. I am thankful you do not stress the "void" for that needs no emphasis. It is too real. Hundreds of men and women have written me, from a sense of the void "which can never be filled." I know I can never fill it. I shall not try. I hope I can carry on in CAB's spirit as long as my own heart beats.

> With unfailing appreciation of your
> affection—Mary R. Beard

Undoubtedly, Lena Madesin Phillips communicated with Mary Beard upon learning of her husband's death. At this time, Phillips was hot on the campaign trail, as the Progressive Party candidate for lieutenant governor of Connecticut. She also served as a national committeewoman for presidential hopeful Henry Wallace's Progressive Party.

129. TO LENA MADESIN PHILLIPS

New Milford
on October 10, 1948

Oh dear Lena an exchange of letters at least again!

I had missed it. Following the news that you are "running" for a political office has interested me of course. It seems to mean that fundamentally you are still physically on your toes.

It is grievous to read the papers in most respects, I agree. More and more I skim the headlines only, for one can be sure what is carried beneath them quite automatically, if one has long been a reader of the press journalism.

Your letter means so much to me for memory is an important part of one's being. You understand this in writing me and in saying what you do about my memory of the long companionship with Charles Beard.

For the mastery of grief and the enrichment of the invisible continuing companionship I intend to try to go on working. This is what I hope the innumerable men and women who have written to me about their deep sense of loss with the death of CAB will do too, as I have tried to say to them on this printed card. I am sending you the card now but with this note attached to tell you again that your and my companionship in better days is an important aspect of my life.

I would certainly urge you and Marjory to drive up to see me now were it not for the fact that I must close my big house by the first of November and go to a warmer climate for the winter. I have so much to do until then that I am overwhelmed with tasks and shall have no liberty for anything else. With my daughter and son I am an Executor of Charles' estate and this is one business which I cannot avoid.

I am going to Baltimore where I shall be close to the great local and the greater Congressional Library, where I can live quietly as one can in a big city, where I can be warm enough, where for an emergency I can get such care, as I might have to have, in that medical center. Naturally my children offer me shelter in their homes and their mates with them are infinitely gracious about this inviting but I know better than to crowd in with the younger people. AND I NEED MY OWN WORK as long as my breath holds out. It is breathing which counts of course for continuity of effort— a bromide remark and yet one of which I am more conscious as truth than I have ever been before.

In the spring let us try to talk together again. I'll be "home" by April. If you win the election, maybe you will have time to let me peep into your office and say at least "Hello."

> I'm much the same queer person
> Mary Beard

●←~

During the year following Charles Beard's death Mary Beard dealt with the flow of words, published and private, assessing his character and impact. Her correspondence with a few of his scholarly defenders, especially Merle Curti and Harry Elmer Barnes, steams with her rage at his detractors. She steeped herself in her own work for sustenance. Her collaboration with Dorothy Brush quickened pace, and she discussed with Brush and with Margaret Grierson the possibility of setting up a Women's Research Institute. The manuscript on Japanese women was in the hands of the Macmillan Company in June 1949; thence it began its travels from one publisher to the next, looking for acceptance. If Beard privately recanted her rash claim in her article of 1929 on "American Women and the Printing Press," that publication was easy and open to women, she did not say so. She was buoyed by the progress of a German translation of *Woman as Force*, writing to Jim Putnam that the woman in Stuttgart assigned to translate the book called it "'one of the most interesting, instructive, objective and tolerant books ever written on a subject the growing importance of which is now getting more and more evident in Germany.'" Beard added, "I smoked a lot of cigarettes to be sure I was not dreaming." [11]

The following letter expresses more personal feeling than usual, because Beard is writing to a friend who also experienced the loss of a beloved husband. Gilbert Roe, a law partner of Robert La Follette, had died in 1929. Mary Beard's occasional correspondence with Netha Roe lasted until the end of her life.

130. TO GWYNETH ROE

New Milford, Connecticut
October 15, 1949

Dear Netha Roe:

The promise and beginning of our direct and still more meaningful friendship is symbolized perhaps in our using each other's personal name. The "Mrs" has its beauty for us both but its stamp of formality we can leave for others less independent of the world's ways. I adore your letter to me written a month ago for it is eternally warm although I have seemed unable to tell you so until this day.

Among the invincible reasons has been the serious illnesses of two brothers and a sister. My older brother, Halstead Lockwood Ritter, now 80, refused to consider a hard attack of coronary thrombosis by leaving his bed after a session in it and returning to his law office in Miami. I doubt whether you know that the Senate impeached him (he was a Coolidge appointment as a federal judge) *without a debate*—a grossly unconstitutional thing to do—by the management of the Democratic presiding officer. Farley was determined to wrest that bench from him to unseat a Republican and turn it over to a Democrat and Farley won. This violation of the constitutional procedure in an impeachment trial was written up in an issue of the Am. Historical Rev. this year as a legal outrage. But this brother Hal, though grieved as he has been entitled to be and rightly as his Brief calling for a review of this trial in the Senate proves, tries to hold on to life as courageously as he can.

My sister was confined to the hospital—Harkness Pavilion—for two months and I made frequent trips to her bedside. Now at long last she is in her home and recovering with remarkable speed. My younger brother died last week. To his funeral in Indianapolis came a throng of men and women representing an ex-mayor, members of civic societies, and a Negro attorney with whom this brother Dwight Ritter had worked in the interest of better conditions for the exceptionally large population of colored folks in that city.

It was for me too a precious thing to find you "in" when I looked for you in Washington that day. I was on my way to the station for a return to Baltimore. I had lunched at the home of George Bussy Hewes and at its end Alice Roosevelt said she would drive me to any place I wished to go. I had her drop me at the Carleton and there I started alone for you. Yes I was at the Statler when Charles made his last public speech. I did not see him kiss you for I slipped up to our room to be there when he came up and do anything that I could to see that he rested, for this speech-undertaking, involving the long trip from Tryon, North Carolina, as well as an effort, not light, of trying to decide what to say, was a tough physical ordeal for many reasons. I had just opened the door of our room when several of his men friends arrived likewise with the intention of seeing him to tell him in that room of their joy in his performance. He was definitely tired by that time but of course the reaction of the audience brought a rebound. I am so happy that you were present and that he could honor both you and Gilbert as he did—a kiss for each of you.

I did live in almost total isolation last winter in Baltimore except for some trips to the Congressional Library. Even there I worked alone. Of course I had to discover whether I had any personal resources left to lift me from grief over the terrific loss to living out my days without the great companionship of nearly half a century. If I had dwelt on the mass of letters which flooded in on me and nearly all of which assured me that I would be lonelier every day ahead, I would have been lost in an ocean of misery. I felt I must surmount their depressive influence. When I found that I was being able to work again, I slipped in to see what you were doing in your bereavement and you buoyed me more than you can ever know.

I am so grateful to you; and our communion, if not of *two* saints, will continue, I trust, as long as we live. We were mates of two extraordinary men. The four of us were and will always remain a mutual admiration society, as we retain the memories of their interrelation to us.

Write me about yourself, though I know your great spirit and love it, in your mental and active labors. If I get a publisher for a Ms I rounded out by June on women in long Japanese history, I will let you know. Macmillan has turned it down for publishing and on this ground: while its editor and its readers "appreciate the aim and scope" of this proposed work, it is their common opinion that it would not interest "the average reader" and so would not be of advantage to a "commercial" publishing house. The House advised me to send it to a University Press. I asked Mr. Couch now head of the Univ. of Chicago Press, whom I know, whether I might send him this Ms to read and consider for publication? He replied that his Press could not afford to take it and it would be futile to submit it because this press can't afford to take something which probably, very likely, would not sell well. He advised me to try Harvard or Princeton or Yale. But those three Presses are so steeped in men's worlds that I know it is useless to try any one of them, even though they are better endowed than the Univ. of Chicago Press.

The literary scout for a new publisher is keen about my theme and likes the way I have treated it but the verdict of this publisher, not having seen my pages, is that it would have to be offered as a "prestige" work—that is without expectation of sales. Another literary agent whom I know and who knows what will sell is a stanch Catholic and I open my Ms with the Supreme Deity in Japan: The Sun Goddess. If I would riddle this deity's supremacy, she might like to promote this book. I won't do that of course. I am not propagandizing for any species of Christian missions. I am trying to describe the Japanese people's own religion—with the one great goddess who has reigned far into the modern age, and who cannot, I believe, be over thrown by fiat.

For Americans who now occupy the land and rule this Oriental people to care nothing about understanding the long force of the Japanese women, which has found new expression (but by no means the first) in their right to vote and their election to both houses of the parliament, is surely contemptible. I shall perhaps turn to Pantheon Books for the next attempt to get a publisher, since this firm has money for printing "prestige" books. But an attitude toward women as less worthy of attention than men may bring a rejection there too.

Before I ask this House to examine my Ms, I shall try to elicit their interest by opening each chapter with some kind of appeal for public interest by diagramming its significance further. I have assumed that one chapter which I call "The Debut of the Lady" would carry its own appeal. But I now realize that it takes an interest in history to arouse that interest, plus a willingness to find woman in history. If I have to put this Ms in camphor for the winter, if I live I shall bring it out next spring and see whether it will be welcomed anywhere then. We should have a great Woman's Press but even our women do not know this. In 1848 at Seneca Falls women denied that our sex was anything but subject of Man the Tyrant through the ages since the Biblical kind of golden age which in fact never existed. Too bad we've been so dumb as to take what those women proclaimed as the truth of history. We put that over on our men and they make the most of it in education, etc.

Well I must sign off and go at tasks of a commanding nature, such as insistent mail, though I feel like talking with you alone, if only on paper, on and on. I'm keeping your stimulating letter before my eyes on my desk so as to get from it the kind of strength that I need.

Mary R. Beard

◦←⌐

In her acknowledgment of Macmillan's rejection of her Japanese manuscript, Mary Beard's sarcastic use of the postwar rhetoric of "free men" is
priceless.

131. TO HAROLD LATHAM, THE MACMILLAN COMPANY

[New Milford]
January 18, 1950

Dear Harold:

I am glad that you gave me your verdict so quickly and so honestly as
to explanation.

I can answer: "So be it." I neither weep nor laugh in this case and that
is a mental-emotional change for me.

In the world of "free men" including men who run the university
presses, I shall operate as a woman free to formulate values in her own
way, fortunate in not having to try to compete with the novelists who
dominate the literary arena.

Your verdict can never diminish an iota our deepened friendship. I appreciate vastly this relation.

Affectionately yours, Mary

◦←⌐

Writing again to her old and respected friend Florence Kitchelt, Beard explains her objection to the ERA and also summarizes what she sees as her
life's work.

132. TO FLORENCE CROSS KITCHELT

New Milford.
March 17, 1950

Dear Florence Kitchelt:

Your remembrance and expression of affection for me, written by
hand, on the circular letter about the Equal Rights Amendment give me
true joy. I have wondered how you are and have hoped to see you on one
of my trips to New Haven to get a medical lookover. But obligations have
steadily claimed first consideration so far. I expect however to have a free
lunch hour when I go again to have my blood pressure tested the last
week of March. As soon as the exact day is fixed, I shall let you know and
hope you can join me at the Taft Hotel for lunch then.

It is hard to write you about the Amendment although you must marvel that it could be hard. Of course I am "interested." What bothers me, and you no doubt think it is silly of me to be bothered, is the difficulty of deciding what "equality" is in countless cases, types of which I cited in my last book, Woman As Force in History. In Japan, where women members of the Diet helped to frame the new Constitution for a democratic age and influence the written principle of "liberty, equality, and fraternity", though these declarations stand as affirmations the applications are far from automatic. In our country, courts of equity and statutes of law embodying many of its principles help to define principles of equality but I foresee the crowding of cases to our courts if this Amendment becomes ratified. It would not, in other words, establish any conception of "equality" as a fixed reality, in itself. Judges even of equity are human—remarkably inclined to seek "justice" in our country. But "justice" like "equality" is not always easy to determine. If you have not looked at my book and examined illustrations of problems in this connection which I cite, should you do that you may understand my attitude better.

I don't like to seem obdurate and hostile to the good life for women. What I have been trying to do for years is to awaken women to the reality of their historic power, direct power, and influence in making all the culture patterns of history. It seems to me that the strongest argument living women can make in their quest for what we think of as equality is the *fact* of their historic force. I think that the 1848 interpretation of women in history as an unqualified subject sex has done immense injury to women's minds. It was not historic truth. It was a fiction useful for reform agitation but harmful in the long run to men's as well as women's understanding of women in the ages of the past. I have written so much about the great tradition of women's self-expressions in history, including the subjection of men as slaves bought and sold by women, in an effort to incite women to realize who and what they have been, with a view to their realizing better who they are and what they are now doing, that I am about written out on this matter. I have aroused much resentment, even anger, among feminists. A review of my last book in a leading newspaper opened with this sentence: "There are two kinds of people who won't like this book: feminists and woman-haters." I have found that true.

To have your remembrance of me still warmed with affection is a testament to your spirit of friendship.

Do let us have a reunion for friendship's sake. This spirit is a boon beyond weight and measurement. We can base it on respect for each other's will to integrity, while we feel a mutual admiration for each other's personality. Here I am asserting what I want to have us both continue to cherish.

I am yours as ever—Mary R. Beard

●←—

Whatever Lt. Weed's question about government and the freedom of the individual was (and that is not clear), it provoked in the letter below a sober philosophical rumination from Beard, who at seventy-four was much less of an idealist than she had been a half-century earlier. Her readiness—parenthetically—to bristle at Henry Steele Commager's evaluation of Charles Beard is typical of her response to evaluations that were not pure praise. (Her additional criticism of the singular in Commager's title is remarkably prescient of later historiographical trends.) Whether fairly or not, Commager actually wrote—in just a small fraction of his appreciative pages on Charles Beard—that his historicism, or admission that written history was delivered by the historian's frame of reference, was "sterile" because it did not provide a constructive path.[12]

133. TO LT. ETHEL B. WEED

New Milford, Connecticut
August 9, 1950

Dear Ethel Weed:

Not knowing how to "answer" your letter of July 20, I have wondered all this time what I could write you. I wouldn't want to "stall" on any question or comment but forging ahead might be as bad as stalling.

I could deal in generalizations relative to democratic ideology and nonconformities in practice but this disparity is not confined to any society or state professing its democratic basis or ideals. The "freedom of the individual," if taken as "perfect" or "absolute" freedom, is an impossible privilege if society is to hold together. At the beginning of this century I was inclined to be a disciple of Prince Peter Kropotkin of Russia whom I met in London when he and his wife were exiles there. He was classified as a "philosophic anarchist" but he had written, in reply to the tooth-and-claw Darwinian conception of life, a treatise on "Mutual Aid" as explanation of social origins, rightly claiming that there never could have been human social order without mutual aid. His solution of modern urban strife was given in his "Fields, Factories and Workshops." He would have planted factories in rural communities and had agriculture developed around them for the sustenance of the workers. That was probably ultra-rational—too rational for the impulsive force of modern human be-ings. He had been reared amid slavery in Russia; he loathed it; he sought a way out of it. But it exists in cities as well as in rural life to this day.

How can I defend our democratic integrity at home, in view of FDR's promises to the people that he would never take our boys out of the coun-try to fight in foreign wars, when he was secretly engaged in conjunction with Churchill to exert their combined power over all the earth? [Henry Steele] Commager, in *The American Mind* (surely there is more than one Am. mind!) which you tell me you have been reading, after some care-fully considered pages on Charles Beard winds up with the charge that Beard was "futile" because he was "devoid of a moral sense" or upshot. Democracy is made up of all sorts of people and minds and with free speech and a free press they can exercise their freedom to write and pub-lish. But Commager like hosts of other writers is fundamentally a Roose-velt partisan. Democracy permits diverse parties as long as civil strife does not explode into war. With war, controls are set up, often total in their range.

How far can individual liberty go, how far should it be allowed to go, if it menaces order to a degree which induces civil war? Democracy cannot sustain itself amid a high degree of violence. Youth is prone to be lawless and to follow or demand a violent leader. We are having in New York awful cases of this among the young boys and girls who have committed some murders in their gang wars. With the brakes off in what may be called non-hypocritical loyalty to democratic precepts, where could a "true" democracy flourish for any length of time?

The alternative is horrible to contemplate, I know. To demand that the Japanese outlaw war forever in their Constitution was unrealistic, in view of the very Occupation itself. The future of such Occupation could have been, and should have been foreseen in the light of the War out of which it came and the foreign policies of the Allied Forces—all of them—which were involved in that war. Democracy can be a cliche like all other ideals. It has risen and fallen many times in history. Its injury comes from many levels of society. The Founders of our Republic knew its history as no other state makers had known it, for they were operating in a growing history-conscious century. Now? So what? History is becoming outlawed as knowledge and interest, where it does not serve a special interest.

Yes I read with intense interest the items in the Nippon Times relative to a peace treaty for Japan. I too wish that the Occupation would end. If it should, do you think that Kawakami was right when he wrote that the Japanese could, alone, take care of themselves? I had hours with him in his home in Washington a short time before he died, after he had written in behalf of complete independence for Japan. He seemed to think that a non-resistance policy, such as Gandhi advocated for India, would be possible and correct for Japan. He wrote beautifully of his philosophy for Japan but did not reckon with the "cold war" policy promoted by the U.S. and the Russian answer to this policy. I did not argue with him. I hoped he was right. Yet he left out of account the Communist cells planted everywhere; reckoned not with their non-democratic objectives nor with the complications they could inject into a non-resistant, non-cooperative, isolationist boycott of Russian imperialism. India now faces that terror itself. Its people might lie down in the streets in protest. Would the Slavs respect that protest? I have doubts.

The sum and substance of this letter to you is my feeling that the horrible mess in which the world is now caught is not soluble by democratic aspirations alone, if at all. I hate persecution in all its forms as much as anybody does or can. I prefer the democratic way of life. But even democracy gives play to insincerities and hypocrisies of all species and these social defects can destroy it. I am forced to be glad that my CAB lies at rest now. He did his best to enlighten our people about the theft of its democratic-republican values. He doesn't have to know how he is attacked as unmoral. He would feel that he was futile, despite self-respect.

It takes all the brains that humanity can muster to operate a democracy. The less brains the better are right for militaristic power when it can thrive on universal conscription including the conscription of women and employ modern weapons for warring. It can dominate the politico and put its agents even in all centers of education. Russia sets the type and the pace for power politics, since the "men of Yalta" built up her aggressive force.

This is not a cheerful way to write you but I don't know how else to write sincerely. You went to Japan as an idealist and have kept loyal to your ideals. I love you for your desire and labor in behalf of human decency. I only keep alive by trying to work for a future revival of Reason coupled with knowledge of history with which I think it must be combined for the strength it needs and will always need hereafter. Superwisdom is required for the adjustment of Liberty with Government. Our conservative wing of trade unionism seems to have discovered that our whole industrial system could be wrecked if strikes were allowed to run an uninhibited course and it has itself been clearing out the reckless leftists who are ready, they think, to side with Russia if she gets the upper hand in the war. That they would get slavery if they did they seem unable to believe. Even Henry Wallace has broken with his Communist supporters; he has some intelligence on which to draw.

I can't ask forgiveness for this kind of letter because it is an honest letter. I do wish, however, that I could write more cheerfully.

I can't yet get a publisher for my book on women in long Japanese history but I shall make yet one more effort. Meanwhile two large portfolios of pictures of Japanese women made by the print artists are in the market at $6 for each. Most of the pictures, perhaps all, are of geisha. A story by Mona Gardner, called "Middle Heaven" about a rural family in war-time Japan is selling well I understand. But the women in my Ms are women whom few readers would want to know enough about yet for the publishers to risk its publishing. These enclosures will indicate that I keep plugging for women's interest in their history.

My true love to you—Mary Beard

⟡

As she settled into her life without Charles, Mary Beard remained intensely interested in the wide world around her, sober and skeptical and yet never defeatist about its chances for redemption through rationality. She imagined plans for educational transformation and discussed them with Margaret Grierson. When Smith College in 1950 appointed a new president, Benjamin Wright, whom Beard had met as a professor at Harvard, she wrote to him praising his inaugural address, "I thought I detected an inclination to approach a truly equal education of young women and young men—an education which is far from a reality as yet." Hoping that Wright might support a venture such as she and Grierson had envisioned, she proposed to him,

> In my opinion Smith College is the perfect seat of learning to lift education to that high level as model for other institutions for the training of women and men. I believe that this modeling would be widely influential. . . . How could a college, such as Smith, start to equalize education? Since no one is yet equipped to integrate the history of women with the history of men in relation to all branches of knowledge, it seems to me that the ideal beginning would be with a Seminar directed to research and reports. If students from Holyoke and Amherst could come to Smith as members of this Seminar, it could partake of the graces and meanings identified with the French salons where men and women mingled in the great discussions of life, as Italian and Greek and Roman men and women had done earlier.

From that challengingly amiable intellectual companionship the greatest conceptual thought of the past developed. A College should now be that kind of discussion center, vastly heightened by access to the world's historic documents and literature and inciting to the spirit of intellectual companionship for perhaps new mental force. [13]

This seminar did not become a reality, but Beard and Grierson continued planning on their own. Beard also established a close friendship with Marine Leland, the woman with whom Grierson shared her home and life. She confessed to Leland at one point that she was "garrulous by nature," and indeed, in her life as a widow, she poured out pages of correspondence to a few trusted friends, as if she were substituting these for the conversations that she had always shared with Charles.[14] Many of these pages were long-winded and repetitive, but some also rose to heights of aesthetic and philosophical appreciation, like the one below. Ruth Woodsmall, whom Beard mentions, was a YWCA executive in the international field.

134. TO MARGARET GRIERSON

This Dec. 28 / 1950
On my hill at 10 degrees below zero
in a magically beautiful landscape
of deep snow on the ground, silver
trees, snow birds, blue jays, etc.

Dear Margaret:

This is a day to pity the poor in the cold and grieve with the tragic lads asked to be battle heroes in frigid Korea and feel angry over the mental weaknesses of power-hungry politicos, etc. Amid the glamorous display of nature's loveliness and with comforts partly provided by my housekeeper who even had taken a course in electrical engineering, I "take my pen in hand" to write you these words of commingled visual delights and invisible but grave distress. Perhaps I would just burn up over the human tragedies, if nature in this form of visual grandeur did not save my spirit for yet a while to live and try to work on for objectives long dominating my mind and heart. Should mortals give up such a struggle, nothing of course in human life would be above human nature in the raw. This is a bromide comment but not as a sleeping pill.

I forgot to answer a question in your letter of Dec. 15 about [Henry Thomas] Buckle's [1858] speech on "The Influence of Women on the

Progress of Knowledge" as to whether it was printed? Yes, it was published. On page 334 of my Woman As Force in History, you can see where and when it was first published and when it was reprinted. In substance he said that men are devoted to collecting *facts*, whereas women are inclined to ask what the facts *mean*. I wish I knew that kind of women. Maybe there were more such women in England in his day? Facts of sex and crime seem to fascinate both sexes today and both flood the book marts with their novels based on these aspects of life.

Judge Sarah Hughes, now national president of the B[usiness] & P[rofessional] W[omen], has accepted the *fact* of woman's force in history, publicly, but appears to neglect the study of its *meaning* while merely declaring that it must be exercised today. There should be a pamphlet exposition of its historic meanings—creative and destructive, "intellectual" and physically violent, etc. Everything seems to need diagramming. But the facts have to precede the diagrams to be convincing as diagrams, do they not?

Thanks for telling me about D. Brush's adoption of the two young Phelps. She sent me a wonderful flowering plant for Christmas with her love and best wishes.

As for Ruth Woodsmall's book on Moslem women, I find it non-historical, Christian-American missionary minded and so I am rather cold about it. Woodsmall and my sister Ruth O'Daniel are close friends and my sister does not take to my point of view easily if at all. Miss Woodsmall has been in this country recently and may still be. I can't ask my sister whether she is still here. When my sister is home, in Bronxville, from holiday visiting with her offspring and their families, I shall do that and let you know.

The Minn. Univ. Press doesn't want my Ms on Jap. women. I shall offer it for inspection now—as a last submission—to the New York House where I have been *invited* to re-submit it by a top official who did not see it before. By request I have sent a carbon copy to Japan. I have asked for a critical reading and verdict there. There are few, if any, Japanese of either sex who know this long and vital history of woman's *public* meanings.

If you would like for *me* to send *you* some suggestions for women to be brought into review in different fields of instruction at Smith, I'll work on that next week.

> Let us work on with strength of
> will as ever in mutual courage
> and love—
> Mary

•◡̶

Mary Beard's name did nothing to help her find a publisher for her manuscript on Japanese women. After rejection by Macmillan, it was subsequently rejected by the houses of Rinehart, Farrar, Houghton Mifflin, Knopf, and Doubleday, and by two university presses, Yale and Minnesota. She did not stop attempting to place it after the date of the letter below.

In June 1951 good news arrived: a Japanese press wanted to publish the work in translation. This version was supposed to come out in the spring of 1952 but actually did not appear until 1953. Also in 1953, a "miracle" happened: an American publisher, Public Affairs Press, accepted the manuscript. "I like the firm with that name as publisher," Beard wrote to Alma Lutz in satisfaction. "My book is all related to public affairs." [15]

The Force of Women in Japanese History (1953) was not Mary Beard's last book, as she threatens below. She also composed a brief biography of her husband, *The Making of Charles A. Beard* (1955). Her extant letters do not reveal when she began work on the biography or discuss her motives for writing it.

135. TO LT. ETHEL B. WEED

New Milford, Conn.
Jan. 19, 1951

Dear Ethel:

Partly to spare you the pain of telling me that you think the manuscript on women in long Japanese history is "punk" as writing, I am reporting now that I can't get an American publisher to take it. I have tried five of them, including the University of Minnesota Press really run by women and Macmillan which published my Woman As Force in History and seemed to me to be the logical publisher for this Japanese story which demonstrates in the history of a single people the thesis of that book of mine.

This manuscript is rejected by the five publishers on these grounds. They all agree that there is no reading public for it and that it would be a foolish financial project on that account. The Editor at Houghton Mifflin wrote, while declining to publish it, that it might be a tragic thing to let go—to bypass—such a story about the Japanese concerning whom we Americans really know so little but assume that we know everything that needs to be known. Another publisher said my Ms was too "diffuse". So is the great story—novel—of Eleanor of Aquitaine and the Four Kings exceedingly diffuse. The Harvard Press published that and it was a best seller for some time. It is a great novel and its author, Amy Kelly, is a professor at Wellesley. She wore herself to shreds with the long and hard research for it and has had to take a year off teaching for a rest in Florida. BUT this historical novel raises no questions today. My Ms raises many no doubt.

I had to stick as closely as possible to the sketches which were sent me from Japan and editors do not find them "interesting."

This is the end of that work tale for me. I shall not work any more on that material. You can do what you will with the carbon I sent you—burn it if no one wants to bother with it. I know that the opening with the Sun Goddess would not be acceptable to Christians and I know that my injection of the elevation of Mary to a place in the Christian Trinity would not "do." But I know what the Sun Goddess still means in Japan as well as what Mary means in Catholicism and that is that and this is this.

I shall never attempt to write another book now at my age. There is no use for my type of work at this ghastly hour of history when sex and crime, Catholic publications celebrating cardinals and "peace of mind" by that religion, and "thrilling" adventure stories of travels, plus the flood of war books constitute the offerings to the public. Reading surveys in the U.S. show that the number of persons who read books of any kind has fallen very low.

I do not question the possibility or the probability that my writing is too dull and otherwise wretched. I know that our reading public is no longer inclined to read straight history. Of Sir George Sampson's wonderful and in my opinion basic enlarged (last) book on The Western World and Japan, the publisher feared he could not sell enough to pay the cost of printing. I don't know how it has been selling—it has not appeared among best-seller lists. But I have read every word and marvel both at his learning and his objectivity. I wish I could listen to his lectures now in Japan.

Well there is neither crying nor laughing on my part about the fate of my effort to tell Americans and the Japanese too what Japanese women have done and been in their long history from the age of myths to this age. Those two women who came to my home last summer knew absolutely nothing themselves, it seemed to me, about the history of their women—not even that empresses had ruled in their own right.

SO BE IT. I have the satisfactions of having learned so much and I love to learn, and of having tried to do my bit for the learning of others.

Please tell Shidzue that my struggle is over and that my true regret is that I could not carry out the publication of the findings accumulated by the research committee which she instigated.

Of current events and what lies ahead I shall not say a word here. What could I say in words?   My love to you does not falter

Mary R. Beard

Mary Beard's correspondence with the president of Radcliffe College fell off about 1947. In 1949 the Radcliffe Women's Archives opened, and Elizabeth Borden was appointed director by President Jordan in 1951. Beard's response to a letter from Borden rehearses some old cavils and expresses much continuing doubt about the likelihood of a Harvard affiliate bringing her vision of women's archives to fulfillment.

136. TO ELIZABETH MCGINLEY BORDEN

New Milford, Connecticut
February 8, 1951

Dear Mrs. Borden:

It will be a privilege to have you in my home in the Spring when you may be able to drive here as you suggest doing. Your letter interests me for countless reasons, not least among them being your invitation to me to suggest people who might take a financial interest in promoting the collection of women's materials for furthering knowledge of their "contributions."

You may not know or even suspect that I not only turned over to Radcliffe data on persons who had helped to disseminate the idea of a World Center for Women's Archives, suggestions for essential documents for such an institution, with suggestions for materials about American women as well as about women in other lands, but I also contributed $1000 for the promotion of an important Archive at Radcliffe. Yet in this letter from you who are now to direct this movement at Radcliffe, I learn for the first time details of its status at this moment. Having lured many women to believe that Radcliffe was the best place in the U.S. for a great collection of books and documents respecting women's roles in American and other history, I have regretted that Radcliffe, as far as I knew, was in no great sense apparently warranting that belief.

As for the Harvard-Radcliffe "university city" and joint setting for a worthy woman's Archive, I found several years ago positive hostility from two high officials at Harvard when, on President Jordan's invitation, I went to Cambridge to pull for such a research library. During a luncheon with Mr. Jordan as host, Dean Buck, who sat beside me, left abruptly after I had begun to present the case for it, saying as he withdrew that he thought it was best or enough for women to be educated for domestic pursuits. He excused his departure on the ground that he had to attend a meeting of the Harvard Corporation but he did not depart without deriding the idea of woman's meaning in a larger sense.

Mr. Metcalf [university librarian] was present at the luncheon. He displayed no unfriendly bias. He asked me how many books I thought the Harvard Library would need to cover the history of women. I was silent for a minute and he asked whether 5000 books would do? I replied that 5000 would be a good beginning. I explained this seemingly crazy remark by affirming that where one begins to study any history is a clue to knowledge of that great subject. If one starts with 1848 as the history of women, I said, it would probably be enough to have the set of volumes on The History of Woman Suffrage which Susan B. Anthony initiated. (I had just seen the room in the Radcliffe Library dedicated to that feminist movement and I had met the woman who provided the pictures and documents for that room. I found everyone almost bending the knees to her.) But, I went on to say, at the luncheon, to Mr. Metcalf and the other persons present, including two women trustees of Radcliffe, if my memory is correct, that if one begins the study of women or men where human history began and comes up through the ages with the study of history, one would need for an adequate research library such an institution as our Congressional Library at least.

At President Jordan's that same evening, after dinner, President [James B.] Conant was graciousness complete. I had given a talk in Longfellow Hall, if that is right as to place, that morning. Before he came to sit by my side in the drawing room he asked Mrs. [Elizabeth] Schlesinger to tell him what I had said. My subject had been the force of women in long history. He seemed really interested and there was what I thought a high conversation on history in its large significances.

But when the committee assigned to draft a statement and plan for a proper education at Harvard in this hour of time presented its [1945] report [General Education in a Free Society], after three or so years of discussion, in effect the plan called for the training of "Christian gentlemen." Just where Radcliffe students, now proclaimed by President Jordan to be "the finest young women in the country", come into the educational program of training Christian gentlemen, I can't even imagine. Nor indeed do I think that Radcliffe has more than a share of the finest young women in the country, although this is not strictly on the point I am making—to the effect that I fear Harvard is of little, if any, help to the advancement of higher education in our country which in my opinion demands that such education take into account the truth and the documentation of the truth that women have been also potent agents in making all the history that has been made, as they are still making all the history that is being currently made.

I have one more comment to make: namely that *much duplication must occur in college libraries* if the dynamic of woman's thought and action in long history is to be studied to any extent on various campuses. Students can neither afford the expense nor the time of running from campus to campus in search of fundamental education in this aspect of life. If they miss it, all they have available will be the assertions of psychologists and the superficial sociology (superficial because lacking time depth) or the narrow biological verdicts about sex as deterministic in women's place in life.

I am aware that I have written too long a reply to your letter to me. But as spring is yet rather far off for our direct communion, I have been moved to put before you at this time my experience in Cambridge—in the university city—and my conception of the problem of educating men and women alike for an understanding of life as the life of both sexes, both potent in creating and in destroying patterns of culture.

I hope you won't feel that you do not want to come to see me after all.

Cordially yours,
Mary R. Beard

Mary Beard's extensive correspondence with Merle Curti and Harry Elmer Barnes—defenders of Charles Beard—shows that she was avidly following the acrimonious reassessment of her husband's life and work. The following is a more temperate letter than most of hers on the subject, and one reflecting her views of the contemporary world, showing how astute her intelligence remained as she neared seventy-five. Curti at the time was working on his presidential address to the Mississippi Valley Historical Association (the original name of the current Organization of American Historians).

137. TO MERLE CURTI

New Milford
on June 6, 1951

Dear Merle:

. . . A presidential address is a terrific challenge also. I don't see how it could be "fun" to write about the fate of Peace and the Government-over-Man conception of loyalty at this moment of time, unless one could be as rough and tough as a Swift. There is room for wit—not for mere humor—and the wits of the past who ran risks of life and limb to riddle follies of humankind are among the immortals. Charles and I read Lucian a lot and with delight. CAB often wanted to try his mind in a satire but his "moral" temper—which was a prime characteristic of his (despite [Henry Steele] Commager's charge in THE AMERICAN MIND that Beard was "futile" in that he was devoid of a moral sense)—held him to the sober tasks of social explorations. If he had lived a year longer, we would have attempted to carry out a plan to go off to the Southwest somewhere and in comparative aloofness from the turmoil try to release him for the wit he had as well as gravity.

I am deeply moved by your longing to write something about him and his work. I have been collecting a miscellany of writings about him but the effusions are mostly angry. When not angry many seem sadly stupid to me. I have not been able to resist attaching notes of mine to some of these writings and I may do more of this from time to time. Morton C. White has promised to come to see me for a talk about Beard and others in his Social Thought in America[: The Revolt Against Formalism (1952)] and has seemed to want to come really after he read Arthur Macmahon's tribute to CAB which I sent him. As yet, however, White has not put in an appearance here. I believe he was amazed at Macmahon's account of the Teacher—writing as he did as a Harvard "philosopher" himself. I except of course that portrait drawn by Macmahon as loving and not angry. There are many many fine letters expressing admiration for Charles but the printed things are mostly frenzied. This is not true of Japanese tributes; they are remarkable for their intense admiration and a fine memorial meeting was held in Tokyo. *The Republic* [1943] was issued in a Japanese translation and other Beard books are in process of translation in Tokyo.

Prof. [Richard] Hofstadter and his wife drove up for an afternoon recently. I tried to make it clear to Mr. Hofstadter that CAB was never a

Populist nor a Party Progressive disciple of Theodore Roosevelt—etc. Well critiques on persons and events are a grand-go-as-one-pleases for the most part.

But the democratic theme could and should be handled with acumen now, in my opinion. The framers of our Constitution, as you know, were not "democrats," although it has become the fashion to think of them as such and write about them as if they had been democrats. In placing checks and balances against a runaway democracy they were historicizing democracy in fact, with a very few exceptions. A press comment on CAB lambasted him for his An Economic Interpretation of the Constitution as an attempt to undermine their democratic ideals. But they read history, many of them, and knew how fragile democracies had been, about mobocracies, about venality, etc. They were afraid of democracy and it rightly is fearful when, as and if it becomes devoted to a demagogue as it has done in the past. To the apathy of our qualified voters in our society—staying from the polls in such numbers as a sign—is to a high degree due the demagogy of our time in the U.S. The fabulously large bureaucracy of this day springs not only from the Executive Dept of our Govt but from the rush of our people to climb on the bandwagon of the part in power; it is not only the USSR that constructs an exploitive bureaucracy; our democracy builds it too.

In my house are many big tomes on Democracy written in recent years, most of them anthologies of statements about democracy; others, descriptions of democracy in America; none, I am inclined to think, without examining all these books for accuracy at this moment, dealing with the critical aspects of universal suffrage as a fiat of law or a partial use of the suffrage. Several years ago CAB and I were asked by the editor of the Encyc. Brit. to write an article on Democracy. We declined on the ground that it should not be lightly undertaken and that singly or together we did not know enough about it as our political system. Max Cohn had no inhibition; he tossed off an article post haste. It was a shallow childish performance. But nothing now seems more important to undertake than a vital analysis of democracy as a way of politics. To discuss it as historiography is not enough, in my opinion. The positive adoration bestowed on the big warrior [Gen. Douglas] MacArthur by the hosts of men and women in our land seems to me to be terrifying as indicative of what mob rule might do; to say nothing here about the terrifying rule by Truman and his coathangers, who keep his mood one of confidence in himself.

Maybe in your presidential address for the Miss. Valley Hist. Assn, you could forecast a superb book of yours on Democracy in historiography and in practice, in the U.S. today. We run the awful risk of having a military man with a world yen for world warring as our next President— MacArthur or Eisenhower. Eisenhower might play that world game if it would put him into the White House. We might get a military dictatorship under a Shogun (non-aristocrat) if we could not become aware of what that would mean, in time to prevent it.

I have hung on my wall a picture of the first Tokugawa Shogun in Japan who founded a dynasty of Shoguns lasting for about 250 years. This first Shogun was named Iyeyasu. He had come to the military top in the feudal medieval fighting. He wrote down his principles grounded in his fighting experiences. The principles were translated by a Professor in the Imperial University of Japan and I have framed them, in his translation and hung them under Iyeyasu's picture. Attached is a copy of Iyeyasu's precepts. He had learned wisdom from hard experiences and applied it remarkably well. He was a Buddhist but not a fatalist.

This is far too long a letter to you and may have no value in it whatsoever. But I indulge myself in this kind of chatter to you, promising before I write you again to put a new ribbon in my typewriter—even do better typing—and try to choke off my verbosity much much sooner than I have done here.

> Love to you and Margaret
> —Mary Beard

In the winter of 1951–52, following the habit she and her husband had established in the 1930s, Mary Beard packed up and went to a warmer climate than New Milford for the winter months. The following sociable letter to friends describes her arrangement in Tucson—where, as ever, her intellectual work dominated her life. Beard liked her location, as she wrote to Miriam Holden, because she was only a three-block walk from the library of the University of Arizona. But she did not repeat the experiment the subsequent year, perhaps because of the disappointing weather.

Beard's mention here of a new book echoes her expression to Jim Putnam of the Macmillan Company in 1949, just eight months after Charles Beard died: "I hope some day and if I live long enough I shall try to do a very different kind of book on men and women—pointing up my belief that when both know the historical background of each the way can and will be clear for a better relation than history ever knew." As is also clear in this letter, she was holding her husband's surviving papers close to the vest. In 1950 she refused permission to Merle Curti to publish his letters in her possession.

Beard had known Nancy Cushman, a sculptor, since at least 1940, when she persuaded her to form a committee of women sculptors to collect documents for the World Center for Women's Archives.[16]

138. TO NANCY AND CHARLES CUSHMAN

> Christopher Square
> 1035 East Main Street
> Tucson, Arizona
> January 1, 1952

Oh my dear Nancy and Charles Cushman!

How wonderful you are to overlook my long silence and greet me so buoyantly at this Yuletide and opening of the New Year.

My silence has been to a considerable extent due to a two-winter struggle to run my big house in Connecticut & my will to stay there and collect and classify my great husband's records. That I have accomplished and no person will hereafter be justified in writing about him with emotion only, when the truths are documented in my files. But neither shall any person have access to them who is not really prepared temperamentally to search for the truth which inheres in these documents. Having gone so far in assembling and classifying them by October 1951, I closed my house and drove to Tucson for freedom *from* domestic burdens and freedom *to* work along the line of my strong and peculiar interests.

The weather here is by no means all that advertising claims for it as steady sunshine. In fact it has been quite cold a lot of the time since I came and old inhabitants here tell me it is usually apt to be cold until February but I have no grouch about the weather myself since here I have a darling two-room and bath cottage for all the privacy I want and a gas furnace to keep me as warm as I need to be. This place is a full block square giving it its name. There are landscaped grounds in which both Inn with its inmates and the separate cottages stand. I have the only cottage for a single person and it has a very large desk which I made a requirement for taking it. It has only a few decorations in it and each one exactly matches my taste. I am infinitely thankful that I can be here and physically fit enough to work long hours every day. I have my car for such diversions as I need for changes. So I am blessed in all sorts of ways.

My chief interests lie in the study of history and I am trying to learn more about women in history—with the hope that I may be able to write another book—this one on the meanings of man and woman in history and its continuation in our time.

I enclose an editorial in the exceptionally fine local paper here which will impress you as it does me, I think. I am sending you so many copies which Nancy may want to help circulate for its inclusion of the emphasis on knowing women in *history* instead of generalizing about her with pure emotions.

You must both come to see me when I am home again in the early spring and have my house open to receive friends. I plan to be there by the middle of April. Please do come to be with me when you can. And meanwhile write me.

> With sincere admiration and very
> best wishes for you individually and
> together—Mary R. Beard

To Mary Beard, the world around her seemed increasingly bleak, yet she retained her vital interest in it. The day after President Eisenhower's inaugural she wrote to Merle Curti, "I hope that the shadow of McCarthyites, etc. . . . will not blacken out the intelligence, courage, and means of survival for the educational enterprise and leave our people in outer as well as inner darkness terror-stricken. The Devil is loose. And appeals to God seem vain. Yet we must live out our days by striving to do our best work. And this effort I make—leaving the consequences to the Fates." She refused to vote for a military man for President, writing frankly to her son, "I see no ground whatsoever for voting for Ike, an ignoramus and a man who had operated on orders and by orders only. I detest his grinning pictures. Stevenson is not a Truman stooge and . . . Stevenson's humor is frequently shrewd. . . . If Ike is popular with the "Ladies" and "Youth" as young as children, that is for me a sign of our public degeneracy and suggests that situation in Germany when Hitler was the kingpin." [17]

Her idea for a women's research institute or seminar at Smith never was realized. Regardless, she kept in touch with new and old friends, by letter and by visit, and she constantly reached out for books on women. She usually had to look to sociologists rather than to historians to find any. Her letters reveal her usually critical opinions on such writers of the early 1950s as Ashley Montagu, Margaret Mead, Viola Klein, and Mirra

Komarovsky. She called Montagu's *The Natural Superiority of Women* (New York, 1953) an "idiotic book." (Perhaps she was especially peeved because it was brought out by her old publisher, Macmillan, who had rejected her Japanese manuscript.) "He is of the huge breed of ignoramuses," she wrote to Miriam Holden, "who know nothing about women in history. That naiveté runs through the flood of books on women in this day." [18] She was no easier on female writers. Her assessment of Simone de Beauvoir's *The Second Sex*, below, is astonishing—yet predictable. De Beauvoir's depiction of woman as "other" stood at the opposite end of the spectrum from Beard's depiction of woman as "force." Beard's refusal to glean anything from de Beauvoir's book, even if she saw it as severely flawed, suggests that her love of learning was operating within rigid boundaries by this time of her life.

Beard seems to have had a minor stroke early in 1953, making it difficult for her to write or type—hence the letter's closing lines.

139. TO MARJORIE WHITE

New Milford
Feb. 9, 1953

Dear Marjorie:

I have Simone de Beauvoir's book and I consider it perfectly ridiculous. The persons from whom she quotes are theoreticians. She pretends to knowledge of primitives, to give long history as background, and says that man *made* woman till the fields. She is a most pretentious person, not profound as the publisher and her translator claims. I can see why he falls for this book—since she plays up man as his sense of the existence of himself as the *One* and of woman as just the *other*. It's utter nonsense in view of actual long history. But no doubt it will have a big sale. Folly usually does.

. . . This is just a note. I can't write much at a time nor very legibly yet but I hope to do better soon. I can't type at all yet.

I am yours—Mary Beard

In 1950 Beard acquired a new correspondent in Margery Steer, who lived on a farm in Ohio and wrote political journalism, especially on peace issues. The two wrote to each other for the next five years.

The following letter shows her still in feisty form. Earlier in the year she had been busy with a "Herculean task," she wrote to Merle Curti, bringing *A Basic History of the United States* up to date for republication by Doubleday.[19]

140. TO MARGERY STEER

[New Milford, Connecticut]
August 5, 1954

Dear Margery Steer:

This is my 78th birthday and I am happy that I can still swing a pen if not good at typing now. Answering first your question about the Radcliffe College Archives, it is a fact that I started the collection there. The President of Radcliffe was delighted but some one of course had to be the Director and the woman in charge did the best she knew how to do about it, since American history was supposed to be the limit. Just before she was given a year off that beat, she initiated a "Workshop Report" consisting of lecture statements about the meanings of the archives. A friend of mine from New York attended that event and requested that the copies of the lectures be sent to me.

They came and I had pains in my soul on reading them. They all began with a background of woman's "rights" as 1848 historiography. It was depressingly evident to me that the women knew nothing about realistic history. They clung naively to the absurd Seneca Falls 1848 interpretation of women which made women the subjects of man through all history since a romantic golden age. The upshot was and still is that anything a woman now "achieves" is rather a miracle. I agree about the miracle but it is still manacled to 1848 after all the intervening decades.

The clipping you sent me about the Advisory Committee's intention to "rescue" the papers of "average, representative women, as well as those of suffragettes and career women" certainly can be encouraged and/or tested as to sincerity or intelligence. Just write to President Jordan in the absence of Mrs. Borden, and ask him whether the archives of church women would be acceptable. Jordan is a gentleman. I know him and we are friends.

Thanks immense for "What Makes Your Community Tick?" Congratulations on its exploration and reportage and the help from Hiram College.

That's a gleeful story about the cow giving powdered milk! I am sure your community ticks with joking as well as with prayers.

At this moment I am summoned to partake of a Happy Birthday cake and I must obey this call.

Happily yours, Mary Beard

[P.S.] Smith College has the finest women's archives in the U.S.—a really wonderful collection of printed and unprinted documents. They are *used* by students—really.

•←

"Work is salvation to me," Mary Beard wrote to Merle Curti early in 1953; two years later she still felt the same way.[20] Which "writing commission"—whether her book on Charles Beard or something else—occupied her at this time is not clear. Florence Hazzard, an author with a special interest in writing about women, had been Beard's occasional correspondent since the time she offered materials on Emily Howland, the pioneer educator, to the World Center for Women's Archives. In this letter Beard's spirit seems indomitable. Not long after, however, age and illness claimed her. After her eightieth birthday, in 1956, she was hardly active; she resided in Scottsdale, Arizona, near her son Bill Beard. She died just after she turned eighty-two.

141. TO FLORENCE HAZZARD

[New Milford, Connecticut]
January 26—55

Dear Florence Hazzard:

Your letter is a marvel of related episodes (shall I call them that?) in your efforts to collect and publish a book on Michigan women—certainly a worthy subject.

I am deeply occupied with a writing commission myself, the subject of which I tell no one until I find whether I can handle it well enough to submit it to a publisher. But work is my physical and mental salvation as it has been for nearly fifty years.

I have often thought of you, hoping you keep well. I am 78 years old and feel that time rushes by. I keep very well. In fact I think I was never ill. But I don't walk like a youth and so have to stick at home—to excess for lack of exercise. Even so—what does that deprivation matter? I go for auto rides, with my domestique as chauffeur, occasionally, and that is bracing.

I am glad that you were moved to write me—at last. Correspondence is not easy to maintain if one has a maze of real obligations which must be met, as you know of course. I don't travel, even to New York any more, except mentally. I don't miss New York, however. I spent more than thirty years there and that was enough for me.

> My best wishes for your health and
> aspirations with affection—
> Mary Beard

Abbreviations

AAUW: American Association of University Women.

AHA: American Historical Association.

ALP: biographical box 4, Alma Lutz collection, Vassar College.

AWA: American Woman's Association.

CU: Congressional Union.

Holden vol.: volume, "Mary Ritter Beard Letters, 1935–1963," box 54, Miriam Holden collection, Princeton University Library.

LC: Library of Congress.

NAACP: National Association for the Advancement of Colored People.

NAWSA: National American Woman Suffrage Association.

NCNW: National Council of Negro Women.

NCPW: National Council for Prevention of War.

NFBPW: National Federation of Business and Professional Women.

NRA: National Recovery Administration.

NWP: National Woman's Party.

NWPSF: microfilm edition, "National Woman's Party Papers: The Suffrage Years, 1913–1920," Microfilming Corporation of America, Sanford, N.C.

NWP 1913–1974: microfilm edition, "National Woman's Party Papers, 1913–1974," Microfilming Corporation of America, Sanford, N.C.

NWTUL: microfilm edition, "Papers of the Women's Trade Union League," Research Publications, Inc., Woodbridge, Conn.

NYPL: New York Public Library.

SCPC: Swarthmore College Peace Collection.

SL: Arthur and Elizabeth Schlesinger Library on the History of Women in America, Radcliffe College.

SSC: Sophia Smith Collection, Smith College.

WCWA: World Center for Women's Archives.

WILPF: Women's International League for Peace and Freedom.

WPA: Works Progress Administration.

YWCA: Young Women's Christian Association.

Notes

1   MRB to Mary Philbrook, Nov. 17 [1936], folder 1936, WPA-Women's Archives Collection; William Beard to Marjorie White, Mar. 25, 1959, vol. 154, box 27, White papers.

2   MRB to Merle Curti, Feb. 18, 1950, Mar. 26, 1950, and Dec. 6, 1950, Curti papers. She criticized the "wicked lack of sensitivity" of the literary heirs of Mark Twain in publishing his love letters to his wife and said she regarded as "disgusting taste" the "gratification of sexual curiosity" in the publication of private letters.

3   Alma Lutz, notes on Mary Beard, Dec. 27, 1939, ALP.

PUTTING WOMEN ON THE RECORD

1   Late in life MRB remarked that the notion of careers for women "trivializes their operations" and, again, that "career women, like career men, are capitalistic entrepreneurs or retainers of the bourgeoisie." MRB to Margaret Grierson, Aug. 13, 1950, and Dec. 10, 1950, box 1, Beard papers, SSC.

2   Beard, *On Understanding Women*, 33.

3   Beard and Beard, *American Citizenship*, vi–vii; MRB, *Women's Work in Municipalities*, vi–vii; MRB to Harriot Stanton Blatch, undated [May 1935], ALP.

4   Turoff, *Mary Beard as Force in History*, 5, quotes an interview with MRB in the Louisville *Courier Journal*, Nov. 2, 1946: "I've never accepted any honorary degrees. I wouldn't be able to stand the things they would say." Thomas Bender has emphasized the Beards' orientation toward the public as audience in "The New History—Then and Now," 617. On changing models of the historian, from publicist to academic professional, see Novick, *That Noble Dream*, 37–53.

5   MRB to Mira Saunders, June 29, 1939, box 9, Saunders collection.

6   Quotation from Hofstadter, *Progressive Historians*, 299. Postwar male scholars assessing Charles Beard's life and work rarely considered the famous volumes bearing both Beards' names to be jointly written rather than the man's work, unlike Ellen Nore, in *Charles A. Beard: An Intellectual Biography*. I am enormously indebted to her study, both for her interpretation of Charles Beard's mind and work and for her acknowledgment of the

couple's collaboration, which makes it more possible than ever before to appreciate their common themes as well as common labors. On the latter point, I have also been influenced by Bonnie Smith's innovative "Seeing Mary Beard," especially regarding Mary Beard's influence on her husband's move toward explicit relativism in the 1930s; see also Bender, "The New History," 612–14.

Sales figures for CAB's and coauthored volumes appear in note 17 to Howard K. Beale's essay, "Beard's Historical Writings," in Beale, ed., *Charles A. Beard*, 310–12.

7   John Higham, "Charles A. Beard: A Sketch," reprinted in Higham's *Writing American History* (Bloomington, Indiana University Press, 1970), 131, from *International Encyclopedia of the Social Sciences* (New York, 1968), vol. 2: 33–37. Although MRB had published three books in women's history between 1931 and 1934 (in addition to the joint works), she was subject to baldly ignorant comments such as this one from a Southern woman in 1935, "I know your husband's work very well. Why don't you do anything yourself?" Mary Beard professed herself "amused" and took some pride in having responded by "smiling only. I think I am moving ahead in my own personality." Copy of MRB to "Dear friends," dated "the morning after" [a major organizing meeting for the World Center for Women's Archives, which took place Oct. 17, 1935], Box 1, pt. 1, Schwimmer-Lloyd collection.

When Harold Faulkner and Merle Curti invited Charles Beard to speak to their students and history colleagues at Smith College—a women's college—in the mid-1930s, they gave no thought to inviting his female coauthor until word got to them that she had accompanied him to Northampton. MRB's *amour propre* then kept her from accepting their belated invitation to campus, on the grounds that the event was her husband's. Merle Curti to Nancy F. Cott, Nov. 3, 1988 (in author's possession).

8   *Current Biography*, 1941; Perry Miller, "Charles A. Beard," *Nation*, Sept 25, 1948, 344–46; Higham, "Charles A. Beard: A Sketch," 131; Beale, "Beard's Historical Writings," 300 n. 44. In *History* (Englewood Cliffs, NJ, Prentice-Hall, 1965), by John Higham with Leonard Krieger and Felix Gilbert, p. 125, n. 15, Higham cites *America in Midpassage* as by CAB without mention of MRB and consistently speaks of it on pp. 193–94 as "his" work, even failing to cite MRB as coauthor in footnotes. Defenders of Charles Beard's reputation did not differ from his critics in their inattention to MRB's contribution to the jointly written works. A recent astute discussion of the attacks on Charles Beard is in Novick, *That Noble Dream*, 281–319.

9   MRB to Merle Curti, Oct. 13, 1950, May 24, 1938, Dec. 2, 1947, and Dec. 17, 1947, Curti papers; Merle Curti to Nancy F. Cott, Nov. 3, 1988 (in author's possession); MRB to Mrs. [Catherine Drinker] Bowen, Feb. 20, 1944; container 1, Bowen papers. MRB repeated the judgment of this re-

viewer (Bernard De Voto) to Curti (Dec. 2, 1947) as though she accepted it, but that was more of her self-deprecation.

10 Mrs. Charles Beard, "The Nineteenth-Century Woman Looking Forward," *Young Oxford* 2 (Jan. 1901): 122; fragment of letter from MRB to William Beard, n.d. [but likely 1951 or 1952], in private collection of Detlev Vagts, Cambridge, Mass.

11 Nore, *Charles A. Beard*, 14–27, esp. 22; MRB to "My dear Son" [William Beard], Aug. 18, 1951, Vagts private collection. The serial *Young Oxford* published at Ruskin Hall tells much about its aims. On women at Ruskin Hall, see Anna Vrooman, "A Ruskin Hall for Women," *Young Oxford* 1 (May 1900): 11–12.

12 CAB, "Cooperation and the New Century," *Young Oxford* 2 (Dec. 1900): 98; MRB, *Woman as Force in History*, 88. Cf. Mary Beard's telling an international congress of women in 1933 that "action without thought is perilous," but "without action, whatever our thought, we are futile. It is not enough to know; action is as essential as knowledge." MRB, "Struggling toward Civilization," address to the morning session of the International Congress of Women, July 17, 1933, in *Our Common Cause, Civilization*, Report of the International Congress of Women (New York, National Council of Women of the U.S., 1933), 28. See Morton G. White, *Social Thought in America: The Revolt against Formalism*. CAB earned the Ph.D. in Political Science in 1904; his first appointment was as lecturer in History, but he soon joined the Department of Public Law and by 1907 was appointed to a new chair in Politics and Government. See Nore, *Charles A. Beard*, 28–37.

13 CAB to Dorothy Kirchwey Brown, Oct. 22, 1917, folder 241, Brown unprocessed collection, SL.

14 MRB to Leonora O'Reilly, Jan. 1, 1912, undated [May 1912?], and July 21, 1912, NWTUL, reel 105; MRB to Jessie Hardy Stubbs, Jan 4. [1913?], NWPSF, reel 1. On her reform work between 1909 and 1913, see also Harriot Stanton Blatch and Alma Lutz, *Challenging Years*, 134–35; Barbara Turoff, *Mary Beard as Force in History*, 22; Ann J. Lane, *Mary Ritter Beard: A Sourcebook*, 22–24; Loretta Zimmerman, "Mary Beard: An Activist of the Progressive Era," 19–22; Nore, *Charles A. Beard*, 46–47, 241 n. 26; MRB to "My dear Son [William Beard]," Aug. 18, 1951, Vagts collection.

15 MRB to Alice Paul, n.d. [1913], NWPSF, reel 6; MRB to Alice Paul, July 26, 1916, NWPSF, reel 30. Documentation of MRB's work with the Congressional Union appears throughout the correspondence of the group. She withdrew from the Executive Committee (the ruling body) late in May 1915 to join the Advisory Council (which served more as window dressing); see Lucy Burns to MRB, June 1, 1915, reel 17. For her attitude on the suffrage pickets see MRB to Jane Norman Smith, Jan. 17 [1917], and June 23

[1917], folder 55, Smith papers; for her resignation from the Advisory Council, MRB to Elizabeth Rogers, Nov. 17, 1917, NWPSF, reel 52. During 1916 and 1917 MRB was also very active in the New York State woman suffrage campaign, which reached success in November 1917; therefore when she resigned from the National Woman's Party she, as a New York resident, was able to vote. For other treatments, see Turoff, *Mary Beard as Force*, 19–30; Zimmerman, "Mary Beard," 22–31; Lane, *Sourcebook*, 22–29. Looking back on her suffragist years much later, MRB readily acknowledged her deep involvement with the Congressional Union but did not remember that she had ever been a member of the National Woman's Party; MRB to Alma Lutz, Apr. 15, 1940, ALP.

16 MRB to Alice Paul, Nov. 30 [1914], NWPSF, reel 13. CAB published four articles supporting the CU position in the *New Republic*, beginning with "Woman Suffrage and Strategy," Dec. 2, 1914, 22–23, and continuing with others in the issues of Jan. 9, 1915, Oct. 4, 1915, and July 29, 1916. He also replied directly and at length to Carrie Chapman Catt, who had conveyed her annoyance at his writings; see copy of CAB to Catt, Aug. 8, 1915, NWPSF, reel 30, where he explicitly favored the "political and partisan" tactics of the CU and derided Catt's adherence to nonpartisanship and "silent influence." In 1916 he voted, as the CU would wish, not for Woodrow Wilson but for the Republican presidential candidate Charles Evans Hughes. See Nore, *Charles A. Beard*, 46–50, 73; Zimmerman, "Mary Beard," 24–29. In MRB to "my dear Son," Aug. 18, 1951 (Vagts collection), she was at pains to explain what she assumed must have seemed to him as a young child "mad wrangling" between his parents over the suffrage question. Since William was born in 1907, these arguments probably took place about 1909–10—unless, of course, MRB's memory had failed her and these arguments took place earlier, only in front of Miriam (born in 1901).

17 Nore, *Charles A. Beard*, 38–66, 241 n. 26; Beard and Beard, *American Citizenship*, vi–vii; Mary Ritter Beard, *Women's Work in Municipalities*; and Charles Austin Beard, *American City Government*. On MRB's instigation of the first coauthorship, MRB to "Dear Son [William Beard]," Aug. 30, 1951, in Vagts collection.

18 See Nore, *Charles A. Beard*, 77–95. Originally published by the Workers' Education Bureau of America in New York in 1920, Mary Beard's book went through at least ten editions; in 1931 it was reprinted as *The American Labor Movement: A Short History* (New York, Macmillan, 1931).

19 Typescript of speech by MRB at opening meeting for World Center for Women's Archives, Oct. 17, 1935, p. 3, box 1, pt. 1, Schwimmer-Lloyd collection; for her views on home economics, see MRB to Eva Hansl [copy], Aug. 11, 1944, with Grierson letters in box 1, Beard papers, SSC; printed book flap, document container 10, Beard papers, DePauw.

In memorable remarks of 1929, CAB characterized the university as having "too much routine, not enough peace; too much calm, not enough passion; above all, too many sacred traditions that must be conserved; too many theories, not enough theory; too many books, not enough strife of experience; too many students, not enough seekers." Quoted in Nore, *Charles A. Beard*, 83; see also Thomas Bender, *New York Intellect*, 298–302, 307–08.

20 MRB to Marjory Steer, Sept. 6, 1954, box 2, Steer papers, states that there are nearly seven thousand books in the New Milford house; MRB to Margaret Grierson, Apr. 23, 1945, box 1, Beard papers, SSC, mentions no telephone in home; but seven years later (and after CAB's death) MRB to Harry Barnes, Aug. 3, 1952, Barnes papers, gives New Milford phone number. Hofstadter, *Progressive Historians*, 287–88, called Charles Beard individualistic, citing his refusal to join either the American Association of University Professors (when John Dewey and others tried to recruit him in 1917) or the America First group of anti-interventionists in the 1940s. Nore, *Charles A. Beard*, however, emphasizes that CAB liked to work with others on collaborative projects; see also Bender, "The New History."

21 MRB was the person chosen to review Eleanor Roosevelt's book *It's Up to the Women* in the *New York Herald Tribune* a year after FDR gained the White House; see Turoff, *Mary Beard as Force*, 1 n. 1. Clippings regarding *Pictorial Review* in folder labeled "NRA, 1934–38," box 3, Phillips collection; *New York Sun* list reported in *Washington Post*, Jan. 1, 1936; on Charles Beard's reputation, see Novick, *That Noble Dream*, 240; Nore, *Charles A. Beard*, 258 n. 45.

22 CAB to George Smith, Jan. 31, 1937, quoted in Nore, *Charles A. Beard*, 266 n. 42; MRB to Florence Boeckel, Apr. 8, 1939, Boeckel correspondence, DG 23, NCPW papers; MRB to Marjorie White, Jan. 18, 1941, vol. 154, box 124, White papers. See MRB, "Is Collectivism the Answer?"; on CAB's changing views of Marx and communism, see Nore, *Charles A. Beard*, 190–93; cf. also John P. Diggins, "Flirtation with Fascism: American Pragmatic Liberals and Mussolini's Italy," *American Historical Review* 71 (Jan. 1966): 493–94.

23 CAB, "War with Japan, What Shall We Get Out of It," *Nation* 120, no. 3116 (Mar. 25, 1925): 312; Nore, *Charles A. Beard*, 172–86; Novick, *That Noble Dream*, 131; MRB to Florence Brewer Boeckel, Apr. 8, 1939, Boeckel correspondence, DG 23, NCPW papers.

24 MRB to Lena Madesin Phillips, Apr. 28 [1935], folder 93, box 4, Phillips papers; MRB to Miriam Holden, June 13, 1940, Holden vol.; MRB to Luella Gettys, Apr. 25, 1941, folder 4, Keys papers.

25 She was Mrs. Charles Beard in her contribution to the Ruskin Hall serial in 1900 but never again. "Mrs. Mary R. Beard, Editor" stated the letterhead of *The Woman Voter* in 1911. Among the bold group of women listed on the

Congressional Union's letterhead of 1914, only she and Crystal Eastman
Benedict used their own full names, while the four other married women
used their husbands'; see CU letterhead in MRB to Miss Dunn, Mar. 12
_[1914], container D13, La Follette Family papers, LC. Quotations from
MRB to Doris [Stevens], Nov. 14, 1935, file B, box 4, Stevens (unprocessed) papers; MRB to Rosika Schwimmer, Oct. 18, 1936, box 1, pt. 2,
Schwimmer-Lloyd collection; MRB to Marjorie White, July 11, 1940,
folder 150a, White papers.

26   MRB to Margaret Grierson, June 22 [1944], box 1, Beard papers, SSC;
MRB to Dorothy Brush, Jan. 18, 1947, ibid.

27   MRB to Mira Saunders, June 29, 1939, box 9, Saunders papers; MRB to
Florence Kitchelt, Aug. 13, 1941, folder 113, Kitchelt papers; MRB to
Margaret Grierson, Mar. 6, 1944, box 1, Beard papers, SSC; MRB to Flor-
ence Cairns, Apr. 19, 1948, "Mary Ritter Beard" folder, Cairns papers;
MRB to James Putnam, Oct. 9, 1948, Beard-Macmillan correspondence;
MRB to Lena Madesin Phillips, Oct. 10, 1948, folder 93, box 4, Phillips
collection; typescript fragment by MRB [to William Beard], c. 1951, Vagts
private collection. On foreign and domestic policy issues see also MRB to
Florence Brewer Boeckel (educational director of the NCPW and former
NWP worker), July 28, 1936, folder 2 and additional letters of the middle to
late 1930s from MRB to Boeckel in folder 11, box 31, NCPW papers;
MRB to Miriam Holden, Mar. 12, 1938, Holden vol., and MRB to Florence Kitchelt, Feb. 22, 1944, folder 113, Kitchelt papers.

28   MRB, "The Twentieth-Century Woman Looking Around and Backward,"
100–04; "The Nineteenth-Century Woman Looking Forward," 119–22.

29   "Points to Wilson's Silence on Women," *New York Times*, Nov. 20, 1914,
6; MRB, *Women's Work in Municipalities*, vi. Her speech to the National
Municipal League was printed as "Women's Work for the City"; see
esp. 204.

30   MRB, "Mothercraft," *Woman Voter* 1–2 (Jan. 1912): 12–13; reprinted
in Lane, *Sourcebook*, 77–79, quotation on 79.

31   MRB to Alice Paul, n.d. [1914], NWPSF, reel 7; on CAB see note 16 above.

32   MRB, "Have Americans Lost Their Democracy?"; typescript reprinted in
Lane, *Sourcebook*, 86–88.

33   MRB, "Votes for Workingwomen," *Woman Voter* 3 (Sept. 1912): 3–5, reprinted in Lane, *Sourcebook*, 80–84, quotation on 83; MRB "The Legislative Influence of Unenfranchised Women," 60.

34   MRB, "Votes for Workingwomen," 81; Hearings before the Committee on
the Judiciary, House of Representatives, 63d Congress, 2d session, serial 11,
part. 1, Mar. 3, 1914 (Washington, D.C., Government Printing Office,
1914), 24–28; MRB to Alice Paul, Nov. 15 [1914], NWPSF, reel 13;
"Hearing before the Committee on Woman Suffrage, United States Senate,
65th Congress, First Session, on S.J. Res. 2, Proposing an Amendment to the

Constitution of the United States Conferring upon Women the Right of Suffrage," Apr. 20, 1917 (Washington, D.C., Government Printing Office, 1917), 40–45.

35 MRB to Elsie Hill, July 10, 1921, NWP, reel 9. On the European trip, see Thomas Kennedy, *Charles A. Beard and American Foreign Policy*, 44–45; MRB, *The Making of Charles A. Beard*, 29; and Nore, *Charles A. Beard*, 95–96.

36 Clipping, "Time to Boast a Bit, Women Told," *Japan Advertiser*, Dec. 2, 1922, pt. 2, Beard papers, DePauw. No other documentation of MRB's views at this time is known to exist.

37 CAB and MRB, *American Spirit*, 412–13.

38 See excerpts from Stanton's "Woman's Bible" in *Elizabeth Cady Stanton/ Susan B. Anthony: Correspondence, Writings, Speeches*, ed. Ellen Carol DuBois (New York, Schocken, 1981), 228–45; on Gilman's attraction to Lester Ward's theories, see Mary A. Hill, *Charlotte Perkins Gilman: The Making of a Radical Feminist, 1860–1896* (Philadelphia, Temple University Press, 1980), esp. 264–72.

39 Anna Garlin Spencer, *Woman's Share in Social Culture*, 2d. ed., esp. 296–302; CAB and MRB, *American Spirit*, 418. See the biographical sketch of Spencer by Louis Filler in *Notable American Women: A Biographical Dictionary*, ed. Edward James and Janet James (Cambridge: Harvard University Press, 1971), Vol. 3, 331–33.

40 MRB to Elsie Hill, July 10, 1921, NWP, reel 9.

41 "Time to Boast a Bit"; MRB, *On Understanding Women*, 17–18; *A Changing Political Economy*, 7–8.

42 Nore, *Charles A. Beard*, 109–11.

43 CAB to Curtice Hitchcock, March 25 [1927], and June 11, 1927, Beard-Macmillan correspondence.

44 MRB to Florence Kitchelt, May 18, [1928], folder 113, Kitchelt papers; MRB to Margaret Grierson, Nov. 10, 1944, box 1, Beard papers, SSC.

45 Quotations from preface to *The Rise*, xii-xiv. I discuss Mary Beard's contribution to *The Rise* in greater depth in "Two Beards: Coauthorship and the Concept of Civilization." In immediately succeeding years, CAB edited two volumes of essays, both adopting the theme of civilization: *Whither Mankind: A Panorama of Modern Civilization* and *Towards Civilization*. The Beards wrote a second high school history text (their first was *A History of the United States* [1921]) in the 1930s, called *The Making of American Civilization*; MRB later commented: "I persuaded CAB to let me plan it as, in effect the drama of our history, because I see all history as a drama." MRB to "Dear Son" [William Beard], Aug. 30, 1951, Vagts collection.

46 CAB and MRB, *The Rise*, 24–28. Beard was likely influenced and informed here by Alice Clark's *The Working Lives of Women in the Seventeenth Century* (1919), which she discussed favorably in *On Understanding*

Women, 501–05. In later years Beard also expressed appreciation for Elisabeth Anthony Dexter's *Colonial Women of Affairs* (1926), but she probably had not read it before *The Rise* was completed.

47   CAB and MRB, *The Rise*, 1: 24–28; 2: 215; 2: 562–65; 1: 181–82, 817–18; 2: 475; 2: 75–77, 404–05, 722–23.

48   See MRB, "The Feminist Progression," "American Women and the Printing Press," and "After Equality, What?" Her assumption that women in the United States had opportunities open to them continued to underpin her essays of the 1930s, such as "A Test for the Modern Woman" and even her series on "Women and Social Crises."

49   CAB to Merle Curti, Apr. 15, 1945, quoted in Nore, *Charles A. Beard*, 111; MRB to Margery Steer, Oct. 31, 1950, box 3, Steer papers. At one point in *On Understanding Women* MRB remarked that "the countless cottages through the Island Empire [of Japan], where women now spin and weave silk from the worms they carefully tend, are unbroken links in the industry probably started by their sex and now their chief source of wealth" (54).

50   E.g., CAB, "A Plea for Greater Stress upon the Modern Period," speech delivered at the Sixth Annual Convention of the Association of History Teachers of the Middle States and Maryland (1908), cited by Novick, *That Noble Dream*, 189.

51   MRB, *On Understanding Women*, 17, 32, 33. As in the rest of the Beards' work, this vision of increasing understanding by means of "widening of historical narration and interpretation" looked toward a social goal—new modes of social arrangement which would "develop the highest powers of men as well as women."

52   CAB and MRB, *The American Spirit*, esp. 53–61.

53   See MRB, *On Understanding Women*, 526; *A Changing Political Economy as It Affects Women*, 8–9; MRB to Marjorie White, Aug. 18, 1948, folder 150a, box 26, White papers; MRB to Mrs. Elizabeth Borden, June 25, 1951, box 1, series 2.1, record group 17, Radcliffe Archives. It is not clear when MRB read the Swiss philologist Johann-Jakob Bachofen, whose *Das Mutterrecht* (1861) served to ground some nineteenth-century women's belief in a primitive matriarchy (although Bachofen himself affirmed the superior value and organization of the succeeding patriarchy). Turoff, *Mary Beard as Force in History*, claims that Alfred Vagts introduced MRB to Bachofen's work in 1928–29. MRB does not cite Bachofen in her bibliography for *On Understanding Women*, however. In 1949 MRB wrote to Marjorie White about her excitement at finding an English translation of Bachofen's introduction to his famous work in an anthology edited by V. F. Calverton. She admitted in this letter that she did not read German easily and speculated why a full translation was not available: "Did Bachofen tell so much that a 'wall of silence' arose and denied him world wide popular

expression at least in the English-speaking world?" She also noted that Briffault referred to Bachofen four times and saw him as a major founder of modern social science in spite of some lapses of judgment. MRB to Marjorie White, July 21, 1949, vol. 154, box 27, White papers.

54 MRB to Dorothy Brush Dick, Aug. 6, 1946, box 1, Beard papers, ssc; MRB, *Woman as Force in History*, 168.

55 *On Understanding Women*, esp. 12–27 (on historians' partiality), 30–31 (quotation).

56 Ibid., 22.

57 MRB, *America Through Women's Eyes*, 5, 7, 126, 479; see also 173, 194.

58 Ibid., 358, 5, 90, 127. On "compensatory" and "contribution" history see Gerda Lerner, "Placing Women in History: Definitions and Challenges," in her *The Majority Finds Its Past*, 145–59.

59 The entry for Beard in *Woman's Who's Who, 1914* (New York, Commonwealth, 1914), 37, noted that she had "resigned from the Woman's Municipal League and other societies to devote herself to suffrage."

60 See Nancy F. Cott, "Feminist Politics in the 1920s: The National Woman's Party," and *The Grounding of Modern Feminism*, 66–81.

61 MRB, "The Feminist Progression," 241.

62 CAB and MRB, *The Rise*, xiii; MRB, "After Equality—What?" 227, 228; "Test," 179, 180; "Women and Social Crises" (Jan. 1935), 31; see also "American Women and the Printing Press." In comparison, Harriot Stanton Blatch judged statistics about women's economic power through her awareness of "the domination of women's finance by men," women's "lack of training and the old inhibitions," which kept them from having real control; Blatch quoted in "Leaders Discuss Women in Finance," *New York Times*, Mar. 15, 1936, sect. 2, p. 9.

63 MRB, *On Understanding Women*, 522, and *America Through Women's Eyes*, 2–6.

64 MRB, "After Equality—What?" 228; see also "The College and Alumnae in Contemporary Life."

65 MRB to Florence Cross Kitchelt [June 29, 1950], folder 113, Kitchelt papers; MRB to Wilbur K. Jordan, Jan. 20, 1944, Beard papers (A-9), sl; Lane, *Sourcebook*, 56. In "College and Alumnae," 11, she also noted, "Within the women's colleges are some teachers who refuse to recognize any value in women's study of themselves; they declare that the time has arrived for a sexless consideration of the world."

66 MRB, "University Discipline for Women—Asset or Handicap?" *Journal of the American Association of University Women* 25, no. 3 (Apr. 1932); reprinted in Lane, *Sourcebook*, 149.

67 CAB, "Cooperation and the New Century," 99.

68 Virginia Woolf, *Three Guineas*, 62, 63, 66, 78–79. Woolf found nothing to encourage her that, for instance, "if we help the daughters to become profes-

sional women we shall discourage war." She found that the professions "make the people who practise them possessive, jealous of any infringement of their rights, and highly combative if anyone dares dispute them. Are we not right then in thinking that if we enter the same professions we shall acquire the same qualities? And do not such qualities lead to war?"

69 Report of Beard speech at NWP banquet taking place on Nov. 4, 1933, in "Banquet Attracts Brilliant Assemblage," *Equal Rights* 19, no. 41 (Nov. 11, 1933): 319; MRB, "Women and Social Crises" (Nov. 1934), 347, 362; see also "College and Alumnae," 15; *A Changing Political Economy*, 7.

70 CAB, "The Myth of Rugged American Individualism."

71 MRB to "Dear Chief," Aug. 20 [1935], folder 93, box 4, Phillips papers; MRB to Rosika Schwimmer, Dec. 27, 1935, pt. 1, box 1, Schwimmer-Lloyd collection.

72 MRB, "A Test for the Modern Woman," 179; "Feminist Progression," 241; "Women and Social Crises" (Jan. 1935), 31; MRB to Alma Lutz, Jan. 29, 1937, ALP (there is also a copy of this letter in folder 45, Alma Lutz papers, SL).

73 Jane Norman Smith to Alma Lutz, Nov. 16, 1932, folder 58, Lutz papers, SL (written in response to MRB's "A Test for the Modern Woman"); MRB to Harriot Stanton Blatch [relating conversation with Doris Stevens], July 16 [1934], ALP; MRB to Doris Stevens, "May Day" [1937], folder B, box 4, Doris Stevens uncatalogued collection. MRB noted in "Women and Social Crises" (Jan. 1935), 8, "When the writer hears women today refer to themselves as 'children,' as 'novices in the fields of social and public affairs,' as persons 'just waking from a long sleep to personal awareness,' it makes her sick to the bone."

74 MRB to Alma Lutz, Jan. 29, 1937, ALP; Dorothy Dunbar Bromley, "'Sponsor' Spurns Charter for Women," *New York World Telegram*, Jan. 7, 1934, 34; MRB to Lena Madesin Phillips, June 3, 1936, folder 93, box 4, Phillips papers. At a meeting on the Women's Charter, MRB reportedly also said, "The social welfare stand toward women and children is just as pale as equal rights"; minutes of "Women's Charter" conference, Sept. 9, 1936, Correspondence Regarding Meetings, Women's Subcommittee on International Labor Organization, Record Group 86, U.S. Women's Bureau papers, National Archives. The U.S. Supreme Court invalidated the New York minimum wage law for women in 1936, to the cheers of the NWP and the despair of the "protectionists"; Beard advocated mandatory minimum wages for both sexes. MRB to Lutz, Jan. 29, 1937.

75 CAB, "Written History as an Act of Faith," 220, 226. E.g., Hofstadter, *Progressive Historians*, 299–304, on "intellectual conversion." I am greatly indebted to Nore, *Charles A. Beard*, 154–171, whose interpretation I follow.

76 MRB, *On Understanding Women*, 13; CAB, "That Noble Dream"; Nore, *Charles A. Beard*, 157–61. On the relativism controversy swirling around

Becker and Beard, see Novick, *That Noble Dream*, esp. 250–278. Bonnie Smith argues for Mary Beard's influence moving her husband toward relativism in an iconoclastic and revelatory article, "Seeing Mary Beard."

77 Croce is quoted in Nore, *Charles A. Beard*, 156, 159–60; see her enlightening discussion of the influences on CAB, including the new physics of the 1920s, Mannheim, and other philosophers and historians.

78 MRB, *On Understanding Women*, 33; CAB, "Written History as an Act of Faith," 225, and "A Historian's Quest for Light" (1931), quoted in Nore, *Charles A. Beard*, 161 (and see generally 158–64); see also Edward Purcell, Jr., "Non-Euclideanism: Logic and Metaphor," in *The Crisis of Democratic Theory*, 47–73. CAB's critics saw him as not only subjectivist but also antiscientific; cf. Hofstadter, *Progressive Historians*, 304–17; Novick, *That Noble Dream*.

79 MRB, *On Understanding Women*, 515.

80 Thomas Bender uses the term "distributive justice" to characterize what both Beards saw as their goal, in his interesting brief reassessment (influenced by Nore), "The New History—Then and Now," 617.

81 MRB to Rose Arnold Powell, Aug. 10, 1935, folder 27, Powell papers.

82 CAB, "Written History as an Act of Faith," 220, 226. Charles Beard at college amused his future bride by reading her passages from de Coulanges, according to Nore, *Charles A. Beard*, 171. Peter Novick notes that the phrase "Pas de documents, pas d'histoire [No documents, no history]" was a hallmark of the "most widely used and influential manual of historical method" among early twentieth-century "scientific" historians, *Introduction aux études historiques* (1898) by Charles Victor Langlois and Charles Seignobos, translated into English the same year. The English version went into many editions and "was the standard handbook down to World War II," according to Novick, *That Noble Dream*, 37–39.

83 CAB, "That Noble Dream," 82; MRB to Mrs. Dorothy Porter, Mar. 31, 1940, folder 1, box 1, series 4, National Council of Negro Women records (there is also a copy of this letter in Beard papers, SL).

84 MRB to Miriam Holden, Mar. 12, 1938, Holden vol.; CAB and MRB, *America in Midpassage*, 462–63. MRB came to a similar conclusion in *Woman as Force in History*, 339: "Despite the barbaric and power-hungry propensities and activities in long history, to which their sex was by no means immune, women . . . were in the main on the side of *civil*-ization in the struggle with barbarism."

85 MRB to Dr. Minnie Maffett, Feb. 22, 1940, box 4, Josephine Schain papers, SSC.

86 MRB to Luella Gettys, Apr. 25, 1941, Luella Gettys Key papers; MRB to Marjorie White, July 19, 1953, vol. 154, box 27, White papers.

87 CAB and MRB, *American Spirit*, esp. 339, 376, 672–73, 197–213; *America in Midpassage*, 942–45. MRB's letters to Harriot Stanton Blatch

of the mid-1930s show how thrilled she was by reading Stanton's manuscripts in the Library of Congress, especially upon finding her critique of the wage labor system.

88 CAB and MRB, *American Spirit*, 672–74. MRB repeated the same formulation of the meaning of civilization in the conclusion to *Woman as Force in History*, 339.

89 Typescript, "A Study of the Encyclopaedia Britannica in relation to its treatment of women," by Mary Ritter Beard, Marjorie White, Janet Selig, and Dora Edinger (her three hand-picked associates on the project), Nov. 15, 1942, folder 150d, White papers.

90 There are telling critiques of *Woman as Force in History* in Berenice Carroll, "Mary Beard's *Woman as Force in History*: A Critique," and in Suzanne Lebsock, "Reading Mary Beard."

91 Albert Guerard, "Cherchez La Femme," *New Republic* 114 (Apr. 15, 1946): 515; Ella Winter, "Eve's Numerous Daughters," *Saturday Review of Literature* 29 (Mar. 30, 1946): 20.

92 See MRB to Anne Martin, Feb. 27, 1947, Anne Martin papers; MRB to Mrs. Powell, July 3, 1948, folder 27, box 2, Rose Arnold Powell papers; MRB to Margaret Grierson, Mar. 26, 1948, box 1, Beard papers, SSC. On MRB's negative reaction to women in the military, cf. her comments on Anna Rosenberg, appointed by President Truman to be an assistant secretary of defense: "While 'Little Anna' who went to Washington is being lauded in Independent Woman [journal of the National Federation of Business and Professional Women] as a woman holding the highest military rank in Am[erican] history, I feel flattened out—almost"; and "Anna Rosenberg! Product of the sheer career idea for woman. Oh God!" MRB to Margaret Grierson, Jan. 25, 1951, and Jan. 17, 1951, box 1, Beard papers, SSC.

93 Huntington Cairns to MRB, Apr. 9, 1946, and MRB to Cairns, Apr. 17, 1946, container 2, Cairns papers.

94 MRB to President Winthrop K. Jordan, Apr. 4, 1947, folder 29, box 2, Beard papers, SL; MRB to Lt. Ethel Weed, May 27, 1947, box 1, Beard papers, SSC; Ferdinand Lundberg and Marynia F. Farnham, *Modern Woman: The Lost Sex* (New York, Harper and Row, 1947).

95 See Lebsock, "Reading Mary Beard"; Carroll, "Critique," esp 33–39; Lane, *Sourcebook*, 65–66.

96 On this generational shift, see Cott, *The Grounding of Modern Feminism*. Cf. Joan Kelly, "The Doubled Vision of Feminist Theory."

97 MRB to Florence Kitchelt, Mar. 17, 1950, folder 113, Kitchelt papers.

98 CAB and MRB, *American Spirit*, 60; cf. Bender, "The New History," 621. On Beard's secularism, she related one anecdote: "My father used to hope when I was very young that I would enjoy the Western Christian Advocate on Sabbath days, but I was more than lukewarm about the matter. I was

frigid." MRB to Mr. Knowlton, Dec. 13, 1948, Beard-Macmillan correspondence.

99 In a review of *Women as Force in History,* that greatly annoyed Beard, J. H. Hexter magisterially exculpated the male historians whom she indicted, stressing that her twenty-six page bibliography showed her reliance on male historians' prior work; therefore, they could not have been as neglectful of women as she claimed. "The Ladies Were There All the Time," *New York Times,* Sunday, Mar. 17, 1946, sect. 7, p. 5.

100 MRB to Margaret Grierson, Nov. 10, 1944, box 1, Beard papers, SSC; MRB to Miriam Holden, Nov. 26, 1936, Holden vol.; MRB to Eva Hansl, Aug. 1, 1944, interfiled with Grierson letters, box 1, Beard papers, SSC.

101 MRB to Merle Curti, Jan. 3, 1950 [actually 1951], Curti papers. See preface.

102 Cf. Joan Kelly, "Doubled Vision"—"Woman's place is not a separate sphere or domain of existence but a position within social existence generally" (221); Michele Rosaldo, "The Use and Abuse of Anthropology"; Judith Newton, "Family Fortune: New History and New Historicism." See also Gerda Lerner's autobiographical tribute to MRB's inspiring influence, in *The Majority Finds Its Past,* xxi–xxiii.

THE SUFFRAGE YEARS

1 For all biographical material, Ann J. Lane, *Mary Ritter Beard: A Sourcebook,* and Barbara K. Turoff, *Mary Beard as Force in History,* are helpful; on MRB during the suffrage years see also Loretta Zimmerman, "Mary Beard: An Activist of the Progressive Era," and Ronald Schaffer, "The New York City Woman Suffrage Party, 1909–1919." Harriot Stanton Blatch and Alma Lutz, *Challenging Years: The Memoirs of Harriot Stanton Blatch,* is the major source on MRB's work with the Equality League of Self-Supporting Women, which was renamed the Women's Political Union.

2 MRB to Leonora O'Reilly, Sept. 7, 1911, NWTUL, reel 104. Seager was the author of *Social Insurance* (New York, Macmillan, 1910).

3 MRB to Leonora O'Reilly [April 1912], NWTUL, reel 104.

4 MRB to Lt. Ethel B. Weed, Sept. 30, 1946, box 1, Beard papers, SSC.

5 When Alice Paul in a personal letter to Du Bois tried to contest the critical edge of the rather generous-spirited report in *The Crisis,* he warned her "that it would be best for the causes in which you and I are both interested, that the matter stop where it is. No one knows, of course, better than you that you yourself were most active and determined in opposition to the participation of colored women in the parade on the same terms as other women." "Politics," *The Crisis* 5, no. 6 (Apr. 1913): 1; W. E. B. Du Bois to Alice Paul, June 11, 1913, NWPSF, reel 3.

6   MRB to "My dear Son" [William Beard], Aug. 18, 1951, Vagts private collection.

7   Turoff, *Mary Beard as Force*, 23. On MRB's activities in the Congressional Union, Loretta Zimmerman, "Mary Beard: An Activist of the Progressive Era," is the most detailed; see also Christine Lunardini, *From Equal Suffrage to Equal Rights: Alice Paul and the National Woman's Party, 1910–1928*, 1–104.

8   Inez Irwin, *Story of the Woman's Party*, 57–60.

9   "Hearing before the Committee on Rules, House of Representatives, Sixty-Third Congress, Second Session, on Resolution Establishing a Committee on Woman Suffrage," Dec. 3, 4, and 5, 1913, (Washington, D.C., Government Printing Office, 1914), 27–32; MRB to Lucy Burns, n.d. [Jan. 1914], NWPSF, reel 7; Lunardini, *From Equal Suffrage*, 130.

10 MRB to Lucy Burns, Jan. 9 [1914], NWPSF, reel 6.

11 See MRB to Alice Paul or Lucy Burns, Jan. 28 [1914], NWPSF, reel 7.

12 "Hearings before the Committee on the Judiciary, House of Representatives, Sixty-Third Congress, Second Session, on Woman Suffrage," serial 11, pt. 1, Mar. 3, 1914 (Washington, D.C.: Government Printing Office, 1914), 24–32.

13 MRB to Alice Paul, Feb. 9 [1914], NWPSF, reel 7; Lunardini, *From Equal Rights*, 57–59.

14 MRB to Alice Paul, Oct. 25 [1915], NWPSF, reel 13.

15 Eleanor Flexner, *Century of Struggle*, 267.

16 MRB to Alice Paul, Nov. 15 [1914], NWPSF, reel 13; MRB to Doris Stevens, Feb. 9 [1915], NWPSF, reel 7.

17 Charles A. Beard, "Woman Suffrage and Strategy," *New Republic* 1 (Dec. 12, 1914): 22–23; "Section Four and Suffrage," ibid., 1 (Jan. 9, 1915): 23; "Historical Woman Suffrage," ibid., 4 (Oct. 9, 1915): pt. 3, 1–3; "The Woman's Party," ibid., 7 (July 29, 1916): 329.

18 See Lucy Burns to MRB, June 1, 1915, NWPSF, reel 17.

19 MRB to Doris Stevens, Feb. 9 [1915], NWPSF, reel 7.

20 Lunardini, *From Equal Suffrage*, 91–93.

21 MRB to Anne Martin, July 26, 1916, NWPSF, reel 30.

22 "President Demands a Child Labor Law," *New York Times*, July 19, 1916, 6; "Child Labor Bill's Passage Is Assured," ibid., July 26, 1916. In accord with the CU's strategy, Charles Beard voted not for Wilson but for Hughes in the 1916 presidential election; Nore, *Charles A. Beard*, 73.

23 See MRB to Alice Paul, Mar. 23, 1916, NWPSF, reel 25; MRB to Alice Paul, Aug. 3, 1916, NWPSF, reel 30.

24 MRB to Alice Paul, Aug. 3, 1916, NWPSF, reel 30; MRB to Jane Norman Smith, June 23 [1917], folder 55, Smith papers.

25 MRB to the Honorable Woodrow Wilson, Nov. 12, 1917, series 4, case file 89, Woodrow Wilson papers, LC; the rally was reported in the *New York Times*, Nov. 12, 1917, 1.

26 Before the Senate Committee on Woman Suffrage in late April 1917, however, Beard testified on behalf of the Susan B. Anthony amendment with a speech detailing the contributions of American women in the Revolutionary War, the War of 1812, and the Civil War and arguing that as battlers for liberty women deserved the ballot. "Hearing before the Committee on Woman Suffrage, United States Senate, Sixty-Fifth Congress, First Session, on S.J. Res. 2, Proposing an Amendment to the Constitution of the United States Conferring upon Women the Right of Suffrage," Apr. 20, 1917 (Washington, D.C.: Government Printing Office, 1917).

THE ACTIVIST INTELLECTUAL EMERGES

1 See "Drafts of the Equal Rights Amendment, 1921–1971," series 3, pt. F, NWP, reel 116. I follow NWP usage in the title "chairman" for its leader.
2 MRB to Elsie Hill, Sept. 15 [1927], Hill papers, Vassar.
3 MRB to Margery Steer, Oct. 31, 1950, box 2, Steer papers, SSC.
4 MRB, "The Feminist Progression," 241; "After Equality—What?" 228; "A Test," 179. See also "American Women and the Printing Press."
5 MRB to Dorothy Detzer, Aug. 25, 1933, box 5, series C, WILPF-US papers.
6 MRB to Maud Wood Park, Mar. 13, 1933, box 5, Maud Wood Park papers, LC. I am indebted to Jacqueline Goggin for bringing this letter to my attention.
7 "Manifesto," in *Our Common Cause, Civilization*, Report of the International Congress of Women . . . July 16–22, 1933, Chicago, Illinois (New York: National Council of Women, 1933), 252–53. MRB's speech "Struggling Toward Civilization" appears on 23–28. Four pages of CAB and MRB's *The American Spirit*, 31–34, were devoted to reviewing the themes of this congress of 1933.
8 Harriot Stanton Blatch to Alma Lutz, Sept. 25, 1933, ALP.
9 Harriot Stanton Blatch and Alma Lutz, *Challenging Years: The Memoirs of Harriot Stanton Blatch*.
10 Beulah Amidon, "For Women Only," *New Republic* 77 (Dec. 27, 1933): 203–04.
11 Edward A. Purcell, Jr., *The Crisis of Democratic Theory: Scientific Naturalism and the Problem of Value*, 130, states that Mary Beard spoke at the rally, but the proceedings of the rally clearly say Miriam; see *The Case of Civilization against Hitlerism*, presented under the auspices of the American Jewish Congress at Madison Square Garden, New York, Mar. 7, 1934 (New York, 1934), 103, 145.
12 "Banquet Attracts Brilliant Assemblage," *Equal Rights* 19, no. 41 (Nov. 11, 1933): 319; MRB to Dorothy Detzer, Aug. 25, 1933, box 5, series C, WILPF-US; MRB to Mrs. A. D. Mizzy, May 11, 1934, box 4, series B,

WILPF-US; MRB to Lena Madesin Phillips, May 11, 1934, folder 93, box 4, Phillips papers, SL.

13 R. L. Duffus, review of *Laughing Their Way: Women's Humor in America*, *New York Times Book Review*, Aug. 19, 1934, p. 1.

14 No salutation appears in the copy of this letter at the Vassar archives, which is a typed transcription by Alma Lutz, as is the whole Beard-Blatch correspondence; perhaps Lutz skipped the beginning of the letter. In the summer of 1990, as this volume was at press, original Beard letters came to light in the possession of Blatch's descendants and were newly donated to Vassar.

15 MRB, *A Changing Political Economy as It Affects Women*, 18, 20.

16 Thomas Kennedy, *Charles A. Beard and American Foreign Policy*, 75.

17 See MRB to Dorothy Detzer, Mar. 5, 1935, box 17, series C, WILPF-US.

18 MRB to Doris Stevens, Nov. 14, 1935, folder B, box 4, Stevens papers. Kirchwey wrote, "She has repopulated the ages with the female members of the human race, and has demonstrated that the place of women in history as it was made has little or no relation to the place of women in history as it has previously been written." *Saturday Review of Literature* 8 (Dec. 19, 1931): 391.

19 MRB to Lois Jameson, Aug. 7 [1935], box 17, series C, WILPF-US.

THE WOMEN'S ARCHIVES BEGINS

1 Rosika Schwimmer to Mary Ritter Beard, July 17, 1935, and two-page typescript, "Sketch of a Plan for Organizing an International Feminist-Pacifist Archive," box 1, pt. 1, Schwimmer-Lloyd collection. The 6–3 decision against Schwimmer at the U.S Supreme Court—*U.S. vs. Schwimmer*, 279 U.S. 644 (1929)—a cause célèbre among civil libertarians, was reversed (in effect) in *Girouard vs. U.S.*, 328 U.S. 61 (1946), but Schwimmer did not subsequently seek citizenship. She died in 1948, the same year in which she was among the nominees for the Nobel Peace Prize. On Schwimmer's life, see biographical sketch by Edith Wynner in *Dictionary of American Biography*, suppl. 4, 1946–50, John A. Garraty and Edward T. James, eds. (New York, Scribner's, 1974), 724–28.

2 Rosika Schwimmer to MRB, Aug. 4, 1935, box 1, pt. 1, Schwimmer-Lloyd collection.

3 The founding of the World Center for Women's Archives is discussed in detail in Turoff, *Mary Beard as Force in History*, 51–60.

4 Personal communication from Detlev Vagts, Sept. 1989.

5 As late as 1952 Alice Paul paid a visit to Mary Beard, still hoping to enlist her support for the ERA. MRB to Marjorie White, Oct. 17, 1952, vol. 154, box 27, White papers.

6 MRB to Lena Madesin Phillips, Dec. 22 [1935], folder 93, box 4, Phillips

papers; MRB to Rosika Schwimmer, Feb. 3, 1936, box 1, pt. 2, Schwimmer-Lloyd collection.

7   "Smith Blasts New Deal as Socialistic . . . ," *Washington Post*, Jan. 26, 1936, 1.

8   Rosika Schwimmer to MRB, Sept. 4, 1935, box 1, pt. 1, and see newspaper clippings in box 1, pt. 2, Schwimmer-Lloyd collection.

9   MRB to Rosika Schwimmer, Apr. 11, 1936 [copy], and typescript, "Confidential discussion for the reasons of Madam Schwimmer's resignation from A World Center for Women's Archives between Madam Rosika Schwimmer, Mrs. Mary R. Beard, and Mrs. Inez Haynes Irwin, at Madam Schwimmer's apartment on May 1, 1936," box 1, pt. 2, Schwimmer-Lloyd collection; MRB to Margaret Grierson, May 18, 1951, box 1, Beard papers, SSC.

10   MRB to Florence Boeckel, Nov. 21 [1936], folder 2, box 31, NCPW, SCPC; MRB to Harriot Stanton Blatch, "Sunday the eleventh" [October 1936], ALP.

11   See Irving Brant, *Impeachment: Trials and Errors* (New York, Alfred Knopf, 1972), 170–77; MRB to Gwyneth Roe, Oct. 15, 1949, ms. 151, folder 2, box 1, Roe papers.

12   MRB to Lena Madesin Phillips, Jan. 21 [1937], folder 93, box 4, Phillips papers; MRB to Miriam Holden, Apr. 14, 1937, Holden vol.

13   MRB to Lena Madesin Phillips, Jan. 21 [1937], folder 93, box 4, Phillips papers. The *History of Woman Suffrage* to which Beard refers was actually published in six volumes, the first edited by Elizabeth Cady Stanton, Susan B. Anthony, and Matilda Joslyn Gage and published in 1881, the last two published and copyrighted by the NAWSA in 1922.

14   MRB to Mary Philbrook, Nov. 17 [1936], folder 1936, WPA-Women's Archives collection.

THE WOMEN'S ARCHIVES CONTINUES

1   White describes herself in an introductory letter to MRB, July 10, 1937, in folder 150a, box 26, White papers; on Holden, see the tribute by Gerda Lerner, "Miriam Holden—in Remembrance and Friendship."

2   Pearl Buck, "America's Medieval Women," *Harper's* 177 (Aug. 1938): 225–32; Genevieve Parkhurst, "Is Feminism Dead?" ibid. 176 (May 1935): 735–45.

3   Carrie Chapman Catt to Alice Stone Blackwell, June 14, 1937, container 4, reel 3, Catt papers, LC.

4   Ruth Savord to Marjorie White, Nov. 6, 1937, and Savord to White, Dec. 22, 1938, folder 150b, box 26, White papers; see also documents in folder 150a; typescript, "Mrs. Mary R. Beard's Talk at World Center for Women's Archives, Nov. 14, 1936," Holden vol.

5 MRB to Miriam Holden, Aug. 30 [1938], MRB to Miriam Holden, Jan. 23, 1939, Florentine Sutro to MRB, Jan. 24, 1939, Holden vol.; MRB to Marjorie White, Jan. 23, 1939, folder 150a, box 26, Marjorie White collection.

6 Camp Fire Girls' Department of Publications to Executives of the Camp Fire Girls, Dec. 31, 1938, folder 22, Beard papers (A-9), SL.

7 See Bettye Collier-Thomas, "Towards Black Feminism: The Creation of the Bethune Museum-Archives," on the collaboration between the NCNW and the WCWA.

8 MRB to fellow members of the Women's Archives Board, Aug. 26, 1939, Holden vol.; MRB to Lena Madesin Phillips, Dec. 9, 1939, folder 93, box 4, Phillips papers.

9 It is impossible to identify from existing documentation whether there was consensus or internal controversy among the white women in the Washington unit on this matter.

10 MRB to Dorothy Porter, Feb. 21, 1940, folder 1, box 1, series 4, National Council of Negro Women Records; copy of Dorothy B. Porter to MRB, Mar. 27, 1940, Holden vol.; MRB to Grace Cooper, Mar. 25, 1940, folder 17, box 1, Beard papers (A-9), SL.

11 See letters of late March and early April 1940, especially Miriam Holden to MRB, Apr. 5, 1940, and MRB to Holden, Apr. 7, 1940, in Holden vol.; MRB to Marjorie White, Mar. 25, 1940, folder 150a, box 26, White papers.

12 MRB to Fola La Follette, Apr. 11, 1940, "Mary Ritter Beard" folder, container E7, La Follette collection, LC; Carol Willis Moffett to Miriam Holden, May 29, 1940, Holden vol.

13 Miriam Holden to Eva Hansl, June 13, 1940, Holden vol.

14 Rosika Schwimmer to MRB, July 5, 1940, box 1, pt. 2, Schwimmer-Lloyd collection.

15 MRB to Margaret Grierson, Oct. 3, 1949, box 1, Beard papers, SSC.

16 MRB to Miriam Holden, Aug. 21, 1940, Holden vol.; MRB to Grace Cooper, Aug. 10, 1940, Sept. 2, 1940, and Sept. 5, 1940, Beard papers (AB-368), SL; MRB to Eva Hansl, Sept. 9, 1940, Holden vol.; Inez Irwin to Members of the WCWA, Sept. 16, 1940, folder 3, box 1, Jeannette Marks papers, SL; Collier-Thomas, "Towards Black Feminism," 52–63.

17 MRB to Florence Kitchelt, Oct. 28, 1940, folder 113, Kitchelt papers.

ALTERNATIVES TO THE ARCHIVES

1 On the Hunter lectures, Mary Ritter Beard to Eva Hansl, Oct. 22, 1940, Holden vol., and Marjorie White to Florence Hazzard, Nov. 4, 1940,

Hazzard papers. On the *Encyclopedia* project, see Lane, *Sourcebook*, 43–49, 215–24, for more detail. Documents of the project are in vol. 154, box 26, Marjorie White collection; see also M R B to Elizabeth Schlesinger, May 30, 1944, June 4, 1944, June 15, 1944 [copy], Schlesinger papers.

2   It was in the spring of 1940 that medievalist Nellie Neilson was nominated as second vice president of the A H A; her victory put her automatically in line for the presidency, which she gained in 1943, making her the only female president of the association before Natalie Zemon Davis in 1987. Program of the American Historical Association, Fifty-Fifth Annual Meeting, New York City . . . Dec. 27, 28, and 30, 1940; Joan W. Scott, *Gender and the Politics of History*, 185–86.

3   M R B to Margaret Grierson, Oct. 3, 1949, box 1, Beard papers, S S C. See also M R B to Marjorie White, July 19, 1953, box 27, vol. 154, White papers.

4   Lillian E. Smith and Paula Snelling, "Man Born of Woman," *North Georgia Review* 6 (Winter 1941): 7–17; "They Say . . . ," ibid. 7 (Spring 1942): inside front cover. Karl Menninger was one of those who praised Smith and Snelling's essay.

5   Ada L. Comstock, "Women in This War," *Yale Review* 31, no. 4 (June 1942): 671–82.

6   For sales figures for Charles Beard's works, including jointly written works, see Beale, ed., *Charles A. Beard: An Appraisal*, 310–12. The guess that Mary Beard's authorship bulked larger in *The American Spirit* than in the earlier joint works appears in Smith, "Seeing Mary Beard," 410–12, and Merle Curti to Nancy Cott, Apr. 5, 1989 (in author's possession).

7   Fortieth Anniversary Report, Arthur and Elizabeth Schlesinger Library on the History of Women in America, Radcliffe College (1983), 2–6.

8   M R B to Margaret Grierson, June 22 [1944], box 1, Beard papers, S S C.

9   Quotation in biographical sketch of Catherine Shober Drinker Bowen, *Notable American Women: The Modern Period*, Barbara Sicherman and Carol Hurd Green, eds. (Cambridge: Harvard University Press, 1980), 97–98.

10 Interestingly, in a 1940 letter to historian Alma Lutz concerning the manuscript of Harriot Blatch's memoirs, Beard maintained, "I was never a member of the National Woman's Party so far as I know. I was deeply involved in the Congressional Union." M R B to Alma Lutz, Apr. 15, 1940, Lutz collection, Vassar. Actually, at the time she withdrew from the Advisory Council, the group had been called the National Woman's Party for almost a year. On the National Woman's Party in the 1940s, see Leila Rupp and Verta Taylor, *Survival in the Doldrums*.

11 Janet Wilson James, "History and Women at Harvard: The Schlesinger Library," *Harvard Library Bulletin* 16, no. 4 (Oct. 1968): 386; Maida Goodwin (archives specialist, Smith College Archives) to Nancy F. Cott, Aug. 19,

1988 (in author's possession); MRB to Eva Hansl, Aug. 11, 1941, copy interfiled with Grierson letters, box 1, Beard papers, SSC; MRB to Marjorie White, Dec. 2, 1937, folder 150a, box 26, White papers.

TOWARD *WOMAN AS FORCE IN HISTORY*

1 Lewis Mumford to the editor, *Saturday Review of Literature* 27, no. 49 (Dec. 2, 1944): 27; see also Henry Steele Commager, "History By Innuendo," ibid., 27, no. 46 (Nov. 11, 1944): 12, and other letters in both these issues.

2 MRB to Margaret Grierson, Oct. 20, 1945, box 1, Beard papers, SSC.

3 MRB to Anne Martin, July 8, 1945, box 1, Martin papers.

4 MRB to Margaret Grierson, Oct. 20, 1945, box 1, Beard papers, SSC.

5 MRB to Mme. Rosika Schwimmer, Sept. 16 [1936], box 1, pt. 2, Schwimmer-Lloyd collection.

6 MRB to Jim Putnam, June 1, 1946, Beard-Macmillan correspondence.

7 Harold Latham to MRB, Dec. 10, 1946, and Dec. 11, 1947, Beard-Macmillan correspondence; Beale, ed., *Charles A. Beard: An Appraisal*, 311.

8 The letter fills one typed page and is unsigned; possibly a second page has been lost.

9 MRB to Harold Latham, Dec. 13, 1947; Harold Latham to MRB, Jan. 15, 1948, Beard-Macmillan correspondence.

THE POSTWAR YEARS

1 MRB to Wilbur K. Jordan, Apr. 30, 1947, presidential correspondence, Radcliffe Archives.

2 MRB to Anne Martin, Apr. 2, 1946, Anne Martin papers.

3 See Baroness Shidzue Ishimoto, *Facing Two Ways: The Story of My Life*.

4 MRB, "Women's Role in Society." See Susan M. Hartmann, *The Home Front and Beyond: American Women in the 1940s*, 101–23, for an excellent discussion of postwar developments in higher education for women.

5 See Langston Hughes' poem "Freedom Train," *New Republic*, Sept. 13, 1947, 27.

6 The volume ran into many difficulties—and rejections from publishers—and was not published until 1954, as Beale, ed., *Charles A. Beard: An Appraisal*.

7 MRB to Harold Latham, Dec. 3, 1947, Beard-Macmillan correspondence; J. H. Hexter, "The Ladies Were There All the Time," *New York Times*, Sunday, Mar. 17, 1946, sect. 7, p. 5.

8 MRB to Alma Lutz, Apr. 11, 1948, Lutz papers, Vassar.

9 "The 102 Great Ideas," *Life* 24 (Jan. 26, 1948): 92–93, 96–102.

10 MRB to Elizabeth Borden, June 25, 1951, folder "Correspondence with Women's Archives, 1951–53," box 1, series 2.1, record group 18, Radcliffe Archives; on Charles Beard's death, see Nore, *Charles A. Beard*, 224, where, however, the date of his death is in error.

11 MRB to Dorothy Brush, Aug. 1, 1949, box 1, Beard papers, SSC; MRB to Jim Putnam, Apr. 13, 1949, Beard-Macmillan correspondence. For MRB's letters regarding CAB's attackers, see the Merle Curti and the Harry Elmer Barnes collections.

12 Henry Steele Commager, *The American Mind: An Interpretation of American Thought and Character Since the 1880s* (New Haven, Yale University Press, 1950), 303–09.

13 Carbon of MRB to President Benjamin Wright, Mar. 23, 1950, with Grierson letters in box 1, Beard papers, SSC.

14 MRB to Marine Leland, Nov. 10, 1950, box 1, Beard papers, SSC.

15 MRB to Elizabeth Borden, June 25, 1951; MRB to Marjorie White, Mar. 1, 1953, vol. 154, box 27, White papers; MRB to Miriam Holden, Mar. 22, 1953, folder 75, box 5, Holden papers; MRB to Alma Lutz, May 7, 1953, Lutz papers, Vassar.

16 MRB to Miriam Holden, Dec. 26, 1951, folder 73, box 5, Holden papers; MRB to Jim Putnam, Apr. 13, 1949, Beard-Macmillan correspondence; MRB to Merle Curti, Dec. 6, 1950, Curti papers; MRB to Nancy Cushman, May 11, 1940, Cushman papers, SSC.

17 MRB to Merle Curti, Jan. 21, 1953, Curti papers; MRB to William Beard, Oct. 13, 1952, Vagts private collection.

18 MRB to Miriam Holden, May 27 [1953 or 1954], box 75, Holden papers.

19 MRB to Merle Curti, Feb. 6, 1954, Curti papers.

20 MRB to Merle Curti, Jan. 31, 1953, Curti papers.

Location of Manuscript Collections

Barnes, Harry Elmer
American Heritage Center, University of Wyoming, Laramie, Wyo.
Beard, Mary R.
DePauw University Library, Greencastle, Ind.
Arthur and Elizabeth Schlesinger Library, Radcliffe College, Cambridge, Mass.
Sophia Smith Collection, Smith College Library, Northampton, Mass.
Bowen, Catherine Drinker
Library of Congress, Washington, D.C.
Cairns, Huntington
Library of Congress, Washington, D.C.
Curti, Merle
State Historical Society of Wisconsin, Madison, Wis.
Cushman, Nancy Cox-McCormack
Sophia Smith Collection, Smith College Library, Northampton, Mass.
Evans, Elizabeth Glendower
Arthur and Elizabeth Schlesinger Library, Radcliffe College, Cambridge, Mass.
Hazzard, Florence
Manuscripts and University Archives, Cornell University Libraries, Ithaca, N.Y.
Hill, Elsie M.
Vassar College Library, Poughkeepsie, N.Y.
Holden, Miriam
Princeton University Library, Princeton, N.J.
Key, Luella Gettys
Arthur and Elizabeth Schlesinger Library, Radcliffe College, Cambridge, Mass.
Kitchelt, Florence Cross
Arthur and Elizabeth Schlesinger Library, Radcliffe College, Cambridge, Mass.
La Follette Family Papers
Library of Congress, Washington, D.C.
Lutz, Alma
Arthur and Elizabeth Schlesinger Library, Radcliffe College, Cambridge, Mass.
Vassar College Library, Poughkeepsie, N.Y.

Macmahon, Arthur W.
  Rare Book and Manuscript Library, Columbia University Libraries, New
      York, N.Y.
Macmillan Company
  Rare Books and Manuscripts, New York Public Library, New York, N.Y.
Martin, Anne
  Bancroft Library, University of California, Berkeley, Calif.
National American Woman Suffrage Association
  Library of Congress, Washington, D.C.
National Council for the Prevention of War
  Swarthmore College Peace Collection, Swarthmore College Library,
      Swarthmore, Pa.
National Council of Negro Women
  National Archives for Black Women's History, Bethune Museum-Archives,
      Washington, D.C.
National Woman's Party
  Library of Congress, Washington, D.C.
Phillips, Lena Madesin
  Arthur and Elizabeth Schlesinger Library, Radcliffe College, Cambridge,
      Mass.
Powell, Rose Arnold
  Arthur and Elizabeth Schlesinger Library, Radcliffe College, Cambridge,
      Mass.
Radcliffe College Archives
  Radcliffe College, Cambridge, Mass.
Roe, Gwyneth K.
  State Historical Society of Wisconsin, Madison, Wis.
Saunders, Mira and Charles
  Huntington Library, San Marino, Calif.
Schlesinger, Elizabeth
  Arthur and Elizabeth Schlesinger Library, Radcliffe College, Cambridge,
      Mass.
Schwimmer-Lloyd
  Rare Books and Manuscripts, New York Public Library, New York, N.Y.
Smith, Jane Norman
  Arthur and Elizabeth Schlesinger Library, Radcliffe College, Cambridge,
      Mass.
Smith, Lillian
  Rare Books and Manuscripts, University of Florida, Gainesville, Fla.
Steer, Margery
  Sophia Smith Collection, Smith College Library, Northampton, Mass.

Stevens, Doris
Arthur and Elizabeth Schlesinger Library, Radcliffe College, Cambridge,
Mass.
U.S. Women's Bureau
National Archives, Washington, D.C.
White, Marjorie
Arthur and Elizabeth Schlesinger Library, Radcliffe College, Cambridge,
Mass.
Women's International League for Peace and Freedom
Swarthmore College Peace Collection, Swarthmore College Library,
Swarthmore, Pa.
WPA-Women's Archives Collection
New Jersey Historical Society, Newark, N.J.

Location of Letters

The letters are published with the kind permission of Arlene Beard, Detlev Vagts, and the libraries cited below. To avoid repetition, library locations are not repeated after first citation, except when collections under the same name are held at more than one library.

TLS = typed letter, signed

ALS = autograph (handwritten) letter, signed

1. To Leonora O'Reilly, Jan. 1, 1912, TLS, NWTUL, reel 105.
2. To Leonora O'Reilly, Friday [Apr. 1912], TLS, NWTUL, reel 105.
3. To Leonora O'Reilly [May 1912], ALS, NWTUL, reel 105.
4. To Alice Paul, Sunday [Jan.–Feb. 1913], TLS, NWPSF, reel 2.
5. To Alice Paul [Mar. 1913], TLS, NWPSF, reel 6.
6. To Lucy Burns, Jan. 18 [1914], TLS, NWPSF, reel 7.
7. To Alice Paul, Feb. 4 [1914], ALS, NWPSF, reel 7.
8. To Alice Paul, Mar. 5 [1914], TLS, NWPSF, reel 8.
9. To Alice Paul, Aug. 15 [1914], ALS, NWPSF, reel 11.
10. To Alice Paul, Aug. 21 [1914], TLS, NWPSF, reel 11.
11. To Alice Paul, Nov. 7 [1914], ALS, NWPSF, reel 13.
12. To Alice Paul, Nov. 30 [1914], TLS, NWPSF, reel 13.
13. To Alice Paul, Dec. 14 [1914], TLS, NWPSF, reel 13.
14. To Alice Paul, May 15 [1915], TLS, NWPSF, reel 10.
15. To Lucy Burns, June 8 [1915], TLS, NWPSF, reel 17. This letter is illegible on the microfilm but the original can be found in Correspondence, container 28, National Woman's Party papers, LC.
16. To Carrie Chapman Catt, June 8 [1915], TLS, NAWSA papers, LC, Congressional Union Subject file, container 48.
17. To Alice Paul, Feb. 21 [1916], TLS, NWPSF, reel 24.
18. To Jane Norman Smith, June 23, 1916, TLS, Jane Norman Smith papers, SL, folder 55.
19. To Alice Paul, July 26, 1916, TLS, NWPSF, reel 30.
20. To Alice Paul, Dec. 21, 1916, TLS, NWPSF, reel 36.
21. To Elizabeth Rogers, Nov. 17, 1917, ALS, NWPSF, reel 52.
22. To Elizabeth Kalb, Apr. 9, 1919, TLS, NWPSF, reel 70.
23. To Elsie Hill, July 10, 1921, TLS, NWP 1913–1974, reel 9.
24. To Curtice Hitchcock, Dec. 25, 1926, TLS, Macmillan Co. records, Rare Books and Manuscripts Division, NYPL, Astor, Lenox, and Tilden Foundations.

25. To Florence Cross Kitchelt, May 18 [1928], TLS, Kitchelt papers, SL, folder 113.
26. To Lena Madesin Phillips, Aug. 3, 1933, TLS, Phillips papers, SL, folder 93, box 4.
27. To Harriot Stanton Blatch [Jan. 1934], copy by Alma Lutz, ALP.
28. To Lena Madesin Phillips, Feb. 26 [1934], copy, Phillips papers, folder 93, box 4.
29. To Harriot Stanton Blatch, July 16 [1934], copy by Alma Lutz, ALP.
30. To Harriot Stanton Blatch, Sept. 7 [1934], copy by Alma Lutz, ALP.
31. To Harriot Stanton Blatch, Sept. 22 [1934], copy by Alma Lutz, ALP.
32. To Harriot Stanton Blatch, Jan. 21, 1935, copy by Alma Lutz, ALP.
33. To Harriot Stanton Blatch, Jan. 30, 1935, copy by Alma Lutz, ALP.
34. To Lena Madesin Phillips, Apr. 28 [1935], TLS, Phillips papers, folder 93, box 4.
35. To Harriot Stanton Blatch [May 1935], copy by Alma Lutz, ALP.
36. To Dorothy Detzer, Aug. 2, 1935, TLS, WILPF-U.S., SCPC, Swarthmore College Library, box 17, series C.
37. To Rosika Schwimmer, July 21, 1935, TLS, Schwimmer-Lloyd collection, Rare Books and Manuscripts Division, NYPL, Astor, Lenox, and Tilden Foundations, box 1, pt. 1.
38. To Rosika Schwimmer, Aug. 6, 1935, TLS, Schwimmer-Lloyd collection, box 1, pt. 1.
39. To Florence Brewer Boeckel, Aug. 10, 1935, TLS, NCPW papers, SCPC, Swarthmore College Library, folder 2, box 31.
40. To Rose Arnold Powell, Aug. 10, 1935, TLS, Powell papers, SL, folder 27.
41. To Lena Madesin Phillips, Aug. 20, 1935, TLS, Phillips papers, folder 93, box 4.
42. To Rosika Schwimmer, Sept. 6 [1935], copy, Schwimmer-Lloyd collection, box 1, pt. 1.
43. To Rose Arnold Powell, Sept. 14, 1935, TLS, Powell papers, folder 27.
44. To Harriot Stanton Blatch, Oct. 28 [1935], copy by Alma Lutz, ALP.
45. To Doris Stevens, Nov. 14, 1935, ALS, Stevens uncatalogued papers, SL, folder B, box 4.
46. To Lena Madesin Phillips, Nov. 17, 1935, TLS, Phillips papers, folder 93, box 4.
47. To Lena Madesin Phillips, Jan. 23 [1936], TLS, Phillips papers, folder 93, box 4.
48. To Lena Madesin Phillips, Jan. 26 [1936], TLS, Phillips papers, folder 93, box 4.
49. To Rosika Schwimmer, Feb. 14, 1936, copy, Schwimmer-Lloyd collection, box 1, pt. 2.
50. To Lena Madesin Phillips, Mar. 1 [1936], TLS, Phillips papers, folder 93, box 4.

51. To Rosika Schwimmer, May 12, 1936, copy, Schwimmer-Lloyd collection, box 1, pt. 2.
52. To Lena Madesin Phillips, June 3, 1936, TLS, Phillips papers, folder 93, box 4.
53. To Rose Arnold Powell, June 14, 1936, TLS, Powell papers, folder 27.
54. To Florence Brewer Boeckel, July 28, 1936, TLS, NCPW papers, folder 2, box 31.
55. To Harriet Stanton Blatch, Jan. 2 [1937], copy by Alma Lutz, ALP.
56. To Florence Bayard Hilles, Jan. 5 [1937], ALS, NWP 1913–1974, reel 58.
57. To Alma Lutz, Jan. 29, 1937, TLS, ALP.
58. To Harriot Stanton Blatch, Jan. 24 [1937], copy by Alma Lutz, ALP.
59. To Doris Stevens, May 1 [1937], TLS, Stevens uncatalogued papers, folder B (miscellaneous), box 4.
60. To Detlev Vagts, Jan. 10 [1938], TLS, Vagts private collection.
61. To Miriam and Alfred Vagts, Thursday [Jan.–Feb. 1938], TLS, Vagts private collection.
62. To Miriam Holden, Mar. 12, 1938, TLS, Holden vol.
63. To Miriam Holden, July 29 [1938], TLS, Holden vol.
64. To Alice Stone Blackwell, July 29, 1938, TLS, NAWSA papers, container 3.
65. To Marjorie White, Nov. 28, 1938, TLS, White papers, SL, folder 150a, box 26.
66. To Miriam Holden, Feb. 6, 1939, TLS, Holden vol., Princeton University Library.
67. To the Camp Fire Girls [1939], Mary Ritter Beard papers (A-9), SL, folder 27.
68. To Juanita Mitchell, Mar. 1, 1939, carbon (initialed), Beard papers (A-9), SL, folder 17.
69. To Miriam Holden, Mar. 9 [1939], TLS, Holden vol.
70. To Lena Madesin Phillips, Mar. 9, 1939, TLS, Phillips papers, folder 93, box 4.
71. To Lena Madesin Phillips, May 11, 1939, TLS, Phillips papers, folder 93, box 4.
72. To Mira Saunders, May 16, 1939, TLS, Saunders collection, Huntington Library, San Marino, Calif., box 9.
73. To Mira Saunders, June 29, 1939, TLS, Saunders collection, box 9.
74. To Dorothy Detzer, Sept. 26, 1939, TLS, WILPF-U.S., series C, box 24.
75. To Dr. Minnie L. Maffett, Feb. 22, 1940, copy, Josephine Schain papers, SSC, box 4.
76. To Sue Bailey Thurman, Mar. 25, 1940, carbon, Beard papers (A-9), SL, folder 17.
77. To Miriam Holden, Mar. 25, 1940, TLS, Holden vol.
78. To Miriam Holden, Apr. 2, 1940, TLS, Holden vol.
79. To Grace Cooper, Apr. 29, 1940, carbon, Beard papers (A-9), SL, folder 17.
80. To Merle Curti, May 14, 1940, TLS, Curti papers, State Historical Society of Wisconsin, Madison.

81. To Miriam Holden, May 25, 1940, TLS, Holden vol.
82. To WCWA Board, June 26, 1940, TLS, Holden vol.
83. To Rosika Schwimmer, July 10, 1940, TLS, Schwimmer-Lloyd collection, box 1, pt. 2.
84. To Marjorie White, July 11, 1940, TLS, White papers, folder 150a, box 26.
85. To Miriam Holden, Aug. 15 [1940], TLS, Holden vol.
86. To Miriam Holden, Oct. 10, 1940, TLS, Holden vol.
87. To Marjorie White, Jan. 18, 1941, TLS, White papers, vol. 154, box 27.
88. To Luella Gettys [Key], Apr. 25, 1941, TLS, Louella Gettys Key papers, SL.
89. To Lillian Smith and Paula Snelling, Apr. 30, 1942, TLS, Lillian Smith collection, Rare Books and Manuscripts, University of Florida Libraries, Gainesville, group 2, correspondence box 1.
90. To Anne Martin, June 21, 1942, TLS, Martin papers, Bancroft Library, University of California at Berkeley, box 1.
91. To Merle Curti, Oct. 18 [1943], TLS, Curti papers.
92. To Wilbur K. Jordan, Jan. 14, 1944, TLS, Beard collection (A-9), SL, folder 30.
93. To Wilbur K. Jordan, Jan. 20, 1944, TLS, Beard collection (A-9), SL, folder 30.
94. To Catherine Drinker Bowen, Feb. 20, 1944, TLS, Catherine Drinker Bowen collection, LC, container 1.
95. To Florence Cross Kitchelt, Feb. 22, 1944, TLS, Kitchelt papers, folder 113.
96. To Margaret Grierson, Mar. 6, 1944, TLS, Beard papers, SSC, box 1.
97. To Elizabeth Schlesinger, June 15, 1944, TLS, Elizabeth Schlesinger Collection, SL.
98. To Walter Yust, Nov. 3, 1944, copy, White papers, vol. 154, box 27.
99. To Harold Latham, Sept. 29, 1944, TLS, Macmillan Co. records.
100. To James Putnam, Nov. 10, 1944, TLS, Macmillan Co. records.
101. To James Putnam, Apr. 8, 1945, TLS, Macmillan Co. records.
102. To Harold Latham, Apr. 18, 1945, TLS, Macmillan Co. records.
103. To James Putnam, Apr. 18, 1945, TLS, Macmillan Co. records.
104. To Harold Latham, May 16, 1945, TLS, Macmillan Co. records.
105. To Mr. Cunningham, July 3, 1945, TLS, Macmillan Co. records.
106. To James Putnam [1945], TLS, Macmillan Co. records.
107. Publicity sketch [1945], typescript, Macmillan Co. records.
108. To Margaret Grierson, July 15, 1945, TLS, Beard papers, SSC, box 1.
109. To Wilbur K. Jordan, Aug. 25, 1945, TLS, Beard collection (A-9), SL, folder 30.
110. To James Putnam, Nov. 5, 1945, TLS, Macmillan Co. records.
111. To Frieda S. Miller, May 6, 1946, TLS, U.S. Women's Bureau papers, National Archives, general correspondence, box 804, file 47.
112. To Dorcas Campbell, Aug. 4, 1946, TLS, Beard collection (368a), SL.
113. To James Putnam, Sept. 18, 1946, TLS, Macmillan Co. records.

114. To Marjorie White, Oct. 17 [1946], TL (no signature), White papers, vol. 154, box 27.
115. To Harold Latham, Dec. 3, 1946, TLS, Macmillan Co. records.
116. To Edward Aswell, Jan. 15, 1947, TLS, Harper and Row collection, Rare Book and Manuscript Library, Columbia University Libraries.
117. To Miriam and Alfred [Vagts], Feb. 5, 1947, TLS, Vagts private collection.
118. To Anne Martin, Feb. 27 [1947], TLS, Martin papers, box 1.
119. To Lt. Ethel B. Weed, Mar. 30, 1947, TLS, Beard papers, SSC, box 1.
120. To Frieda S. Miller, June 15, 1947, TLS, U.S. Women's Bureau papers, general correspondence, box 804, file 47.
121. To Margaret Grierson, Sept. 18, 1947, TLS, Beard papers, SSC, box 1.
122. To Arthur W. Macmahon, Sept. 21, 1947, TLS, Arthur W. Macmahon collection, Rare Book and Manuscript Library, Columbia University Libraries.
123. To Merle Curti, Dec. 2, 1947, TLS, Curti papers.
124. To Merle Curti, Dec. 17, 1947, TLS, Curti papers.
125. To Margaret Grierson, Mar. 26, 1948, TLS, Beard papers, SSC, box 1.
126. To Rose Arnold Powell, July 3, 1948, TLS, Powell papers, folder 27, box 2.
127. To Marjorie White, Aug. 18, 1948, ALS, White papers, folder 150a, box 26.
128. To James Putnam, Oct. 9, 1948, TLS, Macmillan Co. records.
129. To Lena Madesin Phillips, Oct. 10, 1948, TLS, Phillips papers, folder 93, box 4.
130. To Gwyneth Roe, Oct. 15, 1949, TLS, Roe collection, State Historical Society of Wisconsin, folder 2, box 1, ms. 151.
131. To Harold Latham, Jan. 18, 1950, TLS, Macmillan Co. records.
132. To Florence Cross Kitchelt, Mar. 17, 1950, TLS, Kitchelt papers, folder 113.
133. To Lt. Ethel B. Weed, Aug. 9, 1950, TLS, Beard papers, SSC, box 1.
134. To Margaret Grierson, Dec. 28, 1950, ALS, Beard papers, SSC, box 1.
135. To Lt. Ethel B. Weed, Jan. 19, 1951, TLS, Beard papers, SSC, box 1.
136. To Mrs. [Elizabeth] Borden, Feb. 8, 1951, TLS, record group 18, series 2.1, box 1, Radcliffe College Archives, Radcliffe College.
137. To Merle Curti, June 6, 1951, TLS, Curti papers.
138. To Nancy and Charles Cushman, Jan. 1, 1952, ALS, Nancy Cox-McCormack Cushman papers, SSC, box 2.
139. To Marjorie White, Feb. 9, 1953, ALS, White papers, notebook 23, box 4.
140. To Margery Steer, Aug. 5, 1954, ALS, Marjory Steer collection, SSC, folder 14, box 2.
141. To Florence Hazzard, Jan. 26, 1955, ALS, no. 2516, Florence Hazzard papers, Manuscripts and University Archives, Cornell University Library.

Bibliography

N.B. The following is not an exhaustive bibliography for either Mary or Charles Beard. More inclusive listings can be found in Turoff, *Mary Beard as Force in History*, 76–78, and Nore, *Charles A. Beard*, 287–97.

Beale, Howard K. (ed.). *Charles A Beard: An Appraisal* (Lexington, University of Kentucky Press, 1954).
Beard, Charles A. *American City Government* (New York, Century, 1912).
———. *Contemporary American History* (New York, Macmillan, 1914).
———. "Cooperation and the New Century," *Young Oxford* 2, no. 15 (Dec. 1900), 99–100.
——— (with George H. E. Smith). *The Idea of National Interest: An Analytical Study of American Foreign Policy* (New York, Macmillan, 1934).
———. *The Myth of Rugged American Individualism* (New York, John Day pamphlet, 1932), originally published in *Harper's*, 1931.
——— (with George H. E. Smith). *The Open Door at Home: A Trial Philosophy of National Interest* (New York, Macmillan, 1934).
———. "That Noble Dream," *American Historical Review* 41 (1935): 74–87.
——— (ed.). *Towards Civilization* (New York, Longmans, Green, 1930).
——— (ed.). *Whither Mankind: A Panorama of Modern Civilization* (New York, Longmans, Green, 1928).
———. "Written History as an Act of Faith," *American Historical Review* 39 (Jan. 1934): 219–31.
Beard, Charles A., and Mary Ritter Beard. *America in Midpassage*. 2 vols. (New York, Macmillan, 1939).
———. *American Citizenship* (New York, Macmillan, 1914).
———. *The American Spirit: A Study of the Idea of Civilization in the United States* (New York, Macmillan, 1942).
———. *A Basic History of the United States* (New York, Doubleday, 1944).
———. *History of the United States* (New York, Macmillan, 1921).
———. *The Making of American Civilization* (New York, Macmillan, 1937).
———. *The Rise of American Civilization*. 2 vols. (New York, Macmillan, 1927).
Beard, Mary Ritter. "After Equality—What?" *Independent Woman* 9, no. 6 (June 1930): 227–28.
——— (ed.). *America Through Women's Eyes* (New York, Macmillan, 1933).
———. "American Women and the Printing Press," *Annals of the American Academy of Political and Social Science* 143 (May 1929): 195–206.

———. *A Changing Political Economy as It Affects Women* (Washington, D.C., American Association of University Women, 1934).

———. "The College and Alumnae in Contemporary Life," *Journal of the American Association of University Women* 27 (Oct. 1933): 11–16.

———. "The Feminist Progression," *Independent Woman* 8 (June 1929): 241.

———. *The Force of Women in Japanese History* (Washington, D.C., Public Affairs Press, 1953).

———. "Is Collectivism the Answer?" *Independent Woman* 13 (Mar. 1934): 69, 92.

——— (ed., with Martha Bensley Bruere). *Laughing Their Way Women's Humor in America* (New York, Macmillan, 1934).

———. "The Legislative Influence of Unenfranchised Women," *Annals of the American Academy of Political and Social Science* 56 (Nov. 1914), 54–61.

———. *The Making of Charles A. Beard* (New York, Exposition Press, 1955).

———. "The Nineteenth-Century Woman Looking Forward," *Young Oxford* 2, no. 16 (Jan. 1901): 119–22.

———. *On Understanding Women* (New York, Longmans, Green, 1931).

———. *A Short History of the American Labor Movement* (New York, Workers' Education Bureau, 1920).

———. "A Test for the Modern Woman," *Current History* 37 (Nov. 1932): 179–83.

———. "The Twentieth-Century Woman Looking Around and Backward," *Young Oxford* 2, no. 15 (Dec. 1900): 100–04.

———. *Woman as Force in History* (New York, Macmillan, 1946; reprint, New York, Collier, 1962).

———. "Woman's Work for the City," *National Municipal Review* 4 (Apr. 1915): 204–10.

———. "Women and Social Crises," *Independent Woman* 13 (Nov. 1934): 347, 362–63; 13 (Dec. 1934): 376, 400–01; 14 (Jan. 1935): 3, 30–31.

———. "Women's Role in Society," *Annals of the American Academy of Political and Social Science* 251 (May 1947): 1–10.

———. *Women's Work in Municipalities* (New York, D. Appleton, 1915).

Bender, Thomas. "The New History—Then and Now," *Reviews in American History* 12, no. 4 (Dec. 1984): 612–22.

———. *New York Intellect* (New York, Knopf, 1987).

Blatch, Harriot Stanton, and Alma Lutz. *Challenging Years: The Memoirs of Harriot Stanton Blatch* (New York, G. P. Putnam, 1940).

Carroll, Berenice. "Mary Beard's *Woman as Force in History*: A Critique," in Berenice Carroll, ed., *Liberating Women's History* (Urbana, University of Illinois Press, 1976), 26–41.

Collier-Thomas, Bettye. "Towards Black Feminism: The Creation of the Bethune Museum-Archives," in Suzanne Hildenbrand, ed., *Women's*

Collections: Libraries, Archives and Consciousness (New York, Haworth, 1986), 43–66.

Cott, Nancy F. "Feminist Politics in the 1920s: The National Woman's Party," *Journal of American History* 71 (June 1984): 43–68.

———. *The Grounding of Modern Feminism* (New Haven, Yale University Press, 1987).

———. "Two Beards: Coauthorship and the Concept of Civilization," *American Quarterly* 42 (June 1990): 274–300.

Flexner, Eleanor. *Century of Struggle: The Woman's Rights Movement in the United States* (New York, Atheneum, 1968).

Hartmann, Susan M. *The Home Front and Beyond: American Women in the 1940s* (Boston, Twayne, 1982).

Hofstadter, Richard. *The Progressive Historians* (New York, Knopf, 1968).

Irwin, Inez Haynes. *Story of the Woman's Party* (New York, Harcourt, 1921).

Ishimoto, Shidzue. *Facing Two Ways: The Story of My Life*, with an introduction and afterword by Barbara Molony (Stanford, Stanford University Press, 1984).

Kelly, Joan. "The Doubled Vision of Feminist Theory," *Feminist Studies* 5, no. 1 (Spring 1979): 216–27.

Kennedy, Thomas C. *Charles A. Beard and American Foreign Policy* (Gainesville, University of Florida Press, 1975).

Lane, Ann J. *Mary Ritter Beard: A Sourcebook* (New York, Schocken, 1977).

Lebsock, Suzanne. "Reading Mary Beard," *Reviews in American History* 17, no. 2 (June 1989): 324–39.

Lerner, Gerda. *The Majority Finds Its Past* (New York, Oxford, 1979).

———. "Miriam Holden—in Remembrance and Friendship," *Princeton University Library Chronicle* 41 (Winter 1980): 64–69.

Lunardini, Christine. *From Equal Suffrage to Equal Rights: Alice Paul and the National Woman's Party, 1910–1928* (New York, New York University Press, 1986).

Newton, Judith. "Family Fortunes: New History and New Historicism," *Radical History Review* 43 (Winter 1989): 5–22.

Nore, Ellen. *Charles A. Beard: An Intellectual Biography* (Carbondale, Southern Illinois University Press, 1983).

Novick, Peter. *That Noble Dream: The "Objectivity Question" and the American Historical Profession* (Cambridge, Cambridge University Press, 1988).

Purcell, Edward A., Jr. *The Crisis of Democratic Theory: Scientific Naturalism and the Problem of Value* (Lexington, University of Kentucky Press, 1973).

Rosaldo, Michele. "The Use and Abuse of Anthropology," *Signs* 5, no. 3 (Spring 1980): 389–417.

Rupp, Leila, and Verta Taylor. *Survival in the Doldrums: The American Women's Rights Movement, 1945–1960* (New York, Oxford, 1987).

Schaffer, Ronald. "The New York City Woman Suffrage Party, 1909–1919," *New York History* 43 (July 1962): 269–87.

Scott, Joan W. *Gender and the Politics of History* (New York, Columbia University Press, 1988).

Smith, Bonnie. "Seeing Mary Beard," *Feminist Studies* 10, no. 3 (Fall 1984): 399–416.

Spencer, Anna Garlin. *Woman's Share in Social Culture*, 2d ed., enl. (Philadelphia, Lippincott, 1925).

Turoff, Barbara K. *Mary Beard as Force in History* (Dayton, Ohio, Wright State University, 1979).

White, Morton G. *Social Thought in America: The Revolt against Formalism* (New York, Viking, 1952).

Woolf, Virginia. *Three Guineas* (1938; reprint, New York, Harcourt Brace, 1966).

Zimmerman, Loretta. "Mary Beard: An Activist of the Progressive Era," *University of Portland Review* 26 (Spring 1974): 15–36.

Index